Transition from Below

RENATE HARISSON
44 TREMONT STREET, APT H2
CAMBRIDGE, MA 02139

TRANSITION FROM BELOW IS THE
WORK OF A CLOSE FRIEND MINE. FROM
A TRADE UNION PERSPECTIVE, HE
SPEAKS TO SOUTH AFRICA'S STRUGGLE
IN THE 1980'S. LATER HIS THEME
CHANGES TO THE DILLEMAS AND
CHALLENGES FACING THE UNION
MOVEMENT IN POST 1994 SOUTH
AFRICA

HOPE THAT YOU WILL ENJOY
THE BOOK.

SNAKES
2003/07/21

Transition from Below

Forging Trade Unionism and Workplace Change in South Africa

KARL VON HOLDT

UNIVERSITY OF NATAL PRESS
Pietermaritzburg

Published in 2003 by University of Natal Press
Private Bag X01, Scottsville 3209
South Africa
E-mail: books@nu.ac.za
Website: www.unpress.co.za

ISBN 1-86914-029-X

Editor: Sally Hines
Typesetter: Patricia Comrie
Cover designer: Sumayya Essack

Printed and bound by Interpak Books, Pietermaritzburg

Contents

Acknowledgements   vii

Abbreviations   x

CHAPTER 1
   Transition from below: The apartheid workplace, trade
   unionism and local politics   1

CHAPTER 2
   'A white man's factory in a white man's country': The apartheid
   workplace regime   27

CHAPTER 3
   'The Messiah comes to Highveld Steel': The apartheid workplace
   regime and the union challenge   61

CHAPTER 4
   'Fighting everything': Social movement unionism, popular
   alliances and 'ungovernability' in the community   89

CHAPTER 5
   'It was just chaotic': The apartheid workplace regime, political
   challenge and 'ungovernability' in the workplace   119

CHAPTER 6
   'Union of the township, union of the hostel': Social movement
   unionism, contestation and violence among black workers   147

CHAPTER 7
'Freedom is here, apartheid is finished': NUMSA, transition
and the new strategy of reconstruction   181

CHAPTER 8
'The government is ours': Shop stewards, reconstruction and
class formation during the transition in Witbank   205

CHAPTER 9
Fighting for 'the law of freedom': The workplace regime,
incorporation and the strategy of reconstruction   229

CHAPTER 10
'*Amabhova* revolt against the union': The fragmentation and
erosion of worker solidarity   269

CHAPTER 11
'Today I see myself as a human being because of the union':
The future of the workplace, the future of the union   297

Bibliography   309
Index   319

Acknowledgments

Solitary as the task of researching and writing a book such as this is, I have many people to thank for helping me along the way. My trek was punctuated by discussions with colleagues at the Sociology of Work Unit (SWOP) at the University of the Witwatersrand, which helped me to develop, focus and refine my thinking. I would particularly like to thank Glenn Adler, Sakhela Buhlungu, Ian Macun and Eddie Webster for providing the kind of lively, searching and rigorous intellectual environment that not only sustains a project of this sort – especially when it grows beyond imagining into a kind of many-headed Hydra – but also nourishes the hope that it has some kind of meaning and value both to the intellectual community of which we are part and to the labour movement with which we work so closely.

I also owe a deep intellectual debt to Michael Burawoy and Dunbar Moodie – to their own rich writings on workplace change, as well as for their generous commentary on my study. Thanks too to Sam Mkhabela, not only for discussions about ungovernability, but also for persuading me to consider Highveld Steel as the site of investigation. More recently, my colleagues at the National Labour and Economic Development Institute and the Congress of South African Trade Unions have provided a supportive environment for further exploring some of my ideas as well as testing them in practical projects for workplace change.

I am particularly grateful to Eddie Webster, the director of SWOP, who provided me with the opportunity to undertake this study, encouraged me to embark on it, supervised my thesis, ensured that I pursued the project to the bittersweet end, and along the way provided me with judicious advice, tough or gentle as the occasion demanded. His central place in the interpretation of South Africa's labour history over the past two decades ensured that I grappled with his work at every turn, and one of the pleasures of this project has been our discussions and arguments, in which I always had reason to value his generous, open-minded, passionate and knowledgeable mentorship. Indeed, in many ways this book is built on the foundations of his seminal work, *Cast in a racial mould*, which investigated change in the apartheid workplace during an earlier period.

I would also like to thank William Matlala, former shop steward, labour photographer, cultural activist, Pedi migrant and friend, for his companionship, assistance, frequent discussions of trade union and political issues, translation during interviews with Pedi migrants, and insights into rural and migrant Pedi culture which have helped shape some of my arguments in this book.

My deepest thanks must go to the workers, and especially the shop stewards, at Highveld Steel. Their commitment to the trade union and liberation struggles, and their insight into their own history, were a constant source of inspiration. Their lives, experiences, struggles and ideas form in every way the substance of this study. I am grateful to all the shop stewards, workers and union officials who agreed to co-operate with my lengthy 'interrogations' between working tough shifts, union negotiations, meetings and community activities, and particularly to Leslie Nhlapo and Ezekiel Nkosi, chairperson and secretary respectively of the shop stewards committee, for arranging most of my interviews with other shop stewards and workers. Indeed, my solitude was mitigated by the workers and shop stewards of Highveld Steel, because they were always in some sense present, joking, explaining, recounting, dreaming, as I battled to understand and structure the material. I hope this study contributes in a small way to the goals of the labour movement, and I dedicate it to the shop stewards of COSATU who have played so great a role in changing our world.

As a disabled researcher I would have found it difficult, if not impossible, to undertake this journey without the generous practical and logistic support of the administrative staff at SWOP: Anthea Metcalfe, Marilyn Bristow, Thandeka Ndebele and Khayaat Fakir, and students in the Sociology Department, particularly Karl Gostner, Gerald Kabasa, Cecil Macheke, Tshandipiya Dube, Thabo Sephiri, Jennifer Parsley and Paul Truter. I would like to thank, too, Nina and Kate Shand and Suzy Bernstein for their speedy and accurate transcription of interviews; Malehoko Tshoaedi, Cecil Macheke and Fanie Mashego for both translating and transcribing certain interviews;

Philip Daniel and my editor at the University of Natal Press, Sally Hines, for substantial editorial assistance.

I would also like to express my gratitude for the financial support of the Albert Einstein Institute, the Sociology of Work Programme and the National Research Foundation: Division for Social Sciences and Humanities, without which this research project would have been impossible, and to the Friedrich Ebert Stiftung for the grant which made this book possible.

Finally, I would like to thank Adele Kirsten for breaking the solitude of this journey in a different way, bearing with my obsessions and moods, consoling me when all seemed lost, and laughing at me when that seemed necessary.

Abbreviations

ANC	African National Congress
AWB	Afrikaner Weerstandsbeweging
AZAPO	Azanian People's Organisation
BLA	Black Local Authority
COSAS	Congress of South African Students
COSATU	Congress of South African Trade Unions
CUSA	Council of Unions of South Africa
FOSATU	Federation of South African Trade Unions
GMPD	General Maintenance and Planning Department
HAB	Highveld Administration Board
HSVC	Highveld Steel and Vanadium Corporation
KTC	KwaGuqa Town Council
LRA	Labour Relations Act
MAWU	Metal and Allied Workers Union
MITB	Metal Industries Training Board
MK	Umkhonto we Sizwe
MPL	Member of the Provincial Legislature
MWU	Mine Workers' Union
NNP	New National Party
NP	National Party
NTB	National Training Board
NUM	National Union of Mineworkers
NUMSA	National Union of Metalworkers of South Africa
NUSAAW	National Union of Steel and Allied Workers
PAC	Pan-Africanist Congress
PWV	Pretoria-Witwatersrand-Vereeniging
RDC	Reconstruction and Development Committee
RDP	Reconstruction and Development Programme
SABS	South African Boilermakers' Society

SACP	South African Communist Party
SACTU	South African Congress of Trade Unions
SANCO	South African National Civics Organisation
SEIFSA	Steel and Engineering Industries Federation of South Africa
TPA	Transvaal Provincial Administration
UDF	United Democratic Front
UPCO	Unemployed People's Congress
WYCO	Witbank Youth Congress

CHAPTER 1

Transition from below

The apartheid workplace, trade unionism
and local politics

The huge, smoky complex of Highveld's steelworks is situated outside Witbank. It was built in the mid-1960s, and produced steel through the period of high apartheid, through the turbulent period of trade unionism and popular revolt of the 1980s, through the transition, and continues to produce steel in the new democratic South Africa. From outside it looks much the same, although it has expanded and diversified its products – but inside, its dusty, fiery and noisy plants have been the stage for a drama as intense and full of sound and fury as the broader political drama staged outside.

During the 1970s and 1980s, the people who arrived there to work – on the regular day shift or any of the three production shifts that keep the steelworks running 24 hours every day of the year – came from very different points on the social compass. The whites – from the operator or the receptionist to the managing director – came from the comfortable garden suburbs of the white town of Witbank, where Highveld Steel sponsored a housing estate, a sports club and other facilities for its employees. The blacks came from the tiny houses and hostels of Witbank's black township, or other townships in the area, and later in the 1980s, the shack settlements on the periphery of the town. Whites and blacks at Highveld Steel came from different worlds.

The different points of origin of the black people and the white people who entered the steelworks every day were mirrored by their different destinations in production. Workers changed into their work clothes in different change-houses – two for blacks, one for whites. And then, when they went to their workstations in the iron plant, steel plant or structural mill, they went to different jobs. Nonetheless, they worked alongside each other and with each other – which was what distinguished the workplace from the town, where blacks and whites lived far from each other and schooled, travelled, bought stamps or tickets, were entertained, worshipped, went to the toilet, got sick, died and were buried separately. But working together did not undermine apartheid; in some ways the forced proximity generated an even more virulent form of racist domination than in other arenas of society. As they worked together producing steel so they produced the social relations of apartheid in the workplace, forging and contesting the social structure of the apartheid workplace regime.

This is a study of transition from below, of the militant struggle of black workers against the despotism and racism of white power in the workplace, and of their participation in the broader political struggle against apartheid; of the triumphant democratic breakthrough which culminated in the election of an African National Congress (ANC) government in 1994; and of their strategy for reconstruction in the workplace and in local politics – a strategy for building a new post-apartheid future inside Highveld Steel and in the town of Witbank. This book explores the chaos and ungovernability in workplace and community as activists endeavoured to disrupt the order of apartheid, as well as the outlines of a new order that emerged from this turbulence. Simultaneously, it examines the divisions and contestation within the union – between political activists and shop stewards, between migrant outsiders and urban locals – that erupted in open conflict and violence among workers. The struggle against white power was simultaneously a struggle to build trade union organisation in a continuous process of forging and reforging the meaning and 'law' of the union.

Transition

Most of the literature on trade unions in the South African transition has concerned itself with the strategic responses of labour to political democratisation and to economic restructuring and liberalisation. Important themes include the political alliance with the ANC (Adler and Webster 1995; Eidelberg 2000; Götz 2000), participation in corporatist institutions (Baskin 2000; Friedman and Shaw 2000; Maree 1993), and strategies for influencing industry restructuring (Joffe et al 1995). These analyses tend to be framed by the idea of a negotiated transition from authoritarianism entailing a process of elite pacting, and based on the model of democratic transitions in southern Europe and Latin America. Both the political constraints of pacting, and the economic constraints of liberalisation driven by globalisation, limit the scope for progressive redistributive policies, and debate has centred on the degree to which this is so, with Adler and Webster (1995) in particular emphasising the degree of labour influence over the outcome of the transition (Adler et al 1992; Adler and Webster 1995, 2000b; De Villiers and Anstey 2000; Webster and Adler 2000).

This book takes a very different approach, exploring the transition from below at a micro-institutional level. Its subject is change and contestation within institutions, organisations and movements. Such a study reveals the analogy of a 'double transition' (Webster and Adler 1999) – i.e., combining a political transition to democracy and an economic transition towards a liberalised economy – to be limiting, if not misleading. The South African transition entails a third dimension, a transition from apartheid to a post-colonial society. This latter dimension of what is actually a triple transition implies a deeper and broader process of social transformation: a multitude of struggles, compromises and pacts best understood as a process of internal *decolonisation* and *reconstruction* of society. Since colonialism and apartheid penetrated so deeply into South African society, shaping every aspect of social, economic and political life from the most intimate relations to the most public, processes of decolonisation – and protracted contestation over these processes – are correspondingly diverse and far-reaching. They cannot be settled through a quick four-year process of elite pacting at the summit of society, but are engaged at every level of society, in the spotlights of media attention, in obscure corners, as well as in the 'hidden abode of production' (Marx 1976: 279), and may well continue for a long time, even generations. Since the triple transition takes place not only at the commanding heights of society, but also below, it can only be illuminated from both angles. The view from above has received much analysis. This, on the other hand, is a study of transition *from below* – in the workplace, the trade union, the town council, the ANC branch. It is an ideal perspective from which to grasp the contested transformations of post-colonial reconstruction, which constitute a 'war of position' (Gramsci 1971) in the depths of South African society as contestants battle over the preservation, dissolution and recasting of institutions and social structures. The partners to the elite pact are themselves irrevocably transfigured or even dissolved –

one need look no further than the processes of internal change in the ANC and the New National Party (NNP) – by the forces and processes unleashed by their pacting.[1] At these depths, society is fluid, in motion, turbulent and provisional.

Two further features distinguish the South African transition, both of them linked to its colonial nature: working class incorporation and class formation. South Africa's first democratic elections in 1994, constituted the *moment of democratic incorporation* of the black working class (analogous to but more dramatic than the winning of the franchise in the capitalist societies of Europe, since historically the labouring classes there had been incorporated in other ways without parallel in colonial society) which fundamentally altered its relations to other classes and to the state. This book explores the significance of this moment and its impact on trade unionism, worker solidarity and the workplace regime. It argues that, while democratic incorporation at the political level was the founding moment of class incorporation, the terms and mode of incorporation at all levels continue to be a matter of profound contestation – one aspect of the broader contestation over decolonisation and reconstruction. Indeed, the trade union movement's 'strategy of reconstruction' was a strategy for contesting and shaping these processes. Thus, this book is not only a study of transition but of the founding moment of incorporation and the subsequent contestation over the terms and mode of incorporation in the workplace and in local political life.

This approach to workplace struggle implies that *hegemony* is established at the political level, in the relations between classes and between classes and the state, rather than in everyday relations in the workplace as Burawoy and Moodie argue (Burawoy 1985: 259, 1989: 72–4; Moodie 1994: 279n). It is political exclusion or incorporation at this level, and the mode of incorporation – i.e., the formation of the historic bloc that underpins the state – that constitutes the political terrain of the working class and shapes its politics. The transition explored in this study is defined by the dissolution of the old apartheid ruling bloc (led by Afrikaner nationalism and which excluded most blacks, including the black working class) and the formation of a new historic bloc that incorporates the black working class and is led by the forces of African nationalism. This provides the basis for the shift from illegitimacy to legitimacy of the state from the point of view of black workers, and for their new politics of reconstruction.

Workplace incorporation is another matter. The form of workplace incorporation is determined in part by state policy, legislation and so on, but more importantly by the more or less strategic struggles of managers, workers and unions to preserve or reconstitute the workplace regime. Littler provides a model for this kind of analysis with his comparative study of incorporation in Britain, Japan and the United States. He demonstrates that a range of incorporation modes is possible, each constituted in an historical process of struggle, ranging from paternalistic incorporation of work groups (Japan), to smashing the workgroup and incorporating the foreman (US), to failing to incorporate foreman or workgroup, which remain 'as a sceptical corrosive of shopfloor bureaucratisation' (Britain) (Littler 1982: 190).

The process of class formation that characterises decolonisation is a second distinguishing feature of the South African transition. The removal of apartheid created the scope for the rapid formation of a new black elite in the sphere of politics, in social and economic activity, and in the world of work. This process too is accompanied by fierce contestation, and has had a profound effect on the internal life of trade unionism and on the workplace.

The apartheid workplace regime
The concept 'workplace regime' provides the analytic framework for identifying changes and continuities in the South African workplace transition. The concept is derived from Burawoy's path-breaking comparative analysis (1985), with significant modifications. Firstly, for Burawoy a production or factory regime consists of two elements: the labour process shaped by valorisation and technological change, which is the sphere of 'domination and fragmentation', and the 'production apparatuses' – a set of workplace institutions beyond the labour process which 'account for resistance and struggle', i.e., the politics of production. However, this distinction is difficult to sustain. The labour process is itself a socially constructed terrain, an arena of contestation and resistance, structured as much by the workplace regime – and forces beyond the workplace – as by the imperatives of profit and technology. Job design, supervision, hierarchies – the organisation of work – vary with shifts in the workplace regime, notwithstanding continuity of technology and ownership, as this

study shows. The racial structuring of the South African workplace shaped not only the production apparatuses, but also the labour process itself.

Secondly, as Moodie (1994: 6, 112) and Thompson (1990: 117–19) argue, Burawoy's analysis provides little room for the collective agency of workers in struggles for control or reform of the workplace regime. Production apparatuses are virtually absolute in their power to prevent resistance in the case of despotic regimes, or to absorb struggle and render alternatives impossible to imagine in the case of hegemonic regimes. In contrast, I follow Moodie in taking the workplace regime to be a social structure that allocates 'rights and resources unequally within particular historical structures among differently socialised actors':

> Once structures have been established, dominants' maintenance of control as well as subdominants' resistance involves strategic action within established but contested patterns of social interaction on changing historical terrain. Actors experience structures as formally or informally patterned rules of conduct, more or less firmly sanctioned, which exist outside of them, both constrain and empower their social practices and distribute material goods according to regular procedures (Moodie 1994: 275).

Moodie argues that social structures are 'sites of struggle . . . always in contestation and subject to reinterpretation' that 'must be protected by the constant vigilance and strategic shifts of dominants and their agents, who modify them in response to resistance from subordinates and changes in external environments' (ibid: 3).[2]

Finally, Burawoy overburdens the concept 'workplace regime', using it to construct a global periodisation of despotic and hegemonic production regimes. The leap from specific workplaces to global types is too great, and I prefer to use the concept to analyse *national* and *comparative* patterns – and variations – of workplace domination, resistance, incorporation, co-operation and compliance. Thus, this study distinguishes between the apartheid workplace regime corresponding to the era of apartheid, the neo-apartheid workplace regime that emerges as an unstable and decomposing order with the democratic breakthrough in the political sphere, and the struggle between contending notions of the nature of a post-apartheid workplace regime. During much of this period (i.e., since militant black trade unionism emerged in the 1980s), the workplace regime can be regarded as *transitional* – a transition which, as Moodie puts it, 'has been chaotic' (1994: 110). Integral to the idea of chaotic transition is the concept of struggle over bringing a new order into being – a struggle between contending notions of workplace order rather than a struggle to modify an existing structure. Analysis of such a process takes as its object, not the dynamics of workplace order, but the dynamics *before* 'structures have been established' – or the struggles against an existing structure and *through which* a new one is established, struggles in which the actors are not bound into a social structure consisting of 'formally or informally patterned rules of conduct' but rather operate according to contending and mutually incompatible ideas of social structure. Such a study is necessarily concerned as much with states of *disorder* as with order.

In contrast, much of the literature on the South African workplace under apartheid tends to interpret the evidence through the concepts of workplace order provided by metropolitan sociology. This is best illustrated by the work of Webster. In order to make headway against the despotic apartheid workplace order the first shop stewards had to push forward the frontier of control like 'a guerrilla fighter' (Webster 1984: 81). As the negotiating relationship stabilises, the shop steward is no longer described as a guerrilla fighter, but as an agent of order and stability in the workplace (Webster 1985: 235–6, 244), meshed in an 'industrial relations web' that contains and institutionalises conflict, and threatens to insulate economic from political struggles (Lambert and Webster 1988; see also see Pityana and Orkin 1992: 2–6; Webster 2002). Similarly, Maller (1992) filters her workplace analysis through concepts of metropolitan industrial sociology. When, in a detailed study of shopfloor dynamics at Volkswagen SA and other workplaces, the behaviour of shop stewards and workers failed to conform to these expectations, and instead displayed highly disruptive and politicised practices, these are treated as incidental anomalies with external causes, rather than as distinctive features of militant trade unionism in workplaces shaped by apartheid.

It is Moodie's study of *transition* on the gold mines – which draws not at all from the sociological traditions of workplace analysis – which first really investigates the workplace transition from despotism to a collective bargaining order prior to decolonisation. It was a transition in which the National Union of Mineworkers (NUM) sought to replace the despotic order of mine management with a new, negotiated order in the compounds and workplace. However, the terms of a new order between managers and workers were sharply contested and savagely disrupted, with the result that 'this period of transition which still continues today, has been chaotic' (Moodie 1994: 110) – a finding which resonates with Maller's (1992) evidence, though not her argument.

The metropolitan sociology of workplace trade unionism – while inspired by Marx's analysis of production relations during the period of early industrialisation when class antagonism was high – was elaborated in the period of developed capitalism, when the working class had already been incorporated and bourgeois hegemony established. In contrast, under the colonial conditions of apartheid the trade union movement was politically excluded, became a participant in the national liberation struggle to overthrow apartheid, and developed a new strategy of reconstruction in post-apartheid South Africa. What is distinctive, then, about this study of the workplace is that it captures the processes of construction and contestation of workplace order and incorporation – condensed in a very short time span – and focuses on the generation of disorder that characterised these processes, rather than the 'negotiation of order' (Hyman 1975), the 'manufacture of consent' (Burawoy 1979), the 'manufacture of compromise' (Webster 2002) or the 'regulation of labour' (Edwards et al 1994) characteristic of the workplaces of metropolitan capitalism.[3]

Trade unionism in transition

If the workplace regime provides us with a core analytical framework for grasping the transition, the trade union as an institution and movement provides a second. The concept of social movement unionism was developed by progressive scholars in an effort to understand the militant, mobilised industrial unions emerging in newly industrialising countries such as Brazil, South Africa, South Korea and the Philippines in the 1980s (Lambert 1990; Lambert and Webster 1988; Munck 1987; Scipes 1992; Seidman 1994; Waterman 1984, 1993; Webster 1988). The concept has been used to distinguish quite sharply between trade union practices and goals in South Africa and those prevalent in advanced industrial society (Lambert and Webster 1988; Seidman 1994; Webster 1988). Social movement unionism is characterised as a highly mobilised form of unionism based in a substantial expansion of semi-skilled manufacturing work, which emerged in opposition to authoritarian regimes and repressive workplaces in the developing world. Social movement unionism is fiercely independent, but establishes alliances with community and political organisations. It demonstrates a commitment to internal democratic practices and to the broader democratic and socialist transformation of authoritarian societies.[4] More recently, social movement unionism has been used to describe the emergence in North America of more militant trade unionism with a strategic commitment to forging community alliances (Moody 1997).

In this analysis of social movement unionism in the South African transition, the focus is on exploring the meanings, practices and contestations within the social structure of the trade union. Moodie's comments on the social structure of the workplace can be adapted to the internal social structure of trade unionism. Union social structure includes the formal institutional girders of the union – its constitution, offices and resources, the rules and procedures that govern shop steward elections and roles – and the informal relationships, practices and meanings that cohere around them. The social structure consists not only of current structures and practices but also of values and meanings, discourses and repertoires of action, that have been collectively engendered in the past and continue to shape current activities. The social structure of the union constitutes its collective identity, governs the distribution of power between members, shop stewards, officials and its various structures, and defines the processes of decision-making, strategies, goals and organisational culture of the union.

This book shows how trade union collective identity in the 1980s consisted of a complex amalgam of popular, class and workplace identities, many of which – popular political identity and migrant identity in particular – were forged beyond the workplace. These collective identities *both* reinforced each other, generating an extraordinarily intense solidarity, *and* created faultlines between differing conceptions of 'the union law' – faultlines which, when placed under pressure, could become the front line in a bitter and frequently violent conflict over contending notions of union order. Like the workplace regime, the social structure of the union was unable to bind all its members within 'established but contested patterns of social interaction', since social structure was itself the subject of struggle between contending notions of 'the union law'. The result was disorder and ungovernability within the union.

This analysis challenges the orthodox literature on social movement unionism. Where the literature assumes social movement unionism is primarily class-based, this study finds an amalgam of popular and class identities. The literature does argue for the centrality of alliances with community organisations, social movements and other popular and non-class organisations, but it views these as external alliances between independent organisations. This book highlights an interpenetration, a complex and dynamic network of political, community and workplace struggles woven together by a discourse of national liberation struggle. Where the literature sees social movement unionism as characterised by internal democracy, debate and diversity of opinion, this book finds the failure of democratic practices to empower all layers of workers equally, and an intense and even violent conflict over leadership, power and control. Unproblematic solidarity is replaced with internal contestation and the prevalence of what Moore calls 'revolutionary bullying' (1978: 342–3; see also Webster and Simpson 1991). Where the literature fails to investigate the workplace practices of social movement unionism, this book finds distinctive workplace practices of symbolic confrontation and un-governability. Where some studies argue that social movement unionism is a transferable strategy (Moody 1997; Waterman 2001), this research explains union strategy and organisational culture in terms of specific national factors. Indeed, as I argue elsewhere (Von Holdt 2002), the concept of a coherent and widely applicable model of social movement unionism may well be unsustainable. More fruitful is the comparative study of the interplay between movement and institutional dimensions of trade unionism – something which this study attempts for South Africa.

Social movement unionism in South Africa emerged in the struggle against apartheid generally, and white power in the workplace specifically. With the democratic breakthrough of the negotiated transition, there was a fundamental political reorientation within the union, although the workplace regime barely changed. The trade union movement responded with the new strategy of reconstruction. Some analysts branded this strategic unionism because it was in part shaped by borrowings from social democratic unionism via the Australian trade unions, where it was labelled in these terms (Joffe et al 1995). However, the strategy was more ambitious and far-reaching than strategic unionism, which after all had not been designed to deal with the kind of challenges faced by trade unions in the South African transition. This book charts the emergence of the strategy and its impact on the union at a local level, and describes the attempts by the Highveld Steel shop stewards to implement it in Witbank and at Highveld Steel.

The study

Highveld Steel was chosen as a case study[5] for exploring, firstly, the nature of the apartheid workplace regime, and secondly, the potential for a union-driven project for the transformation of this regime. The first aspect of this investigation requires that the workplace be 'typical' in some sense, exploring the causal links between apartheid and workplace relations, since the very notion of an apartheid workplace regime implies a national pattern of workplace practices. The second aspect requires that it be a 'critical case' for the potential of a union-driven project. Highveld Steel appears to fulfil these conditions: like many other companies, during the 1980s it was a site of militant union organisation of migrant and urban African workers with strong links to community struggle; and it had the potential to become a pilot project for union innovation in the 1990s, combining intervention by the union head office with an exceptionally talented and experienced group of shop stewards. Ultimately, however, conclusions as to the significance of, and generalisation from, developments at the company can only be established empirically and analytically through marshalling whatever comparative evidence is available, and through sustained reflection on the evidence.

The case study consists of 60 in-depth interviews with 28 National Union of Metalworkers of South Africa (NUMSA) unionists and former unionists, three with trade unionists from the white Mine Workers' Union (MWU) (one of whom had recently joined NUMSA), two with officials from the Witbank Town Council, and one with the former recruiting officer of Highveld Steel. These interviews, conducted between 1993 and 1998, were supplemented with observations of union meetings and interactions between union members, and numerous informal conversations with union activists. This research methodology facilitated an extended discussion of core themes with key activists over a long period, and created the opportunity to identify complex processes and subtle changes in relationships and attitudes during a period of profound political change.

Highveld Steel management refused to co-operate with this study, referring to the volatile racial tensions in the company and their anxiety about losing control of confidential information. My position at the time, as editor of the labour-aligned *South African Labour Bulletin*, probably also influenced them. As a result I had to interview unionists in the union offices, and in their homes and hostels, rather than at the workplace and was only able to attend those meetings that took place outside the workplace. I was able to enter the workplace three times: for a tour of the steelworks when the company was still considering my request for access; without the knowledge of management, when a crowd of *toyi-toying*[6] strikers surrounded my car and escorted me to the canteen where a general meeting was being held; and when shop stewards drove me into the works without management permission to attend a shop steward meeting.

These incidents illustrate something of the nature of the relationship shop stewards established with myself as researcher. The same status which contributed to management's rejection of my request, established my credibility with the trade union: as editor of the *Labour Bulletin* I was a participant in the labour movement, and a supporter of its struggles for justice and democracy. Shop stewards were willing not only to assist me in every way possible, but also in some cases shared with me their most intimate thoughts and anxieties about their experiences, their union and their political participation. In some senses too, I became a weapon in the struggles of the shop stewards with management, both in the immediate sense of enabling them to demonstrate their defiance of management rules, but more importantly as a way to make known the truth about their treatment by their employer. This required me to remain vigilant and self-reflective in my assessment of the meaning of my research. This book has lost something by the company's refusal to co-operate, but it has gained immeasurably by my status in the labour movement.

The interviews and observations were supplemented with union and management documents provided by NUMSA and by the official history of Highveld Steel (Hocking 1998). For the most part these sources served to cross-reference dates and sequences of events. The substance of the analysis of the social structures of the workplace and the union was derived from the interviews.

The town

Witbank, a city of roughly 250 000 people in the province of Mpumalanga and 150 kilometres east of Johannesburg, developed as a typical apartheid town. In the white town residents elected their own town council, well resourced on a tax base that included businesses and the residential areas of the wealthy, and therefore able to provide its residents with high quality services. The African township of KwaGuqa developed as the site for the regulation, control and reproduction of black labour – and particularly for the implementation of influx control – which served the triple purpose of regulating the African labour market by segmenting it into local urban labour and migrant labour from the rural reserves, of excluding surplus labour and therefore the financial and social burden of unemployment from the 'white' urban areas, and of organising the urban black population into spaces that could be easily policed and controlled.

The Non-European Affairs Department of the Witbank council, and then from 1972 the Highveld Administration Board (HAB), administered the web of regulations through which the residential and working lives of Africans were controlled: the passes, the allocation of houses, the lodgers' permits, business licenses and so on.[7] The municipal police – established by the municipality and then transferred to the HAB – constantly raided the hostels and the township for illegal occupants and for residents with out-of-order documents. Lawbreakers were processed through pass courts administered by the HAB. As in all South African urban areas, Africans in KwaGuqa were only permitted to seek jobs through the local labour bureau, also administered by the HAB, and employment was restricted to those with urban rights. Migrant labour could only be recruited when the labour bureau agreed that there was no local labour to perform the work, and permitted the employer to recruit in the rural areas, through rural labour bureaus. The hostels, where the migrant workers were housed, were also tightly controlled by the HAB. They were fenced off from the surrounding township and access was controlled by the municipal police, whose job was to check passes and hostel permits. A hostel superintendent with clerical staff managed the hostels. Visitors were required to carry a permit, which specified the time allotted for the visit, issued by the superintendent's office.[8]

The Witbank-Middelburg region is dominated by three economic activities. Its coal mines produce over 80 per cent of the coal mined in South Africa, and employ 28 000; the eight power stations burn local coal to produce half of South Africa's electricity and employ 6 300; and the local basic metals, steel and stainless steel industries, which make use of coal and electricity, employ close on 10 000 (Dauskardt 1994).

The black population of Witbank expanded rapidly from the mid-1980s after government abandoned influx control. In 1980 there were 56 000 Africans (roughly 12 000 of them migrant workers living in the hostels) and 30 000 whites living in Witbank. By 1991 there were 89 000 Africans and 40 000 whites living there. During the late 1980s and early 1990s, the KwaGuqa Town Council embarked on a massive programme of expansion of the KwaGuqa township, doubling the number of houses – but this was not sufficient to prevent the formation of large informal settlements. By 1998 the Witbank Town Council estimated that more than 200 000 people – an increase of 123 per cent in the African population over seven years – were living in the townships of KwaGuqa and in informal settlements (Central Statistical Services 1980, 1991).[9] Census figures also give a rough indication of the apartheid distribution of income in Witbank. In 1980, 75 per cent of blacks and 10 per cent of whites earned R2 400 or less, while 59 per cent of whites and 0.5 per cent of blacks earned more than R6 000 per annum. In 1991, 57 per cent of blacks and 18 per cent of whites earned R10 000 or less, while 42 per cent of whites and four per cent of blacks earned R30 000 or more per annum.

Highveld Steel

The Highveld Steel and Vanadium Corporation (HSVC) produces a range of basic metal products. The main complex, the steelworks, is situated six kilometres outside Witbank and produces steel and vanadium slag. Transalloys, which produces silicomanganese and ferromanganese for use in steel alloys, is nearby. Vantra produces vanadium pentoxide and ferrovanadium in Witbank's Ferrobank industrial area, just beyond KwaGuqa township. Rand Carbide, on the other side of town, produces ferrosilicon, also for use in steel alloys, as well as carbonaceous products such as electrode paste and char. The iron ore processed by the steelworks and by Vantra is mined at the Mapochs mine, 140 kilometres north-east of Witbank. All of these plants, with the exception of the mine which employs about 150 people, are major employers: Transalloys 575, Rand Carbide 770, Vantra 600 and the steelworks 4 000.[10] Highveld Steel is the biggest employer in Witbank and has had a corresponding impact on the growth and the economic, social and political life of the town. The corporation established a large housing estate in the town for its white employees, and facilitated home ownership in KwaGuqa for black employees, particularly in the 1990s. In the early 1980s, it accounted for more than 2 000 of the 12 000 migrant workers in the hostels in KwaGuqa.

Highveld Steel is majority owned by the Anglo American Corporation, which was South Africa's biggest conglomerate until it moved offshore in the late 1990s. Highveld Steel is a product of Anglo American's ambition to become a major producer of vanadium, a mineral found in large quantities in the iron ore of the Bushveld Igneous Complex and used to produce high-strength steel alloys. The company bought Vantra in 1959, and established the Highveld Steel and Vanadium Corporation in the early 1960s to build a large integrated steelworks that would smelt iron, draw off vanadium slag, process the iron into steel, and then roll a portion of this into structural steel products. This was the biggest single enterprise ever established by Anglo American, whose then chairperson, the late Sir Harry Oppenheimer, proclaimed the R127 million investment 'a major single act of faith by private enterprise in the future of South Africa' (Hocking 1998: 76, 111). Highveld Steel began production in 1968, and Vantra became a division of the company. Despite early problems, Highveld became the world's biggest producer of vanadium.[11]

In 1976 Highveld Steel bought Transalloys from its parent company. In 1977 a plate mill was established to roll plate from steel slabs; in 1978 the company bought Rand Carbide; in 1982 a strip mill was added to roll plate into hot-rolled strip; and there have been frequent expansions of capacity in the iron plant and the steel plant. The plate and strip mills became the flat products division; a second iron plant was added in 1985. In the 1990s Highveld Steel bought two smaller vanadium companies and extended its activities further into vanadium and vanadium chemical processing. In the same decade Highveld Steel entered into a partnership with Samancor and the Industrial Development Corporation to build Columbus Stainless, the biggest integrated stainless steel producer in the world, at Middelburg. This project, together with the Rheem division that has negligble connections with the Witbank operations, is beyond the scope of this study.

The table below shows the expansion of production, products and profits over the 30 years of Highveld Steel's existence. The years chosen were at the peak of the commodity cycle and of company production and profitability, to illustrate the expansion of capacity.

Indicator	1974	1980	1989	1998
Profit after tax	R9.8 m	R43.9 m	R322.4 m	R216.8 m
Share price (cents)	92	216	892	1 878
Exports	44.4%	44.1%	61.4%	58%
No. employees	3 728	6 795	7 612	5 697
Total iron (tons)	430 000	738 000	1 009 000	911 000
Steel cast	437 000	787 000	1 058 000	985 000
Total rolled steel	316 000	661 000	842 000	722 000
– sections	276 000	379 000	330 000	340 000
– plate	–	263 000	205 000	193 000
– strip	–	–	292 000	189 000
Vanadium slag	35 000	57 000	76 000	70 000
Ferroalloys	–	155 000	176 000	226 000
Carbonaceous	–	232 000	157 000	130 000

Table 1: The growth of Highveld Steel: key indicators (HSVC, Annual Reports).

The picture that emerges is of a successful company, expanding its capacity and product range into higher value-added products such as plate, strip, ferroalloys and processed vanadium. Its profit and share price increased steadily over three decades. Employment also tended to increase over the period, with the exception of 1997–98, when a substantial reduction took place as the company implemented a productivity programme. The table does not illustrate the cyclical downturns characteristic of the commodity market, when production and profit declined sharply, and retrenchments took place.[12]

Highveld Steel accounts for 12 per cent of South Africa's steel production, while the formerly state-owned Iscor accounts for 75 per cent. South Africa produces about 1.3 per cent of world steel and is almost entirely self-sufficient in steel production. The producers are unusually export-reliant because of the relatively small size of the domestic market, and since inception Highveld Steel has exported around 50 per cent of its steel production. While sanctions against apartheid closed the major markets of Europe and the United States, both Highveld and Iscor were successful in penetrating markets in Asia. The domestic market has remained stagnant during the 1990s because of the relatively low level of fixed investment and infrastructural projects, and the global market has become intensely competitive owing to the protection of steel industries in the major markets of the industrialised countries, and the rapid expansion of the steel-making capacity in the developing world (Brazil, Korea, China) (Jourdan 1993; Lings 1990).

South African steel makers are protected by an *ad valorem* duty of three to five per cent on imported steel. Notwithstanding cost advantages and import duties, the opening of the South African market with the transition to democracy, and the surplus steel capacity in the global market, has increased competitive pressure on the South African producers, both in global markets and from cheap imported steel in the domestic market (HSVC, Annual Report, 1998). The intensification of competitive pressure in global and local markets has increased the salience of the quality of product, delivery and service in company performance, which explains the growing concern with these issues by Highveld's management.

This study of workplace trade unionism, managerial practices and workplace culture focuses on the steelworks that were the centre of union activity for the Metal and Allied Workers Union (MAWU) and NUMSA. The process at the steelworks starts at the two iron plants with a mixture of ore, coal and fluxes which is fed into the heated rotary kilns for pre-reduction.[13] The resulting hot charge is transmitted to the furnace bunkers by hot charge cars, from where it is fed into the six furnaces of Iron Plant One and the bigger single furnace of Iron Plant Two. The iron is smelted in the furnaces for a period of 3.5–4 hours, after which it is tapped by teams of tappers on the tap floors beneath the furnaces. The molten iron and slag are separated, and the iron poured into giant ladles and transported to the steel plant. Here vanadium slag is separated from the iron in the shaking ladles, and the iron is then transferred to the basic oxygen furnaces where it is purified of carbon and other minerals by blowing oxygen onto the molten metal, producing steel. From this point on, all production is driven by specific customer orders. Fluxes are added at this stage to produce alloys with specific properties. The molten steel is then transferred to the continuous casting machines where it is cast into blocks, slabs and billets, and cut and cooled.

Production process at the Highveld Steel steelworks.

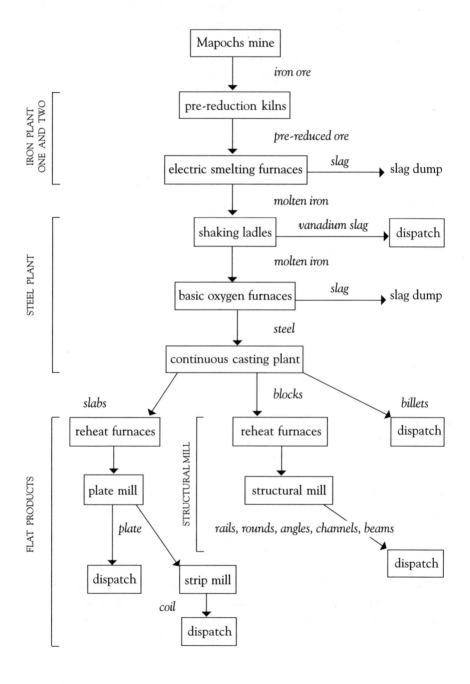

From the steel plant, blocks are transferred to the structural mill. They pass through reheating furnaces and rolling mills to produce channels, angles, rounds, rails and universal beams. These are cut to length, cooled and inspected. Slabs are transferred to the flat products division where they are reheated and rolled into plate. The plate then either passes through a hot leveller and is then cooled and cut to size on the flame cutting bed (for thicker plate) or the shear cutting line, or it passes through the hot reversing strip mill where it is rolled into strip, cooled and wound into coils on the up-coiler. Some of the strip may be passed through a temper mill, decoiled and cut into sheets.

The iron plants and steel plant are continuous process operations, running around the clock 365 days per year. Although not technically necessary, the structural and flat products mills are run on a similar basis. Engineering and maintenance operate on a regular day shift, while production operates a three-shift system (7 am–3 pm, 3 pm–11 pm, 11 pm–7 am).

The National Union of Metalworkers of South Africa

NUMSA – and its predecessor, MAWU – emerged as a highly influential trade union during the 1980s, at the forefront of forging new union strategies during a decade of accelerated change in South Africa: the participation by black trade unions in the industrial relations institutions established by the Wiehahn reforms, in turn shaping in a very real way their development; the dynamic growth of the black union movement from precarious structures with a toehold in scattered factories to the most organised and durable movement among the black population oppressed by apartheid; and the union response to the wave of popular political organisation and mobilisation which characterised the decade. The union was able to blend an emphasis on strong shopfloor structures and workers' control with building a large and complex organisation; mass militancy with sophisticated institutional tactics; and working class independence with support for the national liberation movement, in a creative and dynamic tension. In the early 1990s, NUMSA was again at the forefront of developing a strategic response within the Congress of South African Trade Unions (COSATU) to the challenges of the transition. The explicit attempt by NUMSA to adopt a new strategy in new political and economic conditions, and the internal contestations this provoked, made it the ideal subject for a study of unionism in transition.

MAWU, formed in 1973, was one of the wave of new unions which attempted to organise black workers in the early 1970s, in the aftermath of the wave of strikes that rolled through Durban. While the union remained tiny and weak through the 1970s, the opportunities created by the new legislation recommended by the Wiehahn Commission in the early 1980s provided the space for MAWU to take advantage of successive waves of worker militancy, reinforced by broader mobilisation against apartheid. It grew rapidly. In 1980 MAWU's membership was 10 000; by 1982 it had trebled to 30 000 (Webster 1985: 233). It had become the biggest industrial union of black workers in South Africa, and it was only eclipsed with the growth of the NUM in the mid-eighties. NUMSA remains one of the biggest affiliates of COSATU, and the biggest union in the manufacturing sector, with over 200 000 members.

Thus MAWU's initiative at Highveld Steel, where it began organising in 1981, forms a part of its early expansion from small beginnings. It was only in 1980 that MAWU won its first recognition agreement (Webster 1985: 134, 147–50, 242), and it was recognised by Highveld Steel at the end of 1982. By 1980 two important organisational principles had emerged from the practices of MAWU (ibid: 232 ff). Firstly, the organisation should be built on a foundation of *shop steward committees* in the workplace. Each workplace organised by the union was demarcated into constituencies, and each constituency elected a shop steward or shop stewards – generally one shop steward per 50 members – to the shop steward committee. The shop stewards, who were provided with union education, constituted on the one hand the union leadership in the company, taking up workers' grievances, representing them in disciplinary inquiries and, with the support of union officials, negotiating with management, and on the other hand the democratic foundation of the higher structures of the union. The organisational base of the union was therefore integrally linked to the second principle, that of *workers' control*. The constitution of MAWU stipulated that all the structures of the union were to be constituted by a majority of workers, elected as representatives by their fellow workers and accountable to them. Thus the branch executive committee consisted of two delegates elected by each shop steward committee in the branch, as well as the branch secretary, a full-time official. This was to ensure that decisions and policies were controlled by workers rather than by full-time officials. Despite changes to this institutional structure occasioned by the growth of the union, the principle of worker control has remained important.

At Highveld Steel shop steward committees were established in the steelworks, the other plants around Witbank, and Mapochs mine, each of which elected its own office-bearers. A joint shop steward committee was established, with representation from each of the workplace shop steward committees, to co-ordinate activities and negotiate with the management of Highveld Steel. The workplace structures at Highveld Steel were supported by the MAWU branch office in Witbank, established in 1984, and by head office officials. When the branch structure of the union was later split into local and regional structures to accommodate the huge growth in membership, both the Witbank local office and the Highveld regional office, also situated in Witbank, supported the shop stewards at Highveld Steel.

MAWU merged with two other unions in the metal sector to form NUMSA in 1987. In this study I use the current name of the union, NUMSA, to cover the period of MAWU as well, in order to avoid confusion for the reader.

The United Democratic Front

The evolution of trade unionism in South Africa has always been intimately linked to that of the popular movement against apartheid. Despite the crushing of the liberation movement in the early 1960s and ongoing repression of black political and community organisations, and despite the tight mesh of apartheid control in the workplace, the township and the 'homelands', the despotism of apartheid was not absolute. There were spaces in the system of control, and social resources within families and communities, and within institutions such as churches and schools, which could be utilised to rebuild resistance. Families, communities and exiles could sustain memories of earlier cycles of resistance. Just as the expansion of industry collected workers in factories, schools and universities brought together concentrations of black youth, where they could debate, develop new ideas of liberation, and explore new tactics of struggle over new grievances. The emergence of the black consciousness movement during the 1970s, the Durban strikes in 1973, and the schools uprisings of 1976–77, were all a manifestation of a new cycle of resistance in South Africa.

The confrontations of the 1970s induced not only the Wiehahn labour reforms, but also the political reforms of the early 1980s. The new tricameral parliament consisted of a coloured and an Indian parliament alongside the dominant white parliament, and a limited form of black local government was established with the Black Local Authorities (BLAs). In 1983 a wide range of community, student, youth, women's and trade union organisations launched the United Democratic Front (UDF) to campaign against the reforms on the grounds that they entrenched apartheid. The UDF drew together activists from a wide range of historical, generational and organisational experiences: veterans of the 1950s, survivors of the first MK (Umkhonto we Sizwe – the guerrilla wing of the ANC) guerrilla offensives, former Robben Island prisoners, many of whom had begun political life in the black consciousness movement, and activists who emerged from the new wave of popular organisations during the later 1970s and early 1980s (Seekings 2000; Swilling 1988: 95–7). The bulk of the black trade union movement which had emerged during the 1970s and grown rapidly during the early 1980s, chose not to affiliate to the UDF, fearing to compromise their independence. The dominant 'workerist' current within these unions was sceptical of the 'populism' of the community organisations in the UDF.

Five phases can be identified in the life of the UDF. During the first phase, from its launch to August 1984, it ran a successful campaign to boycott the tricameral parliamentary elections and the BLA elections, establishing its own legitimacy and undermining that of the reforms. During the second phase, from late 1984 to mid-1985, school and rent boycotts coalesced into a sustained urban uprising featuring insurrectionary tactics, which gave rise to 'ungovernable areas' as state authority collapsed in many townships. The urban uprisings opened up a new strategic debate within the independent trade unions, and a trend towards closer co-operation was signalled by the jointly organised stayaway in November 1984 (Labour Monitoring Group 1985; Von Holdt 1988). The UDF adopted an organisational programme to transform 'mass mobilisation' into 'mass organisation'. This programme was cut short by the state of emergency declared in mid-1985, which ushered in the third phase. Increasing repression made formal organisation more difficult to sustain, and activists developed a new strategy to continue undermining state institutions through the insurrectionary tactics of 'ungovernablity' while building grassroots 'organs of people's power' in the form of street committees and people's courts.[14]

A fourth phase started with the second state of emergency in mid-1986, when the state stepped up its repression and by the next year had crushed the political movement in the townships. At the beginning of 1988, the UDF and its key affiliates were effectively banned, and COSATU was banned from engaging in political activities. During this phase the leadership of the popular movement inside the country passed to COSATU. Strike activity was highly politicised, and reached its highest level ever in 1987. In the course of 1988, the democratic movement regrouped in the form of the Mass Democratic Movement (MDM), a loose formation including the clandestine leadership of the UDF and its affiliates, COSATU, progressive church organisations and others. This introduced the fifth phase, that of the MDM's 1989 'defiance campaign' to defy apartheid laws and 'unban' the ANC from below. During this phase the MDM was able to take advantage of confusion and contestation within the state over strategic direction, and the openings created by the adoption of a new reformist strategy, to rebuild the profile of the popular movement. The ANC and other exiled organisations were unbanned by the government in 1990, opening up the phase of negotiated transition.

The growth of the popular movement inside South Africa also raised the profile of the ANC, and in effect brought it into the centre of South African politics. The UDF and the ANC shared a common political tradition, the UDF made it clear that it was not a replacement of or rival to the ANC, and there were clandestine linkages between the two. The ANC was influential within the proliferation of grassroots organisations which constituted 'a revolutionary movement of considerable proportions' (Lodge 1986: 231–2). Its call for 'ungovernablity' at the beginning of 1985 was influenced by the urban uprisings and, in turn, influenced strategic debate within the organisations involved (Mayekiso 1996: 53, 68). Within the ANC a revolutionary perspective developed based on notions of 'people's war', 'organs of self-government' and 'seizure of power'. This existed in dynamic tension with a somewhat different perspective, in which such struggles were regarded as a form of pressure to compel the government into negotiations (Lodge 1989). In either case, though, the ANC was projecting a vision of a new society, of replacing apartheid with democracy and ending black oppression rather than reforming the apartheid political and social order.

This study explores the changing relationship between the trade union movement and this popular movement at a grassroots level in Witbank, examining in particular the impact of popular political identities forged in community struggles on the collective identity of the trade union.

*   *   *

Having taken a necessary detour through the conceptual terrain of this study, taking in as well thumbnail sketches of the town, the company, the union and the popular movement, let us return to the brooding, smoky complex of the steelworks outside the segregated town of Witbank; let us pass through the perimeter fence, the security checkpoint and the booms, let us pass into the hidden abode of production, that grimy, fiery place where steel is produced and where apartheid was forged, challenged and partially dismantled in the contestations between black workers, white workers and managers as they contended over their local transition.

Notes

1. Adler and Webster's (1995) analysis of the role of COSATU in the South African transition neglects to consider the ways in which the transition transfigured COSATU and its strategies, and assumes instead the continuity of a strategy of 'radical reform' between the 1980s and the 1990s.

2. This exposition of workplace social structure is virtually identical to the concept of 'frontier of control' elaborated by Edwards (1990).

3. Moore (1978: 16–18) uses the idea of an 'implicit social contract' to describe a similar process at society-wide level, which Moodie incorporates into his concept of 'moral economy' for the South African gold mines.

4. Not surprisingly, with analysis focused on a diversity of national realities scholars have emphasised different qualities of social movement unionism. Thus Munck (1987) defined social movement unionism by its linkages with social movements outside the formal proletariat; Waterman (1993) adopted a more normative approach which emphasised the qualities associated with new social movements such as grassroots

activities, non-hierarchical relationships and the articulation with other class or non-class democratic and political movements; and South African scholars focused on the forging of alliances with the highly politicised community organisations and the national liberation movement. More recently, Seidman (1994) has defined social movement unionism as a struggle to raise living standards for the working class as a whole in the context of authoritarian industrialisation; while Moody (1997) emphasises reaching out to other sectors of the working class combined with democratic practices, militant collective bargaining, and political independence.

5. For a discussion of case-study methodology as applied to the workplace, see Edwards et al (1994).

6. A 'struggle dance' or 'war dance' accompanied by chanting and the singing of freedom songs.

7. Under the 1952 Native (Urban Areas) Amendment Act every African was required to carry a pass that specified his or her status in the urban areas. Those who had been born in an urban area, or who had worked legally and continuously for the same employer for 10 years, or resided legally in the urban area for 15 years, and the wives and children of men who qualified under the above, qualified for permanent urban status in the specific urban area (they were not permitted to reside in a different urban area). All other Africans were barred from staying in an urban area for longer than 72 hours.

8. Interview, Adam Engelbrecht, 12/5/98; interview Leo Makwakwa, 12/5/98. The figure for Africans in the 1991 Census is probably an undercount.

9. Interview, Adam Engelbrecht, 12/5/98.

10. The refusal of management at Highveld Steel to co-operate with this study has made it difficult to arrive at precise employment figures in Witbank, and especially in the steelworks. The company's Annual Reports aggregate figures for the Highveld group as a whole (excluding Columbus Stainless, which is a joint venture) include Rheem, which is not part of this study. The figures used in this paragraph pertain to the late 1980s and are taken from Hocking (1998: 284–7, 294–5). They include black and white employers.

11. This and the following paragraph are based on HSVC, Annual Reports, and Hocking (1998).

12. More specifically, the contribution of Rheem to the aggregate employment figures, and of Rheem and Columbus Stainless to share price and profitability, is obscured.

13. The iron ore of the Bushveld complex is rich not only in vanadium but also in titanium, which makes it impossible to smelt iron with conventional blast-furnace technology. The company developed an innovative process for overcoming this problem by putting the iron ore through pre-reduction kilns, which partially reduce the iron before it is smelted in submerged arc furnaces.

14. Swilling (1988), writing at a time when the full impact of state repression was not yet clear, identifies four phases over the period covered in this paragraph, and concludes on an optimistic note about the prospects for building 'organs of people's power'. I have reduced this to three phases.

CHAPTER 2

'A white man's factory in a white man's country'

The apartheid workplace regime

> When this man sees you, he does not see a human being. You're just an ordinary thing that maybe thinks sometimes, or need not think and just do the job. This was seen as a white man's factory, this was a white man's country. *Joe Mokoena, shop steward*

The apartheid workplace regime

Apartheid existed not only in the residential and social segregation of the town of Witbank, but also in the social and occupational structure of the Highveld Steel workplace. The workplace regime allocated skill and authority on a racial basis. The racial structure of power was characterised by racial insults and racial assault. This apartheid workplace regime had deep historical roots in the evolution of labour regimes, work practices and the racial structures of power within settler colonialism, and was underpinned by the educational and labour market policies of apartheid. There were no mechanisms for workplace incorporation of black workers: on the contrary, the broader political and social exclusion of blacks was mirrored by workplace exclusion and oppression.

This chapter analyses the internal dynamics of the apartheid workplace regime, and traces processes of change brought about by skill shortages and by the beginnings of a new 'cycle of contention' (Tarrow 1998) by black school students and workers.[1]

The racial division of labour

Black workers at Highveld Steel were labourers, artisan assistants, and later

27

semi-skilled operators, whereas whites monopolised the more skilled operating and artisan jobs, and managerial positions. In production, there were black labourers supervised by a black *induna* or *baas-boy* under the authority of a production foreman, as well as an increasing number of black semi-skilled operators from the mid-1970s. The more skilled operating jobs were reserved for whites, and the first line of management, the production foremen, were all white. On the engineering and maintenance side, there were black labourers working as artisan assistants under the direction of white artisans. There were no black artisans during the 1970s. Above artisan level, the line of managerial authority ran upwards from leading hand to chargehand to foreman.

Thus there was a clear – albeit shifting over time – ceiling on the skills level that black workers could reach, and none except for *baas-boys* on the production side exercised any sort of supervisory or managerial authority.[2] A number of blacks were employed as clerks and assistant training officers in various administration and training departments. But here too there were strict limits on what kinds of jobs they could occupy. For example, black assistant training officers could only train black workers; they were supervised by white training officers, who also trained white workers.[3]

The rightless and tightly controlled black workers, occupying the less skilled jobs, constituted a cheap labour force. The white workers, monopolising the skilled and supervisory jobs, constituted an expensive labour force. The racial division of labour replicated the broader class and racial inequalities of apartheid. Black hourly-paid workers and white hourly-paid workers were on separate payrolls, with different rates and benefits. Staff payrolls were also segregated on racial lines, with different salaries and benefits and this remained the case in the early 1990s (Hocking 1998: 194–6).[4]

Racial 'job reservation' was enforced by the broader industrial relations regime in the form of the 1956 Industrial Conciliation Act and Industrial Council collective bargaining agreements. While the racial division of labour secured an abundant supply of cheap unskilled labour for capital, it also protected the privileges of white workers, who used their trade union power and their access to political power to monopolise the more skilled and better-rewarded jobs. Even when management at Highveld Steel, under pressure from the scarcity of white skills, sought to promote black workers into semi-skilled jobs, it was forced to negotiate these shifts with the white unions and white workers on the shopfloor (Hocking 1998: 108, 177; HSVC, Annual Reports, 1973, 1976, 1978). Nonetheless, while the racial division of labour was rigid, it was not static. The racial boundaries shifted over time in response to changing production processes and changes in the labour market.

In reality, black workers had acquired skills that were essential to production but these were not formally recognised in the grading and wage system or in the racial structure of power on the shopfloor. Blacks acquired these 'tacit skills' (Leger 1992) because they were required to do tasks employers were reluctant to recognise and pay for; because their white superiors were frequently too lazy or too ignorant to perform their own work; and because the absence of job demarcations for blacks meant that they were required to perform a wide range of tasks.[5] Thus black 'unskilled' workers possessed production knowledge essential for running the plants, which they often had to pass on to new white recruits who then became their supervisors. This was a source of bitter comments by black workers: 'after you have guided a *boer* from the farms, a man who cannot even write his name, he becomes your boss' and then 'you will see the white man come after you, saying you are not working'.[6] The racial distribution of power allowed whites to claim skills they did not have and denied blacks the skills that they had – but at the same time ensured that those skills were made use of.

Racial segregation of facilities
The entire social life of Highveld Steel was structured by apartheid, as the company now acknowledges:

> Change-houses and canteens remained segregated. Rates of pay were calculated differently and Highveld Club had a whites-only membership. Production parties and long service award ceremonies were held separately. Blacks were necessarily excluded from Highveld housing schemes within Witbank . . . Segregation reflected a wide social gap between whites and blacks. Following general South African practice black workers were registered by number rather than by name (Hocking 1998: 194–5).

These practices were established by legislation such as the Factories Act, which stipulated that employers had to provide separate facilities, as well as by the 'convention' of workplace practices.[7] While the legal requirement for segregated facilities was removed when the Factories Act was repealed in 1983, racial segregation of facilities continued in practice into the 1990s. The company has claimed that it took the initiative during the 1980s to remove this kind of segregation (Hocking 1998),[8] yet in the experience of black workers management remained extremely reluctant to enforce a policy of workplace desegregation until the transition to democracy and increased pressure from NUMSA made this unavoidable in the mid-1990s. Even then desegregation depended on militant union action to break the control of white workers over access to facilities.

Such shifts and continuities illustrate the way racial identity in the workplace was constructed by legislation, by company policy and by workplace practices. Labour legislation reform – an alteration in the national regime of labour regulation – did not necessarily translate into change in the workplace regime. Racial identity was constructed by white political, managerial, trade union and social power, rather than by the law alone, and it was the basis of that power. Power in the workplace was *racially constituted*.

The racial structure of power in the workplace

The racial structure of power in the workplace constituted the factory as a place of white power and black powerlessness, ensuring that black workers understood they were working in 'a white man's factory':

> You didn't enjoy going to work because it was like bussing yourself to a prison. They took an uneducated Afrikaans-speaking person, and this man would want to please his foreman or superintendent. He would push you the way he wants to . . . When this man sees you, he does not see a human being. He's the only human being, you are just an ordinary thing that thinks maybe sometimes, or need not think and just do the job. We were called 'kaffirs' for instance. Obviously there is 80 per cent chance of violence. That's violence itself, to be called a 'kaffir'. That is why some people were not happy to go to work. It scares you away sometimes. This was seen as a white man's factory, this was a white man's country.[9]

In the white man's factory, 'all whites saw themselves as supervisors for all black employees . . . apartheid was rife'.[10] A migrant worker, who had worked at Highveld Steel since 1977, explained:

> If I may speak the truth, if a white man gave you a job, you were not supposed to know whether he was a foreman or where he worked, you just had to follow him, listen to what he was telling you . . . He had a right of just taking you and saying follow me to fix that machine even if you were not working with him. If you refused, you had refused to obey that man's rules.

Asked whether this meant he would get into trouble with his regular foreman, the worker responded that blacks were interchangeable and expendable, like overalls:

> It depended on the one who took you away. If you impressed him he might protect you by saying it is true, he was with me. Otherwise he could just keep quiet and you could be fired for having stayed away from your work. We were like overalls, mere overalls. We did not have lockers, we just put our overalls together in one place. If you came across another overall, whether it was a different size, you could just put it on.[11]

The relationship between managerial authority and the racial structure of power was complex. Not all whites were managers. However, any white had the 'right' to issue instructions to any black. This meant that there was no clear line of managerial authority or job demarcation – at least, as applied to black workers.[12] White men made the rules and the cardinal rule for black workers was to 'obey that man's rules', however arbitrary or senseless. For black workers this spelt extreme insecurity: one white man's rules might contradict another's, and in trying to follow both a worker was bound to transgress one or other instruction.

The 'right' of any white to issue instructions to any black had deep colonial roots and was closely associated with the idea that blacks were the servants of whites. Thus, it was also customary at Highveld Steel for black workers to be instructed not only to do company work, but to make tea or buy cigarettes for whites, or wash their cars: 'Any foreman, any white, if he wanted to send you to a café, he didn't ask. He just came and said, man, go and buy me cigarettes.'[13]

It was an instruction that had the same status as other work instructions:

> We worked badly because you will be fired for a stupid thing. Sometimes the white man will say, make me some tea. If you are not willing he will take you to the office so that they could fire you because you refuse to work. When you arrive, they will say if you do not obey your boss, well, work is over for you. And when you ask how can you fire me for tea, the answer is, 'A white man is a white man. If you do not listen to him, it is over with you.' When he says go and wash my car and you refuse, he will go and tell the firm that you refused to work.[14]

By blurring the distinction between tasks of production and tasks of personal service, these workplace practices constituted whites as masters and blacks as servants.[15] They implied not only an employment relationship with the company but a personal obligation to serve whites. This was not an ordinary master-servant relationship, though, structured by the reciprocal obligations of paternalism, it was a relationship that constituted blacks as non-sentient 'things', expendable and interchangeable like 'mere overalls', 'kaffirs' rather than human beings. On the other hand, 'a white man is a white man', the tautology expressing the self-evident truth that being white conferred the right to make the rules. There was a constant assertion of white domination and black subordination, suggestive of the anxiety of a settler minority which owed its position to conquest and dispossession, and which, surrounded always by the conquered, had an acute sense of its own insecurity.[16] These workplace practices blend into a racial culture that is perhaps best described as white *baasskap*.[17]

White *baasskap* was maintained by frequent dismissals, by fear and by the threat of violence. A migrant worker from Lebowa, who started working at Highveld in 1975, remembered that 'Highveld was employing and dismissing. No one could talk, because the Highveld's gate was very open. You come in and get out'.[18] Worker after worker emphasised that there was no code or procedure governing discipline or dismissals:

At the time, to lose a job was very easy . . . A supervisor could say to you, go – then you're gone. No inquiries, nothing. Nobody would be interested to hear exactly what the problem is between you and this supervisor.[19]

Arbitrary dismissal was linked to the assertion of *baasskap*. For a black worker to show disagreement or resentment, to challenge a decision, even to return the gaze of a white man, meant that he 'thinks he is white'. Transgressing workplace rules in this way warranted dismissal:

If your foreman did not like you, he came and said, hey, why are you looking at me? Seemingly you become white now, hey? All right, you go and collect your money, you must go. Nothing can be discussed.[20]

Just as any white could issue instructions to any black, so it seemed that almost any white could dismiss a black worker without reason. 'You could be dismissed by a simple artisan, every person who was white had jurisdiction to dismiss you', or, 'one of the clerks there at the clock station, you could anger him and he could also fire you without people at the plant knowing what you were fired for'.[21]

Even where a worker might think that he had come to a clear agreement with a supervisor, he had no guarantee that it would be honoured:

Sometimes you may excuse yourself to go home, when you are away the white man will report you, saying you dodged from work, meanwhile you agreed. When you come back, if they decide to fire you, they fire you.[22]

Racial assaults were part of the fabric of the workplace regime, an expression of the need to continually assert white domination and black subordination: 'People were kicked or *klapped*[23] as whites liked and nothing would happen.'[24] Managers colluded in this violence.[25]

The lack of rights or procedures, the racism, the assaults, dismissals and arbitrary behaviour of supervisors and whites created an atmosphere of fear:

People by then were so scared, in the sense that even to look at the boss is an offence. He might chase you away from work . . .[26]

Another worker remembered: 'You were just afraid of every white man, not knowing who is your divisional manager.'[27] An artisan who was in the first batch of apprentices in 1981 remembered his surprise at seeing labourers racing up ladders with heavy loads: 'It was because the foreman was waiting for him up there – it was because of fear . . .'[28]

The racial structure of power in the workplace was also institutionalised by the industrial relations order. White workers had trade union rights and access to industrial relations institutions such as industrial councils. African workers were denied these rights by the simple mechanism of excluding them from the definition of an 'employee' in the relevant legislation. During the 1970s, the unions active at Highveld Steel were the racially exclusive industrial union, Yster en Staal, two small, whites-only craft unions, and the South African Boilermakers' Association which was an industrial-craft union with white, coloured and Indian members. African workers had no union, no representation and no access to collective bargaining.

The existence of unions for white workers not only ensured that relations between white workers and management were governed by a collective bargaining regime, in contrast to the despotic and arbitrary regime for black workers; it also empowered white workers in relation to black workers. 'The white people were defeating us with their unions,' said one labourer. The white unions would support members in any dispute with a black worker, and add their pressure – should it be necessary – to the white managers' inclination to support their fellow whites. Many white foremen were union members, which further implicated the white unions in the control of black workers.[29]

In addition to the mechanisms of control provided by racial domination in the workplace, foremen and managers had access to more traditional management tools for controlling workers – in particular, withholding the payment of bonuses, the allocation of overtime and therefore the opportunity for supplementing wages, and control over promotions (the latter appears to have become more important during the 1980s as black workers were placed in more skilled jobs). Workers could lose their bonuses for coming late, sleeping on duty, insubordination, absence and other offences. Supervisors 'could wield a lot of power' over workers' earning power – which, as with most aspects of white domination at work, was wielded in arbitrary fashion.[30]

Black baas-boys

The apartheid workplace regime did not rely only on direct control of black workers by whites. Racist coercion created barriers to its own effectiveness as a way of managing production. Apartheid created great social distance between whites and blacks. White supervisors could seldom speak an African language, and many black labourers could speak little English or Afrikaans. Even if they could, language could become a means of resistance, through feigning incomprehension, or communicating with other workers in a language impenetrable to white supervisors. Management needed black 'eyes, ears and hands' (supervisor quoted in Webster 1985: 124) to ensure effective communication, and to police black workers in the thickets of their language and social networks, to which they could always retreat in order to frustrate white authority.[31] To this end it created a layer of black junior supervisors called *indunas* or *baas-boys*:

> Before the chargehand would come to me as an ordinary labourer, he'd go to the *induna* and say, 'This man has been to the toilet for an hour. What's happening to him?' Now the *induna* would come knocking on all the doors in the toilet to find out where I am, and then he'd report to the chargehand that I'm in the toilet.[32]

These terms provide interesting clues to the nature and ideology of the apartheid workplace regime. *Induna* is a Zulu word denoting a village headman or a military leader, a leader rooted in traditional institutions of leadership. The deployment of the term in colonial, and later apartheid, workplaces reflects white efforts to affirm, strengthen, or if necessary even create traditional and ethnic identities for blacks as a bulwark against 'modernisation', and its attendant demand for modern rights such as democracy or trade unions.

The second term is more blunt. In colonial discourse all blacks were denoted by the term 'boy' to indicate their imputed state of permanent childhood, irresponsibility and need for adult (i.e. white) guidance, a state that signalled they could not be entrusted with supervisory responsibilities. How then could one refer to a black who, despite this, was given a supervisory role, albeit limited? The solution was to yoke it to the term used to identify a white *baas*, creating an ambiguous term that suggested a 'boy' imbued with some of the qualities of a *baas* – strictly by delegation – while underpinning the racial hierarchy by indicating that he was the 'boy' of the *baas*:

> That's why they were called *baas-boy*, meaning therefore he's a *boy* belonging to a *baas*. He's still a *boy*, but he's a *baas-boy*, the others are just *boys*.[33]

Many workers omitted to mention the *baas-boys* when asked about workplace relations before the union came, as if they were peripheral to the substance of management-worker relations. Among those who did mention them, there was universal scorn.

> Supervisors, especially at the iron plant, would be very strong, powerfully built men who have got no brains. The reason why such men were made supervisors, was because of the system at the time where they were looking for someone who would put fear into the workforce to get the job done. You must be very big, strong, tall and threatening. Actually, we didn't even call them supervisors, we called them *baas-boys* – they were the boys of the *baas*. The type of a person who would never take anything from you, but will always come down to you with something that the *baas* says. He was subordinate to the *baas*.[34]

The relationship of the *baas-boys* with whites meant they were not respected: 'You buy cigarettes for your *baas*, then you get the position of being a *baas-boy*.' Nonetheless, they were part of the regime based on fear.

> If he tells you to do this you must do it at the very same time *and do it fast!* . . . If the *baas-boy* himself felt that you are not doing the job properly, he had the right to report you to the foreman. Because that was the only solution: if you don't want to listen, *jy is harde gat,*

jy moet net uit gaan.[35] They don't want that type of a person, because you might spread this thing among the other employees.[36]

The ambiguous position of the *baas-boy* – delegated a great deal of despotic power by the foreman but completely subject to his decisions – contributed to the arbitrary quality of management. A worker told this story to illustrate the point:

> The *baas-boy* tells a group of workers that they will be cleaning a particular area, and that they should wait for him to bring the necessary tools. A white foreman comes by and demands: 'Hey, why are you standing here?' The workers start to answer but the foreman stops them: 'No, no, no – I don't want your answer, you are fired. You don't want to work.' The workers try to explain that they are waiting for shovels, brooms and wheelbarrows. 'No, no, no – you don't want to work, you could have come to me.' The *baas-boy* also says, 'Ja, you don't want to work, you could have gone to the foreman,' because he is afraid. But when workers do go to the foreman, and tell him they have been allocated work but haven't got the tools, and ask him to provide them, he responds: 'You think you are white. You are too clever, you are fired.'[37]

Despotism, racial etiquette and efficiency

The apartheid workplace regime was clearly despotic, with coercion and fear playing an important role. Yet despotism in the workplace cannot be absolute. Managers need the compliance of production workers. Fear, coercion and the threat of dismissals can be powerful mechanisms for ensuring compliance but the complexity of production tasks, the tacit knowledge and experience that workers have and the inability of managers and supervisors to be everywhere at the same time, creates space for 'working the system', for workers to pace tasks, to engage in bargaining – explicit or implicit – with white workers, foremen or *baas-boys*, to exchange favours, to buy cigarettes for the *baas* in exchange for light work, and to work slowly or sabotage a task to show dissatisfaction with bad treatment.

As in all workplaces there was some scope for black workers to negotiate aspects of their domination and their work effort: 'If you are an *induna* you are a big person. Workers would bribe you for things, like for time off. You are the only person who has access to the immediate supervisors.'[38]

This was recognised, and exaggerated, by some managers:

> Everything was done by consensus . . . once an accord was reached they all accepted it and waited for you to deliver. If you played to their rules they were fantastic, but if you let them down you were in trouble (Hocking 1998: 221).

Although a degree of tacit negotiation took place *within* the constraints of a despotic workplace order imposed by whites, it would be wrong to conclude that workplace order was negotiated or that workers could rely on managers to play according to the rules. There were workplace codes but the cardinal rule was that rules were made by whites, and that blacks had to obey such rules. The result was that whites could make decisions about tasks, dismissals, bonuses, overtime or promotion without reference to any procedure or code to which blacks could appeal for 'fair' treatment.

The absolute power of dismissal and the practice of racial assault underpinned white power and black powerlessness. The threat of violence, racial insults and the constantly re-enacted rituals of white superiority and black inferiority were woven into the fabric of workplace relations. The racial distribution of power in the workplace was not constructed in isolation from broader social structures beyond it. State control of hostel and township regulated workers' lives beyond the workplace. Police repression of organised resistance secured these interlocking institutions. This was captured in the remark of a migrant that when NUMSA began to organise, it was difficult to recruit members because 'the majority took it like we were going to be arrested like the Mandelas when we join the union'.[39] Throughout the 1970s, attempts to organise trade unions met with harsh repression from management and state alike (Webster 1985: 127–55).

White rule-making was buttressed by an elaborate code of racial etiquette (Gordon 1977) that affirmed white domination and black subservience. Blacks had to agree with everything the *baas* said. If a black worker pointed out inconsistencies, asked questions or showed independence, he was threatening the white conception of the racial order and the place of white and black in it: being told 'you think you are white' or 'you are too clever' was a warning to adapt his behavior to that perception or be dismissed from the 'white man's factory'. As a white foreman put it: 'In the past, the black, if he's calling "Gert, Gert" there was shit. It was "*baas* Gert" or otherwise nothing.'[40] A white worker could hit a black worker 'as a joke'; it was not a joke that could be played in the other direction.[41]

Black workers knew these codes and knew they had to conform. In the case of a Namibian mine compound, Gordon notes that blacks could conform simply to avoid trouble or, more proactively, manipulate the codes to achieve specific goals – promotion, patronage, etc. But no matter how hard they might try, it was impossible for black workers to always avoid trouble or enjoy the fruits of successful manipulation (1977: 122). At Highveld Steel workers' testimonies give an overwhelming impression of the capricious and unfair nature of management and white behaviour towards them.[42]

The existence of a degree of tacit negotiation, and compliance with racial etiquette, does not imply a workplace characterised by 'hegemony' or a mutually constructed 'moral economy'.[43] Indeed, it is the absence of such qualities – what Sitas calls 'domination without hegemony' (1983: 282, 431) – that explains the aggression of white behaviour, the constant need to assert white dominance and demand black deference. Violence, and the threat of violence, was never far from the surface since domination could not be rendered invisible nor cloaked in legitimacy through consensual processes.

What was the relationship between the practices of white domination in the workplace, on the one hand, and the exigencies of capitalist production on the other? The coercive and despotic regime secured the compliance of black workers to hard, dangerous work and low pay. It also secured an apartheid form of flexible labour, where workers could be hired and fired at will, or shifted from task to task or from department to department, as the need arose.[44] On the other hand, the lack of clear lines of managerial authority, the 'right' of any white to give instructions, and the arbitrary nature of those instructions, produced endless inefficiencies in the allocation of labour – as well as opportunities for black workers to 'disappear' and 'loaf'. The rigid social hierarchy also generated numerous skills shortages: blacks with ability who could not be promoted or trained, blacks who were denied the opportunity to use their production knowledge to the full, and incompetent whites who were trained or promoted beyond their ability.[45] The result of these practices was significant black and white overstaffing. The apartheid workplace regime, then, was not highly efficient or productive (which does not mean it was not highly profitable). The practices of white domination were aimed as much at ensuring black deference as at the efficient organisation of production.[46]

The differentiation of black labour: migrant and urban workers

The differentiation of the black working class into migrant and urban workers was reflected in the division of labour in the apartheid workplace. After 1948, the system of migrant labour became the cornerstone of the National Party's apartheid labour policy, perpetuating a system that had begun with the arrival of diamond and gold mining in the nineteenth century.[47] Around 1980, more than half the black workforce at Highveld Steel were migrant workers who lived in hostels in KwaGuqa and the nearby hamlet of Oogies. The greatest number of these were Pedi-speakers from Lebowa, followed by Xhosa-speakers from the Transkei. Although some migrant workers with higher levels of education were employed as clerks, operators or drivers, the great majority were employed as labourers in the toughest and least-paid jobs such as tapping the furnaces.[48] Township residents were employed as artisan assistants, low-level operators, drivers, loaders, clerks, messengers, assistant training officers and so on during the 1970s. When increasing numbers of black workers were employed in more skilled positions during the 1970s, urban workers benefited most often.

The process of recruiting black workers at Highveld Steel was based on an explicit differentiation.[49] The personnel department would receive information about labour requirements from the company's various divisions and in conjunction with a black recruiting officer it would be decided if these were best met by local township residents or migrants recruited from the Bantustans. Migrants were preferred for jobs in hot, dangerous places such as the iron plant tap floors or the steel plant furnaces, and for hard labour 'because local residents were afraid of such jobs'. Locals were preferred for 'softer' jobs – such as artisan assistants (for which both locals and migrants were recruited) – and jobs that required literacy, such as drivers or crane drivers. If no one suitable could be found locally, migrants could be recruited for such positions.

In the case of local labour, the recruiting officer would make a selection of those with suitable qualifications from the list of registered work-seekers kept at the labour bureau in the Highveld Administration Board (HAB) offices in KwaGuqa. In the case of migrant recruitment, the first task was to confirm with labour bureau officials that there were no suitable local candidates. An application to recruit migrants then had to be sent to the regional HAB office for approval and, once this had been obtained, the recruiting officer could make arrangements with the relevant authorities in the rural areas. In the case of Lebowa, where most of Highveld's migrants were recruited, this meant phoning the magistrate's office, informing it that a certain number of labourers were to be recruited, and setting a date. The message would go out to the villages and on the designated day a crowd of men wanting work would gather, and the recruiting officer would arrive at the magistrate's office to make his selection. Over the years these men from the rural villages had formed part of the industrial working class in the mines and factories of South Africa. Many had experience and skills that could prove valuable for Highveld Steel, despite being classified and paid as unskilled workers. In the words of the recruiting officer:

I would explain the conditions of work, the good and the bad. I explained that conditions on tap floors and the furnaces were dangerous, and that a person must be physically fit and healthy to work there. I asked whether anyone had experience of working at Iscor,[50] and told them to stand on one side. I would also check whether anyone had experience of bricklaying, or laying tracks for the railways – there were similar jobs at Highveld Steel. Also whether anyone had experience as an artisan's assistant. I was looking for experience. I would then call each one forward to talk to me, show me if he had any references, check his reference book to see how long he had worked at Iscor. I had a box next to me, and if I dropped his reference book into the box then he knew he had been selected.

The men were desperate for jobs: 'Sometimes a thousand people would arrive for the selection, while I was only looking for 50. There was always conflict; they were starving. Sometimes I had to jump in my car and move off in a hurry if they were very angry.'

Once his selection had been made, the clerks at the magistrate's court would write out 12-month contracts and the workers would be told to return in a couple of days with their blankets and clothes, to catch the railway bus to Witbank. On arrival they would be taken to the hostels, put through medical and aptitude tests, and assigned to their workplaces. Once again, the company would benefit from the different work experiences and work attitudes among the migrants, and they were differentiated accordingly:

> Workers on the tap floors earned lower rates than those on the casting floor or slag-fishing in the steel plant because the latter was a more advanced process. Workers would therefore be allocated to the steel plant on the basis of a better IQ result or experience. Workers would be allocated to the iron plant on the basis of their strength and fitness, and ability to deal with heat. The Lebowa guys were suitable for the iron plant, the Transkei guys as well; they were tough, many had mining experience. Artisan assistants would be selected on the basis of previous experience or education – they should have the potential for training. If the tests showed someone had a low IQ or poor health, they were allocated to garden maintenance or housing maintenance. Pay was lower there.

If the company needed to recruit 'more literate people' from the rural areas, such as clerks or crane drivers, the recruiting officer would arrange a special visit and meet a much smaller group summoned by the magistrate's office.

This differentiated recruiting strategy was related to control, discipline and cost in the workplace. For migrant workers, pressed upon by the large reserve army of labour penned up in the Bantustans, and desperate for work, dismissal or non-renewal of a contract would be a disaster. This imposed on them the discipline to accept the toughest and most grueling work, at the lowest pay, and under harsh treatment. As a more skilled migrant at Rand Carbide observed: 'People were working very hard. Even people who are in prison, I don't believe they work in the way people were forced to work in the plant. People who are staying here in the township, they couldn't work like that.'

Labourers on the tap floor and in the drum plant at Rand Carbide worked under such awful conditions and under such pressure from white foremen and operators, that youngsters and township residents would simply 'run away' before finishing their first day on the job. But older migrant workers could not afford to do this:

> The person who has been working for a longer period, those called *madala-boy*,[51] he has got the family to look after. He has been taken by the contract from his place, and it is difficult for him just to leave the job. He starts thinking about his children, about his family . . .[52]

Workers who did not have rights to live in urban areas could only get access to jobs through the rural labour bureaus, such as that at the magistrate's office used by Highveld Steel, and the only jobs they had access to there were heavy, unpleasant and low paid. Urban residents, on the other hand, had access to a much wider range of jobs and could afford to avoid such work. A young black apprentice from the township commented:

> Since I came into Highveld there is one thing that one grew to know. There is a place there, the tap floor, where it is hot and dirty and conditions are very bad. Seemingly that place was only reserved for those who come from far away areas. You would not find a person staying in the township working on that tap floor.[53]

This differentiation within the black working class in the workplace was intimately linked to residential differentiation within the township. The migrant workers lived in rows of long single-storey hostels administered by, in turn, the Witbank municipality, the HAB and the KwaGuqa Town Council (KTC). The hostels were initially built on the edge of KwaGuqa township, but as the township expanded more houses were built beyond them so that eventually they were surrounded by houses. The hostels were generally arranged in squares around central structures with facilities for washing and ironing clothes. Some hostels had communal kitchens attached; in others the kitchens were located in the central block. They all had a derelict, uncared-for look. The ground was bare and dusty, with patches of unkempt grass. Cars had to negotiate bumpy, pitted tracks. There was an intense social life, with groups of men talking, listening to music, drinking, washing or cooking.

Highveld Steel rented hostels from the HAB – the rent being deducted from pay – and managed them, employing staff to keep them clean. In accordance with the ideology of apartheid, hostels were demarcated for different ethnic groupings – Pedis, Zulus, Xhosas, Ndebeles, Swazis, Shangaans.[54] Two hostel *indunas* were appointed by the company, one a Pedi from Lebowa and the other a Xhosa from Transkei, as well as a clerk to keep records. The *indunas*, who were accountable to the personnel manager, had disciplinary powers over drunkenness or fighting, and could issue warnings or refer cases to the company. They selected a hostel committee, with five Pedis and five Xhosas as members, to help with discipline.[55] Workers made bitter comments about living conditions in the hostels. A man who had worked for the company for 20 years commented:

Hostel life is not life, it's the type of life which is led by the poor . . . A hostel is not a place where people are supposed to stay. As a human being I must have my own yard.

Although the company rented the hostels from the municipality, 'they were bad, nobody is taking care, it does not show that we have employers'. Workers complained about broken windows, taps not working, leaking drains, broken lights and electric points. With the pinpoint clarity reserved for milestones in a workers' life, a worker from Lebowa recalled arriving at the Highveld hostels on 13 January 1978 'because I was told that I will make steel. I was promised everything, food, accommodation . . . Those things were nowhere to be found'. When workers complained, instead of taking responsibility the company offered to cease deducting rent from their wages. 'Up until today the hostel is still that type of hostel . . . the stoves, when they are broken, we fix them on our own. We collect some money and find somebody to fix them so that we can cook.'[56] In the memory of migrants, the hostels have always been unpleasant places to live, neglected by the company and government alike.[57]

The hostels were also strictly segregated from the townships, surrounded by fences and the gates guarded by municipal police. Only hostel residents were allowed to enter.[58] Residential segregation reinforced tensions between migrants and township residents. A township resident said that this encouraged the perception that 'you and them are not the same people, that you must not allow them to get into your place'. His comrade added:

There has always been that perception that people from the hostel are different. I think this led them to develop an inferiority complex against the people in the township. They would easily get robbed in the township because they are not known and they do not know anybody from the township.[59]

Another reported that hostel dwellers were regarded as 'uncivilised' by township residents, while a Pedi-speaking township resident described how township residents, whether Pedi- or Zulu-speaking, used insults to refer to migrant workers, for example *amaMpokwane*, meaning 'those whose ears have been blocked with stones', because 'in the homeland it's full of stones, mountains – those big stones, they close their ears, that's why they don't understand. It's a vulgar word. Then we start fighting.'[60]

Complex factors combined to produce the experience of difference between township residents and migrant workers.[61] They faced different labour market opportunities and constraints, frequently had different jobs in the workplace, were segregated in the community and lived under very different conditions. Many migrant workers retained links to rural productive resources, and their engagement in the urban economy was a strategy to preserve their 'rural integrities' (Moodie 1994). This entailed different family structures and a different relationship to traditional (albeit changing) cultural practices and social institutions, which increased the salience of ethnic divisions between predominantly Zulu locals and Pedi or Xhosa migrants. Apartheid policies sought to freeze, institutionalise and deepen these differences. The result was a history of tension between township communities and hostel communities located in their midst or on their periphery. While the contours of this tension were submerged most of the time in the language, attitudes and practices of daily interaction, in times of heightened political and social activism they have frequently emerged in open conflict.

Witbank and Highveld Steel were no exception. The tension between migrant and urban blacks was an integral part of the apartheid workplace regime and the wider apartheid regime. A union organiser remembered a violent clash between migrants and township youths in the late 1960s. 'Now, whenever we discuss this hostel issue, we remember that incident.'[62] Such incidents provided a repertoire of memories, meanings and actions that could be drawn upon over and over again in response to current issues.

This was the context in which NUMSA began to organise workers at Highveld Steel, and the union was to be profoundly shaped both by the ability of migrants and township residents to unite as workers, and by the tensions between them. The changing relations between migrant and urban workers and their union – and their relation to broader political struggles – is a central theme of this book. The centrality of migrant labour to the apartheid workplace regime makes this unsurprising.

Change in the apartheid workplace regime

Although the apartheid workplace regime was an extremely rigid social structure in its distribution of power and occupations, it was not static. Changes in the production process, in the labour market and in the broader political arena all introduced new dynamics. Two of these were the shifts in the racial division of labour brought about by the scarcity of white skilled labour, and the early tremors of black assertiveness in the workplace and the attempts to meet this by incorporating black workers through weak forms of 'consultation'.

The changing racial division of labour

Throughout the 1970s, Highveld Steel expressed concern at the scarcity of skills and the high cost of white skilled labour. In 1971 the company called for a change in government labour policies. In 1973 it reported that agreements had been reached with the (white) trade unions on increasing the number of occupations that could be filled with black workers. In 1974 it called again, not for the end of the racial division of labour, but for a shift in its lines of demarcation: 'The semi-skilled white workers must be trained as artisans and as first line supervisors, and black workers must be used in a far wider range of operating jobs.' To facilitate this, training centres should be established for black workers. In 1977 Highveld Steel commented on the need to negotiate with the trade unions for the opening of more skilled jobs for blacks, and in 1979 announced its success in removing the closed shop for white unions in the more highly paid occupations (HSVC, Annual Reports).

Inside the plants, managers – frustrated by high turnover and absenteeism among white workers who knew they were in high demand – experimented cautiously with employing black workers in semi-skilled positions: as crane drivers in Transalloys in the later 1960s and in the steel plant in the early 1970s, followed by casting machine operators in the steel plant a couple of years later. When the new plate mill was commissioned in 1977, the corporation 'broke with tradition' and employed a number of black semi-skilled operators (Hocking 1998: 108, 161, 177, 192, 220, 224). By the 1980s, there were black furnace and kiln operators. Frequently there was white resistance but since there was no shortage of demand for white workers they tended to move out of occupations as blacks moved in. Managers were pleased with the commitment and performance of this vanguard of black semi-skilled workers, which was in strong contrast to the work attitudes of the whites they replaced. Across industry in the 1960s and 1970s, there was similar growth of a stratum of black semi-skilled workers (Crankshaw 1997).

Highveld Steel's concern was not only about operators but also about shortages in artisan skills, which were driving up wages and hampering production. In the late 1970s and early 1980s, the company was driven to undertake large-scale recruiting campaigns overseas and, by 1982, 20 per cent of its artisans came from the United Kingdom. It was such pressures that led the government-appointed Wiehahn Commission to recommend in 1979 that apprentice training should be opened to Africans. The legislation that prevented this was repealed in 1980 and in January the following year 17 of Highveld Steel's 300 apprentices were Africans.[63] In 1984, after the first group of black apprentices qualified, the company could boast that 12 of its more than 800 artisans were black. This grew to 32 the following year. The fact that apprentices had to have passed the formal educational level of standard 7 was a constraint, so in 1982 the company also started inducting black workers who had developed skills on the shopfloor – as artisan helpers or operators – into the journeyman recognition scheme.[64]

By 1994, these initiatives had significantly altered the composition of the black workforce: 23 per cent (about 185) of the artisans at Highveld Steel were black, as were 45 per cent of the approximately 330 apprentices, 74 per cent of the skilled operators and 24 per cent of technicians and technicians-in-training. In addition, a new emphasis – coinciding with the first democratic elections in South Africa – on promoting blacks into supervisory roles meant that 9.5 per cent of first and second line supervisors were black.

All the new apprentices and artisans, and most of the semi-skilled workers, were recruited from the ranks of urban black workers rather than migrants. Most of the 'black advancement' into more skilled jobs took place through internal promotion and favoured the local black workers who had a higher level of education. When such workers were recruited from outside, influx control regulations dictated that local workers were preferred. In 1986, when influx control was abolished, the company ended its recruiting in the rural areas. From 1990, recruitment was restricted to those with a standard 6 or higher level of education – partly as a response to the increasing use of computerised technology in production. These changes produced a gradual shift in the proportion of migrants in the workforce. During the 1970s, migrants constituted a majority of the black workers, their numbers peaking at above 2 000; by the 1990s migrants were a minority, albeit a large one, with Highveld Steel still paying rent for almost 1 500 workers in the hostels.[65] The growing numbers of black semi-skilled and skilled operators, and the emergence of a new stratum of black apprentices and artisans, increased the internal differentiation of the black working class, and reinforced the existing differentiation into migrant and urban black workers.

Apart from changing the composition of the black workforce, these changes in the racial division of labour disturbed the structure of power in the apartheid workplace regime. In the early 1980s, the Department of National Education refused permission for the Witbank Technical College to accept Highveld Steel's black apprentices – partly because of resistance from the mining companies in the area[66] – and Highveld Steel, together with other metal companies in the area, had to establish its own in-house facilities for theoretical training.[67] Black apprentices also encountered racism and a refusal to co-operate from white artisans on the shopfloor (Hocking 1998: 223–4).[68]

Despite these significant shifts, the racial division of labour remained a relatively rigid system. The majority of highly skilled workers were still white in 1994, and the overwhelming majority of supervisors and managers were white. The workplace remained strongly characterised by a racially structured distribution of skill, authority and income.[69]

The beginnings of resistance

In the long history of settler colonialism and apartheid in South Africa, the ruling classes have consistently sought to create, maintain and defend a variety of despotic workplace regimes – slavery, indentured labour and controlled black labour. Throughout this history, workplace despotism has been contested and there have been moments of resistance, rebellion and reform. With the emergence of an industrial economy, there were periods of sustained mobilisation and organisation by trade union and quasi-union structures. Periods of successfully reproduced coercive despotism have alternated with periods where despotism has had to accommodate organisation and negotiation.

The despotism of the apartheid workplace regime – which was so clearly apparent at Highveld Steel – was secured by the repression of the early 1960s, which saw the banning and destruction of the national liberation movement and the harassment and collapse of the South African Congress of Trades Unions (SACTU). In this way, the state resolved the problem of growing popular resistance and trade union activity during the decade of the 1950s. Management control and white power were secured in South Africa and in the workplace. But, over time, this regime, based on a specific configuration of national and international forces, would feel the impact both of changing external conditions as well as new dynamics generated by its own successes. Thus rapid industrial development, based on domestic and foreign investment, created the conditions for the emergence of a large, semi-skilled, black working class – and also made South Africa more vulnerable to international pressure. The Durban strikes of 1973, and the persistence of the new unions' efforts to establish a foothold in industry in the face of management intransigence and government repression, were a signal that change would come. The 1976 student uprisings in Soweto and elsewhere indicated that in the broader society as well, the despotism of apartheid would be challenged by a new generation concentrated in the institutions of apartheid education. The shackles of fear were being broken.

These national stirrings were felt inside the Highveld Steel complex, both in the form of isolated instances of worker resistance, and in the formative efforts by management to head off unionisation by establishing a liaison committee. It was no coincidence that the first sign of a new assertiveness among black workers occurred in the new plate mill, opened in 1977 just after the student uprisings, and where the company 'broke with tradition' by employing large numbers of young black workers in semi-skilled positions. Ezekiel Nkosi was one of the young township men employed in the new mill. For six months he worked as a hotbank marker. Then followed jobs as hotbank operator, clerk on the new shear-line, crosscut shear operator and side-trimmer cutting the steel plates to size. Nkosi, and many of his colleagues in the new plant, had participated in the school uprisings the year before after hearing about June 16 in Soweto. The hated administration offices in KwaGuqa were 'burnt to ashes'. Nkosi participated in student organisation and was detained for two days. Friends of his were detained for up to six months and three students were killed. With education at a standstill, many were looking for work in 1977 – the year Highveld Steel opened its new plant.

In the plate mill, 'most of us were youngsters from school, and we had this militancy of students. We did have some strikes and actions, before we even knew about unions, or about this thing called NUMSA'. Nkosi became an informal leader of the workers on the shear-line. They 'started fighting about things that were not right for us, feeling that the company was doing things wrong against us, then we would fight'. One night they managed to find their wage rate cards in a manager's office – and discovered that they were supposed to earn R1.50 on their machine, not the 95 cents that Highveld was paying. They protested. 'We did demand things and win things as workers. We went on wildcat strikes, work stoppages of two or three hours, even at night, just workers organising ourselves.'

Management started to dismiss troublemakers in ones and twos. When it came to Nkosi's turn he was accused of being drunk after quarrelling with his supervisor on a Saturday and sent home. 'When I came back on Monday, I found they had already written a discharge for me. I showed some of my friends. They striked immediately, for about two hours, because we knew the company was trying to weaken the power we had.'[70] Nkosi was reinstated. The beginnings of collective resistance were being forged, although they were isolated in flat products and particularly on the shear-line.

J.J. Mbonani was an Ndebele-speaking migrant worker but he had also been affected by the 1976 uprisings when he lost his job as a teacher in Springs on the East Rand. He started working at Rand Carbide in Witbank in the same year. In 1978 Highveld Steel bought Rand Carbide. Management told workers that the pension fund – to which they contributed with monthly deductions from their wages – was bankrupt. The workers demanded their money. Highveld offered to transfer the pension fund to its own pension scheme. Workers were puzzled and suspicious: if the fund was bankrupt, how could money be transferred to the Highveld scheme? 'We didn't agree with that. I was the one who was pushing the hardline not to accept that. We demanded our money. I had to draw the people together. We decided that the best thing was to demand our money, or else we would not proceed with the job.' The company managed to persuade some of the older workers who were close to retirement not to withdraw their money. 'But most of us, more especially the young ones, we demanded the money.' Their collective solidarity paid off and they received between R600 and R900 each.[71]

Mbonani saw his actions as a product of his political consciousness. His experiences of racial oppression had made him an angry man. As a 14-year-old he saw his uncle being *sjambokked*[72] by a farmer, all the while being encouraged by his grandfather, who was fearful that he would be evicted from the farm. For Mbonani it was a defining moment. 'That's when I started to see that no, no, no, something must be done. I don't believe this is the way. Sooner or later I will also be taken to this farmer to work for him, six months without any pay. At the very same time I must be *sjambokked* for not coming to work! But I couldn't do anything about that pain because I was still young.'

Mbonani was also influenced by his grandfather, who used to talk about the ANC, about 'the history of Nelson Mandela and his fellow guys'. The young Mbonani decided that 'I like the name ANC, fighting for the poor people'. He also loved to go to church where he learnt about Moses and the oppression of the Israelites. The discovery that people so long ago had experienced similar oppression strengthened his resolve to find ways to fight:

I started to be so aggressive to every white guy. Even if he wanted to fight me, I was prepared to fight with him. When I am inside the working place, or outside the working place, or at his farm. I cannot live under this pressure. If I might die then that will solve the problem, rather than living under this pressure. We are being pressured at work, we are being pressured where we are staying, we are being pressured everywhere. There is no respect for us. Even if one is walking on the streets, police come demanding passes. No, no, no, I said. No. Absolutely no.

Mbonani was recognised as a leader. At school he was elected to a committee of students. When he worked as a teacher in Springs he was elected as a town councillor. Dismissed as a teacher in 1976 for encouraging the students, he organised the pension demands at Rand Carbide. Recognised 'as a bullfighter' for his role in this struggle, Mbonani's fellow workers elected him to the liaison committee at Rand Carbide when it was taken over by Highveld Steel.[73]

Ezekiel Nkosi and J.J. Mbonani became conscious of their oppression and the possibilities of rebellion in their experience of apartheid outside the workplace – at school, in the community, on the white farm.[74] On the one hand, they had access to older generations' memories of previous eras of resistance, as well as moral resources such as the Bible; on the other hand, they were conscious of being a new generation, the 'youth'. It was a 'white man's country' – but this had to be challenged. The 1976 uprisings showed that the white order could be challenged through collective action, and it became a symbol of the youth and their will to resist. The seeming solidity of apartheid had been cracked. They brought their anger and their consciousness with them into the 'white man's factory'. There they found things were also unfair: the company was doing 'wrong things'; it was cheating them of their correct pay; it claimed that their pension money had disappeared. They experienced the injustice of apartheid at work as much as outside work. They got together with their fellow workers to challenge 'wrong things'. They were participants in the spirit of the times.

Despite its despotism, there were strategic resources within and outside the apartheid workplace regime that workers could use to mobilise collective solidarity and challenge managerial and white domination. One of these was their strategic power in production – when they stopped work, or threatened to do so, managers listened. Given the skills shortage at Highveld Steel, this was not surprising. Another resource was their consciousness of national oppression, the history of resistance and the potential of black solidarity.

The liaison committee: an attempt at incorporation

After the 1973 Durban strikes, the government amended labour legislation to provide for liaison committees in the workplace. These were joint management-labour committees, with equal representation from both, and the chairperson appointed by management. The committee could 'make such recommendations concerning conditions of employment as the committee may at any time deem expedient'. The committees ensured management control over worker representation and were clearly designed to pre-empt unions. Employers responded with enthusiasm: by the end of 1974 there were nearly 1 700 liaison and works committees in place (Webster 1985: 134–5).

Highveld Steel established a liaison committee in the mid-1970s, an indication that management was aware that the despotism of the apartheid workplace regime could not be sustained indefinitely.[75] If the threat of a union challenge to the workplace order were to be headed off, the company would have to find ways to reform the workplace regime and give it greater legitimacy in workers' eyes. The liaison committee would be a forum where workers could air their views and be consulted.

In elections for the liaison committee candidates for each division of the company were nominated by employees in that division. Those whose nomination was supported by at least 10 workers became candidates. Each candidate had his or her own ballot box, to which an enlarged photograph of his or her face was fixed. Workers were let in one by one to vote.[76] Despite the appearance of democracy, the liaison committee proved to be powerless. 'It was used as a mouthpiece for management. If they wanted to say something to the workers, they used to say it through the liaison committee.'[77] The committee was not allowed to hold meetings with workers. The only permitted avenue for communication was to summarise the minutes and place them on the company notice boards, and for individual workers to approach their representative.[78] In the words of the bullfighter Mbonani, it had no power 'to change the decisions or the oppression made by this management'.[79]

The liaison committee 'kept on complaining about the dismissals and how they were handled' until the company produced a disciplinary code which stipulated that workers were entitled to a fair hearing before dismissal.[80] This did not empower the liaison committee: 'We started representing workers as a liaison committee but because we were not trained we did not know what argument to prove. It was just tokenism.'[81] Another worker remembered: 'Those guys were like messengers. They wouldn't go there to represent you but just to interpret proceedings.'[82] The new procedures did not alter the reality of white power: 'When the liaison officers were going to represent you, they would tell you straight that they must go down on their knees and plead for you. Even if maybe the white man was wrong they would take it as if the white man is right and you must plead because he is white.'[83]

The members of the liaison committee realised they had no power. It did not give workers any rights, nor did it shift even slightly the balance of power in the workplace. It was not in any real sense a reform of the workplace regime. What the liaison committee did achieve, though, from its members' point of view, was to cast a shadow image, like the negative of a photograph, of what real rights and powers, and real representation, might look like. Wage negotiations cast this shadow image most clearly. After the white trade unions and the company had completed their wage negotiations, the liaison committee members would meet the managing director in the boardroom where they would be informed of the increase agreed by management and the unions, and receive copies of the agreement. The liaison committee 'had no impact whatsoever'. Only white workers were allowed to be members of trade unions, 'so our understanding of this liaison committee was that it existed on the basis of the law that was not allowing blacks to be members of a union'.[84] When the liaison committee tried to table wage proposals, 'we were told that wages and conditions of employment are negotiated at the Industrial Council with the unions, and we are not a union, and in order to come into the Industrial Council we have to go via a trade union.'[85]

The liaison committees were an attempt to incorporate black workers into the apartheid workplace regime. At Highveld Steel this attempt failed, as it did in most workplaces (Webster 1985), because it did not affect, in any significant way, the balance of power in the workplace. Management was as much as telling the liaison committee that they would have to organise a union if they wanted to negotiate with their employer. The only option inside Highveld Steel was the South African Boilermakers' Society (SABS). Although a number of black workers had joined SABS when it opened a branch for black workers at Highveld Steel in 1979, liaison committee members felt it was racist because it had separate branches for black and white workers, and black members had fewer rights than white members.[86] A black industrial officer at the company approached Frank Boshielo and Bob Moloi and 'mentioned the name of a trade union, and the name of that trade union was NUMSA'. The liaison committee then mandated Boshielo and two others to look for the National Union of Metalworkers of South Africa.[87]

Notes

1. This chapter should be read together with *Cast in a racial mould*, Webster's (1985) study of the racial division of labour, the changing labour process and changing forms of trade unionism in the metal industry. The parallels are striking.
2. Interview, Frank Boshielo, 9/93.
3. Interview, Charles Makola, 8/5/94; see also interview, William Sehlola, 5/6/94.
4. Interview, Frank Boshielo, 9/93.
5. Adler (1993) describes virtually identical processes at Volkswagen SA during the 1980s.
6. Interview, Tshagata, 26/5/94; interview, Ephraim Kgole, 10/95. One of the new black apprentices of the 1980s remarked on how he relied on black labourers to teach him, and a rigger – and former rigger assistant – described the skills of the rigger assistants. Interview, Sam Mkhabela, 1/6/94; interview, Hong Kong Kgalima, 3/7/94.
7. The history of the Factories Act and workplace segregation sheds interesting light on the relation between law and workplace practices. The original Act in 1918 did not specify separate facilities, but the department of manpower noted in 1928 that such facilities were often provided, which encouraged employers to employ workers of a single colour because of the expense of duplicating facilities. In 1941 government proposed an amendment introducing compulsory segregation. This was officially supported by the Trades and Labour Council and the Cape Federation of Labour Unions, and vociferously by the National Party, then in opposition, but withdrawn in the face of strong resistance from left-wing trade union groupings, and possibly because of the cost implications for capital. The National Party cited instances of racial mixing in canteens and toilets in support of segregation, but Budlender argues that cases of integration were infrequent and that when the amendment enforcing segregation was finally passed it reflected rather than imposed workplace practices (1983: 33–4).
8. When the plate mill was established in 1977, the company decided not to label the segregated facilities with the stipulated signs. According to the company, it decided to end the segregation of facilities after the law was changed in 1983, but then

discovered that steelworks fell under the Mines and Works Act rather than the Factories Act, and was threatened with prosecution by one of the white unions; however, 'the group went ahead with more reform', including the first mixed social function, a long service awards ceremony, in the late 1980s (Hocking 1998: 194, 278–9).

9. Interview, Joe Mokoena, 12/10/95; see also interview, J.J. Mbonani, 31/5/94. Compare this quote with the words of the Minister of Bantu Affairs in 1955: '. . . There will always be thousands of Bantu on the white farms, in the mines, in industry and also as servants in the white houses. The difference however, will be that the natives will be there, not as a right, but at the bidding and by the grace of the whites. At best they will be visitors in the white area . . .' And in 1966 the Minister said: '. . . even if they were born here in the white areas . . . the Bantu has always been subject to restrictions not because we regard him as an inferior being . . . [but because] we regard him as being present in another man's country' (quoted in Sitas 1983: 213–14).

10. Interview, Bunny Mahlangu, 8/11/93.

11. Interview, Jerry Mogoleko, 10/95; see also interview, J.J. Mbonani, 31/5/94; interview, Charles Makola, 8/5/94.

12. Gordon notes similar practices on a Namibian mine, where despite the formal rule that a worker should only obey his/her supervisor, informal 'house rules' made it clear that blacks should obey any white who gave them an instruction, whether he was a mine employee or not (1977: 98).

13. Interview, J.J. Mbonani, 31/5/95; see also interview Charles Makola, 8/5/94.

14. Interview, Tshagata, 26/5/94.

15. The Masters and Servants Act, which criminalised breaches by black workers of the employment contract, and had its origins in the Masters and Servants Ordinance of 1841, was only repealed in the mid-1970s. The Industrial Conciliation Act of 1956 excluded Africans from the definition of an 'employee' and thereby from trade union rights (Friedman 1987: 13–14, 34; Keegan 1996: 125–6).

16. Apartheid, of course, was a strategy to resolve these anxieties by partitioning South Africa into black Bantustans and a white South Africa where blacks would be present only to the extent that they were needed to labour for whites – see the quotes in note 9 above.

17. *Baasskap* literally means white bosshood. *Baas* is the Afrikaans work for 'boss', but it has much stronger connotations of patriachy, deference and the servility of the addressor. The colour of power is suggested by the word used by black workers to denote a manager, *umlungu*, which literally means 'a white person' in Zulu/Xhosa.

18. Interview, Johannes Phatlana, 15/4/94; see also interview, Frank Boshielo, 9/93.

19. Interview, Bob Moloi, 10/7/94; see also interview Ezekiel Nkosi and Philip Mkatshwa, 9/3/94; interview, Jerry Mogoleko, 10/95; interview, Albert Makagula, 24/3/94. Management described this regime as 'autocratic' – a man could be fired if you 'didn't like his face', but claimed that this applied equally to black and white workers (Hocking 1998: 195–6).

20. Interview, J.J. Mbonani, 31/5/94.

21. Interview, Mosi Nhlapo, 12/95; interview, Jerry Mogoleko, 10/95.
22. Interview, Tshagata, 26/5/94.
23. *klapped*: 'given a blow' in Afrikaans.
24. Interview, J.J. Mbonani, 31/5/94.
25. Management described 'a *klap* on the ear' as a highly effective form of discipline, and also acknowledged a culture of racial insult and assault on the shopfloor (Hocking 1998: 221–2, 250–3). See also interview, Phineas Mabena, 12/5/94; interview, J.J. Mbonani, 31/5/94.
26. Interview, J.J. Mbonani, 31/5/94. Gordon quotes a Namibian mineworker explaining an identical fear: 'Outsiders would say our behaviour is full of humbleness, but in reality it is fear – fear of being fined or beaten up and fear of our family's starving' (1977: 121).
27. Interview, Jerry Mogoleko, 10/95.
28. Interview, Mosi Nhlapo, 12/95.
29. Interview, Tshagata, 26/5/94; interview, Charles Makola, 8/5/94.
30. Interview, Sam Mkhabela, 1/6/94.
31. Compare Gordon on the importance of 'acting dumb', pretending not to understand what whites were saying, and answering to several different names, as strategies for black workers (1977: 125–7).
32. Interview, Mosi Nhlapo, 12/95.
33. Ibid.
34. Interview, Bob Moloi, 10/7/94.
35. *jy is harde gat, jy moet net uit gaan*: 'you are hard-arsed, you must just get out'. During interviews, workers would frequently break into Afrikaans when explaining how supervisors or managers insulted them, dismissed them or gave them instructions. Afrikaans was the language through which the attitudes and practices of white *baasskap* were defined. Black workers used the Zulu word *ububhunu* – 'the quality of being a *boer* [i.e. an Afrikaner]' – to denote behaviour that was racist, rude, bossy or lacking respect (see interview, Veli Majola, 26/10/95).
36. Interview, J.J. Mbonani, 31/5/94.
37. Ibid.
38. Interview, Mosi Nhlapo, 12/95.
39. Interview, Tshagata, 26/5/94.
40. Interview, Gert van der Merwe, 29/11/95.
41. Interview, J.J. Mbonani, 31/5/94. Gordon notes very similar codes between blacks and whites in a mining compound in Namibia (1977: 120 ff).
42. Compare Gordon's description of the 'low credibility of all whites' who 'sometimes make formal rules which they do not implement, and at other times they implement rules of which blacks are unaware'; who also 'differ in the way they apply the laws' and 'do not always do what they say they will do when a law is disobeyed' (1977: 96–7).
43. Moodie (1994), in his excellent study of the workplace regime in the mining industry, does attempt to characterise the workplace in these terms, mistakenly in my view. In

Thompson's work 'moral economy' refers to an autonomous plebeian culture, rebellious yet defending the traditional, which emerged in resistance to new market relations that were undermining a customary system of reciprocal obligations. Popular expressions of moral economy comprised the 'exertion of force at the margin of legitimacy and illegality' (Thomson 1991: 1–15, 258–351). Moodie gives the concept a subtly different meaning, using moral economy to describe a mutually acceptable and mutually understood social order, thus privileging a narrative of order and hegemony over one of contestation (see Von Holdt 2000: chapter 1). It is in any case questionable whether the concept of customary relations of reciprocal obligation can be smoothly transposed from the English setting to a South African context of colonial dispossession.

44. COSATU's September Commission made the connection between flexibility and 'apartheid forms of employment' (COSATU 1997: 132).

45. The new black apprentices noticed many signs of the shortage of skills in the workplace: the shortage of competent artisans, the preponderance of journeyman artisans, vacancies in the machine shops, the recruitment of immigrant artisans, the frequency of 'jipping' and shoddy maintenance (interview, Sam Mkhabela, 1/6/94).

46. Gordon argues that this is typical of colonial society, citing Colson in Gordon (1977: 120). Sitas also cites recurring bouts of managerial concern from the 1920s to 1950s at the low productivity of black workers that was the result of 'domination without hegemony' (1983: 207–20).

47. Migrant labour has been a central feature in the evolution of labour supply in the South African economy. It took shape on the diamond and gold mines in the nineteenth century, when taxation and land dispossession forced Africans into wage employment on the mines and farms and in urban industrial and service sectors, while pass laws prevented the majority from settling in the urban areas. A series of rural Bantustans emerged, governed indirectly through traditional (albeit often restructured by the colonial powers) tribal authorities, as impoverished labour reservoirs for cheap labour sectors of the economy. Migrant labour was enshrined as the cornerstone of apartheid's labour policy by the National Party government elected in 1948, and was regulated by means of the influx control system and government housing policy, specifically the hostel system.

48. Interview, Frank Boshielo, 9/93; interview, Moses Nkabinde, 12/5/98.

49. This account of the company's recruiting practices is drawn from an interview with the company recruiting officer, Moses Nkabinde, 12/5/98.

50. The state-owned steel company, privatised in the late 1980s. Highveld Steel also recruited around Newcastle in KwaZulu-Natal, looking specifically for workers who had experience in the Iscor works at Newcastle.

51. This term for an old black man illustrates how racist discourse permeated the workplace. As noted before in the discussion of the term *baas-boy*, all blacks were 'boys' in white discourse. How then could this discourse identify some men as older than others? One solution was to co-opt terms from African languages: hence '*amadala*', Zulu for

'old men' and incorporating a tone of respect, was yoked to 'boy' to create a uniquely disrespectful means for addressing an older man.

52. Interview, J.J. Mbonani, 31/5/94.
53. Interview, Mosi Nhlapo, 9/11/93.
54. Interview, Tshagata, 26/5/94.
55. Interview, Moses Nkabinde, 12/5/98.
56. Interview, Tshagata, 10/95; interview, Jerry Mogoleko, 10/95; interview, Ephraim Kgole, 10/95.
57. Sitas (1983: 255) and Webster (1985: 210) note similar conditions for migrant workers in hostels on the East Rand in the late 1970s and early 1980s. According to the Highveld Steel recruiting officer, though, conditions were good when the company managed the hostels itself; it was only during the uprisings of the mid-1980s, when it withdrew and handed responsibility back to the KTC, that conditions deteriorated.
58. Interview, Sam Mkhabela, 1/6/94.
59. Interview, Mosi Nhlapo, 9/11/93.
60. Interview, Charles Makola, 8/5/94; interview, Hong Kong Kgalima, 3/7/94.
61. Sitas (1983), Webster (1985) and Mamdani (1996) all discuss the difference and tension between township residents and migrant workers in the context of trade unionism.
62. Interview, Barney Mashego, 13/10/95.
63. All figures in this and the following paragraph are from HSVC, Annual Reports.
64. The journeyman recognition scheme provided a route for workers to qualify as artisans through practical training on the shopfloor, rather than through the traditional apprenticeship route that combined practical and formal training examined through trade tests. Entry into the journeyman scheme did not require a specific level of formal schooling.
65. Interview, Moses Nkabinde, 12/5/98; figures supplied by Witbank City Council housing department.
66. Interview, Sam Mkhabela, 1/6/94.
67. Similar problems were experienced at Boksburg Technical College (HSVC, Annual Report, 1981).
68. The external borders of settler colonialism drew internal borders within the workplace regime: a trainer linked the racial tensions between black and white apprentices to the fact that the whites 'were fresh out of the army' where they'd been 'on the border where blacks had been the enemy' (Hocking 1998: 223). One of the black apprentices recalled the attempt of Professor Nic Wiehahn, who had chaired the Wiehahn Commission, to justify the blurring of apartheid barriers to his predominantly white audience when he addressed an annual apprentice function in Witbank: 'He wanted to impress upon the parents of the apprentices and other members of the broader Witbank community that being an artisan was a very respectable occupation – sort of trying to generate some enthusiasm for that, firstly – and then secondly he argued that the birth rate of whites was approaching zero – which I interpreted as an attempt to justify the recruitment of black apprentices' (interview, Sam Mkhabela, 1/6/94).

69. This was uppermost in workers' perceptions. For example, in 1993 shop stewards in the flat products division remarked that the highly skilled operating jobs in the strip mill were reserved for whites (interview, Ezekiel Nkosi, 9/3/94).
70. Interview, Ezekiel Nkosi, 9/3/94, 5/5/94, 10/7/94.
71. Interview, J.J. Mbonani, 31/5/94.
72. *Sjambok* is Afrikaans for a rawhide whip, to flog with such a whip.
73. Interview, J.J. Mbonani, 7/6/94.
74. This should not be construed as an argument that rebellion or trade unionism at work will only develop where there is experience of rebellion outside work. For many workers at Highveld Steel joining NUMSA was their first experience of rebellion against oppression. Sitas (1983) finds that migrant workers first experienced unity in the workplace. Adler (1994) reveals the important role played by underground ANC activists in organising the union at Volkswagen. There was clearly a complex blend of factors in the formation of the new unions among black workers in South Africa.
75. At the time the company congratulated the government on 'strengthening' the liaison committee system, adding that it was also necessary for black workers to be represented in industry level negotiations (HSVC, Annual Report, 1977).
76. Interview, Frank Boshielo, 9/93; see also interview, Bob Moloi, 10/7/94.
77. Interview, Bob Moloi, 10/7/94.
78. Interview, Frank Boshielo, 9/93.
79. Interview, J.J. Mbonani, 31/5/94.
80. Interview, Frank Boshielo, 9/93.
81. Ibid.
82. Interview, Bunny Mahlangu, 8/11/93.
83. Interview, Tshagata, 26/5/94.
84. Interview, Bob Moloi, 10/7/94.
85. Interview, Frank Boshielo, 9/93.
86. Ibid.
87. Ibid; interview, Bob Moloi, 10/7/94.

CHAPTER 3

'The Messiah comes to Highveld Steel'
The apartheid workplace regime
and the union challenge

> The shop stewards started to defend the workers, they were seen to
> be defending them and, once some cases had been won, gradually
> people started to see their Messiah having now arrived in the
> workplace.
>
> *Bunny Mahlangu, chairperson, shop steward committee (1986–87)*

The Wiehahn reforms: a strategy of incorporation

By 1981, when the liaison committee mandated its members to find the
National Union of Metalworkers of South Africa, the conditions for trade
unionism had improved substantially compared with those in the mid-1970s
when the committee was established at Highveld Steel. The tenacity of the
new black trade unions in the face of repression, the growing international
pressure for change and the shock to the apartheid system of the national
school student revolt of 1976–77, had impelled the regime to consider
reform. In 1977 the Wiehahn Commission was established to investigate
labour reform. Five years of intense public debate, private lobbying, drafting
and redrafting culminated in a new Labour Relations Act (LRA) in 1981
that extended trade union rights to African workers. Employers and
government had concluded that trade unions could no longer be suppressed
and a more fruitful strategy would be to incorporate them into the industrial
relations system, and to encourage a controlled form of trade unionism
that could be insulated from the political struggle for liberation. In this
way managerial control could be maintained, the apartheid workplace
regime could be modified and the broader apartheid system defended.

Initially intended as a strategy for controlling the new unions, the Wiehahn reforms ended up endowing them with considerable legal, organisational and collective bargaining rights. This was a substantial departure from colonial and apartheid ideology. The new LRA constituted African workers as industrial citizens – in 'a white man's country' where they were denied the political rights of citizenship. It was not clear what this would mean in the workplace – in the 'white man's factory'. The LRA allowed unions with African members to register and participate in the industrial relations machinery – Industrial Councils, conciliation boards and the Industrial Court. It also laid down prescribed procedures for dispute resolution and legal industrial action. While legal strikers were not entitled to any protection from dismissal, illegal strikers could face prosecution for breaking the law. The only right it established inside the workplace was protection against victimisation for belonging to a trade union. Indeed, the Wiehahn Commission envisaged that unions would be active exclusively at the industrial level, and that at workplace level workers would be represented through works councils modelled on the old liaison committee structures. Employers in the metal industry concurred with this strategy (Webster 1985: 238–9). In 1981 the chairperson of Highveld Steel, Leslie Boyd, who was also president of the Steel and Engineering Industries Federation of South Africa (SEIFSA), announced: 'We are trying to encourage the development of black trade unionism in a disciplined manner along the registration route and bring it successfully into the industrial council' (Sitas 1983: 178).

However, an amendment to the LRA in 1982 gave the Industrial Court increased powers. This encouraged the unions to use the court to define workplace rights through its judgements on what constituted unfair labour practices. The labour court established that workers had the right to be protected from any dismissal that was procedurally or substantively unfair, and that a fair procedure entailed the right to a fair hearing and to representation; that retrenchment had to be preceded by consultation; and that selective rehiring of striking workers was unfair. While it ruled that there was no duty on employers to bargain, on occasion it did reinstate legal strikers who had been dismissed (Benjamin 1987).

In effect, the LRA did establish workplace rights for unions via the Industrial Court, and the main focus of union activity in the early 1980s was on establishing recognition and collective bargaining at enterprise level, rather than on participating in the Industrial Council system (Webster 1985: 255). While this was extra-statutory in the sense that it was not regulated by the LRA – and indeed it contradicted the thrust of the Wiehahn reforms – it was facilitated by the general climate of reform in industrial relations. Recognition agreements established a set of codes regulating trade union rights in the workplace, which contributed to workplace reform.

These reforms created a new industrial relations system for African workers, ending despotism at the level of formal industrial relations. However, industrial relations constituted only part of the national regime of labour regulation; apartheid labour market policies, in particular influx control, remained intact despite relaxation of aspects of the racial division of labour. Neither did these reforms translate directly into reform of the apartheid workplace regime – indeed the intention in many respects was to *insulate* the workplace from change. Nonetheless, they constituted new strategic resources for workers seeking to challenge the apartheid workplace regime.

External conditions therefore favoured the initiative of the liaison committee members. The outcome, as will be shown, was a period of transition characterised by instability and disorder, rather than a new, reformed workplace order.

Union recognition at Highveld Steel
Joining the union
The liaison committee's search for NUMSA began unpromisingly – not only did they not know where it was; they did not know how it could help them. 'We didn't even know where the NUMSA offices were, we didn't know anything,' one said. They went to Johannesburg on a fruitless expedition to find the union. However, a member of the company's finance department had contacts in the new union movement and eventually the liaison committee met with the NUMSA general secretary, David Sebabi, in the Highveld hostels. Sebabi 'started telling us about the union and what it was doing. And from there, we started recruiting'. They then paid a more successful visit to the Johannesburg offices, meeting other union officials.[1]

The building of a union organisation entailed establishing a network of union activists, recruiting a majority of the black workers in the company and forging a shared understanding of the meaning of the union among workers. Frank Boshielo, Bob Moloi and the 'bullfighter' from Rand Carbide, J.J. Mbonani, initiated the organising efforts, recruiting other activists from among the migrant clerical staff and labourers and from the militant young workers in Highveld Steel's plate mill, especially those with a reputation for challenging managers.[2] There were different layers of union activists, some directing operations in the background, to protect the nascent organisation from victimisation.[3]

Boshielo's room in the hostel became the meeting place for the union officials and he became known as the organiser. 'When the official came from Germiston, he came to me in my room. He left the joining forms with me. I was responsible for collecting and distributing them. All the information came via us, and in the evenings, in the hostel, we used to call meetings.'[4] The concentration of workers in the hostels, the difficulty of recruiting in the township where workers were scattered, and tight managerial control over workers in the plants, made it the obvious place to start organising. A migrant worker remembered:

We were the first people to join the union. They mainly organised us in the hostels. They would call a meeting and organise us. And then at work as well, when we were together with those from the township, they would organise us whenever there was time, like at the clock station.[5]

On the shopfloor the hostility of supervisors to unionisation and the tight control of the apartheid workplace regime made it more difficult. As a result, staff with relative mobility became an important resource for recruiting, building networks and maintaining communication. Personnel clerks and wage clerks like Frank Boshielo and William Sehlola, and assistant training officers like Bob Moloi, Benson Khumalo and later Charles Makola, could move from plant to plant without the close supervisory control that hourly-paid workers experienced. This was particularly true after the union was recognised and many of the staff activists were elected as shop stewards.[6]

Boshielo recalled that it was 'very easy' to recruit members because of the oppression they experienced: 'There was no specific method to persuade the workers. They joined very quickly in big numbers. Within three weeks we managed to bring 700 workers into the union.'[7] Others remember it as more difficult, 'tense' because of the fear of victimisation.[8] There was a large core of workers who readily joined up, but beyond that there was real caution and fear.[9]

However, a new cycle of contention had emerged in various spheres of South African life. The fact that black unions were now legally recognised also helped. Within a year, a majority of the black workers at Highveld Steel were NUMSA members. Alongside the building of an activist network and the recruitment of members went the process of forging a shared understanding of the meaning of the union. Even those who had first contacted NUMSA were unsure what the union was, as Bob Moloi commented: 'Our understanding of the unions was nil. The only idea that I had in my mind was that maybe this organisation, NUMSA, would sort of negotiate with management over the rights of the workers. We used to call it an insurance, to insure our stay in this company, at least our jobs would be secured.'[10]

Members were recruited with the promise that the union would protect them from unfair treatment and dismissals. A migrant worker in flat products explained:

> I only joined it when I heard that it can stand for me at work, like when you are just fired without any reason, like when you are just taken and made to work there in a manner which is improper, as well as getting injured at work. All those reasons were explained to us, that the union will do something like that . . .[11]

The presence of other unions in the workplace also encouraged workers to join NUMSA. A migrant labourer observed that whites were empowered by their unions, and hoped that NUMSA would be similar 'so that we could have control like them'. A migrant crane driver had joined the South African Boilermakers' Society (SABS) when it opened membership to African workers in 1979 and initially he was confused when NUMSA started to recruit. But the black members of the SABS were not satisfied with their union, and started to notice that NUMSA was different, calling frequent meetings and explaining to workers how it functioned:

That's where I saw, this one can save me, and that one cannot save me. Because if you asked Boilermakers questions, they said no, no, no, we are in a hurry. But NUMSA was just relaxed and answered the questions. That's where I saw it was better to leave Boilermakers and join NUMSA.[12]

Ezekiel Nkosi and his township friends from flat products had also joined the SABS. When they heard about NUMSA, they 'found it was going to fight for the very same things that we were fighting for before the unions came in'. They decided that the SABS was not a 'fighting union' and joined NUMSA, 'especially the youth'. NUMSA was beginning to distinguish itself in the workplace through its grassroots organising, its empowering of workers through discussion, meetings and information, and by bringing them together and promising to challenge the racial structure of power.

However, the forging of collective solidarity was not without tension. NUMSA's base in the hostels made some township workers suspicious: 'Some of them were even questioning, what is the union? What is it all about? Not realising what we were doing. After some time, gradually, we integrated . . .'[13] Inside the hostels, the union had to contend with ethnic identities. The *indunas*, appointed as ethnic representatives, were hostile to the union, fearing that 'the trade unionists were going to take their leadership' because the NUMSA activists ignored them and approached workers directly. The union activists successfully averted a clash between Pedi and Xhosa workers. One of them, a Pedi, remembered:

We are thankful because, on the arrival of the union, we were about to clash with the Xhosa group. We are the ones [i.e. the union] who were solving that conflict. To take this people and unite them into one thing, that is really difficult.[14]

With the support of an external organisation, the trade union, workers had found ways of levering open the regime of white domination within Highveld Steel. These efforts were based on the sense of injustice and oppression among workers, and the bravery and leadership qualities of individuals. The emergence of a new generation of workers forged in the crucible of 1976 was a source of energy. The memories of earlier resistance, safeguarded in families and communities, also helped. The increasing number of black workers in more skilled jobs, particularly the handful of black apprentices, disturbed the symmetry of the racial division of labour and the ideological construction of blacks as unskilled 'boys'. Their increasing importance in production gave them potential bargaining power, as had become clear in the localised struggles at flat products and Rand Carbide, and numbers promised voice. Numbers would give them access to the rights contained in the LRA, and numbers would defend them from management victimisation.

Recognition: institutional power and collective power
The union first sought recognition at the beginning of 1982. In line with SEIFSA policy, the company refused until, later in the year, NUMSA agreed to join the Industrial Council. By the end of the year Highveld Steel had agreed to recognise NUMSA and give the union stop-order facilities. The union officials met with management to hand over membership lists for stop-order deductions and the liaison committee ceased to exist when its members withdrew.[15] The union and the company agreed that there was no need for a formal recognition agreement, since they were now both members of the Industrial Council and collective bargaining in the company was governed by the existing house agreement. NUMSA could now participate, together with the other recognised unions, in the annual collective bargaining process.

In the first shop steward elections each constituency – which generally corresponded to a division of the company such as the iron plant or the steel plant – could elect one shop steward per 50 members, as stipulated by the union constitution. The new shop stewards attended union training programmes because 'we didn't know actually what is the job of a shop steward, what is expected of him, or how to approach a disciplinary enquiry'.[16] Only then did they feel ready to take up their tasks. 'There was one guy who was dismissed and we had a meeting of the shop stewards and we elected four people to oppose management, telling them that we represent this guy. That is how we got recognised.'[17]

A workplace regime consists of both *formal* and *informal* relations, institutions and practices. Recognition of NUMSA provided workers at Highveld Steel with a set of formal, institutional rights. These demarcated an organisational space and provided them with the strategic resources they could use to challenge the practices of the apartheid workplace regime, and constituted therefore a significant reform of the workplace regime.

However, this *formal* reallocation of rights and powers between the different agents in the social structure of the workplace did not in itself alter the social structure of the apartheid workplace. This consisted of a dense mesh of coercive and racist practices and conventions – dismissals, assaults, insults, linguistic and behavioural codes, apartheid labour flexibility, the institution of *baas-boys* – which was impervious to formal rights. White managers, for instance, would have to implement the new procedures, preside over hearings and make findings – and they could simply entrench the racial structure of power, as they had always done.

Workers, NUMSA and the new shop stewards in particular would have to give content, meaning and shape to their new formal rights, and in so doing hack into the dense undergrowth of the apartheid workplace. To do this they would have to forge their own independent base of collective power from which to challenge the racial structure of power in the workplace. It was in these circumstances that social movement unionism was born at Highveld Steel.

Confronting and reforming the racial structure of power
Towards a new order: challenging baasskap with procedure
The struggle to regulate the arbitrary power of management was focused on the disciplinary code, and particularly on using the code's procedures to protect workers from arbitrary dismissal. A verbal warning could be issued by a foreman but a written warning could only be issued by a disciplinary inquiry chaired by a senior manager. A worker called before a disciplinary inquiry had the right to be represented by his shop steward and to call witnesses. The third written warning was the final warning; any further offence would result in dismissal. The role of the shop stewards in disciplinary inquiries was probably the single most important tool for demonstrating the new power of the union in the workplace.

Initially it was difficult because 'at that time we could not say anything to the managers'. But with union training courses and growing experience, the new shop stewards became more confident.[18] In contrast to the liaison committee representatives, shop stewards began to defend the workers, who were dramatically empowered by their shop stewards' ability to master the code and its procedures:

> So for the first few years after the union was introduced, people were still trying to understand more about this union, trying to see if it has got some teeth. And then they realised that if you have a problem with your supervisor, the approach was not as it used to be where he would simply say to you, now go! You will have an opportunity to go and get somebody to come and represent you, and then people sit around the table and listen to your arguments. Most of the line management were not very clear about the disciplinary code of the company so they used to make lots of mistakes and then the shop steward used to shoot them down. That made the employees see that this union seems to be doing fine, so we can fight them for more . . .[19]

Despite the recognition of the union and the existence of new disciplinary codes and grievance procedures, managers on the shopfloor expected to carry on as before, wielding their own arbitrary power. It was the shop stewards who made company procedure a reality in the workplace, an instrument for curbing and regulating the despotic power of supervisors and whites. They would meet to discuss cases, share experiences and exchange advice. They studied the disciplinary code carefully. They were able to outwit managers again and again, probing for procedural errors, inconsistent evidence, lies or bias:

> At times you would find a manager coming to the disciplinary inquiry with ready-made decisions. As a shop steward you had to fight that because we understood an inquiry had to establish the facts as to how this happened. That was a battle. As time went on, they started to respect how the union was operating, they started to respect the shop stewards and the disciplinary inquiries.[20]

In an extended discussion of the role of the shop stewards during the 1980s, Charles Makola, who was the vice-chair of the shop stewards committee at the time, described the tensions and power struggles on the shopfloor.[21]

The shop stewards played a crucial role in giving voice to the grievances of workers, showing that racial power could be challenged, and forging collective solidarity:

> The conditions demanded militancy, but people suppressed their feelings because they were afraid of their bosses. But if a leader emerged, a shop steward who would lead some campaigns, then the workers would support the shop steward. If he intervened once and he succeeded, the workers would have confidence in him and he would become the driving force. That is why shop stewards would be targeted by management as people who were causing problems.

Makola was shifted from the steel plant where he was an assistant training officer because the manager 'hated shop stewards in general, he did not want to be told that something did not go according to the procedure, he just didn't want that'. But the steel plant workers wanted their shop steward back. They staged a wildcat strike and Makola returned. Shop stewards knew that it was only the unity of their members, and their preparedness to take action, that protected them:

> You are in direct confrontation with your boss. You are going to be victimised, there is no doubt about that. You are only relying on the strength of the workers. That is how the trade union movement survived because there was a serious attack on the part of the managers. The managers could not believe that an ordinary worker could be in direct confrontation with himself as the manager. The LRA was something that was not even known to him. The shop steward is protected by the LRA. The workers here also didn't care about the LRA, but they would immediately stop the tools and demand that their leader be brought back, and that would happen.

This was an effective tactic because management could not dismiss large groups of workers. Their increasingly strategic location in the production process gave black workers more leverage to defend and build their organisation. The result was that no shop stewards were dismissed, other than after the 1987 lockout/strike.[22] When management tried to dismiss a shop steward, they were forced to reinstate him, as in the case of Joe Mokoena, which is recounted below.

Thus organisational power based on collective solidarity was integral to the ability of the shop stewards to make institutional power a reality; in turn, institutional power provided the space to build organisation. The recognition of NUMSA did not produce a new, negotiated order based on agreed procedures or the new law, but rather ushered in a period of unstable and fiercely contested transition. The union challenge to the arbitrary power of management and white workers was simultaneously an attack on racism and racial oppression in the workplace:

> It was something unimaginable from the workers to see a shop steward fighting management, who was a white person, that nobody would dare to challenge at that time, fighting to defend another worker. So the union was this new thing that had come to challenge the system.[23]

As shop stewards grew more confident, confrontation between them and supervisors 'had a racist element in it because it is a white supervisor who is actually instructing people – and the workforce see a white person who is trying to oppress them there'.[24] This gave a 'political element' to trade union struggles in the workplace. Enforcing the new procedures was seen as an attack on apartheid. Although the union was not explicitly political in the early period, the challenge to the racial order in the workplace was in some sense implicitly political from its beginnings – and understood to be so by both sets of protagonists.[25] This accounted for the intensity of the power struggle between white managers and shop stewards. Managers 'did not want the power of the union to grow. There was that power struggle, they thought that the shop stewards had taken over'. Management was careful with experienced shop stewards but would try to suppress the inexperienced ones.[26]

Nevertheless, the union won rights and enforced the application of procedures in the workplace. Workers could no longer be dismissed without following these procedures.

Racial assaults: collective action and the limits of procedure
Nothing dramatised white *baasskap* in the workplace as much as racial assault. Used jokingly, it constituted a ritual affirmation of white domination and black subservience. Used in earnest, it maintained the racial discipline and fear that was the basis of the apartheid workplace regime. Formal company policy after NUMSA was recognised was that anyone guilty of assault would be instantly dismissed, irrespective of position or colour. However, the racial solidarity of white managers meant that this was seldom implemented against whites. Disciplinary inquiries tended to issue warnings to whites accused of assaulting black workers, and to dismiss black workers accused of assault.[27] To make progress on this front, shop stewards had to go beyond seeking redress through disciplinary or grievance procedures and use the power of collective action. They saw this as using their power to force the company to follow its own policies.[28] Workers told two stories which illustrate the point.

The first mobilisation that J.J. Mbonani led at Rand Carbide, in late 1984, was to demand that a foreman who had assaulted a black worker, and received a final warning, be dismissed. When Mbonani reported the outcome of the inquiry to a general meeting of workers, 'they were dissatisfied, and then I started to mobilise them, and then we started singing, dancing towards the management office'. Management and shop stewards were unable to reach agreement. Meanwhile, work had come to a standstill as NUMSA members continued *toyi-toying* outside the offices. Workers started searching through the factory for the white foreman, armed with iron bars. Mbonani warned management that the foreman's life was in danger and the police were called to escort him out. The company transferred him to another plant but the union continued to object to his presence and eventually he left.[29]

The second story concerns a demand for the reinstatement of Joe Mokoena, a black shop steward dismissed in 1985 for hitting a white foreman who was physically harassing him.

> That was a physical war. Once you are trapped into a situation like that you lose your head. I had to repay in fighting. I hit him. I hit him very bad. Then security came to search for me and I was dismissed.

The shop stewards appealed against his dismissal but this was disallowed. Shop stewards felt the union was under attack so they organised the first full-blown strike across the Highveld group, mobilising in the hostels. After three days the workers won their demand and Mokoena was reinstated.[30]

In neither case were the formal rights of the union sufficient to change the pattern of racial assaults in the workplace. The new rules and procedures could not penetrate all the structures of racial power. Workers had to resort to their collective power to resist the workplace 'customs' surrounding assault, launching illegal strikes to force the company to adhere to its policies. The result was scepticism about the new procedures: 'You have people that have a law but they will drive it to suit themselves, like the police.'[31] These confrontations had a profound racial and political significance for the participants:

> You will get the wildcat strike immediately out of the foreman assaulting a worker. It could spread to the other divisions of the company, depending on whether it was resolved or not. They were very major political events. The demand that a foreman or a manager or a superintendent be dismissed was not a simple struggle. Management would not agree to dismissing one of their senior people because it was demanded by workers, more so because he was white. There were no cases where we managed to get the manager dismissed but there was an effect because they had to reprimand that manager. It was a serious power struggle.[32]

Despite this impact on management behaviour, confrontation over racial assault continued into the 1990s at Highveld Steel, suggesting that the confrontation between the collective power of the union and the racial structure of power in the workplace remained unresolved.

The reform of the apartheid workplace regime (1): removing the baas-boys

The baas-boys in the frontline of racial despotism became extremely vulnerable once the collective solidarity of black workers had become a reality in the form of the new union. Racial identities were central to workers' understanding of solidarity and struggle. Workers would confront the baas-boys:

Workers would say, 'Who are you? Are you white, or black like myself? And if you are black, brother, why do you follow me this much? I don't want to take orders from you.' Workers started defying the *indunas* and their role eventually disappeared. Then they would go to management and say, 'We're having problems now, these workers no longer want to recognise us. What do we do?'

Baas-boys were also physically assaulted: 'During strike action workers would say, these *indunas* are full of shit, they look for us when we're in the toilet, therefore they must be *sjambokked*.'

Management attempted to protect the *baas-boys*. They were renamed 'supervisors' and classified as staff employees. But workers 'could still recognise those people' and continued to attack them. Many were scared to accept 'supervisor' positions and management was forced to give them new jobs. Some became 'tea-boys' making tea for foremen and superintendents, and helping in the stores, selling cooldrinks to workers. 'They are still there, with no clear job description, just roaming around.'[33]

In a workplace where power was structured on racial lines, the *baas-boys* had no power. They were delegated the despotic power of whites, which they were able to wield by virtue of their location *inside* the black workforce. When black workers constructed their own collective solidarity in the union, the despotic exercise of power ceased to be possible. Whites remained empowered by their positions in the racial division of labour and in the structure of managerial authority, and by their collective racial identity as dominants in 'a white man's country'. But the *baas-boys* had no independent function in production; their power was completely dependent on the despotic aspect of white power, and their 'insider' knowledge of black workers. When they were denied access to these sources of power and knowledge, their function withered away, as happened to black councillors and policemen in the townships. *Baas-boys* were agents of despotism, an institution that had evolved with the labour regime of settler colonialism and apartheid in South Africa. They could not survive the coming of the union.

The reform of the apartheid workplace regime (2): from baasskap to management

Establishing the rule of procedure as a way of ending despotism and regulating management behaviour had a significant impact on supervisory practices on the shopfloor. White workers who were not supervisors lost their authority to issue instructions: if a black worker refused to obey, the white worker had no recourse to a disciplinary procedure. Nor would an instruction to make tea or wash a car have any standing. This meant that workplace practices no longer constituted black workers as the 'servants' of whites. They became 'employees' with the rights and obligations this entailed. As employees they fought to 'own' their jobs: they no longer accepted that they could be instructed to do any job by any foreman. Shop stewards argued that each worker was employed to do a specific job, which entailed accountability to a specific supervisor. Foremen and other managers could hardly argue against this, so disciplinary inquiries upheld the views of the shop stewards. Infringement of these new job rights would immediately be challenged by shop stewards:

It was a clash between black and white. The role of shop stewards was to monitor the relationship of supervisors to workers, how they give instructions, how they treat workers, whether those instructions are correct, whether that worker should do what the supervisor requested. Because some were given duties that were not part of their job, like sending a person to the shop, like insisting that one worker should go and wash a manager's car, like an artisan helper who did more than what he was supposed to do. Actually, a shop steward even took the role of a supervisor because before a worker followed instructions he would consult with the shop steward. If the shop steward said 'no, I don't think you are supposed to do that', the worker wouldn't do it. There was an acceptance that there would be a foreman but the shop steward would just check whether the foreman is working within his powers, he is not overstepping his authority, then the shop steward would intervene. The shop steward became a very powerful instrument to secure the workers. If they said they were calling a shop steward, especially if it was a powerful shop steward, the foreman or the superintendent would start to shiver. At that time reasoning was not an issue, a shop steward would be elected on the basis of his aggression, his braveness to face the supervisor, the guts to say 'no, what you are doing is wrong'.[34]

The new power of black workers meant a substantial renegotiation of relations within the apartheid workplace regime. It was no longer a despotic regime. White *baasskap*, the power to constitute blacks as 'servants', had been displaced into managerial authority – an authority constructed by the union rather than by management – to manage employees, who in turn were located in specific jobs. The foreman had to remain 'within his powers'. Workers were allocated specific 'work duties' and could refuse to go beyond these. Shop stewards played a crucial role in establishing these new realities. The implication of the new order was that black workers, at least in some respects, were industrial citizens.

Contesting the racial order: disorder and counter-order
While the Wiehahn reforms and the formation of NUMSA at Highveld Steel produced reforms in the apartheid workplace regime, the racial ordering of the workplace remained intact. The result was an ongoing contestation, a continuous clash, over the nature and legitimacy of order in the workplace.

Establishing procedure, rejecting procedure
The preceding sections have demonstrated that it was the shop stewards who enforced the new procedures and codes and bound management to the 'rule of law' on the shopfloor. At the same time, shop stewards and workers frequently rejected the constraints of these new institutions:

> Following procedures in terms of the LRA, declaring disputes and so on, was not on the agenda of the workers at that time. They would simply stop if there was a problem. They would simply walk off their jobs.[35]

There were several reasons for this. Firstly, the rule of the new procedures was highly unstable and fiercely contested throughout the 1980s. Managers did not know the procedures and did not want to be constrained by them:

> We were in war with management. We were moving from totally different premises. Our members did not even know whether they had rights or not, and the bosses were not happy about the rights

extended to our members. We had to fight for the recognition of the rights that we already had, which were not recognised.[36]

This 'war' was charged with racial tension over the structure of power in the workplace. Confrontation between managers and workers was simultaneously confrontation between white and black. Workers came to reject *any* notion of dismissal as unfair. In this context, procedure was unable to define a body of fair practices acceptable to both sets of protagonists; instead it was used in an instrumental fashion by either side when it suited them.

Secondly, as the section on racial assault demonstrated, there were limits to the effectiveness of procedure in curbing white despotism. This discredited procedure and encouraged workers to fall back on the immediate impact of collective action. Finally, the reforms in the apartheid workplace regime, significant though they were, remained embedded in the racial structure of the workplace.

A young worker who was a youth activist before being employed at Highveld Steel in 1985, two years after NUMSA was recognised, put this very clearly:

Before I was employed at Highveld, when we talked about apartheid I was looking at the township where I was staying. But I didn't taste apartheid or feel it – I was young and I felt that was the way of living. Until I went into Highveld. It was the first time I came into close contact with a white man. And you could see the way they treated us – this is inhuman. There were some jobs that were only reserved for whites. They were proud, saying that because you are black you cannot do this – and I wondered but how can this be? Even in the toilet there was this thing of whites only, you could not go there. That's actually where I started to get more involved – because I could now feel apartheid, I could taste it.[37]

Racial discrimination remained institutionalised at Highveld Steel until the 1990s. Despite the recognition of the union, and despite the repeal in 1983 of the legislation that made separate facilities for black and white workers compulsory, Highveld Steel continued to provide segregated change-houses, toilets and canteens for its black and white employees.[38] Apartheid was more strongly embedded in the structures and practices of the workplace than in the law. Black and white workers continued to be on separate payrolls. Incomes, managerial authority and skills continued to be racially distributed. On the shopfloor blacks were controlled by whites, and racial insults and assaults still took place. Thus black workers were in some respects incorporated as industrial citizens, and in other respects remained blacks in a workplace structured by apartheid. Black workers continued to see this regime as illegitimate. It had lost a crucial dimension – that of despotism – but this did not give it legitimacy. Furthermore, the persistence of the racial order in the workplace was linked to the wider racial order of apartheid beyond it.

Although the shop stewards were the agents in making disciplinary procedure a real factor on the shopfloor, the company's disciplinary and grievance codes had not been negotiated with them. Both the company and the shop stewards were wary of negotiating such procedures. Without consulting the shop stewards, the company drew up a new code after NUMSA was recognised. There were differing views among the shop stewards on how to respond. Some wanted to negotiate the whole document; others wanted to avoid involvement in formulating the disciplinary procedure so they would not be bound by it. Then a general meeting of NUMSA members at Highveld rejected any participation in drafting the procedures. Since NUMSA and the company had agreed that a recognition agreement, 'which would have bound us to some procedures in terms of disputes', was not necessary, the result was 'the only procedure was the disciplinary code and the grievance procedure – which people said, those are not ours, those are management procedures, we are not going to abide by them'.[39]

This episode revealed both management's deep resistance to negotiating the basis of a new workplace order with unions, and the profound unwillingness among workers to concede any legitimacy to managerial notions of order or to accept constraints on their activities. The reality was that, instead of incorporating black workers via trade unionism into an 'orderly' and 'disciplined' collective bargaining regime, the Wiehahn reforms had unleashed a fundamental struggle over the nature of workplace order.

However, relations between union and management were not

characterised only by conflict and confrontation. In the midst of the turmoil of racial confrontation and power struggle there were substantial reforms to workplace practices that served as the basis for elements of negotiated order to emerge. Managers' attitudes towards the shop stewards were ambivalent. Their presence was an affront to their authority but they were forced to live with them. The result was grudging acceptance. Shop stewards 'had to operate, and somewhere, somehow, legitimately they would bring forward the complaints of the members'. The development of collective bargaining relationships also led to areas of co-operation, and management 'would rely on a shop steward to resolve certain matters' or to communicate with workers.[40]

Shop stewards were closer to the new rules and procedures than rank-and-file members because they were constantly using them and negotiating with management. This led to a division of labour between them and a new structure, the strike committee (which is discussed in detail in the next two chapters), with shop stewards operating in disciplinary inquiries, and the strike committee organising action if that failed. Boshielo remembered:

> The strike committee were the first people to know if someone was dismissed because most of the members knew where they met. They would get your report that you have been dismissed. They would ask, 'Have you been to the shop steward?' They would give the shop stewards a chance to go various steps in terms of the internal disciplinary procedure and they would be the first people to know when negotiations have deadlocked. And they would take it up, saying, 'Hey, no, we had better organise action. Let's talk to the shop stewards and organise an action immediately'.[41]

This separation of roles between shop stewards and strike committee would lead to profound divisions in NUMSA.

Workers' control of discipline

The relation of black workers to discipline was more complex than a simple rejection of the authority of management. Boshielo went on to qualify the willingness of the strike committee to organise action: 'They usually did that, provided they were convinced that there was unfairness there.' He then told the story of a worker with a drinking problem, who was frequently absent from work. His manager, fearing a strike if he took disciplinary action, complained to the shop steward who discussed the problem with members of the strike committee:

> The following day that guy was the first person to come in the workplace, even before the buses came. Management wanted to know how this was? They said, 'We fixed it. He won't give you problems anymore.' The strike committee [had gone] to him and threatened him in a way. The strike committee were saying, 'We are sick and tired of people staying away from work, they get dismissed and we must take action. Before we take action, we must know why he was dismissed.'[42]

The story indicates that workers recognised management might have a fair complaint. They did not want to have to take the risk of strike action to defend such cases. The solution was to take charge of discipline themselves, removing it from management's hands, and developing their own disciplinary procedures and penalties. Mosi Nhlapo, an artisan who became a shop steward in 1987, located this alternative approach in the original rejection of management procedures:

> The first procedure that the company brought to the union, the union refused to sign – they said that as a union we've got our own procedures. All those guys that are said to be misbehaving, bring them to us, we'll know how to correct them. It was not done in a very formal way but the strike committee took it upon itself to deal with such people. One of their tasks was to deal with those workers who were acting very irresponsibly, like coming to work drunk or stealing company property, or doing something that was obviously wrong. People said there's no way we can believe in these procedures but sometimes we ourselves are misbehaving. That is wrong. Therefore, instead of him going to an inquiry, we'll rather discipline him. We'll make sure that he doesn't get dismissed, if necessary by striking – but rather than striking over people that are getting drunk,

we'll go into the hostel and *sjambok* him for having come to work drunk.[43]

The result, according to another shop steward, was that 'there was a time when Highveld Steel did not know what it was like to have people absent from work, people coming late to work, people coming to work drunk. That was a time when Highveld enjoyed about 99.9 per cent attendance'.[44]

Thus, the first principle of workers' approach to discipline was that no worker should be dismissed and that management disciplinary procedures had no legitimacy – although they readily used procedures to constrain management. In other words, the management notion of 'fair dismissal' was rejected. Workers did, however, regard certain kinds of behaviour as 'wrong' or 'irresponsible'. Having established their collective power to resist management, workers rejected what has been called 'informal resistance' (Cohen 1991). Partly this was because such behaviour could not be defended in disciplinary inquiries but only with strike action, and they wanted to avoid striking for trivial reasons. But workers also seemed to be critical of such behaviour on moral grounds: it was 'wrong', 'irresponsible' and 'misbehaving'.[45] One of the shop steward leaders, Ambrose Mthembu, argued that workers' implementation of their own disciplinary process was linked to the idea of NUMSA's discipline and moral superiority, and the idealism of a struggle for a new society. Individual strategies of 'informal resistance' undermined union organisation and the new sense of worker discipline and morality that accompanied it:

It was because we wanted our members to be disciplined. We wanted to dignify the union, that the union must go and represent cases where our people have been aggrieved by management. We also wanted to show that if we take over the government, people will be expected to work, people will be expected to co-operate. So we must show management that we are willing, we can behave, we can work and we are disciplined, so that once we take over they cannot say that we will fail. It's a socialist principle and we were influenced by socialist principles as NUMSA.[46]

Nhlapo and Mthembu make it clear that the disciplining of workers by their comrades was seen as part of the new collective identity and order introduced by the union 'with our own procedures' counterposed to those of management. Workers' control of discipline was a manifestation of their rejection of the illegitimate order of the apartheid workplace regime, but it also met management's objective of reducing absenteeism and could produce an informal negotiated accommodation on aspects of discipline – as it did in the case described by Boshielo.[47]

However, it was not the shop stewards but an informal structure, the strike committee, that asserted this form of discipline and to do so they used violent means, the *sjambok*, rather than the non-violent means associated with democracy. Ironically, such practices would lead to deep divisions and NUMSA's loss of legitimacy among a section of workers at Highveld Steel towards the end of the 1980s.

Go-slow in a white man's country

This desire among union activists at Highveld Steel to demonstrate that union members were disciplined did not extend to their role in production. The formation of the union eroded the despotic power of foremen and managers and in so doing ended the climate of fear that drove workers to work hard. Before the union ended control through fear, 'people worked very hard, but they never felt responsible for the work they were doing'. Then:

After the union was introduced workers started saying, 'but the union is there to protect us'. Then they started resisting the bosses. They started to show lack of respect even to their immediate supervisors. It became clear to each and every worker that here we are being exploited and therefore there was no motive for him to work hard. So therefore you'd always duck and dive and not do your work properly.[48]

A highly articulate and assertive artisan who became a shop steward in 1987 described the erosion of fear in his workshop:

You'd know that at 8 o'clock the manager would go past our shop and it was a rule from the foreman and the superintendent, if he goes past no one must be standing, you must look busy. I did that a couple of times. Then I said one day, 'I'm going to challenge this thing'. The manager came past and I stopped working and I watched him. And it was the first time I noticed who he was, and I said, 'This is the guy, but then why should I work hard when he comes past?' Then I said to the other workers, 'Today I never worked when the manager came past'. Their response was that sometimes they don't work when he passes, but they don't stand around so he can see them, they go and hide behind walls. I said to them, but you can still stop working in front of his eyes, I don't think he'll do anything. And that developed in the workshop. The manager just became an ordinary person eventually.

The vanquishing of fear meant that workplace behaviour had to be negotiated in new ways. When the foreman and superintendent became aware of the workers' new behaviour they called a meeting and explained that it was important to appear to be busy when the manager walked past otherwise he would refuse to sign requisitions for overtime – and everyone had a common interest in overtime pay. They summed up: 'So please, if you still want to work more overtime, can you attempt to be working when the manager is going past?' This was a different way of looking at the issue. 'And then that was a good reason why we should work when the manager comes past because we're not going to get overtime. So we went back again and worked when he came past.'[49]

The shop stewards mobilised their members around the fact that they were working in a 'white man's factory' in a 'white man's country' so they had no reason to work hard:

What you should preach to the workers is that they must do as little work as they can. They are not paid as whites are paid and management is reaping profits. Mandela is still in prison. We'll make sure that we work as slowly as possible, we don't care, this is not our country.[50]

The result was that black workers were engaged in a permanent go-slow and white foremen no longer had the use of baas-boys to monitor and discipline black workers.

Workers were on a go-slow, which is why management complains that we've got a lazy workforce in South Africa. In flat products sometimes they waited for an hour for a crane driver to come and remove a plate so that other plates could come through because the crane driver might have gone to see his friend. At the tap floor, when it's tapping time the foreman must go and look for Tshagata. Tshagata might not be there, he might be in the canteen. Or Veli might have gone to see his friend. To me, that was how apartheid capitalism was frustrated by workers because they were not taking full responsibility for their activities.[51]

The contrast with white workers made clear their different relations to the apartheid workplace regime:

Whites were always there, in place, on time. That is why you had them as foremen. They would stay together in Witbank. When they came in the morning they would plan the job together, excluding us. Blacks would just receive instructions through job cards. There's what you call *kak* job and *lekker* job,[52] and the *kak* jobs would come to us and the *lekker* jobs would come to them. They have already agreed which *lekker* jobs they must get. If you go to a toilet which is written Blacks, it's always occupied. We'd go to toilets for two hours. If you go to a toilet which is written Whites, it's less occupied. If you go to the showers, by half past three the black showers are already full, guys have skipped jobs and gone to shower an hour before knocking off time.[53]

The permanent go-slow of black workers, in contrast to whites, was the manifestation in production of the inability of the apartheid workplace regime to incorporate black workers once coercion and fear had been curbed. Management was unable to impose or negotiate a new workplace order.

Conclusion
The Wiehahn reforms failed in their attempt to incorporate and control the emerging black trade unions: the broader context of political exclusion, and the racially oppressive structures and practices of the apartheid

workplace regime were too great an obstacle to incorporation. Nonetheless, the reforms created opportunities and provided resources for the nascent union movement to establish itself in the workplace, and shopfloor trade unionism did lead to workplace reforms.

It was the shop stewards rather than managers who fought for and defended these reforms, and in doing so they constructed from below the outlines of a new, reformed workplace order. New industrial relations legislation and institutions – and even new company policies – were just so many paper tigers without this innovative activity from below, which in turn depended on an emerging collective solidarity and willingness to mobilise among workers.

Notwithstanding these formative struggles to create new rights and procedures, the result was not a new negotiated order. The union and management constantly contested the meaning and legitimacy of the various elements of this new order, which remained embedded in a workplace regime still profoundly structured by racial discrimination and confrontation. Far from containing conflict within the confines of a new negotiated accommodation, the trade union became a movement that deepened and extended conflict to every aspect of the workplace regime. The result was instability, contestation, incoherence and disorder inscribed in the inner workings of the workplace social structure. This is not to say there was a complete absence of negotiated order in the workplace. The process of negotiating accommodation and the process of challenging this order coexisted in tension with each other. Confrontation and ungovernability erupted through the bounds of negotiated order. The contours of new rights and procedures emerged from the storms of confrontation. Nothing was settled.

This was the paradoxical dynamic of reforming the apartheid workplace without removing the broader apartheid system: institutional participation and radical challenge were bound together in mutual and contradictory interdependence. The qualities of mobilisation and confrontation, and of institutional innovation, that characterised social movement unionism were born out of workplace conditions. They were deepened and extended in response to the wider apartheid context – which we turn to in the next chapter.

Notes

1. Interview, Frank Boshielo, 9/93; interview, J.J. Mbonani, 31/5/94.
2. Interview, Bunny Mahlangu, 8/11/93.
3. Interview, J.J. Mbonani, 31/5/94.
4. Interview, Frank Boshielo, 19/6/94; interview, Charles Makola, 8/5/94.
5. Interview, Jerry Mogoleko, 10/95.
6. Interview, Sam Mkhabela, 1/6/94; interview, Joe Mokoena, 12/10/95; interview, William Sehlola, 5/6/94.
7. Interview, Frank Boshielo, 9/93; see also interview, Bob Moloi, 10/7/94.
8. Interview, William Sehlola, 5/6/94.
9. Interview, Tshagata, 26/5/94.
10. Interview, Bob Moloi, 10/7/94.
11. Interview, Jerry Mogoleko, 10/95; see also interview, Albert Makagula, 24/3/94; interview, William Sehlola, 5/6/94.
12. Interview, Johannes Phatlana, 15/4/94, 7/9/94.
13. Interview, Frank Boshielo, 19/6/94; interview, Charles Makola, 8/5/94.
14. Interview, Tshagata, 10/95; see also interview, Ezekiel Nkosi, 5/5/94.
15. Interview, Frank Boshielo, 9/93.
16. Interview, William Sehlola, 5/6/94.
17. Interview, Frank Boshielo, 9/93.
18. Interview, William Sehlola, 5/6/94; interview, J.J. Mbonani, 31/5/94.
19. Interview, Bob Moloi, 10/7/94.
20. Interview, William Sehlola, 5/6/94; see also interview, Bunny Mahlangu, 8/11/93; interview, J.J. Mbonani, 31/5/94.
21. Interview, Charles Makola, 8/5/94.
22. Ibid.
23. Victor Kgalema in interview, Bunny Mahlangu, 8/11/93.
24. Interview, Charles Makola, 8/5/94.
25. Victor Kgalema in interview, Bunny Mahlangu, 8/11/93; see also interview, Frank Boshielo, 19/6/94; interview, Albert Makagula, 29/3/94.
26. Interview, Charles Makola, 8/5/94.
27. Ibid; interview, Phineas Mabena, 12/5/94; interview, Johannes Phatlana, 15/4/94.
28. Interview, Johannes Phatlana, 15/4/94.
29. Interview, J.J. Mbonani, 31/5/94.
30. Interview, Joe Mokoena, 12/10/95.
31. Ibid. Managers saw discipline asserted with a 'klap' (a blow) as highly effective, and described the 'no klap rule' as a 'revolution'. They also acknowledged the difficulty of changing the culture of racial assault and insult on the shopfloor. They claimed to have taken a firm line in enforcing the new rule, but actually reinforced the impression of leniency by, for example, suspending a foreman instead of dismissing him (Hocking 1998: 251–2).
32. Interview, Charles Makola, 8/5/94.
33. Interview, Mosi Nhlapo, 12/95; see also interview, Bunny Mahlangu, 8/11/93; interview, Bossie Bezuidenhout, 29/8/95.

34. Interview, Charles Makola, 8/5/94; see also interview, J.J. Mbonani, 31/5/94; interview, Tshagata, 26/5/94.
35. Interview, Charles Makola, 8/5/94. In fact, during the four years between NUMSA's first wage stoppage in 1984 and the defeat of the 1987 lockout strike (see chapter 7), at Highveld Steel NUMSA virtually never used the statutory conciliation procedures or the legal institutions provided by the LRA, but relied exclusively on workers' collective power. A consistent flouting of disciplinary procedures is also observed by Maller (1992) at Volkswagen and at Jabula Foods in the late 1980s; see my discussion of this in chapter 1, and more fully in my thesis (Von Holdt 2000).
36. Interview, Ambrose Mthembu, 22/10/95; see also interview, William Sehlola, 5/6/94; and quotes earlier in the chapter.
37. Interview, Jacob Msimangu, 22/10/95.
38. See chapter 2, pp. 29–30.
39. Interview, Bob Moloi, 10/7/94; interview, Bunny Mahlangu, 12/5/94.
40. These points are drawn from interview, Charles Makola, 8/5/94.
41. Interview, Frank Boshielo, 19/6/94.
42. Ibid.
43. Interview, Mosi Nhlapo, 9/11/93; see also interview, Hong Kong Kgalima, 10/7/94; interview, Frank Boshielo, 19/6/94.
44. Interview, Ambrose Mthembu, 22/10/95.
45. Shop stewards at Mercedes Benz SA expressed similar attitudes to discipline: 'You cannot use the militancy of workers to defend a drunken person' (Von Holdt 1990: 37).
46. Interview, Ambrose Mthembu, 22/10/95.
47. Maller describes a similar case at Jabula Foods, where supervisors referred problems to a disciplinary committee consisting of shop stewards without involving management in disciplinary procedures. The committee would sentence offenders to stay at home for between one and two weeks, forfeiting their pay for the period. While supervisors made use of this alternative procedure – thus constituting it as a form of negotiated order – management opposed this innovation on the grounds that discipline was a management function, and succeeded in wresting control back to the formal disciplinary procedures. This did not resolve the problem of discipline, as the legitimacy of the tactics of each party was fundamentally questioned by the other (Maller 1992: 37–8). Other cases of union involvement in discipline have been observed during the 1990s, and are discussed in chapter 9.
48. Interview, Mosi Nhlapo, 12/95.
49. Ibid.
50. Interview, Mosi Nhlapo, 10/7/94.
51. Interview, Mosi Nhlapo, 12/95.
52. *kak* job and *lekker* job: 'shit job and nice job'.
53. Interview, Mosi Nhlapo, 12/95.

CHAPTER 4

'Fighting everything'

Social movement unionism, popular alliances and 'ungovernability' in the community

The night before the stayaway, there was a lot of commotion in the township – the following day, there were barricades in the street. Who called the stayaway? Why exactly was the stayaway called? There was this fear of the unknown. And, yes, some of us were beginning to even be afraid of our own comrades and there were no open and free discussions around these things.

Meshack Malinga, rank-and-file NUMSA member and later shop steward

The emergence of the popular movement

The re-emergence of resistance politics in Witbank

The new cycle of popular contention that erupted in political turmoil across South Africa in the 1970s made its mark in the townships of Witbank. Black students were at the forefront of the action and they responded to the 1976 uprisings in Soweto by launching their own protests against inferior education. As in Soweto, the targets of their resentment and hostility were not confined to the education system but were directed towards 'collaborators' such as black policemen and community councillors. The Highveld Administration Board (HAB) offices were 'burnt to ashes'. Numbers of students were detained for periods of between a few days and six months, and some were killed in police action. Although much of their activity appears to have been spontaneous in the sense that the students were not members of formal organisations, there had been a history of ANC and Pan-Africanist Congress (PAC) activism in Witbank during the 1950s, and some of the students were aware of this history.[1]

After 1976 young men who had participated in the uprisings like Ezekiel Nkosi went into the factories and participated in nascent forms of resistance there. Others became active in black consciousness organisations at schools and in universities. Joe Mokoena wanted to 'go out and join MK and fight'. Others did, including his younger brother.

In 1980 the Azanian People's Organisation (AZAPO) was launched to fill the gap left by the banning of black consciousness organisations in 1977, and many of those who had been active during 1976 joined the Witbank branch. But when the United Democratic Front (UDF) was launched in 1983 most of them followed a group of national AZAPO leaders in defecting from the black consciousness organisation to the 'non-racial', ANC-aligned UDF. In Witbank activists formed the Co-ordinating Committee in 1984 to stimulate the formation of the sectoral (student, youth) and issue-based organisations (detainee support organisations, for example) that characterised the UDF, and to co-ordinate struggles in the community. Although the Co-ordinating Committee was never formally constituted as a UDF structure, it was regarded as the local representative of the UDF, and its activists attended UDF meetings in Johannesburg. The Co-ordinating Committee liaised with churches, the unions and black business, organised lawyers for detainees, printed pamphlets, called mass meetings, and organised mass actions such as marches and consumer boycotts. Its organising efforts bore fruit in the second half of 1985 when the Witbank Youth Congress was formed and affiliated to the South African Youth Congress, and a local branch of the Congress of South African Students (COSAS) was established (although by the end of the year COSAS was banned). The Detainees' Support Committee, the Detainees' Parents' Support Committee and a Witbank Parents' Crisis Committee were also launched, all affiliated to national structures, as well as the Unemployed People's Congress (UPCO). National campaigns and meetings galvanised local activities.[2]

During this period Witbank activists practised the distinctive UDF 'style of politics', focusing on issue-specific campaigns that involved mass protests as well as some negotiation with the authorities. Activists attempted to negotiate student demands with school authorities, secure the release of detained students, negotiate with business over boycotts and with the town council over rents and evictions. They marched in support of petitions and demands; they threatened and then organised stayaways and consumer boycotts.[3]

Ungovernability in the township

During 1986 the confrontation between the popular movement and the forces of the apartheid state grew increasingly intense in KwaGuqa. Groups of youths and activists targeted black 'collaborators', as well as state property, for violent action. The state used the provisions of the second State of Emergency, declared mid-year, to detain and harass activists, ban organisations and launch frequent armed patrols through the township, as it did across South Africa. It became extremely difficult to sustain formal organisation. In KwaGuqa several leading activists in the Co-ordinating Committee were detained, harassed, put on trial or forced to flee the township.[4] Formal organisational structures and procedures effectively collapsed. Tightly knit groups of 'comrades' continued to meet clandestinely to plan activities or campaigns despite being disrupted by detentions, 'internal exile' and trials.

Activists took to the streets to confront the enemy. Sporadic reports in the Witbank News reflect the mood of the times. There were frequent clashes and police seemed to have little compunction in opening fire on 'mobs' armed only with stones. The most frequent targets of attack were government vehicles and property, police on township patrols and black collaborators such as policemen and town councillors. Vehicles belonging to white businesses were secondary targets. The attackers were mostly young men in their teens and twenties and, despite being outgunned, the youths appeared to be relatively successful. In April 1986 municipal police guarding the house of the mayor of KwaGuqa accidentally shot and killed his son when they opened fire on youths who were stoning the house (Witbank News 2/5/86). In May a KwaGuqa town councillor resigned after four petrol bomb attacks on his house (Witbank News 16/5/86, 23/5/86). On Republic Day, 31 May, a black policeman attending the funeral of a friend 'was attacked by a spade-wielding mob', thrown into an empty grave and buried alive (Witbank News 6/6/86). A week later a second black policeman died at a soccer match at the stadium in KwaGuqa after being attacked by a mob with knobkerries and lengths of pipe and then necklaced with a burning tyre. Policemen living in KwaGuqa had been issued with handguns and their homes were protected against petrol-bomb attacks (*Witbank News* 13/6/86), but the police were unable to keep control. The army was brought in and camped in KwaGuqa for a month, forcing the comrades into hiding. When the soldiers left, the attacks resumed.

Industrial action by workers was seen as part of the general 'unrest', and had similar characteristics: the arrival of police, confrontation, stoning, shooting and arrests. Several National Union of Mineworker (NUM) officials, including the regional treasurer Clement Zulu, were arrested after a clash with police at Bank Colliery when workers commandeered the store owner's vehicle, and workers at Landau Colliery 'set upon' a police car carrying two black officers and burnt it after they fled. Zulu was said to be a member of the Witbank Youth Congress, and police said that a 'striking committee' of mineworkers had been formed to protect him (*Witbank News* 7/2/86).

A worker at Highveld Steel, who became active as a comrade in the township, described the *modus operandi* of struggle under these conditions:

> There's a block of shops where all these people used to meet, the youngsters and the big bosses. You get instructions there, how must we conflict the police when they come into the township at night. We had some whistles which we blew to call that we are this side, this side. The police would also know that if they hear such a whistle it means there we are. Then we stone them, petrol bomb them, in the darkness. Every house must be dark. The youngsters used to switch all the electric poles off, until the sellouts reported who is doing that. We fought against the rent. Most of the old people could not afford rent now, so the council wanted to chase them out of the house. So we *toyi-toyied* against the town council. We stopped paying rent, we stopped paying electricity. Some of the people who were not working said, well that's the only way we can survive. Our aim was only to fight everything, the police, the government, the town councillors.

The comrades used violence against the repressive order imposed by the state. They also used coercion to impose a new order in the community, policing collective actions such as rent or consumer boycotts, and punishing those who broke ranks:

Once we see a house with the light on, we know that you are paying rent. Then we'll come to your house and we want you to explain that to us. There were some of our brothers working in the offices – they would tell us who has paid rent or electricity. Then we'll come to your house and petrol bomb the house. So most of the people stopped paying electricity. Even a person who is working in a furniture shop, he couldn't bring furniture in here, they'll burn the car, burn everything.[5]

During this period UDF activists in Witbank, as in the rest of the country, were operating according to a two-pronged strategic vision: 'rendering apartheid unworkable or rendering ourselves ungovernable', and establishing 'people's power, seizure of power'. The two were closely linked. For example, the 'targets of the youth congresses were all the collaborators who were obstacles to people's government – the power of the local authorities had to be broken, councillors would be called upon to resign and ultimately forced to resign. And then people should form the civic association which would be the true representative of the people in the township'. In the field of education, the unilateral control of the state should be broken, and students should prevent the teaching of government propaganda. Building people's power meant building student representative councils and parents' structures so that students and parents 'should have a voice' in running the schools and 'people's education' could be implemented. There was an 'intersection' between ungovernability and the 'imperative of taking control', in that ungovernability would erode or break state control and create the space to build popular organisation and establish popular control.[6]

However, the state assault on the UDF and its affiliates made the building of organisation and 'people's power' all but impossible, although attempts were made. In KwaGuqa, for example, community activists tried but failed to build and sustain a civic organisation towards the end of 1986.[7] A second and more successful example was the Highveld Steel bus service. As the *Witbank News* reported, many of the Highveld Steel buses were stoned or burnt out, especially during boycotts or stayaways. However, activists also took to commandeering the buses if they needed transport for meetings. They also prevailed on the bus drivers to transport the children of KwaGuqa to and from their schools between ferrying workers to and from work. This was done without any negotiation with the company, which in the end formally adopted these practices as a service to the community.[8]

Rudimentary forms of authority were exercised by groups of youths and other activists. This was applied in the first instance in the campaign against collaborators, but also in the monitoring and policing of mass actions and campaigns such as stayaways, consumer and school boycotts. It was also extended for a time to issues such as family quarrels and even witchcraft, through the 'people's courts'. Although this authority had legitimacy and popular support in its confrontation with the apartheid regime, the coercive and arbitrary way in which campaigns were sometimes organised and policed gave rise to anxiety and fear, and its intrusion into the sphere of the family was probably regarded as illegitimate by the majority of township residents. A Highveld Steel worker and township resident recalled the climate:

> The police and the councillors were the prime targets, and I supported this. We had very corrupt police. The councillors were legitimising the system of apartheid. Therefore I supported that they be removed. But you would often see people being carried into the kangaroo courts, and then they would be given their punishment. I didn't like that very much. On one particular day I said, let me just go and see what is happening there. There was an old lady, she was charged with witchcraft. Two youngsters were giving evidence. I feared for the life of that old lady. I could not stop intervening, I stood up and said I wished we had evidence, but there was nothing. I appealed that the old lady be released until there was evidence. I was thinking that she was going to be killed, so I left. Later I heard that my intervention caused a big confusion, and she was released. I was terribly disturbed. Many people exploited the situation for their own self-interest. I wouldn't say there was popular support for these activities. It brought a wave of terror. People were saying, yes we are fighting the enemy. But our methods of fighting are in fact not affecting the enemy, but affecting us.[9]

This form of authority was rudimentary in that it only applied to limited aspects of social life; it was also precarious and could not last for long because of state repression. Neither could ungovernability, in the form of frequent violent confrontation with forces of the state, be sustained for more than a year and a half in Witbank. The local newspaper reported very few violent clashes during 1987. By this time the armoury of repression – shotguns, detentions and trials – had gained the upper hand over the stones and petrol bombs of resistance.

Yet in another sense ungovernability was successful. The boycott of rents and services by township residents soon mired the KwaGuqa Town Council (KTC) in financial difficulties. Capital funds had to be drawn on to pay salaries, and later the Transvaal Provincial Administration (TPA) had to fund salaries. The massive extensions to KwaGuqa in the late 1980s had to be financed with loans from the National Housing Trust, and were never repaid. The government's reform strategy for the 1980s, to use the Black Local Authorities (BLAs) to force communities to pay for their own services and infrastructure, collapsed. The other wing of the reform strategy, to outflank the popular movement by providing a controlled form of self-government via the BLAs, also collapsed.[10] While most councillors in KwaGuqa resisted the pressure to resign, some fled the township and those who didn't had to live under constant threat. The TPA made funds available to install perspex windows and high barbed wire fences, and there were regular patrols by municipal police. Black policemen who remained in the township had to live under similar conditions. Council activities in the township – fixing pipes, maintaining infrastructure, refuse removal – could not take place.[11]

The council also lost control of the hostels. Council personnel at the hostels had to be guarded by municipal police. The walls surrounding the hostels were broken down by youths at night. They were replaced with barbed wire fences, which were in turn demolished at night. Crowds of youths clashed repeatedly with the municipal police guarding the hostels, and eventually the council gave up trying to control access.[12] 'Ungovernability' succeeded in breaking the tight regime of government control over the township, making the influx control institutions and laws unworkable. The regulation of residents via lodgers' permits collapsed. The HAB and KTC evicted residents from their houses for failing to pay rent, demolished shacks, controlled access to the hostels, or prevented migrants from finding accommodation in the township or the informal settlements.[13]

The diminishing ability of the apartheid state to control the township was also related to the incoherence of its own internal reforms. In 1986 the government, faced by similar ungovernability and incoherence in townships across the country, abandoned influx control.[14]

The destruction of resistance did not mean that the apartheid state was able to re-establish its own control, merely that through coercion it had made the township a 'no go zone' for the comrades, rather than vice versa. The township social structure became 'ungovernable' in the sense that there was no legitimate authority that could establish an acceptable social order.

The unions and the popular movement
Organised workers and the community: four phases
Alliances between trade union movements and popular organisations are generally regarded as the defining feature of social movement unionism, particularly in developing countries. The relationship between organised workers and UDF structures in Witbank were characterised by both contestation and co-operation, and went through four distinct phases.

Phase 1: The Co-ordinating Committee and the unions[15]
The Co-ordinating Committee comprised individual activists rather than a structure representing organisations. Several of them were trade unionists. The chairperson, Benson Khumalo,[16] was one of the first shop stewards at Highveld Steel where he was known as a militant leader. He recruited Charles Makola to the committee when the latter joined NUMSA at Highveld Steel, before he became a shop steward. When Khumalo was moved to another division of Highveld Steel he ceased being a shop steward and devoted himself to community activism. Makola, on the other hand, while retaining his role in the committee, became increasingly involved in the union movement: he was elected shop steward, became vice-chairperson of the Highveld Steel shop stewards and the first chairperson of the COSATU local. An apprentice at Highveld Steel, Sam Mkhabela, came into the committee independently of the union, via the Young Christian Students, and left the factory to become a full-time UDF activist at regional and national levels. Barney Mashego was a NUM shop steward and activist at Rietspruit Opencast Collieries. He also joined the committee, and focused

on community activism after he was dismissed during a strike at the beginning of 1985.

The committee was formed at a time of growing organisation and activism in the mines, factories and communities of Witbank. Although these began as separate initiatives, they were starting to interconnect both locally and nationally.[17] Highveld Steel was the first company organised by an affiliate of the Federation of South African Trade Unions (FOSATU – predecessor to COSATU) in the area. A NUMSA branch was formed in 1984, with Frank Boshielo as its first official. The Highveld Steel shop stewards spent weekends and evenings helping Boshielo to organise other factories (not only in the metal sector but also for other FOSATU affiliates) as far afield as Nelspruit. The NUM started organising the coal mines around Witbank in a separate initiative by the rival federation, the Council of Unions of South Africa (CUSA).

The escalation of union organisation and industrial struggles generated large numbers of militant worker activists who inevitably became involved in the proliferation of community structures and initiatives. Although several workers and trade unionists were active on the Co-ordinating Committee, the relationship with the unions was informal rather than formal. The understanding in the committee was that Khumalo would be the link with NUMSA and Mashego the link with the NUM on the coal mines around Witbank, but the committee regarded them as community activists rather than as representatives of their unions. Trade unions had no formal means for making their views known in the committee or participating in its decisions. This led to tension between unionists and community activists, but these were muted. At this stage community struggles did not have a great impact on organised workers.

The workers who participated in community structures did not advocate a specific working-class politics. Some brought with them the confidence, militancy and organisational experience they had gained in the unions; others came to politics directly through community organisation. Some with union backgrounds deepened their involvement in the unions; others drifted away to become community activists. Workers were found on both sides of the sometimes tense divide between unions and community organisations. Indeed, the figure who came to symbolise most clearly the practices which unionists found objectionable in community activists was the former Highveld Steel shop steward, Benson Khumalo. There was no necessary link between an individual activist's workplace and union experience, and the organisational or political practices he or she adopted.

Tensions in Witbank were linked to broader tensions at national level between the trade union movement and the UDF and within the trade union movement over 'workerism' and 'populism'.[18] NUMSA unionists in Witbank were aware of criticisms of their union for not participating in community and political campaigns initiated by the UDF. But political shifts, centred in the Pretoria-Witwatersrand-Vereeniging (PWV) region, were taking place within the union movement. The November 1984 stayaway in the Transvaal, jointly co-ordinated by the trade unions and UDF structures, was indicative of this (Labour Monitoring Group 1985; Von Holdt 1988), but the unions in Witbank felt they were too small and too new to participate, and they were criticised locally for this. They began to engage directly in community struggles a year later, driven by two factors: the formation of COSATU in November 1985, signifying a new political direction for labour; and the direct participation of members in the escalating local struggles.

Phase 2: The COSATU local and the Co-ordinating Committee
LAUNCHING THE LOCAL

When unionists from Witbank attended a regional meeting of the newly launched COSATU in Germiston on the East Rand, they were encouraged to set up a local shop stewards' council. The regional leadership 'were emphasising that we must participate in community structures'. The local was launched and sent a delegation, led by its new chairperson, Charles Makola, now no longer simply a worker on a community structure but a representative of organised workers in the town, to meet the Co-ordinating Committee. 'We introduced ourselves, we were welcomed, and we found that the main guys in the meeting, the chairperson and the secretary, were our members from NUMSA, people like Benson Khumalo. So the relationship was well facilitated.' But before the formal relationship between the COSATU local and the Co-ordinating Committee could be consolidated, the community was plunged into a seven-day stayaway. The unions 'were thrown into it because our members responded'.[19] This kind of mass action *did* affect workers and their unions.

THE SEVEN-DAY STAYAWAY[20]

Late on a Sunday afternoon in February 1986, crowds of youths, workers, unemployed residents of KwaGuqa and activists converged at the township stadium for a meeting convened to put UPCO's employment demands to the black personnel officers of some of the bigger companies in the Witbank area. Grievances included allegations that the personnel officers insisted on bribes for jobs, and that no new jobs were being created for the unemployed in Witbank. The personnel officers, including a nervous Highveld Steel recruiting officer, were escorted to the stadium by the comrades.

At the stadium voices were raised demanding that the companies cease recruiting migrants from elsewhere, and that they recruit unemployed KwaGuqa residents 'who pay rent here'. UPCO wanted any new jobs to be channelled through itself, so that its members would be first in the queue.[21] The Highveld Steel recruiting officer tried to explain that they 'should send a delegation to get an answer from the managers because we did not have the authority'. Some in the crowd proposed that the personnel officers' houses should be burnt down. Then the police arrived and surrounded the stadium. Some of the activists managed to escape but others were arrested and some were beaten by police inside the stadium.

One member of the Co-ordinating Committee, the former NUM shop steward Barney Mashego, was late because he had been assigned to attend his church and request the minister to mention the plight of detainees in his sermon. He was called out of the church service and told what was happening. Heading for the stadium he was warned by a comrade that he was being sought by the police. From a nearby house he watched the police loading their captives into trucks. Mashego and Benson Khumalo contacted a businessman and asked him to buy food and deliver it to the police station for the prisoners. A lawyer was called to start negotiating with the police. Word began to go around the township that there was to be a stayaway, starting the following morning, and that it would last seven days. This process was 'spontaneous', meaning that it arose out of meetings of small groups of activists rather than from a formal structure, and was fuelled by popular anger. What this meant was captured in the story told by J.J. Mbonani, the 'bullfighter' at Rand Carbide:

I was knocking off from work at 11 o'clock that night. When I arrived at the hostels, Benson [Khumalo] was waiting for me outside, together with another guy. We went into the bushes. We planned the seven-day stayaway. We discussed all the plans. We started thinking about other people whom we might involve. I was saying, we mustn't get more people, we might be arrested. In the morning, there were some other people who were acting. We didn't know where they came from. They said, you are not going to work. Sleep! Sleep! Everybody was sleeping. And the police had problems getting hold of those people who called the stayaway.

Khumalo and Mbonani were not meeting as members of a formal organisation but each knew the other as a 'fighter' from union struggles at Highveld Steel. Both had been at the stadium earlier; Khumalo had addressed the meeting and then left and Mbonani had left when he noticed the police arriving. Clearly, similar discussions were taking place in other networks.

Either later that evening or the following day, the Co-ordinating Committee met and decided to issue a pamphlet endorsing the stayaway. The youths raised barricades and monitored participation. The police patrolled the streets. On the Tuesday they *sjambokked* residents and warned them to go to work – which only strengthened the stayaway. Mbonani was detained and assaulted by the police when they raided the hostels looking for a list of instigators. The man who had identified him, a resident in the hostels, was attacked by Mbonani's comrades and narrowly escaped death by necklacing.

The stayaway was seen by the activists who organised it not simply as a response to specific grievances but an attack on the apartheid system as a whole.[22] White Witbank also saw the stayaway as a time for 'Europeans' to pull together. Under the heading 'We can cope!', the *Witbank News* reported that 'despite current unrest in the black township and the Seven Day Stayaway, European employees are keeping the ball rolling'. A spokesman for Highveld Steel was reported saying that 'with no black workers, European employees are covering the work which needs to be carried out, and we will not let it get us under' (*Witbank News* 21/2/86).

Brave words, but the Highveld Steel recruiting officer recalled the stayaway as 'a big problem' for management. 'All the companies came to a standstill.' He himself begged the station commander to release those who had been arrested. Managers also put pressure on the police and pleaded in court for an immediate release. Two days later, a marathon court session lasting into the night processed all the cases on charges of attending an illegal gathering. Fines were paid with money collected from residents in the township and hostels. By the end of the day everyone had been released. But the stayaway continued for the entire seven days.

The stayaway caused tensions between COSATU and the community organisations. There were heated meetings at which the unions complained that they had not been consulted and that workers had not been given sufficient time to prepare themselves. Community activists regarded the stayaway as a spontaneous expression of popular anger, and that there had been no choice but to hit back at the state. COSATU was reluctant to prolong the stayaway beyond the release of the people who had been arrested but 'the community guys took a hard line, saying even if the guys are released we continue with our stayaway up to seven days'.

HOSTEL DWELLERS AND THE SEVEN-DAY STAYAWAY[23]

It was not only the length and manner of organising the stayaway that generated conflict between COSATU and community activists, but also the demand that companies should cease recruiting migrants and employ local residents. One migrant, a NUMSA shop steward, recalled the stayaway as an expression of 'tribalism, where the belief is that the hostel dwellers must go back home because they take the jobs of the township people here'. After the stayaway began, members of the Co-ordinating Committee wrote to companies in Witbank repeating the demand. This letter 'nearly caused chaos'. Many NUMSA members were very angry and wanted to withdraw from the stayaway. The union leadership and activists in the hostels opposed this, fearing division and conflict with the community organisations. Police played up these tensions, using megaphones to announce from their 'hippos' (armoured personnel carriers) that the shop stewards had called off the stayaway. Eventually, hostel dwellers agreed to continue the stayaway, partly because several migrants had attended the stadium gathering and been arrested along with the others, and because they hoped that if they demonstrated their support of township residents the latter would support their demands for urban rights under 'Section 10'.[24] Although the immediate problem had been resolved, it remained as a symbol of the tension between hostel dwellers and township residents: 'Time and again, when there was a conflict, then the hostel dwellers would refer to that letter because that was very divisive.'

The stayaway had the effect that the unemployed had demanded, at least at Highveld Steel. The company decided to cease recruiting migrant workers and to test whether locally recruited workers could cope with the tough conditions in areas of the workplace previously reserved for migrants, such as the Iron Plant One tapping floor. From then on Moses Nkabinde, the personnel officer responsible for recruitment, 'never went to recruit workers in Lebowa or Transkei. I would simply phone the local labour office to send 25 workers, and then we would test them. The existing migrants became permanent workers like any other worker'. This shift in employment policy was partly a response to the mass pressure in the township demonstrated by the stayaway, but it was also a response to broader developments in the township regime of control as well as in production. In 1986 influx control was abandoned by the government, and the administration boards that had administered it were disbanded. Migrants were no longer denied the right to live in urban areas by the notorious 'Section 10', so they too won their demands. The rapid influx of blacks from rural areas, and the explosion of informal settlements around Witbank, meant that there was increasing unemployment – which may explain why township residents were now prepared to take jobs previously reserved for migrants.[25]

Changes in the production process also played a part. In 1985 a second iron plant was commissioned at Highveld Steel. Using more advanced computer technology, it required fewer labourers and they worked in better conditions than in Iron Plant One. Moreover, increasing numbers of black workers were being promoted into semi-skilled positions or being trained as artisans. From 1990, the company only recruited workers with a standard 6 or above.[26] Township residents were more likely to have the required level of education than Bantustan residents.

THE COSATU LOCAL SHOP STEWARDS COUNCIL AND THE COMMUNITY

The seven-day stayaway was an impressive display of militant solidarity. Many activists and unionists claimed with pride that it was the longest stayaway organised by any community in South Africa. It pressured the police and courts into the speedy processing and release of the detainees. Politically, it demonstrated the cohesion of the popular movement and the isolation of the white town. But for many residents, the seven-day stayaway was experienced as a mixture of confusion, fear and disempowerment. Meshack Malinga, at the time a rank-and-file NUMSA member at Highveld Steel, recalled this vividly:

> We didn't know how the stayaway was called. We heard that people were arrested by the police. We were all antagonistic towards the police as the instruments of apartheid, but there was no general meeting where we took a decision that there was going to be a stayaway. Instead, the night before the stayaway, there was a lot of commotion in the township. The following day there were barricades in the street. The police were moving around with their hippos. It was clear from the look of things that it was a stayaway. You would hear people saying 'Azikwelwa!' – meaning nobody would ride to work. One didn't know exactly what the demands were. Who called the stayaway? Why was the stayaway called? It lasted for seven days, and you would sleep not knowing whether you would be going to work the next morning or not. There was this fear of an unknown.

Having become accustomed to democratic decision-making in the union, where shop stewards were mandated by general meetings, Malinga felt the contrast keenly. Instead of building solidarity, the practices of the community activists generated anxiety and mistrust. Fear of the repressive forces of the state started to blur with fear of the coercive actions of the comrades:

> And, yes, some of us were even beginning to be afraid of our own comrades. You wouldn't know who to trust. You would be afraid to say this thing is wrong because you would be identified as someone who is opposed to the struggle. That could mean you are seen as an enemy agent. No one was prepared to take that risk.

The strategy of ungovernability could undermine the apartheid system, but it could also produce disorder, confusion and tension within the community. Although all were united in their antagonism towards the police, the community was composed of various strata with different concerns – hostel dwellers, youths, political activists, shop stewards – and there was no 'visible leadership' to construct an alternative social order among them. This disorder persuaded the shop stewards to look beyond workplace issues and start engaging in the community – and the new COSATU local gave them the platform to do so:

> The shop stewards at that time were addressing worker issues. The youths had taken full control. But immediately after that time COSATU started realising that we need to take a role in the political activities in the township. That is where some of us started emerging. We were beginning to be able to intervene. If a person was calling a stayaway, we would say no, we are supportive of the cause, we are in struggle ourselves, but no one can call a stayaway without consulting with COSATU.[27]

After the stayaway COSATU and the Co-ordinating Committee had 'serious meetings', described by one unionist as a 'power struggle', about the trade unionists' complaints. Stayaways were a particularly important issue for the union federation since every stayaway produced 'casualties' in the form of dismissals. These would have to be contested by the unions and their shop stewards, without help from community structures. Ultimately, agreement was reached that 'there should not be any stayaway unless COSATU is fundamentally involved', establishing the unions as an alliance partner that could influence organisational practices and strategies in the community.[28] During 1986 COSATU and the Co-ordinating Committee worked together on protest actions and political campaigns. Nonetheless, the contestation between unionists and community activists over organisational practices and culture continued.[29]

These differences were partly attributable to greater repression and weaker organisational structures in the community but they were also rooted in different conceptions of struggle and organisation. The structure of the township as an organisational terrain, the political imperative of challenging the apartheid state, the psycho-social features of the youth and the unemployed, the repression directed against the formal structures and leadership of the UDF, and the rapid escalation of the urban uprisings, had combined to produce a set of practices among the surviving activists centred on clandestine networks, the insurrectionary tactics of 'ungovernability', quasi-military confrontation and dramatic and symbolic actions. Violence against the enemy was seen as necessary, and violence to enforce community solidarity and punish transgressors was regarded as legitimate. Building stable organisation, consultation and accountability were not highly valued, but were associated instead with 'hesitancy and lack of militancy'.[30] Activists were representatives of the revolution and 'the Movement', as the ANC was known, not of organisations and constituencies. These practices have been variously described as vanguardism, populism and millenarianism.[31]

For trade unionists, however, democracy, strong organisation, consultation and accountability were core values and practices. Workers' empowerment was directly dependent on strong, structured and democratic organisation to give them a voice. Only through asserting these values and practices in the community could workers and trade unions gain a voice on this different terrain and protect their organisational and other interests. These concerns also resonated with ordinary residents who experienced 'ungovernability' as a climate of disorder and fear. Of course, coercion and the construction of social order are inseparable, and unionists did not object in principle to the use of a degree of coercion to enforce collective decisions and to police collective action in the community.[32] Their objection was to violence that, in their view, was excessive and illegitimate, for example to enforce a decision which had been made undemocratically.

Trade unionists did not at this stage define a distinct political project. They had been drawn into the popular movement as its scope widened. They tended to support the ANC and the UDF, and regarded themselves as participants in the national liberation struggle against apartheid. The racial conflict in which trade union struggles were embedded led to a high degree of political consciousness among workers. Although they 'could not articulate the principles of non-racialism, democracy or international solidarity', when they were *toyi-toying* or on strike they would chant slogans and songs – about Mandela, the ANC, and the armed struggle – that were 'more political than worker related'.[33] For Hong Kong Kgalima, a footsoldier rather than a leader, the community and union struggles were one and the same. 'We are all in NUMSA. I can say we are all ANC, we want rights and we want a living wage for each and every person. The union is us people living in the community.'[34]

What the shop stewards contested, therefore, was not political symbols or ideology but organisational culture, practices and tactics.[35] Nor did all workers and union members automatically adopt the practices and attitudes articulated by the union leadership. Many shop stewards and members had their own independent links to the youth and community movements, and brought their practices and perspectives into the union movement. Workers' collective identity was not a given, but was in a continuous process of formation and contestation within organisations and movements.

The seven-day stayaway illustrates this tension between the formal structures of NUMSA and the activism among some of its members. Frank Boshielo recalled that 'shop stewards were attending community meetings' and, like J.J. Mbonani, mobilising action together with community activists. 'I was a union official but I didn't even know where they were meeting or what they were planning. Because of the state of emergency, nobody would admit that he was involved.' Whether the union liked it or not, members and shop stewards were increasingly active in the community. Participating in community structures and mobilisations, they were adopting the style and tactics of the community activists. Either the organisational structures and culture of the union would be undermined, or it would have to find ways to intervene and influence community struggles.[36]

Thus the alliance between the union movement and the community organisations – regarded in the literature as the defining feature of social movement unionism – was not a simple or straightforward matter. The specific alliance forged between township youths and migrant workers demonstrates this quite clearly.

YOUTHS AND HOSTEL DWELLERS[37]

A close relationship developed between youth activists and the hostel dwellers during this period. In 1986, when the army camped in KwaGuqa and conducted house-to-house searches for activists, many of them sought refuge in the hostels. Youth activists started to realise the importance of working closely with the hostel dwellers to counter the police strategy of exacerbating the tensions that had arisen in the course of the seven-day stayaway. Their aim was to 'integrate' the hostel dwellers into the community and 'mobilise' them in the struggle. They demolished the walls and fences around the hostels. They were able to build on relationships which had been forged in the struggle to organise NUMSA at Highveld Steel, such as that between J.J. Mbonani in the hostels and Benson Khumalo who had become a youth activist. Mbonani started accommodating youth meetings in the kitchen of his hostel block because they 'were running away from the police in the township, and the police did not visit this place'. A youth who became active in COSAS as a student remembered the hostels as a place where the unions and the ANC were 'campaigning and having meetings'. The result was that 'we had a very good relationship with the hostels, we never ever broke with the people there'.

With time the youth and the hostel dwellers were able to mutually influence each other. The migrant workers appreciated the physical courage of the youths: 'The hostel guys realised that the youths were in the forefront, fighting the battle, face to face with the cops.' Hostel dwellers themselves became increasingly involved in mass action. At the same time they were able to argue that the youths should not call stayaways or community actions on their own, but should develop a broader base of consultation and decision-making, explaining that workers faced the danger of dismissal and that relying on intimidation rather than winning worker support would drive a wedge between workers and youths. At first 'when we talked to these young ones they didn't want to listen, they didn't want to understand what we were saying'. But eventually they accepted that all organisations needed to be part of decision-making, and when an action was planned a committee would be elected with delegates from each organisation. The result was that when a stayaway was called 'the people in the hostel were actually more exposed to political issues than the people in the township, so you would have 100 per cent stayaway from the people in the hostels'.

Activists were well aware that the close bond that developed between youths and migrant workers in Witbank was highly unusual.[38] They explained it in terms of the strength of NUMSA in the hostels, and the efforts to 'organise the ANC' – referring to the active presence of the youth in the hostels from 1986. It is also significant that the majority of migrant workers were Pedis, with insignificant numbers of Zulu-speakers. Not only did this mean there was no Inkatha[39] presence to serve as a basis for opposition to the popular movement in the hostels, but Pedi migrants had a history of participation in ANC-linked campaigns and organisations during the 1950s. Particularly important for the Pedi was Sebatakgomo, initiated by the South African Communist Party (SACP) and closely linked to the ANC, which was launched as a 'peasant's movement' in 1955. It became a vehicle linking Pedi migrants in the towns to the rural struggles that culminated in the Sekhukhuneland Revolt in 1958. There had been an active Sebatakgomo branch in Witbank during the 1950s (Delius 1996: chapter 3 and 112, 114). Many of the migrants in the KwaGuqa hostels would have been predisposed, therefore, to support organisations and struggles associated with the ANC. They would also have been aware of the youth mobilisation in their home villages in Sekhukhuneland in 1985 and 1986, and although tensions developed between rural youths and older generations as these struggles became more violent (ibid: chapter 6), Pedi migrants may have been more sympathetic than other migrant workers to the militant youths.

The result was that a large contingent of NUMSA's members at Highveld Steel, the migrant workers, forged a collective identity as militant supporters of the ANC/UDF, and as allies of the youths in confronting the apartheid regime. This would become an important factor in internal contestations over the culture and practices of the union.

This study reveals the alliance between social movement unionism and popular organisation to have been less an alliance between independent organisations with common interests, than a complex mesh of networks and identities. The trade union movement not only sought to influence community politics, but was itself profoundly shaped by identities and their associated practices forged beyond the workplace, in the community and in the popular movement. As we shall see below, this generated internal contestation over the collective identity, goals and practices of the union. The collective identity forged by social movement unionism was not a straightforward class identity, but a complex amalgam of class and popular identities which emerged through interaction between different organisations on varied terrains.

Phase 3: COSATU takes the lead

By 1987–88 COSATU was taking the lead in community struggles in Witbank. This was partly because the strength and organisational ability of the union structures was becoming increasingly clear to community activists, and partly because repression was taking a heavy toll in the community. The Co-ordinating Committee appears to have ceased functioning. The COSATU local became the most important political decision-making forum, and representatives of the youth, UPCO and church organisations started attending it. When the UDF was effectively banned at the beginning of 1988, COSATU became the only organisation able to operate openly.[40] This situation in Witbank mirrored COSATU's political influence nationally.

This led to a 'fundamental difference' in the way that stayaways or boycotts were called:

> When COSATU was leading there would be no stayaway unless it had been thoroughly discussed in the affiliates of COSATU and brought back to COSATU. You had more worker involvement when COSATU was leading.[41]

In Witbank the COSATU local served as the core of the Mass Democratic Movement.[42] The 1989 Defiance Campaign was led by COSATU and 'the entire community was supportive, and it was voluntary, we discouraged intimidation'.[43]

Phase 4: political conflict

During the fourth phase, which lasted from 1988 to 1991, NUMSA shop stewards in Witbank developed a more assertive political agenda. This phase saw heightened political contestation within NUMSA, and between COSATU and the community activists.

POLITICAL STRUGGLES WITHIN NUMSA

Within NUMSA political tensions gathered around Benson Khumalo and Barney Mashego. Both were community activists and leading figures in the Witbank Youth Congress (WYCO), and had come to politics through trade unionism. Both were subject to repression, had gone into hiding and left Witbank for a while. Khumalo had been charged in the Witbank terrorism trial[44] but was acquitted. For both, employment as organisers in NUMSA in early 1988 provided a stable organisational base.

Within Highveld Steel a new group of artisan shop stewards, Mosi Nhlapo, Meshack Malinga and Ambrose Mthembu, emerged as forceful leaders after the defeat of the 1987 lockout (described in chapters 5 and 6). Together with a handful of long-standing shop stewards – Charles Makola, William Sehlola, Johannes Phatlana and J.J. Mbonani – they rebuilt the union at Highveld Steel, which had always been the leading Witbank factory in NUMSA and in COSATU. The new Highveld Steel leadership became highly influential in NUMSA and COSATU locals, and in the NUMSA region. Malinga was the chair at Highveld Steel; Nhlapo was elected chair of the NUMSA local and Makola was still the COSATU local chairperson and the vice-chair of the NUMSA region.

Initially, Nhlapo was not interested in community meetings: 'I was a shop steward and I had to make sure that workers were defended in the factory.' He was also nervous about politics, and particularly about the ANC:

To some of us, the ANC in exile was something unknown, something huge that can destroy you. Barney Mashego was the guy who was more political in NUMSA, and the way he was talking about the ANC you would see guys that are dangerous, guys that can even kill you. I didn't want to be involved with these guys. Seemingly once you make a mistake, you're gone.[45]

However, once Nhlapo was elected as chair of the NUMSA local he became more directly involved. The group of shop stewards would discuss developments and strategies. They would use NUMSA 'as a springboard' for giving direction to COSATU and then engaging with community organisations. As a local leader, Nhlapo attended NUMSA national meetings where he 'started understanding debates'. NUMSA emphasised political independence and organisational democracy, and was prepared to criticise the ANC:

I supported that view myself, that the ANC must not act as God here, we as workers must not follow at their heels. They should bring an agenda and we'll discuss it. Our people are not hopping around following the ANC wherever it is.[46]

The group of NUMSA shop stewards in Witbank 'took it upon ourselves that it is our responsibility to make sure that NUMSA's democratic policies and practices are being implemented wherever we go'. This project, informed by NUMSA's distinctive politics, was a far more assertive and self-conscious worker project than earlier phases of COSATU's engagement in the Witbank community. In Nhlapo's view, community activists in Witbank lacked direction and were failing to build a grassroots, democratic organisation. 'Ungovernability' exacerbated this problem:

One started thinking clearly about the difference between political responsibility and ungovernability. When do you become ungovernable? Do you say, when the traffic light is red I'm just going to cross because the ANC is banned? Or, because the traffic light is there and the cars are coming, I'll wait until it's green and then I'll pass? We started to differentiate these things.[47]

Despite their assertiveness, the NUMSA shop stewards were not presenting a political *alternative* to the UDF and the ANC but rather an alternative way of organising the popular movement.

This assertive union strategy was not well received by the community activists; nor was it welcomed by the two NUMSA officials most closely involved in community activism. The officials were regarded by the leading shop stewards as fomenting opposition to the NUMSA strategy and undermining its policy of worker control. In a regional shop stewards' council the chairperson had to admonish Khumalo for insisting that shop stewards should adopt his views because, he claimed, he 'was speaking for the ANC, and shop stewards might not know the deep politics of the ANC'. Although his views were considered, they were eventually rejected by the shop stewards. Khumalo then resigned from the union, accusing it of 'misleading' the workers.[48]

Mashego ran foul of the shop stewards when he and other organisers were questioned by workers at a regional congress about their arrangements for closing the office over the summer holidays. 'Barney and some other organisers accused us of trying to be bosses.' Tension increased, and the shop steward office-bearers – including Makola and another Highveld shop steward – called Mashego to a disciplinary hearing after an 'exchange of words'. He was given a warning. Political conflict intensified. Mashego would oppose NUMSA policies both within the union and in meetings with community activists. Shop stewards felt that he threatened them with retribution from the ANC if they persisted in their views. Some of them started planning to dismiss him for undermining the union. Mashego was aware of the threat, and was able to use his support among NUMSA members in the hostels – a legacy of his days as a youth activist – to block it.[49]

The union attempt to reshape practices within the popular movement generated a struggle within the union over its policies and practices. The shop stewards found that the various forces they had to contend with in the community – the youth, the political activists, the migrant workers – were also present within the union. Chapter 6 shows how this conflict escalated in 1990/1 into a power struggle for control of the union, which split the shop stewards at Highveld into two committees, and involved the township youths.

POLITICAL CONFLICT IN THE COMMUNITY

In the community, too, the strategy of the NUMSA shop stewards ran into trouble.

The NUMSA national views were seen by most people as being contrary to ANC policies, the ANC way of operating. There were very serious tensions between us and people from other organisations. NUMSA was a threat to most people because how NUMSA wanted to practice democracy – in terms of clear consultation, mandate-giving and reporting back – was totally different from how other organisations saw democracy. People believed in executive powers more than involving the masses.[50]

Nhlapo was so disturbed that he began to suspect that the policies of the union, and the training courses it ran, were wrong because 'why should everyone be against us?' He discussed this with national officials, who told him that union leadership was encountering similar problems in most locals and regions.[51]

In 1989 the NUMSA national congress adopted a detailed resolution on the need to build strong organisations in the community based on a union model, and resolved to deploy its shop stewards and leadership to help implement this. An amended version was adopted by the COSATU national congress later the same year. The COSATU local took this up, initiating a planning forum with four delegates from each COSATU affiliate: four from UPCO, four from WYCO and a number of political activists from the community. Makola and Nhlapo were among the NUMSA representatives. Its purpose was 'to establish a civic, because we never had a formal civic association'. The planning forum met in December and, after some discussion, set a date in January for a second meeting.

However, over Christmas, Benson Khumalo, who was then working in Johannesburg for the UDF, met with about 10 of the delegates on the planning forum and formed a new structure, an interim committee to relaunch the UDF in Witbank. Some of the trade unionists attempted to challenge this but the committee went ahead and relaunched the UDF. Then, as anticipated, the ANC was unbanned. 'Immediately we had to form the structures of the ANC, but it was not possible to form it as a team because of the conflict between ourselves as activists around Witbank.' Once again Khumalo intervened. He established an organising group and started recruiting members. An interim branch was established with Khumalo as chairperson, which enabled him to attend a regional ANC conference in Nelspruit where he was elected to the regional executive. The NUMSA shop stewards had been outmaneuvered – temporarily.[52] But the story of their rise to leadership of the Witbank branch of the ANC is told in chapter 8.

Conclusion

This chapter explores the dynamics of the alliance between social movement unionism and the popular movement at a local level. Instead of a relation between autonomous organisations, it reveals a series of networks that linked the popular movement and the trade union, and the meshing of collective identities woven together in the struggle against apartheid. Thus, while unionists influenced the popular struggle, the popular struggle shaped the union – which itself came to be defined by an amalgam of popular and class identities. The result was contestation, not only over the practices of the popular movement, but also within the trade union movement itself.

These contestations went through different phases in Witbank. However, through all these phases it was the ANC and the UDF that provided overall leadership in terms of the conception, goals and strategies of the struggle. Trade unionists did not provide a political alternative, but attempted to shape organisational practices and tactics within the popular movement. Even when the COSATU local provided organisational leadership after community organisations had disintegrated, as well as in the phase of a more assertive NUMSA project, what was notable was the absence of a political alternative to the ANC/UDF-led national democratic struggle.

Indeed, the tactics that came to prevail in the community under the hammer blows of repression – the tactics of ungovernability, violent confrontation and intimidation – were imported into the trade union together with the popular political identities forged in community struggles. The result was workplace disorder as well as disorder and ungovernability within the structures of the union, as we shall see in the next two chapters.

Notes

1. This and the next paragraph are drawn from interviews with Ezekiel Nkosi and Philip Mkatshwa, 9/3/94; Ezekiel Nkosi, 5/5/94, 10/7/94; Joe Mokoena, 12/10/95; Sam Mkhabela, 1/6/94.
2. Interview, Sam Mkhabela, 1/6/94; interview, Charles Makola, 14/5/94; interview, Frank Boshielo, 9/93.
3. Interview, Sam Mkhabela, 1/6/94.
4. In 1987, 30 activists from Witbank were detained and charged with terrorism, sedition and public violence under the Internal Security Act, as well as with murder. Amongst other things, the state alleged that the accused had formed COSAS to further the aims of the ANC, replaced COSAS with the Witbank Youth Congress when the former was banned, and conspired in these aims with senior COSATU officials, including the general secretary, Jay Naidoo. Most of the accused were community activists, but they included the regional chairperson of the NUM, Clement Zulu. The trial dragged through 1987 and finished in 1988. Six of the accused were discharged, 12 were convicted and 12 acquitted (interview, Sam Mkhabela, 1/6/94).
5. Interview, Hong Kong Kgalima, 3/7/94. 'Revolutionary bullying' is 'liable to be a crucial aspect in the formation of loyalties where conflict is severe and the risk of allegiance high, that is, in any significant struggle' (Moore 1978: 342–3, 489). The role of the

youth in enforcing collective actions such as stayaways or boycotts was regarded by many, including unionists, as legitimate (see, for example, interview, Charles Makola, 8/5/94).

6. Interview, Sam Mkhabela, 1/6/94. Mkhabela was active both in Witbank and at a national level in the UDF. See also Mayekiso on the relation between ungovernability and building 'organs of people's power' (1996: 74, 89–90): 'Ungovernability became a catchword for challenging the regime ... For while ungovernability was aimed at hitting state organs, the next step beyond ungovernability was to build organs of people's power... We were firstly trying to make the township and country ungovernable, and secondly sowing seeds so that, given the opportunity, we would actually have something in place to solve the problems.' This account differs from Bozzoli's (2000) argument that the erosion of state hegemony during the era of 'racial modernism' meant that the township uprisings produced an almost immediate 'legal and moral vacuum' to which the youth responded with a semi-millenarian and authoritarian repertoire of activities. I argue that the UDF activists sought to construct an alternative, i.e. a counter-hegemonic order. This continued to influence youth activists, albeit in a distorted form, once repression had destroyed organisations and their constraining influence.

7. Interview, Charles Makola, 14/5/94; interview, Sam Mkhabela, 1/6/94; interview, Joe Mokoena, 12/10/95.

8. Interview, Leo Makwakwa, 12/5/98.

9. Interview, Meshack Malinga, 14/5/94.

10. The black local authorities, including the KwaGuqa Town Council, were established in 1983. Prior to this the black townships and the influx control system were administered by the central state through a network of Native Affairs Administration Boards, which had in turn taken over these functions – including the municipal police who enforced them – from the white local authorities in 1972. From 1983 to 1987 when the administration boards were finally disbanded, the townships were jointly administered by the boards and the BLAs while functions were transferred from the former to the latter. In the face of the escalating urban uprisings which were sparked off in part by the establishment of these BLAs and the increase in township rents which they imposed, the role of the municipal police, their name unchanged since they had been established by the white municipalities, was expanded from the policing of influx control to the protection of the new councillors and council personnel and property. When influx control was abolished in 1986, the municipal police became solely concerned with these latter tasks. It seems to have been at this point that they were transferred to the BLAs (interview, Adam Engelbrecht, 12/5/98; interview, Leo Makwakwa, 12/5/98).

11. Interview, Adam Engelbrecht, 12/5/98; interview, Leo Makwakwa, 12/5/98.

12. Interview, Adam Engelbrecht, 12/5/98; interview, Charles Makola, 8/5/94; interview, Leo Makwakwa, 12/5/98; interview, Barney Mashego, 13/10/95.

13. Interview, Sam Mkhabela, 1/6/94.

14. The Administration Boards continued to administer the institutions and regulations of influx control after 1983 when the BLAs were established, but the intention was to phase out the Boards when the BLAs were fully operational (interview, Adam Engelbrecht, 12/5/98). It was not clear what would happen to influx control regulation when this happened, or whether the BLAs would be expected to implement the pass laws – which would have been the kiss of death to any popularity they may have managed to garner. The legislation governing the formation of the BLAs was, for example, silent on whether the municipal police – a key institution in influx control – would be taken over by the BLAs once the Administration Boards were phased out (interview, Leo Makwakwa, 12/5/98). By the time the Boards were disbanded at the end of 1986 and beginning of 1987, influx control had been abandoned as government policy. The municipal police were in fact handed over to the KwaGuqa Town Council; however, their function was no longer to police the pass laws, but to protect council property and personnel against the popular uprisings (interview, Adam Engelbrecht, 12/5/98). Thus, on the one hand, the escalation of popular resistance made it increasingly unlikely that the state would be able to retain its influx control policies, while on the other, the 1982 reforms rendered the township regime of control increasingly incoherent. It is unclear whether state reformers in 1982 already envisaged ultimately abandoning influx control, or whether the gaps and contradictions in the reforms were simply a sign of the unravelling of the apartheid system.

15. Interview, Charles Makola, 8/5/94; interview, Sam Mkhabela, 1/6/94; interview, Barney Mashego, 13/10/95.

16. Not his real name.

17. The formation of the UDF aimed to link together a range of community and union organisations in joint national campaigns. Neither NUM nor NUMSA were part of the UDF, and were affiliated to rival national federations, the Council of Unions of South Africa (CUSA) and the Federation of South African Trade Unions (FOSATU). The union unity talks would bring the two unions together in COSATU at the end of 1985, when the NUM broke away from CUSA. One of the factors that would contribute to this drive for worker unity was the interaction of union activists from different traditions together in local community structures such as the Witbank Co-ordinating Committee. The involvement of shop stewards in local community structures also played a decisive role in the shift of the union movement towards more overt political involvement. See Von Holdt (1988) for an account of similar processes on the East Rand.

18. The biggest bloc of trade unions refused to affiliate to the UDF when it was launched in 1983. They were accused of 'workerism' and in turn accused the UDF of 'populism'. As the popular movement gained strength, the political dynamics within the labour movement shifted, and the conflict between 'workerism' and 'populism' became an internal rift within COSATU. See Baskin (1991) for an overview, and Foster (1982), General Workers Union (1983) and Njikelana (1984) for trade unionists on this debate. This chapter constitutes a local study of the practices that gave rise to such tensions.

19. Interview, Frank Boshielo, 9/93, 19/6/94.
20. This account of the stayaway is drawn from interviews with Frank Boshielo, 9/93, 19/6/94; Meshack Malinga, 14/5/94; Barney Mashego, 13/10/95; Charles Makola, 8/5/94, 14/5/94; J.J. Mbonani, 31/5/94, 7/6/94; Moses Nkabinde, 12/5/98; Johannes Phatlana, 7/9/94; William Sehlola, 5/6/94.
21. During this period a similar organisation of the unemployed, the *Amalova* ('the loafers'), was operating in Springs on the East Rand. It worked closely with the Springs COSATU shop stewards local, and together with them negotiated an agreement with the employers in the town that all new jobs would be channelled through *Amalova* (Von Holdt 1988).
22. See, for example, interview, J.J. Mbonani, 7/6/94.
23. This account of tensions between hostel dwellers and township residents is drawn from interviews with Frank Boshielo, 9/93; Barney Mashego, 13/10/95; Moses Nkabinde, 12/5/98; Johannes Phatlana, 7/9/94; William Sehlola, 5/6/94.
24. A key section of the influx control legislation defining different categories of residential rights for Africans.
25. Chapter 1 charts the massive growth of the black population in Witbank after influx control was abandoned.
26. Interview, Moses Nkabinde, 12/5/98. All of the black interviewees in this study who were recruited from 1986 on were either artisans or young township men who started as labourers – often in the 'testing' conditions of the Iron Plant One tapping floor – and were then promoted to semi-skilled operators.
27. Interview, Meshack Malinga, 14/5/94.
28. Interview, Charles Makola, 8/5/94. The calling of stayaways without consulting the unions was a key grievance. See interview, Meshack Malinga, 15/3/94; interview, J.J. Mbonani, 7/6/94; interview, Ezekiel Nkosi, 26/5/94.
29. Interview, Charles Makola, 8/5/94, 14/5/94; interview, William Sehlola, 5/6/94.
30. Interview, Sam Mkhabela, 1/6/94.
31. See Morris (1990) on the township terrain, the psycho-social features of the unemployed, and the phenomenon of 'vanguardism', and Bozzoli (2000) on millenarianism and the nature of the township as a social institution. The term 'populism' was used by those in the 'independent worker' currents of the trade union movement to describe activists who subscribed to the strategy of 'national democratic revolution'.
32. See, for example, interview, Charles Makola, 8/5/94.
33. Interview, Charles Makola, 8/5/94.
34. Interview, Hong Kong Kgalima, 10/7/94; see also interview, Charles Makola, 14/5/94; interview, J.J. Mbonani, 31/5/94.
35. This distinguishes the Witbank case from other areas – particularly metropolitan urban centres where the influence of union ideologues was stronger – where the tension between unions and community organisations was sometimes articulated in the more political terms of conflict between socialist and national democratic revolutions. What

makes the Witbank case interesting is the absence of this more explicitly political dimension, with the result that organisational themes come to the fore.

36. Interview, Frank Boshielo, 19/6/94.
37. This account is drawn from interviews with Charles Makola, 8/5/94; Barney Mashego, 13/10/95; J.J. Mbonani, 7/6/94; Jacob Msimangu, 12/8/95, 22/10/95.
38. See Bonner and Ndima (1999), Mamdani (1996) and Segal (1992) for accounts of the alienation of Zulu migrant workers on the East Rand from COSATU.
39. The KwaZulu-Natal based movement led by Gatsha Buthelezi that mobilised traditional Zulu identities against the ANC.
40. Interview, Charles Makola, 14/5/94. The organisational activities of the UDF and a number of its affiliates were banned at the beginning of 1988, and COSATU was banned from taking part in political or community activities – a ban which it disregarded.
41. Interview, Charles Makola, 14/5/94.
42. With the banning of the UDF and its key affiliates, the Mass Democratic Movement was formed as a loose coalition incorporating COSATU, former UDF organisations and activists, and progressive church organisations.
43. Interview, Meshack Malinga, 14/5/94. This is not to say that the COSATU local was free of conflict over political practices during this phase. Some of the newer, smaller unions – often closely aligned with the UDF, and staffed by organisers drawn from youth and student activists – would attempt to propose major resolutions such as a five-day stayaway in the COSATU local, despite their small size. They would have 'quite a different style and tactic' to the bigger unions, more similar to youth structures. The chair of the local would also have to be vigilant in preventing organisations with observer status, such as UPCO and other community organisations, from moving or seconding resolutions (interview, Charles Makola, 14/5/94).
44. See note 4 above.
45. Interview, Mosi Nhlapo, 8/5/94.
46. Interview, Mosi Nhlapo, 6/3/95.
47. Ibid.
48. Interview, Mosi Nhlapo, 12/95.
49. Interview, Ambrose Mthembu, 15/3/94; interview, Mosi Nhlapo, 12/95; interview, William Sehlola, 5/6/94.
50. Interview, Mosi Nhlapo, 12/95.
51. Interview, Mosi Nhlapo, 9/11/93, 8/5/94, 6/3/95.
52. Interview, Charles Makola, 14/5/94.

CHAPTER 5

'It was just chaotic'

The apartheid workplace regime, political challenge and 'ungovernability' in the workplace

> The aim was political, it was simply to overthrow the government of the day. Everything rallied around that point, that this government has to be brought down to its knees and replaced by a democratic government.
>
> *Charles Makola, vice-chairperson of the shop steward's committee, chairperson of the COSATU local*

The rise of the popular movement in KwaGuqa forged a collective political identity around the idea of a black community challenge to the oppressive and illegitimate apartheid regime. This black political identity was forged not only in ideas, but also in political practices and strategies – violent confrontation with the institutions and forces of apartheid, symbolic defiance and ungovernability, the organisation of a counter-order in the form of 'people's power', and the legitimacy of coercion in maintaining the unity of the people. This chapter explores the impact of popular political identity and its associated practices on social movement unionism in the workplace. The trade union was deeply shaped by political identities forged beyond the workplace. Social movement unionism was regarded as a component of the insurgent black popular movement. Trade union activities became part of the larger political drama of black resistance to white power.

The political dimension of social movement unionism

During the mid-1980s there was a growing sense of 'chaos' at Highveld Steel. Bunny Mahlangu, who was chairperson of shop stewards at the height of the confrontations during 1987, described the atmosphere:

Between 1985 and 1987 Highveld Steel was one company that was militant, and it was so militant that office-bearers or leadership couldn't even stop the militancy. It was just chaotic, that militancy. In 1985 we had these mini-strikes where people would just scare management and then get scared themselves and go back to work. 1986 was not so quiet. But 1987 was the worst. That was the year we had a strike almost every week. Unfortunately I was elected the chairperson of the shop stewards' committee and I found myself in this mist, having to resolve strikes almost every week. But the real problem was that in 1986 we formed what we called a strike committee. It was all these really militant guys, guys that would always like to see action, and for any petty thing they would just stop people and say, 'No, today we are not going to work – there's a strike'. So strikes were just spontaneous. Sometimes, as the chairperson, I would come to work and find there is a strike and I didn't know about it.[1]

Political and industrial relations issues were interwoven through these strikes – wage demands, challenges to dismissals, a response to the killing in a faraway town of the wife of a unionist who had been involved in community resistance to forced removals, and another to the arrest of a fellow worker, the protracted Witbank stayaway and participation in nationwide stayaways. Interspersed with these strikes were dozens of shorter stoppages over political and workplace issues: a two-hour stoppage to hold a prayer service for a community activist killed by the police, a wildcat strike to demand the dismissal of a white manager or the reinstatement of a black worker. The range of actions and grievances, and the political symbols, songs and rhetoric that accompanied them, reinforced the linkages between workplace, community and political struggles. Industrial action was charged with political meaning and racial confrontation. The challenge to white management in the workplace was a challenge to apartheid in general.

Charles Makola, who was active in community structures as well as being the chairperson of the COSATU local and vice-chair of the shop stewards' committee, put this quite explicitly:

The aim was political, it was simply to overthrow the government of the day. Everything rallied around that point, that this government has to be brought down to its knees and replaced by a democratic government. All these actions, boycotts, stayaways were directed at that objective. Before the Harare Declaration[2] the concept of negotiating was out of the question. There was no differentiation between the state and the companies. Apartheid was more practical in the working environment than anywhere else. *At company level the negotiations were not strictly speaking negotiations.* Although it was unavoidable to articulate our demands, and put them before management for discussion, our approach was one of confrontation. We would simply demand that June 16 be recognised as a public holiday, and that's it.[3] It is not going to be negotiated. On June 16 we will not come to work. We were planning outside the company with other structures that June 16 is a stayaway. From time to time we would have to deal with management, but we never trusted them as they never trusted us. We would put forward demands and strike the following day. We were reluctant to use the Industrial Council or the procedures of the LRA. We strike whether it's legal or illegal. We used to argue that there is no such thing as a legal strike on the part of the workers. We were not only challenging the individual employers, we were even challenging the state [author's emphasis].[4]

Activists were reluctant to participate in institutions or negotiate in a way that would imply legitimacy. This created tensions for trade unionism: it sought the overthrow of the entire apartheid system and, at the same time, it was necessarily involved in negotiations with management. So negotiations were at the same time 'not negotiations'. Industrial action not only served to put pressure on management to accede to workers demands; it also undermined the economic base of apartheid:

We were faced with the system of apartheid, which was working hand in hand with capitalist exploitation and naturally, as the union, we had to resist. One way of resisting was through industrial action – strikes, stayaways, go slows, overtime bans. We were not concerned about productivity. We were not concerned about the economy. In fact, we wanted to see this economy in South Africa suffering because it had no significance for us other than keeping the very system of apartheid alive.[5]

The political nature of trade union struggle was influenced both by the racial nature of power relations in the workplace, and by the political oppression experienced by black workers outside the workplace. The political collective identity forged beyond the workplace in the struggle for national liberation shaped the collective identity forged within the workplace by social movement unionism in the struggle against white management:

The struggle for liberation was a pillar of the unity of the people inside, and even outside the factory. It was not a trade union struggle for wages and conditions. Dismissals were not seen in isolation from the political arena, they were seen as perpetuating racial discrimination.[6]

The struggle in the factory took on some of the qualities of a liberation war. As a migrant worker put it, describing the meaning rather than the concrete practices of action: 'We never negotiated. We would just go into the bush and when asked why, we would tell them to release Mandela first.'[7] The image of 'going into the bush' had several layers: it referred to strike action and linked this to the idea – extolled in many of the political songs sung by workers – of going into 'the bush' to join the freedom fighters of the liberation movement; this in turn resonated with the old wars of resistance fought in 'the bush' against colonialism.

In this atmosphere, 'the strike was the order of the day', because there was not 'any mutual agreement on any issues' between workers and management.[8] There was, in other words, an absence of 'established patterns of social interaction' or 'rules of conduct', whether formally or informally patterned. As one migrant worker put it: 'That we were breaking any law didn't bother the workers at all, since most of the things that management wanted from workers it got by force.'[9] Rather than a jointly constructed and mutually understood framework within which conflict and contestation between workers and management could be structured, the apartheid workplace regime was under assault by an insurgent union movement which questioned its fundamental premises. Ungovernability prevailed.

The intransigence of management at Highveld Steel meant that 'those strikes were always resolved by a threat of mass dismissal'. In the shop stewards' view only one or two of the strikes 'achieved any objectives' because of this hardline approach.[10] But the point of striking was not necessarily linked to collective bargaining. Experiencing their collective power was in itself a goal: 'Our strength could be seen! And our membership started to grow.'[11] Downing tools, walking off the job and *toyi-toying* together with a mass of fellow workers in the white man's factory gave a profound sense of power to black workers insulted and oppressed by whites. Just as the apartheid workplace regime was characterised by the continual assertion of white dominance, so resistance took the form of an assertion of defiance and power by black workers. The symbolic potency of this experience, and of disempowering the whites, was as important as collective bargaining over concrete goals. This is how J.J. Mbonani described it:

When we went on strike the managers tried to do our jobs, especially on the tapping floor. After our strike we will find some of them in hospital, burnt or injured. Then people are laughing, saying it's nice to see these white guys being involved in accidents. We have been slaves for such a long time, we want to see what happens when we strike.[12]

They were demonstrating that they would no longer collaborate with the production of apartheid in the workplace. Strikers were reluctant to return to their workstations; it was worth losing wages to experience this power: 'Even if we are not paid for three days we don't care, now the whites can see what is going on, so they won't be able to come and talk the way they like.'[13]

The meaning of industrial action for workers demonstrates the inseparability of politics and industrial relations at the time. Conflict between workers and managers was simultaneously confrontation between blacks and whites in 'the white man's factory', and social movement unionism became a part of the popular movement through which black workers could launch an assault, in the name of democracy and freedom, on the apartheid regime. In this it was linked to the movements beyond the factory: community organisations, armed resistance, and over the borders, the ANC.

Ungovernability, 1986–87

The 'struggle holidays' – mainly June 16 and May Day – were moments of acute political symbolism, days of defiance on which the black oppressed people could demonstrate their rejection of the entire regime that maintained South Africa as 'a white man's country'. Thus they could be treated as events outside the collective bargaining framework, as non-negotiable (although increasingly, and often with success, the unions also drew them into the collective bargaining arena by including the demand for them to be paid holidays in their wage demands). The Highveld shop stewards used these days as an opportunity to avoid negotiating or reaching an agreement with the oppressor, to flout procedures, and to defy white managerial authority. As in the township, black solidarity had to be maintained, and transgressors faced violent punishment.

Charles Makola has already described how negotiations over June 16 were not really negotiations: shop stewards would demand the day off, and simply stay away. A lengthy company affidavit, prepared for a case against NUMSA in 1988, describes in detail how the company experienced this lack of negotiation. In 1986 the black workforce at Highveld Steel participated in national stayaways on both May Day and June 16. The company complained that 'neither NUMSA nor its shop stewards consulted Highveld in order to advise it that they intended to participate in illegal absence from work'. The following year Highveld anticipated a stayaway on 16 June and called a meeting with the shop stewards for 12 June to discuss the matter. The shop stewards 'denied all knowledge of the stayaway or other industrial action planned for that day', so Highveld asked them to give sufficient notice if they did plan any collective absence from work. On 15 June the shop stewards demanded an immediate meeting with management and informed it that they had arranged a mass meeting of all NUMSA members at midday in the shift canteen to discuss the stayaway for the following day. NUMSA's members were already on their way to the shift canteen. Contrary to procedure, no permission had been requested. After the meeting the shop stewards told the company that no black workers would attend work the following day, and demanded that this be made a public holiday. In response to a company request, the shop stewards assured it that no employee would be victimised for failing to heed the stayaway.

While close on 4 000 black workers stayed away the next day, a handful did report for work. Two days later the shop stewards demanded a meeting 'on very short notice' at which they wanted to know the names of black employees who had worked on 16 June, and also demanded that Highveld dismiss them as they had 'acted in breach of an agreement to observe the national stayaway'. The company refused, and shop stewards informed it that a meeting would be held in the canteen at lunchtime where 'the workers would decide what action needed to be taken'. After the meeting the shop stewards presented management with a list of six black employees who had worked during the stayaway and demanded that they be dismissed without disciplinary inquiries. When management refused, the shop stewards 'stated that NUMSA would punish them'. When questioned whether NUMSA had advised its members 'against taking illegal action', the shop stewards 'stated that they only acted as spokesmen and that they did as they were told by the NUMSA members'. According to the company, the workers who had worked during the stayaway were then assaulted (Highveld Steel 1988: 10–12, 14–18).

Defiance and confrontation were not limited to distinctly political moments like the 'struggle holidays'. Collective bargaining was also fraught with confrontations, exacerbated by NUMSA's strategy of trying to mobilise its members around national demands in main agreement negotiations at the Industrial Council, including those like Highveld Steel who negotiated house agreements at company level.[14] Thus at Highveld Steel the union would be simultaneously negotiating in the house agreement forum and mobilising members to participate in national stoppages over the main agreement negotiations.

In 1986 the dismissal of four workers at Highveld Steel after one such stoppage provoked a full-blown 12-hour strike and reinstatement of the dismissed workers.[15] Three weeks later, on 12 June, the same day that the second State of Emergency was declared, 4 368 workers downed tools for 24 hours. The company was left in the dark about the reason as 'neither NUMSA nor its shop stewards' committee consulted . . . nor was any demand made'. It assumed the 'illegal stoppage was apparently in support of NUMSA demands made at the negotiations on the main agreement' and complained that Highveld 'is not a party' to those negotiations (Highveld Steel 1988: 11).[16] Notwithstanding these actions without any anchorage in negotiation or demands at Highveld Steel, collective bargaining in terms of the house agreement successfully concluded with a signed agreement.

During 1987 collective bargaining broke down completely. By the time of the first meeting in the house agreement negotiations at Highveld Steel, NUMSA had already declared a dispute at the national Industrial Council over the main agreement negotiations. According to the company, the union refused to bargain in good faith, 'failing to participate actively in the negotiations' and exhibiting 'an inflexible approach'. The union strategy of focusing mobilisation on the industry level negotiations of the main agreement was clearly informing its approach to company level negotiations at Highveld. NUMSA shop stewards and organisers informed Highveld that it intended to participate in the union's national strike ballot from 6–8 July and was told that a strike on the main agreement would be illegal as it had no relevance to the company. According to the company, the senior NUMSA official at the meeting 'advised Highveld that NUMSA had already decided what to do irrespective of the outcome of the strike ballot'.

Despite its warnings and reservations, management felt compelled to meet the union on the morning of 6 June to discuss balloting facilities. It again asked the unionists whether they had informed their members that a strike would be illegal, but 'NUMSA did not answer'. Highveld then arranged for a strike ballot to be conducted in the car park but, 'in breach of the agreement and without obtaining permission to use a new venue, NUMSA conducted the strike ballot in the change-houses . . . NUMSA has never advised Highveld of the results'.

In the context of resistance to apartheid, balloting was invested with a new, symbolic meaning. In addition to the pragmatic goal of meeting formal requirements for a legal strike, it provided an opportunity for mobilising workers and defying management, rather than a set of rules for regulating industrial action. Collective bargaining was located in a workplace still structured by apartheid. Thus collective bargaining processes shifted back and forth between pragmatic negotiation over concrete ends and symbolic confrontations invested with political meaning.

On 13 July, the shop stewards informed Highveld management that its members would participate in NUMSA's national strike over the main agreement negotiations, due to start the following day. However, the government moved to pre-empt what would have been the first national strike in South Africa's metal industry. The Minister of Labour extended the life of the previous year's agreement, thus rendering the planned strike illegal. NUMSA called off the strike, and spent the next 24 hours desperately trying to communicate its decision to more than 600 factories.

That day workers gathered outside the entrance to Highveld's steelworks. They abandoned the strike after management addressed them on the decision of the government. However, on the other side of town, at Rand Carbide, some 700 workers went ahead with the strike. Three shop stewards from Rand Carbide drove to the steelworks and accused Mahlangu, the shop steward chairperson, 'of acting contrary to an official NUMSA position to conduct a strike on that day'. There were similar scenes at metal factories across the country as the union worked to persuade reluctant members, who had mobilised for action, that the strike should be aborted (South African Labour Bulletin 1987).

The confusion over calling off the national strike sparked further action at Highveld Steel. Ferrometals, a big smelter in Witbank owned by Samancor, did strike on 14 July. Sixteen strikers were dismissed.[17] The Ferrometals shop stewards then approached their comrades at Highveld Steel as well as community forums:

The whole township at that time was centered around Highveld Steel. The guys from Ferrometals went to some meetings in the township to complain that the problem was Highveld Steel. Ferrometals management was dismissing them by pointing out that Highveld did not strike. Highveld Steel was seen as the company that may help Ferrometals. So there was pressure, not necessarily from Ferrometals, but from the whole community, that 'you guys must sort this thing out', because once Highveld Steel guys go on strike there is chaos, definitely.

The next evening the Highveld shop stewards called a mass meeting in the hostels. Company buses taking workers home were diverted to ensure all workers attended the meeting. The following morning the strike started. At the first meeting with management, the shop stewards demanded that a delegation of shop stewards and managers meet with Ferrometals management to persuade it to reverse its disciplinary action against NUMSA members. Highveld offered to ask the company chairperson, Leslie Boyd, in his capacity as a leading member of SEIFSA, to discuss the matter with the chairperson of Samancor. The strike continued the following day as the shop stewards demanded to know the 'exact contents of the discussions between Mr Boyd and the chairperson of Samancor'. Eventually the company agreed that its chairperson would come to Highveld to report to the shop stewards. Bunny Mahlangu recalled the workers' sense of power in that moment: 'Boyd was about to go to London and he had to drop that treat, and come straight to Highveld to sort out the mess.' Boyd reported on his discussion with Samancor, and the union, assured that the Ferrometals workers would be reinstated, agreed to end the strike.

This was an extraordinary display of worker power. The Highveld Steel workers had fought successfully for the reinstatement of workers at a company to which it had no links other than it being in the same town and its workers belonging to the same union. The intensity of this solidarity within social movement unionism can be explained by the overlapping of industrial, community, racial and political identities within worker struggles. It was in the community, where black solidarity against the owners of 'white men's factories' could be invoked, that the solidarity of Highveld workers with Ferrometals' workers was forged.

These overlapping meanings of worker identity and workplace struggle intensified confrontation and ungovernability at Highveld Steel. From early 1987, shop stewards were flouting procedures and interfering in management decisions. They compelled 'security personnel not to carry weapons and to refrain from searching employees, although this was an established and lawful practice'. They also 'interfered with canteen staff by ordering the cooks to prepare certain food in preference to preparing other food. As a consequence canteen costs were increased'. Shop stewards used company materials and photocopying machines to produce notices, and placed them on notice boards without asking permission; they increased the number of shop stewards without consulting Highveld and 'adopted an obstructive and uncooperative approach with regard to the carrying out of disciplinary inquiries'. During the Ferrometals solidarity strike, food – including 600 kgs of beef and chicken – and, more ominously, butcher's choppers and knives disappeared (Highveld Steel 1988: 12–13, 29). The political temperature was rising. Several times shop stewards demanded that management take steps to end the raids of municipal police in the hostels (ibid: 26, 30). Petty issues blew up into major confrontations.[18]

With increasing boldness workers forged and asserted their own notion of order and discipline. 'The guys in the strike committee would be our police, checking on those who go to work when everybody is on strike, or when there is a stayaway. They would take you and *sjambok* you for doing that.'[19] Simultaneously with the assertion of their own discipline, workers rejected the discipline of management. 'People were refusing to be disciplined, even if they were wrong' because 'no dismissal was fair in our view'.[20]

There was an increase in the violent intimidation of workers. During the Ferrometals solidarity strike workers who defied the strike were phoned at work and told to join the strikers outside; those who did not were 'forcefully removed' by a group of 40 to 50 strikers. Security guards 'were forcefully removed from their posts at the main gate, drawn into the midst of the crowd and assaulted'. During the strike a 'people's court' was set up which sentenced strike-breakers to beatings with a *sjambok*, and the company claimed that a total of 24 workers had been assaulted, one of whom had to be hospitalised for several days. Two white employees 'were stoned by NUMSA members' (Highveld Steel 1988: 24, 28–9).

During August two workers were taken separately to the change-house by groups of workers where they were whipped with *sjamboks*, hit and kicked. The following day the company conducted a disciplinary inquiry against the workers accused of the assaults but was unable to proceed because a 'mob of some 150 people' gathered in the passage, forced open the door of the room where the inquiry was taking place, 'attempted to drag the complainants into the group', and then *toyi-toyied* in the parking area outside 'maintaining a general atmosphere of intimidation and terror amongst Highveld staff'. One of the accused then addressed the crowd 'and was carried away by NUMSA members of the crowd at shoulder height'. The next day two women workers were taken from Highveld to the hostels where a 'people's court' convicted them of working during a stoppage. They were sentenced to beat each other with *sjamboks*. A day later another Highveld employee was taken from his house to the hostels where the strike committee found him guilty of working during a stoppage and sentenced him to a lashing with a *sjambok*. The worker laid a charge with the police, who arrived

at Highveld's Vantra plant at about 11 pm and arrested one of the alleged
assailants (Highveld Steel 1988: 30–3).

This incident led to the 'midnight strike', famed among workers for its
militancy. Bunny Mahlangu was working night shift that night. He was
phoned by the Vantra shop stewards and told that a member of the strike
committee had been arrested and Vantra wanted to strike:

> The fear was that, if you allow the police to do this the chance is
> they are going to arrest quite a lot of our people, particularly the
> guys in the strike committee who were, in our thinking, helping us
> strike to sort the company out. So I started to phone shop stewards
> in all different departments, told them of the problem and asked
> them to address it with the workers.

After two hours the Vantra shop stewards phoned again to report that
their divisional manager had arrived but they were making no progress:

> And now I was inundated with telephone calls from every plant
> asking what is the situation, is the guy released, what is happening?
> So you could see that guys were now geared for action. Around
> about half-past-two I had to give the orders. It was amazing, really,
> co-ordinating a strike at that time of the night. I communicated
> with the guys at Mapochs mine, Transalloys, Vantra, Rand Carbide,
> Spitzkop. The whole Highveld Group was on the ready.

Mobilised by their shop stewards, the workers marched out of the plants,
toyi-toying and singing:

> At that time of the night the foremen and superintendents, once
> they are sure that work is going well, they go to their offices and
> sleep. At that time the whole plant was quiet. They must have been
> awakened by this noise from the workers. One could see that there
> was chaos coming. They started running around, and they called in
> the general manager. Everyone was looking for me, the commander-
> in-chief. Once I noticed that, I ran away, and we got a car and went
> to all the different divisions to see what was going on, and we found

that everyone was on strike. I stayed at Vantra. These guys were looking for me – they wouldn't have a meeting until I was there. They knew I was on shift but they couldn't find me.

Mahlangu went back to the steelworks to meet the morning shift:

The first bus arrived and people were amazed, coming to work and finding people already on strike. But the guys on the strike committee wouldn't ask a damn what is going on, as long as he sees guys *toyi-toying*, then he joins and gets information on the line. That is no problem for him. It took us almost the whole day to resolve this strike.[21]

Management met with the shop stewards, who accused the company of collaborating with the police and demanded the immediate release of their comrade. During the meeting management heard that workers were being assaulted in the change-house, and suspended the meeting. The management account of the strike is filled with images of violence and coercion. When two white management employees approached the large group of striking workers gathered near the clock station at the steelworks 'to investigate reports that employees were being assaulted in their midst', part of the group 'charged at them in a threatening manner whilst exhibiting a red flag with NUMSA inscribed'. Some of the workers swore at the managers and 'shouted that they should be grabbed'; they 'feared for their lives' and retreated. Meanwhile, 'angry mobs danced around whilst exhibiting a red NUMSA flag'.

At some of the other plants, according to management, strikers used force to extend the strike. At Rand Carbide strikers 'armed with sticks and iron bars entered the administration block and forcefully removed black staff members from their places of work'. At Transalloys 'a large group of employees armed with *sjamboks* forced their way through the security gate' and 'rounded up all employees at work and escorted them to the steelworks'. At the steelworks strikers 'threatened the kitchen staff and demanded to be fed'.

Meanwhile, shop stewards and managers were trying to find a solution, and eventually the charge against the strike committee member was withdrawn. Thus, with 'militancy at its best',[22] black workers united to defend the structure of order and discipline they had collectively constructed, and used their workplace power to defeat the agents of the racial order of apartheid, both in the workplace and in the state. This was a confrontation between workers' counter-order embodied in social movement unionism, and management order: workers' discipline versus management discipline, workers' punishment (the *sjambok*) versus management punishment (dismissal) and the workers' police in the form of the strike committee versus the police and courts of apartheid. The clash between contending notions of order produced a disorder in the workplace similar to ungovernability in the township. The black workers at Highveld Steel had never seemed stronger. Management was 'starting to lose their authority because people refused to abide with whatever was said by them'.[23] But, in reality, workers were deeply divided over questions of order, discipline and the meaning of the union. Management, too, was preparing a counter-attack to re-establish the order of the apartheid workplace regime.

The limits of ungovernability: the 1987 lockout/strike

On a Monday morning in September, managers summoned the Highveld Steel shop stewards from their various workstations to a meeting where they were told that the company was instituting a lockout against NUMSA's hourly-paid members. Lawyers explained what a lockout was, and that the purpose was to induce the union's members to accept the company's wage offer. The shop stewards were 'stunned' and 'confused'. Inside the plants, managers were distributing letters to all NUMSA's hourly-paid members informing them that they were locked out with immediate effect, but that the lockout would be withdrawn against those individuals who were prepared to sign that they accepted the company's offer. The workers refused to sign and when they discovered that none of the shop stewards were present, 'started to walk out of the plants and converged at the gates'. When shop stewards arrived and addressed the workers, they explained that they had to leave the company premises. NUMSA's members among the staff and semi-staff (which included shop stewards like Makola and Moloi), shocked by this turn of events, decided to strike in solidarity with their hourly-paid comrades.[24]

This was the first time an employer had made use of the lockout provisions in the Labour Relations Act since the Wiehahn reforms, so for employers and unions it was something of a test case. In the shop stewards' assessment, the lockout was a response to the workplace militancy and disorder produced by the union and the strike committee, a management counter-offensive to restore order in the workplace.[25] It took place in the context of a broader escalation in militancy and confrontation between unions and employers during 1987 – a year marked by the highest level of strike activity in the country's history. August had seen the historic three-week confrontation between the National Union of Mineworkers and the Chamber of Mines. This was the biggest strike in South African history, which had been 'as much a battle for physical control of the workplace as it was about wages', in the words of an executive from Anglo American, the company which spearheaded the mining employers and which also owns Highveld Steel. The NUM was particularly well organised and militant in the coal mines around Witbank (Baskin 1991: 225–6, 230–1).[26]

In the weeks before the lockout, leading shop stewards at Highveld Steel had feared that the increasing confrontation with management and within the union held dangers for NUMSA. Growing numbers of workers were alienated by the violence and tactics of the strike committee, and by the loss of wages brought about by frequent stoppages. Senior shop stewards had held an 'informal discussion' on the weekend before the lockout and decided to convene a formal shop steward meeting to recommend that shop stewards persuade members to drop their wage dispute and accept the company offer.

> It was as if we were sensing that a problem was coming. Our people had been going in and out of strikes. We came to the conclusion that if we went on a long strike our people were going to split, and that would cause bigger problems for us as a committee.[27]

But the shop stewards' attempt to regain the initiative was pre-empted by the company lockout. It was now impossible to recommend to angry members that they drop their dispute, since that was precisely what management was demanding. 'People were furious because they were doing their work without going on strike themselves – management had taken them out on strike forcefully. So we never made our recommendation.'[28]

The shop steward leadership's assessment was correct. The lockout/ strike was to lead to deep divisions among workers and a defeat that all but shattered the union, but the disorder at Highveld Steel rendered them powerless to take charge of the situation. Management's action removed the union from the company, creating conditions in which the shop stewards' voices were drowned out by the militant workers organised in the strike committee. As far as the workers were concerned, 'if the company does not want to accept our offer, we are not accepting theirs'. The lockout became a strike as well: employer offensive met with worker counter-offensive.[29] The confrontation made it even more difficult for the two parties to engage in negotiations.

The company gave the union three days to accept its offer. Management had expected the lockout to be over in the first few days (Hocking 1998: 270), but the first meeting between company and union only took place after some two weeks as neither side wanted to make the first move. At one point the company communicated its decision to extend the deadline for acceptance of its offer by showering the workers in the hostels with pamphlets dropped from a helicopter. Eventually the shop stewards, fearing that frustrated workers might start drifting back to work, requested a meeting with management 'just to break the ice'. Several meetings were held over the next two weeks but the deadlock could not be broken. The wider disorder epitomised by the lockout surfaced in the meetings between the two parties. Mahlangu remembered one encounter:

Virtually we were fighting over me pointing a finger at him, and him saying something to me, and my colleagues demanding that he withdraw what he said to me, and him demanding that I apologise for pointing a finger at him [laughter]. That was a petty thing, but everyone was standing and we were on the verge of a physical fight. But we, you know, were negotiating, and eventually we sat down again and tried to carry on with our negotiations, though we were not making progress.[30]

During this period, production was kept going, albeit at low levels, with a skeleton workforce, including white pensioners and schoolboys from Witbank. The company intensified pressure on the union by employing some 1 500 Zulu strikebreakers from KwaZulu-Natal and repeatedly threatening to dismiss the workers (Hocking 1998: 270–1).[31] As the gravity of the situation impressed itself on the shop stewards they 'began to be sober' and 'scared' and began looking for ways to end the strike.[32] The survival of the union depended on a return to the company and the employment relationship, and on reviving both the production of steel and some sort of negotiating relationship with management, but a strategic assessment of the relative balance of power, the resolve and unity of workers, and the strength and intention of the employers was rendered extremely difficult by the issues at stake in the struggle – nothing less than the nature of social order in the workplace.

The management offensive was designed to restore stability to the social structure of the apartheid workplace regime through defeating and breaking the power of the union. Workers recognised this and, fired not only by the injustice of management's immediate actions but also by the injustice of apartheid, wanted to do battle. The shop stewards, too, were swayed by anger, and, according to Bunny Mahlangu, the result was 'bound to be failure'. Workers and shop stewards were torn between the advisability of a tactical retreat to avoid defeat and to secure a negotiated accommodation in the workplace, and their desire not to submit to the power of white management.[33]

Officials from NUMSA's head office also seemed relatively powerless to help the shop stewards. Although the national organiser travelled to Witbank almost daily, sometimes sleeping over, union officials do not loom large in shop steward or worker accounts of the lockout. In retrospect, the shop steward leadership felt the officials failed to provide direction or to help resolve the strike. Some believed this was because of the significance of the Highveld Steel lockout to industrial relations nationally; others believed that the national union was unable to provide direction because 'it was also operating the way we were operating at the factory – you don't need to think over issues, just disrupt anything that comes your way'. Accordingly, the head office's message to the shop stewards was, 'Guys, don't give up, keep on fighting'.[34] Thus the union *outside* Highveld Steel had little impact on the response and strategies of workers, shop stewards and the strike committee to the lockout; this was shaped primarily by the internal dynamics among workers at the company.

The workers had discovered the limits of confrontation and ungovernability in the workplace. The company had the power to dismiss workers and destroy the union; the workers were powerless to evict management. The shop stewards 'felt that we no longer have much power, we felt that we need to go back to work'. The problem was 'how to concede without showing some weakness, because the power struggle with management meant weakness would be followed with dismissals'.[35]

On its side management was also desperate. The skeleton workforce was exhausted, morale in the plants was low, and the company was losing money (Hocking 1998: 271). Although a capitalist workplace regime distributes power unequally between workers and employer, there are also limits to the power of the employer. Highveld Steel had the power to dismiss its entire black workforce and hire another, but it could ill afford to lose the accumulated experience and skills of some 4 000 black workers in one blow.[36] As the biggest employer in Witbank, many of whose workers lived in the township, the prospect of large numbers of dismissed and bitter residents held obvious dangers. Thus the company repeatedly backed off from its threats to dismiss the locked out workers.

At this point the company played its trump card. The union was notified that its members in the hostels were to be evicted as they were no longer working at Highveld Steel or paying rent.[37] This could be a mortal blow for the union: 'Our members would be scattered all over. We wouldn't know who is where, we would be unable to meet as a collective, the bargaining power would diminish and we would lose one another.'[38] A shop steward delegation consulted with union lawyers. The lawyers advised that a legal challenge to eviction would take a long time. Prospects for victory were uncertain and in the meantime the eviction would come into force. It would be preferable to settle. The delegation recommended to the full committee that management's offer be accepted and workers return to work. The shop stewards agreed.

Management had already indicated that those found guilty of intimidation would be dismissed. When workers raised the question of whether all of them would return, Frank Boshielo, the regional secretary, warned them that when soldiers go to war, they know that not all of them will return. The recommendation was accepted by a general meeting of workers where discussion centred on a commitment 'to carry on fighting inside the company', both for those who might remain outside, and for the demands that had led to the lockout/strike. The company was informed of the union's decision. Highveld Steel dropped its demand that individual employees sign letters accepting the company's offer but made it clear that a significant number of workers would be suspended, pending disciplinary inquiries, for intimidation and violence.[39]

Four weeks after they had walked out of the Highveld Steel plants, workers returned with some bravado, singing and *toyi-toying* on the buses. But when they entered the company premises they were left in no doubt that they had been defeated, and that they were returning on management's terms. There was a strong police presence to secure management's power. Workers from each division had to queue and file past their divisional manager. He checked them against a list, and those identified as militant activists were grabbed by police and bundled onto waiting buses to prevent them from communicating with their comrades. One hundred and seventy-one workers, including the chairperson, secretary and vice-chairperson of the shop steward committee, a number of other shop stewards, and numerous members of the strike committee, were suspended on allegations of 'misconduct' pending disciplinary inquiries. The rest were let through.

The union had secured a relatively orderly surrender, but in the workplace 'it was smashed completely, there were no longer meetings, there was nothing'.[40] This defeat had a deep impact on workers:

> Prior to the lockout Highveld Steel was solid, there was unity. Afterwards people were dejected, they lost interest and felt we're not going to crack this management. The lockout killed the spirit of everyone until today. Every time you discuss their problems with people at Highveld Steel, they'll tell you, 'Let's start from what happened in 1987'. Every time. That in itself tells you that all the problems emanated from 1987.[41]

Rebuilding the union: new tactics, new strategies

Those shop stewards who survived the disciplinary process in the aftermath of the strike had to find a way of rebuilding the organisational structures of the union, and develop new strategies for challenging management in the context of worker fear. The first task of the remnants of the shop steward committee was to defend the 171 workers who had been suspended. Charles Makola, the highly experienced vice-chairperson of the shop stewards, was initially suspended but was reinstated when management could not produce evidence of misconduct despite attempting to bribe two of his colleagues to testify against him. Mosi Nhlapo was also reinstated. Eventually 87 of the suspended workers were dismissed, including the chairperson of the shop steward committee, Bunny Mahlangu, and its secretary. Many strike committee activists were dismissed but some, including its chairperson, survived.[42]

Only a small group of active shop stewards remained. The shop steward committee had 'disintegrated', as most of its leadership had been dismissed or became inactive. Disillusioned and victimised by management, many of the more experienced shop stewards 'just vanished'. Workers were deeply demoralised and fearful: 'Many people started saying, "this union can do nothing". They just couldn't understand. They lost their faith in the shop stewards, they lost faith in the trade union.' Management reasserted its control of the workplace and production, and 'made a concerted effort to show that the union no longer exists'. Minor offences led to disciplinary inquiries, dismissals and threats of dismissal. Previously active members were shown photographs of themselves *toyi-toying* during the lockout/strike and threatened that these would remain in their files. Shop stewards were obstructed from performing their duties. The deduction of union dues was no longer reflected on payslips. Workers were fearful of being elected as shop stewards, and scared of being seen talking to them. Fear isolated the shop stewards from their base: 'It was tough because most workers did not co-operate with the shop stewards or support them.'[43]

It was a priority for the remaining group of shop stewards to demonstrate both to management and to workers that NUMSA was still alive at Highveld Steel. They insisted that management resurrect its monthly meetings with shop stewards, and the first demand they made was for union dues to be reflected once more on payslips. Management refused but backed down after the union pointed out that the house agreement stipulated that dues should be reflected, and threatened legal action. It took several months to win this small victory but it meant workers could see, 'Oh, the union is still here'. New shop steward elections were held and a nucleus of activists emerged, including experienced shop stewards such as Charles Makola (vice-chairperson), William Sehlola (secretary) and some shop stewards from the hostels, such as Johannes Phatlana and J.J. Mbonani, together with new artisan shop stewards, Meshack Malinga (chairperson), Mosi Nhlapo (vice-chairperson) and Ambrose Mthembu.[44]

Given the context of worker fear and management hostility, the union had to develop a new strategy for rebuilding organisation and confidence among workers. National officials advised the shop stewards to 'start launching grievances, drag management to the courts, drag them to the Industrial Council, that process will tie them down and they'll start recognising you'. So, for the first time, NUMSA shop stewards at Highveld Steel began to develop expertise in using the grievance, dispute and unfair labour practice procedures provided for by the LRA, the Industrial Council and the Industrial Court.[45] The shop stewards developed a strategy that Makola called 'the strategy of leadership quality', in contrast to the earlier failure of leadership:

We had to build strong leadership that would no longer rely on going back to the workers to mobilise for a strike, because you won't get a strike. We became a very powerful committee challenging management. We were no longer using the power of the workers, we relied now on the intellectual skills and experience that we had, in order to defend workers' rights.[46]

According to Nhlapo, the national union was digesting the lessons of the defeat at Highveld Steel, where the strategy of militant confrontation and disruption had resulted in a lockout, protracted legal contestation over dismissals, and pressure to raise funds for the casualties. The union drew up a code of conduct making it clear that it did not condone assaults, and that it would not support workers guilty of such practices. It also switched policy on strike committees, discouraging rather than encouraging them.[47]

The shop stewards declared disputes on every point they could: disciplinary decisions, dismissals, wages, management amendments to the disciplinary code, a management decision to introduce a new grading system, management's unilateral decisions to increase the wages of artisans outside the structure of collective bargaining, and so on. They used the larger framework of rights and powers contained in the national labour relations regime to frustrate management's attempts to curtail the rights of workers and shop stewards in the workplace. They successfully adapted their strategic and tactical skills, which in the early and mid-1980s had been applied in the workplace procedures of the company, to the institutional terrain beyond the company.[48]

After the lockout/strike, management amended the company disciplinary code, removing the right of workers to appeal against disciplinary decisions and effectively weakening workers' right to representation by their shop stewards. The shop stewards lodged a dispute at the Industrial Council against the company for amending the disciplinary procedure unilaterally. They also launched disputes over every single disciplinary decision. For example, if a worker was issued with a written warning, the shop stewards would write a letter demanding that it be withdrawn and that management meet with them to discuss the demand. When management ignored their letter, they would refer the dispute to the Industrial Council, which would be obliged to convene a dispute resolution meeting requiring shop stewards and managers to travel to Johannesburg. If the matter was resolved shop stewards would have demonstrated their ability to constrain management's disciplinary powers. If it was not, the union had the option of going to the Industrial Court, or balloting for a legal strike.

This strategy snared management in time-consuming and legalistic processes, frequently embarrassed them at the Industrial Council, forced them to recognise the shop stewards, and raised the constant possibility of a legal strike, leaving them uncertain as to whether the workforce was as weak as they imagined. Eventually management agreed to drop its amendment of the disciplinary code and reinstated workers' right to appeal and shop stewards' powers in the disciplinary procedure. Shop stewards had successfully used the rights and institutions created by the Wiehahn reforms to limit management's power in the workplace and create space for rebuilding the union.[49]

The shop stewards also used the strategy of accumulating disputes against the company to bargain over the fate of the 87 workers dismissed for misconduct. The legal process in the Industrial Court would clearly be time-consuming and costly, and the dismissed workers, many of whom continued to stay at the hostels, were impatient for some relief. In an out-of-court settlement, Highveld eventually agreed to increase the payout per worker to R8 000, on condition that the union withdrew all its disputes with the company. As the shop stewards put it, the union sold the disputes for a better settlement for the casualties of the lockout/strike.[50]

Having used disputes and procedures to establish the presence of the union in the workplace, the shop stewards worked to rebuild organisation and confidence among workers. It was difficult. The militant spirit of Highveld Steel had been broken. Workers no longer participated in stayaways. 'Struggle holidays', once a symbolic highpoint of confrontation with management, were now ignored. It was only in 1990, when the union succeeded in negotiating it as a holiday, that workers again celebrated June 16, the most important of these days. Although workers balloted in support of the three-day stayaway against the amendments to the Labour Relations Act in 1988, they actually worked through what was the biggest stayaway in the country's history. They also ignored the overtime ban called by COSATU in the struggle against the LRA amendments. The quiescence of workers at the biggest company in Witbank had a serious impact on the political mood in the town.[51]

However, throughout 1988 and 1989, the shop stewards worked to revive workers' confidence and bring them together – representing them in cases, talking to them in ones and twos, and beginning to convene general meetings in the hostels again. A fund was established, financed with a contribution of 20 cents a month by every member, to pay for the costs of frequent trips to Industrial Council hearings in Johannesburg by shop stewards – a sign of their relative success in winning worker support.[52] In the shop stewards' assessment, what distinguished the new approach was that it relied on intellectual skills; it was strategic and tactically sophisticated. It could not replace organisation, but it provided space for rebuilding it:

In spite of the fact that we were very weak on the ground, we ensured that the rights of the workers were still secured, and that the union was still recognised. We used that strategy to keep management busy and build the union.[53]

But the shop stewards were ambivalent about the implications of this new strategy of using procedures: inasmuch as they forced management to recognise them, they in turn were extending recognition to management, which remained the embodiment of white power in the workplace. This ambivalence surfaced in the reflections of one of the leading shop steward strategists: on the one hand, 'we were becoming co-operative to management by following these routes', but on the other hand:

> I never saw myself as co-operating with management, I saw myself as engaging management. When we went to the Industrial Council with management, we never came back empty-handed. We'd always win. Maybe why one could easily accept this approach was because the militancy was gone. We had no alternative.[54]

Even under these circumstances, shop stewards found ways to avoid conceding the legitimacy of management's role in the company. After overcoming management's attempts to reduce worker rights in the disciplinary procedure, the shop stewards put forward a list of demands for amending the disciplinary code:

> The company then re-drafted the procedures and brought them back to us and said, 'Are you happy with this?' We said, 'Yes we are happy with most of the content, but this is where we disagree.' Then some of these things were changed, and some were not changed, and the company said, 'This is how we're going to operate.' Then we took them to the Industrial Council and said we don't believe these procedures are right, and outlined those procedures which we believed in. Those things were changed. And after they were changed, they said, 'Now, please sign these procedures'. And we said, 'No we don't believe that you must punish workers, we still believe that workers must be punished by us. The fact that we've made inputs does not necessarily mean that we are bound by these procedures, we can still do things the way we want to do them.' We refused therefore to sign those procedures. Although we negotiated them, we were not bound by them.[55]

Once again, negotiation was not truly negotiation. The shop stewards were simultaneously engaged in rebuilding the social structure of negotiated accommodation in the workplace – engaging, recognising and negotiating with management, defending the procedural allocation of rights and powers – and rejecting the legitimacy of the apartheid workplace regime. In the context of the apartheid workplace and the broader apartheid order, the union continued to embody the idea of a workers' counter-order opposed to the order represented by management.

Conclusion

This chapter has shown how the popular political identity of social movement unionism forged in the broader struggle against apartheid shaped union practices on the shopfloor. The workplace disorder identified in chapter 3 as a characteristic feature of social movement unionism in the apartheid workplace was deepened and extended by the collective identities and practices forged through the alliance of social movement unionism with the popular movement described in chapter 4. The result was an escalation of ungovernability generated by contending notions of legitimate order in the workplace. Recognition of NUMSA at Highveld Steel opened up a period of long transition marked by confrontation and disorder, very different from the 'negotiation of order' (Hyman 1975), the 'manufacture of consent' (Burawoy 1979) or the 'regulation of labour' (Edwards et al. 1994) identified by the metropolitan sociology of the workplace in advanced industrial societies.

Notwithstanding the dynamic of disorder, processes of institutional participation and negotiated accommodation continued to shape elements of a new workplace order. After all, despite the interruptions of strikes and particularly the four-week lockout/strike, Highveld Steel continued to produce steel and profit most of the time, and workers and managers continued to co-operate in this production. The persistence of order was particularly clear in the aftermath of the lockout/strike – which tested the limits of ungovernability – when shop stewards fought to re-establish the union and workers' rights in the workplace. The tension between confrontation and negotiation was not easy to manage in the turmoil of the 1980s; indeed, it reached deep into the social structure of the union, generating division, violence and turmoil within the organisation.

Notes

1. Interview, Bunny Mahlangu, 8/11/93.
2. The Harare Declaration was a document setting out the conditions for a negotiated settlement of the South African conflict adopted by the Organisation of African Unity, which was drafted in an extensive process of consultation between the ANC and the internal democratic movement, including COSATU, and which was endorsed by the United Nations during the latter half of 1989 (Baskin 1991).
3. June 16 was the first day of the 1976 Soweto uprisings, and was commemorated by the anti-apartheid movement as the most important 'struggle holiday'.
4. Interview, Charles Makola, 8/5/94.
5. Interview, Meshack Malinga, 14/5/94.
6. Interview, Charles Makola, 6/8/95.
7. Interview, Albert Makagula, 29/3/94.
8. Interview, Charles Makola, 6/8/95.
9. Interview, Albert Makagula, 29/3/94.
10. Interview, Frank Boshielo, 9/93, 19/6/94.
11. Interview, Ambrose Mthembu, 14/5/94.
12. Interview, J.J. Mbonani, 7/6/94.
13. Interview, Charles Makola, 6/8/95; interview, J.J. Mbonani, 31/5/94, 7/6/94.
14. Wages and conditions for workers in the metal industry were negotiated in the Industrial Council main agreement negotiations. Certain large companies like Highveld Steel were deemed to have specific conditions and conducted separate house agreement negotiations under the auspices of the Industrial Council.
15. Interview, Frank Boshielo, 9/93, 19/6/94; interview, Bunny Mahlangu, 8/11/93.
16. This stoppage was unlikely to have been a direct response to the declaration of the state of emergency; a wave of workplace stoppages did take place around South Africa, but only a week to four weeks after the declaration and were generally a response to the detention of union officials or shop stewards (Green 1986).
17. This account of the solidarity strike with Ferrometals workers is drawn from interview, Bunny Mahlangu, 8/11/93; interview, Frank Boshielo, 19/6/94; Highveld Steel 1988: 23–30.
18. Interview, Bunny Mahlangu, 8/11/93, 12/5/94.
19. Interview, Bunny Mahlangu, 8/11/93.
20. Interview, Bunny Mahlangu, 12/5/94; interview, Charles Makola, 6/8/95.
21. Interview, Bunny Mahlangu, 8/11/93.
22. Interview, Bunny Mahlangu, 15/8/95.
23. Interview, Bunny Mahlangu, 12/5/94.
24. Interview, Bunny Mahlangu, 4/5/95; interview, Charles Makola, 8/5/94, 6/8/95; interview, Bob Moloi, 10/7/94.
25. Interview, Bob Moloi, 10/7/94; interview, Bunny Mahlangu, 12/5/94; interview, Ambrose Mthembu, 14/5/94. Management presents the lockout in a more low-key

way as an attempt to 'seize the initiative'. There were doubts and differences of opinion among senior managers about using the lockout option (Hocking 1988: 268–9).

26. The NUM had declared 1987 'The Year Mineworkers Take Control', and managers reported 'disruptions . . . to a point where supervision comes to a grinding halt . . .' and that workers were 'breaking down the supervisory structure . . . existing disciplinary procedures and channels of communication'. Targets included '*indunas*, tribal representatives' and other supervisors. The NUM also formed strike committees to ensure discipline and reduce disruption during the strike. See Baskin (1991: 225–31). The parallels with ungovernability at Highveld Steel are obvious.

27. Interview, Bunny Mahlangu, 4/5/95.

28. Ibid.

29. Interview, Bob Moloi, 10/7/94; interview, Mosi Nhlapo, 9/11/93.

30. Interview, Bunny Mahlangu, 4/5/95.

31. Interview with a group of shop stewards, 2/9/93.

32. Interview, Bunny Mahlangu, 4/5/95.

33. For the discussions on which the argument of this paragraph are based, see interview, Bunny Mahlangu, 4/5/95; see also interview, Bob Moloi, 10/7/94; interview, Mosi Nhlapo, 6/3/95.

34. Interview, Bunny Mahlangu, 15/8/95; interview, Bob Moloi, 10/7/94; interview, Mosi Nhlapo, 6/3/95.

35. Interview, Charles Makola, 8/5/94.

36. One manager commented: 'Some of our people had suggested we should fire everyone and start again. But that wouldn't have been fair or wise. Just think of the problems we'd have to train a completely new workforce' (Hocking 1998: 272).

37. Hocking does not mention the eviction notice, but reports that the strikers' resolve evaporated in the face of a threat from blacks who wanted to work 'to call in the Zulus to sort them out', a particularly stark example of management's propensity – part of the workplace culture of the apartheid workplace regime – for explaining workers' behaviour in terms of ethnicity (Hocking 1998: 271).

38. Interview, Charles Makola, 6/8/95.

39. Interview, Bunny Mahlangu, 4/5/95; interview, Charles Makola, 6/8/95; interview, Bob Moloi, 10/7/94; interview, Mosi Nhlapo, 9/11/93.

40. Interview, Charles Makola, 8/5/94.

41. Interview, Bunny Mahlangu, 15/8/95.

42. Interview, Charles Makola, 6/8/95; interview, Bob Moloi, 10/7/94; interview, Jacob Msimangu, 12/8/95.

43. Interview, Charles Makola, 6/8/95; interview, Bob Moloi, 10/7/94; interview, Ambrose Mthembu, 15/3/94; interview, Phineas Mabena, 12/5/94; interview, William Sehlola, 5/6/94; interview, Tshagata, 26/5/94.

44. Interview, Charles Makola, 6/8/95; interview, Ambrose Mthembu, 15/3/94.

45. Interview, Mosi Nhlapo, 6/3/95; interview, Ambrose Mthembu, 15/3/94.

46. Interview, Charles Makola, 8/5/94, 6/8/95.

47. Interview, Mosi Nhlapo, 6/3/95.
48. See chapter 3.
49. Interview, Charles Makola, 6/8/95.
50. Interview, Charles Makola, 8/5/94, 6/8/95; interview, Ambrose Mthembu, 15/3/94.
51. Interview, Ambrose Mthembu, 15/3/94.
52. One shop steward estimated that R400–R500 per month was raised for this fund, implying a membership of 2 000 or more (interview, Ambrose Mthembu, 15/3/94).
53. Interview, Charles Makola, 6/8/95.
54. Interview, Mosi Nhlapo, 6/3/95.
55. Interview, Mosi Nhlapo, 12/95.

CHAPTER 6

'Union of the township, union of the hostel'

Social movement unionism, contestation and violence among black workers

We were thrown out forcefully. They said this is a state of emergency, so we are suspending the union constitution.

Ambrose Mthembu, shop steward

Social movement unionism at Highveld Steel was shaped by a range of collective identities forged beyond the workplace (political/community/ youth, racial, migrant and ethnic identities), as well as by those forged within the workplace (worker/trade union identities, and different occupational/ skill identities). Some collective identities were reinforced both within and beyond the workplace – especially racial identities in the context of the apartheid workplace regime, also migrant/urban identities that overlaid occupational/skill identities. Thus the social structure of NUMSA took the form of a complex amalgam of popular and class identities, each associated with a distinct set of goals, meanings and practices, rather than a straightforward class identity. This could *both* intensify the solidarity of the trade union movement *and* generate internal fracture lines between contending identities and the conflicting goals and practices that distinguished them.

Generally, analysis of social movement unionism has concentrated on the role of the union in the community. In contrast, this book focuses on the impact of community alliances on the union social structure, and conceptualises the popular alliance as an interpenetration of movements, a complex and dynamic network of political, community and workplace struggles woven together by a discourse of national liberation struggle. In effect, the community was inside the union.

In place of the democracy and open debate identified in the literature as a core feature of social movement unionism, this study highlights a coercive approach to solidarity at Highveld Steel and the failure of democracy to empower unskilled migrants in the union. The result was a fierce and recurring internal struggle over power, leadership strategies and practices. This was not primarily a power struggle driven by personal ambition but rather a contestation – based on contending collective identities – over the meaning, strategies and practices that defined the collective identity of the union. At its height, this struggle broke into open violence between factions and an inability to accommodate diverse views.

The formation of the strike committee

The shop steward committee was involved in the formation of the strike committee in early 1986, and initially it was seen as supplementing the role of the shop stewards. The strike committee emerged from the most militant workers among the rank-and-file, those who 'would sing, dance, give morale to the workers who were on strike, moving around with placards'.[1]

The idea was introduced to workers at a general meeting, with the motivation that the union would 'remain weak at Highveld, because you don't have a backup for the shop stewards'. The strike committee remained an informal structure – workers 'were urged to join' rather than elected. The role of the strike committee was to keep order and discipline among workers during strikes and stoppages, especially when the shop stewards were negotiating with management, and to ensure that all workers attended union meetings in the hostels or the workplace.[2]

Many workers believed the strike committee was formed on the understanding that the negotiating relationship with management needed to be supplemented with more forceful action. The young worker who became its chairperson remarked: 'Our shop stewards said we have got to have a sort of committee that would be more violent against Highveld than what they are doing.'[3]

The use of violence against Highveld Steel included the use of coercion to maintain discipline among workers, and most shop stewards colluded in this. As one put it:

We used intelligence teams to go and check the situation in the plants during strikes. They would report to us as shop stewards that 'there are people working, what are we supposed to do?' We said, just go and form your committee, don't come to us and ask what you are supposed to do. We are Highveld representatives, we can't tell you. Take the stick and do punishment. So that is where the strike committee came from. It managed the situation. You can blame the strike committee for doing a lot of corporal punishment, but they managed to build the union.[4]

Thus many shop stewards gave implicit or explicit support to a structure that would operate outside the negotiating relationship with management, and without being constrained by the procedures that tended to bind shop stewards to the negotiation of order. A degree of coercion, or 'revolutionary bullying',[5] was therefore implicit in the collective construction by workers of the union as a social structure in opposition to the management order. This social structure blended consent and coercion. If an individual broke the code of behaviour agreed by the majority, physical punishment was legitimate. As one worker put it: 'The strike committee came there to teach people what union law is.'[6]

Quite rapidly, however, the 'union law' itself became subject to contestation. This took the form of growing conflict between the shop steward committee and the strike committee. The shop stewards were in an ambiguous position, both negotiating and enforcing procedures, and challenging and rejecting the racial order. In their role as agents of negotiation and procedure, they came to be identified at times as 'sellouts', traitors to the law of the union. The chairperson of the shop steward committee at the time of the formation of the strike committee, Bob Moloi, saw the tension over procedure, and mistrust of the shop stewards, as inscribed in the very formation of the strike committee:

The shop steward committee was aware of the disciplinary code and the procedures of the company, and was finding it very difficult to cope with the demands of the workers who were now saying 'away with your procedures, if we're saying we want this, we want it tomorrow'. If you talk to the shopfloor about a procedure, they don't know anything about procedures, they have never been subjected to any procedures in their past. Now all of a sudden, when the union is introduced, you come and tell him about procedures – then they showed mistrust to the shop stewards, and that mistrust led to the formation of the strike committee.[7]

Frank Boshielo, then branch secretary of NUMSA, commented on the complex structural pressures on the shop stewards that produced this conflict:

There would be an action, and the shop stewards would start negotiating with management. They would find somewhere that management is convincing them, saying your strike is unlawful, unprocedural, and threatening dismissals. They would start to change their approach, and tell the workers, 'We are facing a danger here. We need to retreat'.[8]

The result was that many workers began to suspect that shop stewards were 'selling out'. Jacob Msimangu, who became chairperson of the strike committee, explained how this perception developed, and linked it to the specific intransigence of management at Highveld Steel:

We felt that ever since the union was formed we never won anything. We felt as if these people were betraying us, because whatever our demands, when they came back we get nothing. Even when we would go on strike for about two days, the shop stewards would come back from negotiations and say the strike is not legal, so we've got to go back to work, there's a court order. Most of us were not educated, so it was very difficult to understand this.[9]

The strike committee and the shop steward committee were no longer complementary power centres maintaining and defending a commonly constructed social structure under the overall direction of the formally elected union representatives, the shop stewards. The strike committee started to develop its own autonomy, seeking to discipline and control the shop stewards, and organising industrial action independently of them. A fierce contestation opened up within the social structure of the union over leadership and power, tactics and practices, and organisational culture or 'union law'.

The chairperson of the strike committee described how it began to assert its control over the shop stewards, organising wildcat strikes and using 'violence' against Highveld Steel. The fact that the shop stewards had blessed its formation was of significance but beyond that it did not acknowledge the structures or procedures of the union – it was without 'guidelines':

We had no guidelines, so we felt that we could do whatever we wanted, because we had been given the green light by the shop stewards. We had our own meetings, excluding the shop stewards, and we even elected a chairman and secretary from among ourselves. So it changed. The shop stewards were getting uneasy and they wanted to know what we were discussing. We refused, saying the only thing is that they must take from us the instructions as to how they must operate. Before they report to the members, they must come and meet us. Nobody should talk to the management without consulting us first.[10]

Shop stewards who objected were intimidated, and some were assaulted by strike committee members. Bob Moloi was accused of being too conciliatory, and resigned as shop steward chairperson. He was replaced by the more militant Bunny Mahlangu. At one point the strike committee appointed several of its members to accompany the shop stewards to negotiations to monitor whether workers were being sold out. When they reported back they had to admit that shop stewards were negotiating 'in good faith'. Nevertheless, the tension continued.[11]

'Violence' against Highveld Steel took a variety of forms. The strike committee would organise wildcat strikes, for example to demand the reinstatement of a dismissed worker, by gathering at the bus station outside the plant early in the morning and preventing people from entering. They would disrupt an inquiry if they thought it was unfair. They used coercion to reinforce worker solidarity and to strike at production. The chairperson described an expedition to Mapochs mine to bring it out in support of a strike at the steelworks:

We decided, let's go and disturb production at Mapochs, without
even consulting with our shop stewards. We went there in four
Kombis, about 60 of us. We went into the hall at Mapochs, we
called the people from the hostels to a meeting, and then we danced
and went straight to the plant. Then we didn't only sing, we pulled
people out from the plant and beat them, that they must come and
join us. We beat them, we stopped the plant.[12]

While many of the shop stewards were political activists and led or supported
confrontation, they were also involved in a negotiating relationship with
management. Following negotiating procedure undermined their role as
worker leaders because many workers did not understand 'the law of the
strike' or 'the meaning of strike':

People didn't understand the meaning of wildcat strike. We take
this wildcat strike because we want to force management back to
the negotiating table. Okay, management agrees. When we tell the
workers, let's go to work because management has accepted to return
to the negotiating table, they say, fuck you. Now there is a quarrel
between workers and their representatives.[13]

This in turn undermined shop stewards' relations with management. The
strike committee became an alternative power base to the shop stewards,
and shop stewards frequently found themselves at a loss to explain or justify
strikes to management.[14]

The strike committee rapidly grew to be a movement within the union.
At its height it had anywhere between 800 and 1 800 members/supporters,
identified by distinctive maroon T-shirts and *sjamboks*. The membership or
supporters of the strike committee consisted of migrant workers from the
hostels, and militant young workers from hostels and township. The hostels
were known as its base.[15]

Bunny Mahlangu argued that the majority of NUMSA members did
not support the actions of the strike committee but, like the shop stewards,
were intimidated by it:

We thought the strike committee was going to be a limited number
of people. Eventually we saw a very big giant that was now

uncontrollable, coming and attacking us viciously. Can you imagine 800 people coming from one side with sticks and everything, that's a very large number. They could take up a very big space in a general meeting. And if one person talks and the 800 clap hands, the rest get frozen. They scare the shit out of you. So the people who would have maybe supported us were scared.[16]

Shop stewards were also scared. The attempt to reconcile the conflicting pressures in their role was extremely difficult:

The ungovernability of Highveld in 1987, I really don't think it was condoned by the shop stewards. We sort of played hide-and-seek as shop stewards, not really coming up with what we believed as individuals was the real situation. Fear was always there in people's hearts. You would speak with caution. In the shop stewards meeting I would say, let's be frank and open, if what we intend doing is not taking us anywhere, please say so. But people would first look around, to see who's there and who's not there. The team that we had then was mostly comprised of people who were literate, people who when they sit down with management, their understanding broadens. It then becomes difficult when you have to go to these illiterate people where you've got to narrow your understanding to their understanding. So most of the time, as shop stewards we'd sit and discuss things and completely disagree with the membership, but no one would have the nerve to go and put it to the membership. Because you know that once you do that then you're in for a hiding. Once people see you as literate, they easily target you to be a softy. People would want a leader who talks a lot of insulting language in the meetings, who would go to management and shout at management. Given the political climate, if they saw a white person they didn't trust him. The whole of Highveld management was seen as untrustworthy.[17]

Hostel dwellers and township residents
Mahlangu's comment points to the centrality of tension between migrant ('illiterate') and local ('literate') workers in understanding the strike

committee. The base of the strike committee was known to be the hostels. Deep tensions between migrants and urban workers were a feature both of the apartheid workplace regime and the apartheid township. From its inception at Highveld Steel, NUMSA was shaped by this tension. NUMSA was initially organised in the hostels, which came to be seen as the union headquarters. Township residents first tended to see the union as a hostel organisation, and joined later than the migrant workers. Throughout the 1980s, the general meetings of NUMSA members from Highveld Steel were held in the hostels.[18]

Inscribed in NUMSA's origins, then, was the tension between different places of residence, and the different lives led by the workers in those places, a difference reflected too in the occupational structure in the workplace. This gave rise to an internal contestation – played out over the following decade and a half – over the meaning and ownership of the union. Hostel dwellers felt they had founded NUMSA and it should remain based among them. NUMSA was a powerful movement, not only for protecting them from managerial oppression, but also for collectively asserting their interests in an urban society that disempowered and demeaned them.[19]

Township shop stewards described the impact of this contestation:

> The union may have been seen by a number of workers from the township as a thing of the hostel. Some of the workers who lived in the hostel also perceived the union as their own organisation that is there to defend their own interests, as the hostel dwellers. They wanted the leadership, for instance the chairperson, to come from the hostels. There was a word that was used – kgoro – and choosing someone from outside would be taking the union outside the kgoro.[20]

A migrant leader in the hostel, on the other hand, felt not only that township residents were prejudiced against hostel dwellers, but also that they did not understand the meaning of the union:

> They think that those from far must have their own union and they must have their own. That made me aware of the fact that they knew nothing about the union, how it functions. Truly, they were saying we won't be run by somebody from rural areas. They were lost because of lack of understanding.[21]

Over time the township shop stewards came to dominate the shop steward committee: their generally higher level of education enabled them to engage effectively with complex procedures and negotiations, as well as to manage the increasing paperwork and communication demands within the union.[22] Union democracy empowered workers differentially – indeed, it dis-empowered unskilled migrants. Here, for example, is how disciplinary procedures generated tension:

> The guys who were not as literate, they'd go to a disciplinary hearing and not argue the facts, but just make a lot of noise. So they never advanced arguments that were convincing. Eventually the person would be dismissed. And we'd take up the appeal case and win. That shop steward would then start to think you are a collaborator with the employer. Why was this person reinstated when you represented him? So they were seeing us as management's people.[23]

Practices that produced victories in terms of trade union goals could be regarded with suspicion from the perspective of confrontation with white power. These tensions played into hostel-township differences because 'the shop stewards who were perceived to be literate, and the senior shop stewards, those who talk a lot when meeting management, would be the shop stewards from the township'.[24] The result was that the shop steward committee itself was divided. The strike committee then became an alternative powerbase for migrant workers in the hostels, through which they could assert their power and their notion of social order within the union.[25] The tension over procedure also explains the strike committee's preference for direct action in the form of wildcat strikes reinforced by coercion, rather than relying on disciplinary and negotiating procedures, or the internal democratic procedures of the union: it was these very procedures that disempowered them and allowed the union to slip through their hands.

Migrant workers brought their own cultural practices and notions of male discipline and collective solidarity, deeply rooted in their rural communities, to bear on the construction of union solidarity. Pedi migrant workers referred to the hostels as *kgoro*, not only in Witbank but also on the East Rand.[26] *Kgoro* is a Pedi word referring to a meeting place for men.

In the rural areas of the Northern Province male friends met every evening and morning at their *kgoro*, to converse, discuss problems and advise each other. Village headmen convened their more formal *kgoro* to solve disputes or try cases. At a more senior level, chiefs presided over district *kgoro*. The most common forms of punishment meted out by the *kgoro* to those found guilty of repeated offences was beating with a *sjambok* or payment of a fine in the form of livestock.

The hostels were also places of men. Pedi migrants habitually referred to the hostels as *kgoro*, which had significant implications for the trade union. The *kgoro* was a place of men, where men acted, debated and took decisions according to the codes of discipline, honesty, trust and bravery of men. Township men were different: they would go home and discuss issues with their wives, thus subverting the clarity and discipline of the *kgoro*. Therefore, they were not to be trusted with the leadership of the union. The traditional notions of manhood that Pedi migrants brought with them and reproduced within the hostels, and by extension in the union, became a source of tension between them and urban workers resident in the township.

Furthermore, the traditional forms of community governance in the rural areas implied distinctive notions of solidarity, discipline and punishment. If necessary, the *kgoro* had the duty of maintaining community relations, order and morality by administering punishment, and this was accepted by all in the community as a legitimate form of community governance. Everyone in the community was subject to the decisions of the *kgoro*. The Pedi migrant workers took their traditional form of collective discipline and punishment – the *sjambok* – and their traditional notions of collective solidarity – that it is not voluntary, but applies to everyone in the community – and applied these to their new form of collective organisation in the workplace. They used the *sjambok* as an instrument of discipline when they appropriated discipline from management. The *sjambok* became a means for building black solidarity. These practices tended to distinguish migrant workers from local urban workers and became a source of conflict within the solidarity of black workers. The strike committee became the agent for this migrant notion of social order in the union.

The words of some of the workers at Highveld Steel suggest that traditions of fighting and military discipline could be valuable cultural resources in building trade unionism in the struggle against employers, as well as mobilising in the liberation 'war' against apartheid, especially from the bases of male identity in those modern *kgoro*, the hostels:

> My department is full of Pedis. If we want to make a strike, we know how to punish each other. We discipline you very quick without anybody knowing that you've been disciplined. And you'll hide that thing, you won't tell somebody – it's yours. If you spread it out, you'll be disciplined twice. It's what we do. If we said we're going to fight a particular nation, they must never hear a word from us concerning when, or how. That's how we can overcome each and every nation. We're very strict.[27]

Migrants regarded the township residents as unreliable, people who lacked the resolve to stand firm in struggle. Thus, during stayaways, company buses had to be burnt in the township – mostly by militant youths – to prevent residents from going to work; it was unnecessary to burn buses at the hostels because the hostel dwellers would stand firm.[28] Township residents, on the other hand, became susceptible to the argument that hostel dwellers' willingness to strike sprang from their 'lack of responsibilities' – the pressure to pay rent or bonds, and hire-purchase contracts, which made township residents count the cost of every stoppage. And so the conflict fed on and confirmed mutual prejudices: township residents were cunning, sly, untrustworthy, unreliable and weak; migrants were mindless, rough, uncivilised, 'illiterate' and impervious to reason.

For most workers, the primary factor in the division between them was tension between hostel dwellers – 'those from afar' – and township residents – 'those from here, from Witbank'.[29] The opposing terms of this formulation carried layers of meaning: a distinction between locals and outsiders, between urban and rural, schooled and unschooled, modern and traditional, between different family structures and different community structures. Although most workers, shop stewards and officials argued that ethnic identity played a very limited part in the conflict among workers, it was woven in with the other elements of identity. The majority of the migrants were Pedi, the majority of township residents Zulu. Language mediates ethnic identity, and tension around language certainly surfaced at times, with demands by hostel dwellers that shop stewards speak Pedi, not Zulu.[30] Ethnic identity could inform other collective identities – such as the identity of the union – even subconsciously, as Bunny Mahlangu argued:

> Sometimes it just happens subconsciously to some people, and once you look at it from far you start to say, Oh, but these are Xhosas, these are Pedis. But the people involved, you find that they think they are doing it in the interest of the union, not being conscious about their nationality and ethnicity. Everyone thinks he's doing it for the good of the union.[31]

The important point is that the hostels formed a place where solidarity could be mobilised based on several overlapping identities – forged beyond the workplace in rural villages and urban communities, in families and in the popular movement – and where a particular set of practices and networks developed and acquired a shared meaning. It was also at the hostels that the militant township youths forged an alliance with the migrant workers, as described in chapter 4.

There were parallels between the migrant practices and the practices and culture that evolved among the militant youths of the township: a notion of community solidarity defined by an ethos of war against the oppressor and girded with coercive discipline. The militant youth were capable of an extreme and almost ritualistic brutality directed at *impimpis* (traitors), the enemy within, which served to reinforce the unity and solidarity of 'the community'.[32] There were also parallels between the tactics of ungovernability implemented by the youths in the township, and the preference of the migrants for militant wildcat action rather than negotiation. These cultures and practices provided the basis for the alliance – the 'singing togetherness' – of migrants and township youth.[33]

Thus the strike committee became the focus not only of the contestation over power between migrants and township workers, but also of the politics of ungovernability. In the words of its chairperson, Jacob Msimangu:

> We used that workplace. We knew, even in our general meetings, that whatever happens at Highveld Steel, it's going to have an effect on the government. We felt that whatever we do in the township

against the apartheid regime, we can also use that at Highveld Steel against the management. Even burning the buses. We said to ourselves, let us now try and destroy whatever we can. We identified the personnel block, that we must set fire to it. Unfortunately, we didn't. After striking, we would get a brief from management that this and this had been damaged. We felt that if that strategy was successful in the township, why not apply it at Highveld Steel?[34]

This was another source of tension with the shop steward leadership, some of whom felt 'the strategy in the township would be different from the strategy we can apply in the factory'.[35] The hostels therefore provided a concrete location where those with grievances – migrant outsiders, dismissed workers, disempowered shop stewards, union officials with complaints and even youth activists – could mobilise power in the union.[36]

Despite repeated outbreaks of antagonism and conflict between migrants and local residents, several leading unionists in the region argued that the Highveld region, and Witbank in particular, was unique in NUMSA for maintaining the allegiance of migrant workers. Trade unionists offered two explanations: that the union had started in the hostels – which was, however, also true of the East Rand where many migrants had become alienated from the union by the late 1980s; and the role of the youth in forging a strong political alliance with the hostel dwellers.[37] It seems likely the political tradition of the Pedi migrants, discussed in chapter 4, was the critical factor: their historical role in linking the urban-based ANC to the rural areas, and building ANC-linked organisation there. The absence of a rival political movement mobilising rural identities in opposition to the ANC allowed urban/rural contestations to play themselves out *within* the union and the popular movement, rather than in antagonism to them.

Contending notions of order

While the shop stewards interpreted the rise of the strike committee and its tactics as something 'uncontrollable', a breakdown in the order of the union, it was actually an expression of contending notions of social order among workers. At the heart of this conflict were competing views over the nature of worker solidarity or the 'law' which governed the social structure of the union, and the nature of the interaction with management, and whether this should also be governed by procedures or 'law'. The different perspectives on the social structure of the union are starkly captured in the diametrically opposed meanings of the *sjambok* to different workers. For activists in the strike committee, the *sjambok* was a means of building the union. For the shop steward leadership, the *sjambok* threatened to destroy the union.

For the strike committee, the 'union law' was founded on the solidarity of black workers, and this law was inscribed in the act of joining the union. Transgression could legitimately be punished with force:

> The strike committee was elected by the shop stewards – they said you must guide people, they must not break things or steal things. During those days people were punished for disobeying the orders or instructions of NUMSA. It builds the organisation. That's our agreement, you have joined NUMSA and you have agreed to the structure of NUMSA. Then you get punished, very severely.[38]

Other workers from the hostels explained that the strike committee was a force for maintaining order and peace among workers.[39] As conflicts increased between the two structures, members of the strike committee increasingly saw themselves, not as an opposition to the union, but as the upholders of the 'real' union against the shop stewards who were unaccountable, untrustworthy and too close to management.

In contrast, the shop steward leadership saw the strike committee as an agent of disorder – uncontrollable and 'out of hand'.[40] It undermined democracy and the elected structures of the union: 'Democracy is not about *sjambok*, it is about negotiation and talking.' Coercion meant that workers could not debate issues freely. The shop steward committee, elected by workers in the various constituencies into which the workplace was divided, was the backbone of democracy in the union, the structure on which all other constitutional structures were based. Yet the strike committee tried to control the shop stewards, subverting democracy and the union constitution. But when shop stewards raised these issues they were seen 'as people who were destroying the union. The moment you say this *sjambok* thing is not right, they say, you see, he is destroying the union now'.[41] The union officials were powerless to intervene and restore order because the strike committee refused to meet with them.[42]

These tensions among shop stewards, and between them and the strike committee, revealed workplace ungovernability to be more complex than it first appeared. The shop stewards who flouted procedures and appeared to organise and lead violent wildcat actions were responding to complex forces and pressures from management and from workers, negotiating their way between contradictory and ambiguous notions of 'union law', legitimate practice and union goals. Their leadership was precarious, and at times they were held hostage by the militant ungovernability of the strike committee. This generated internal tension and contradictory behaviour, as Bunny Mahlangu acutely observed:

> Once I believed that this was the right thing we were doing I became carried away with events. So sometimes I would come out shouting loud because I believe in what we're doing. Maybe people then thought that Bunny was a militant, but they never looked at the other side of Bunny. The next moment I'll be discouraged because deep in me I'll know that what we're doing now is really not going to work. And even if you say it, no one is going to listen. So people shout, 'Bunny! Bunny! Bunny!' But when I get to the meeting with management I'll be morally down. Then it's easy for management to convince me, because I know that what they're telling me is in fact true.[43]

Ultimately, it seems the strike committee did degenerate: in the words of its chairperson, it 'went sour' and became a 'kangaroo court', which individuals used to take up grudges against each other, or to interfere in family disputes. In this it resembled the trajectory of the 'people's court' in the township, adopting practices that lacked general legitimacy. This behaviour alienated a growing number of NUMSA members, in the hostels and the township.[44]

The 1987 lockout/strike

The 1987 lockout/strike, as described in the previous chapter, was accompanied by a high level of violent coercion and internal conflict. As it dragged on, the social structure of the union came under increasing strain. The striking workers met at the hostels every day, listening to speeches, *toyi-toying* and waiting for news. The tasks of the strike committee included maintaining discipline and unity among workers and keeping their spirits high, chairing the daily mass meetings, and preventing scabs from working. Ostensibly, the organisational work of the strike committee freed the shop stewards to plan and strategise, meet union officials and lawyers, and negotiate with management, but in reality the strike committee took control of the strike. It made increasing use of the *sjambok* to maintain unity and discipline. All workers were required to report daily at the mass gathering in the hostels; those who failed to do so, or who arrived late or drunk, were sentenced to lashes with the *sjambok*.

Groups of strike committee activists sought out workers who were absent without permission, took them to the hostels and administered punishment. Strike committee members also found their way into the Highveld Steel plants, especially at night, looking for strike-breakers, and either assaulted them then and there or confronted them when they attended the hostel gathering in the day. Another task was to keep an eye out for *impimpis* who might be passing information to management. One man who was found to be attending meetings with a tape-recorder and microphone strapped to his body was badly beaten, and only the efforts of a head office official who happened to be present prevented him from being killed. Other suspected *impimpis* were taken into the bush and beaten, and four were instructed to resign from Highveld Steel or watch their homes being petrol-bombed. Bands of strike committee members also gathered at the entrances to the hostels while workers were meeting, to monitor the movements of the police and prevent them from interfering with the meeting. Later, when the company employed 'scabs' from the nearby town of Middleburg and from KwaZulu-Natal, the strike committee organised attacks on their transport and places of accommodation.[45]

In these ways the strike committee maintained order among workers, but it was an increasingly coercive order with a shrinking basis in collective consent. The strike committee insisted that the strike should continue until management made some shift to increase its wage offer, and took control of worker meetings to prevent discussion of alternative strategies:

> You had to be very careful that you don't say something against the strike committee. I remember a guy who took an initiative by

suggesting, 'Let us fight while having food on the table for our children.' Then one member of the strike committee said, 'Can you clarify exactly what you mean by that?' The guy said, 'I think let's go back to Highveld, let us fight for our wages but while working.' And then he had very good support. People clapped their hands to show that they agreed. After the meeting the strike committee came to him and said, 'Now please, we would love to see you.' They took him to Block 6, and there he was accused of dividing the workforce and he was flogged. Everybody was now aware that to be safe is to support what the strike committee was suggesting.[46]

The strike committee also tried to control the shop stewards' access to workers: 'They would insist that before we talked to the membership, we must talk to them. The problem was that once you've met with them, they could position themselves to influence the bigger meeting.'[47]

However, as the crisis within the union deepened, the shop stewards began challenging the stranglehold of the strike committee. Lives were in danger as more workers began to work at Highveld clandestinely at night. The union was in danger of 'breaking into a physical fight between the township people and the hostel people'. The shop stewards were strengthened by a sense that the majority of workers wanted the regime of the strike committee to end. They refused to continue reporting to the strike committee, and started asserting their accountability to the membership.[48]

The strike committee was losing its power as its support base shrank and its activists themselves became demoralised. In the words of its chairperson: 'The shop stewards were now back in control, because we were tired and we were looking at them to give us the direction. Then we asked them to be open and to tell us exactly whether we were losing or not. They said, "We are losing and we've got to go back to work".'[49]

With the return to work, many strike committee activists were dismissed. Some, including its chairperson, survived. They felt insecure and betrayed.[50] The lockout left a deep legacy of divisions among workers, particularly between the migrants in the hostels and the shop steward leadership from the township. Most of the workers who were finally dismissed after the disciplinary inquiries were hostel dwellers, and they felt betrayed by the union and the shop stewards. This feeling was shared by many of their fellow migrants, often fellow Pedi-speakers, who remained as workers inside the company. A Pedi-speaking migrant, a man who was a founder member of the strike committee and was briefly a shop steward during the 1990s, articulated this feeling with great clarity:

> When we were supposed to go back to work, Boshielo said that some soldiers would be left behind. That shows us very well that we were fooled somewhere. That is why we say shop stewards are not trustworthy, and Boshielo himself as an organiser. It was a mistake, we were not yet finished the strike. It was not those from here [i.e. Witbank] who were fired, it was those from the rural areas, so that really showed us that the union had a problem. Actually we cannot say it is the union, it is the shop stewards. Most of them were residents of Witbank, that is why there was a problem of hating us in the hostel.[51]

Township residents, on the other hand, resented the intimidation they had suffered at the hands of the hostel dwellers, and were alienated from the union as a result.[52] The strike committee chairperson agreed that the strike committee 'really damaged the union up until now', leaving a legacy of bitterness and distrust between workers.[53]

Reforging a cracked union

The task of the new shop steward leadership that emerged in the aftermath of the lockout/strike was not only to re-establish some kind of social order in the workplace to constrain the power of management, but also to rebuild the union which had been devastated by the divisions and violence among workers. The remnants of the strike committee, and some of the shop stewards, still believed that the union should be re-built with the *sjambok*: 'They believed that as long as we don't *sjambok* these workers, we are going to be weak, but once we *sjambok* them then things will start flowing smoothly.' On the other hand, many workers, particularly those from the township, had been driven away from the union by the activities of the strike committee:

> You would try to organise people and they would say, No, that

NUMSA of yours may be good in other places, but not here because here it belongs to the hostel. We from outside the hotels have got no right to participate, so what is the point of joining the organisation?

The shop stewards tried to explain that 'what is happening in Witbank and at Highveld Steel is not in accordance with the policies of the organisation and the constitution of the union, we are not supposed to be doing what is being done here'.[54] For the new group of shop stewards, therefore, 'the first task was to destroy that strike committee'. Their new chairperson, Meshack Malinga, recalled:

We started breaking that tradition. We started reintroducing the principles of democracy and we started preaching that every person has the right to talk, even if he doesn't make any kind of sense. The first thing we had to do away with was the *sjambok*. That was a struggle, we had to trample quite a number of people.

The shop stewards started gaining support for their vision of the union, but this support was – at least partly – articulated in terms of hostel, township and skill differentiation within the workforce: 'I gained some popularity from those people who saw the union as a threat, as something driven by "mindless" people from the hostel, as they saw it.'[55]
According to another artisan shop steward:

Some people started gaining confidence in the shop steward committee, because they started seeing artisans there, and they believed artisans are more responsible people than these other guys, so they started confiding in us individually. You could clearly see that the union was taking a very different direction now.[56]

The position of artisans as shop stewards in the organisation was a contentious one. Many unskilled workers felt that the artisans were an elite who did not understand their grievances – a perception fuelled by the fact that artisans exercised supervisory powers over unskilled artisan assistants in the workplace.[57] Thus, in the process of rebuilding the union, the cleavage between migrant and urban workers was inscribed in the new distribution of organisational power, its tactics and culture, and its leadership style. Township residents were beginning to feel more at home in the union, while migrant activists were feeling disempowered and alienated.

The tension was exacerbated by the focus of the shop stewards on the new strategy of 'leadership quality' which meant using procedural channels requiring specific skills; thought had to go into how to phrase a grievance or declare a dispute; the process itself was complex, and a case could be lost on technicalities. Shop stewards who were illiterate or whose English was poor could not cope with these tasks, so the strategy itself disempowered them. The artisan and staff shop stewards, on the other hand, were not only confident and extremely effective in using formal procedures, they were also guided by one of their number – the vice-chairperson, Charles Makola – who was studying industrial relations by correspondence course and for whom making effective use of the procedures was a challenge.[58]

Thus, as the union was rebuilt at Highveld Steel, the same factors came into play as before the lockout/strike: the contradiction between negotiated accommodation and political confrontation, the disempowering of less literate and articulate shop stewards within the formal structures of the union and the formal procedures of industrial relations, and the consequent alienation of migrants in the hostels. Added to this, though, was the bitter legacy of the lockout/strike, and its impact on divisions between migrants and local residents.

The union splits

Towards the end of 1988 and the beginning of 1989, rumours began to circulate in the hostels that the shop steward leadership from the township was misusing the workers' fund. In part, this had to do with different perceptions about the purpose of the fund. According to the shop stewards, the fund was supposed to finance their frequent trips to the Industrial Council in Johannesburg, while the dismissed workers who had simply stayed on in the hostels argued that the fund should support them.

Another rumour, revealing the suspicion among migrant workers about the role of shop stewards in negotiations and their willingness to use formal procedures, was that the township shop stewards were bribed by, or too close to, management: 'The manager did not come to the hostel, he would go to the township to speak to shop stewards there. After that, when we held a meeting we could not agree on what we talked about the previous day. The shop stewards from the township no longer had power to face management.'[59] This echoes the general refrain that those from the township were untrustworthy, susceptible to alien influences – whether from their wives or managers – that could undermine the unity of purpose of workers. Such rumours meshed with the feeling among some of the migrants that the township shop stewards were looking after the interests of local workers and discriminating against migrants. The presence among them of the dismissed workers, who had used up their payout and were bitter because they felt the pledge by shop stewards and workers to carry on fighting for them from within the company had not been adhered to, reinforced this perception.[60]

A group of hostel-based shop stewards brought allegations of corruption and 'selling out' against the township shop stewards, and demanded that they be removed from office. A fundamental disagreement emerged between the two groups over the interpretation of the union constitution and the practice of democracy. The shop steward leadership and union officials pointed out that the constitution laid down specific procedures for the removal of shop stewards. Each shop steward was elected by a particular constituency, only that constituency was entitled to initiate proceedings to replace their representative, and the constituencies of the accused shop stewards were opposed to removing them. The hostel group, feeling that the constitution was being manipulated and that the shop steward leadership was undermining democracy, wanted to remove them by voting in a general meeting of all NUMSA members at Highveld Steel, where their own support could be mobilised.[61] They were hostile not only to the township shop stewards but also to some of the officials, particularly the regional secretary, Frank Boshielo, because of his advice to end the lockout/strike and because he insisted on a constitutional approach to the tension among shop stewards; and the former shop steward chairperson, Bunny Mahlangu, who had been employed by the union as a local organiser in preference to a candidate from among the dismissed migrants.[62]

Eventually, in 1990, the group in the hostels declared that the shop steward leadership had been suspended and elected new office-bearers. To those who pointed out that this was 'unconstitutional', they responded that the union constitution had been 'suspended' because 'there was a state of emergency at Highveld Steel' – a telling adoption of the rhetoric of the National Party when the social order of apartheid was under attack.[63] This signified a complete breakdown in the social order of the union. The constitution, which was the formal expression of the social structure of the union and laid down mechanisms for resolving conflict in accordance with the principles of democracy, had become unworkable.

During this period the meetings in the hostels became extremely tense. Violence and the use of the *sjambok* reappeared, a sign – like the 'suspension' of the constitution – that workers were no longer governed by a coherent social structure, but that this had been replaced by a violent 'war' over contending versions of internal union order. Confrontation between 'mindless' migrants and 'sly' locals escalated.[64] One member – a township resident – who raised 'relevant questions' in a meeting was later dragged off the bus after work, taken into the hostels, 'seriously beaten' and landed up in hospital. A handful of township shop stewards, 'out of high emotions' marched into the hostels, though 'there was a threat of being killed', and confronted the leadership there. They were able to identify some of the perpetrators and insisted on the company taking action against them.

After a disciplinary inquiry that saw rival shop stewards on opposing sides, one of the assailants was dismissed, and the township shop stewards were now 'seen as total villains, branded as anti-NUMSA people who were representing the evil forces'. The shop stewards felt 'we had no choice, we had to respond directly to the situation and eventually the truth would prevail'.[65]

One night, a petrol bomb was thrown through the window of William Sehlola's bedroom while his family was sleeping. He managed to extinguish the fire with blankets, but agreed to his family's pleas that he withdraw from union activities. Sehlola was a founder member of the union, a Pedi migrant and staff employee, who moved into a township house in the mid-1980s. One of his fellow shop stewards described his dilemma: 'He is a Pedi and he was living in the township so he actually never knew which side to choose, but he chose the correct side, he belonged to us.' He was therefore 'suspended' along with the other township shop stewards. His colleague said that the migrants felt Sehlola had betrayed them: 'They nearly killed him, they burnt his house, seeing that he has moved from their culture and has joined the township culture.' [66]

The union at Highveld Steel effectively broke in two: 'a union of the township and a union of the hostel'.[67] For a while each group of shop stewards held its own general meeting, one in the hostels and one in township venues.[68] In a move reminiscent of the formation of the strike committee, the hostel-based shop stewards organised the election of 'marshals' in all departments 'for the protection of shop stewards' and to maintain order in meetings.[69] Highveld Steel management accepted the suspension of the shop steward leadership from the township, which the latter saw as evidence that management was actively fostering the division in an attempt to undermine their efforts to rebuild the union. Attacked on all sides, and disillusioned by the inability of the regional office or head office of the union to intervene, the township shop stewards decided 'to keep a low profile' and became inactive.[70]

Although most interviewees saw the split as coinciding with the division between migrant workers and local workers, these divisions were not monolithic. Several township workers supported the hostel group.[71] Nor did all the hostel-dwellers support the hostel group of shop stewards, but it was difficult for them to attend meetings in the township without being noticed.[72]

The conflict was also shaped by the political contestation within the union and within the community described in chapter 4. Township youth structures became involved in the dispute, particularly the ANC Youth League after it was launched in Witbank. The youths were a force that could instil fear.[73] The workers' fund bankbook was confiscated from the township shop stewards by members of the Youth League on the request of the hostel shop stewards. Likewise, when the township shop stewards tried to meet in the township, 'it was not anyone but ANC people, especially the Youth League guys, who entered with knives and pangas and said, "We don't approve of this meeting" and escorted us to the hostels'.[74]

The split in the union seemed to render the NUMSA regional structures incapable of resolving the crisis. Most of the union's officials were former Highveld Steel shop stewards, and the shop stewards were important figures in the regional executive. Cross-cutting allegiances paralysed these structures. Eventually, however, the continuing violence, unprocedural stoppages and the paralysis in the union persuaded the NUMSA head office to intervene.[75] A Highveld Steel Commission of Inquiry was established, consisting of head office officials. It found one incident of 'misuse of R500' and negligence concerning a shortfall of R590, but no evidence of dishonesty or corruption. It did, however, identify major organisational problems and personal struggles. The commission reprimanded various individuals and structures, recommended leadership training programmes for regional office-bearers and shop stewards, proposed that the two groups form an interim joint negotiating team and ordered fresh shop steward elections to be held before the end of the month in accordance with proper procedures (NUMSA, Commission Report).

Although none of the individuals named in the report felt that the findings against them were fair, the commission did serve to assert the authority of the national union over the protagonists from both sides, and so re-establish a formal framework of agreement within which the social structure of the union could be rebuilt.[76]

Fresh shop steward elections were held. Sehlola was prohibited from standing but had already decided to withdraw after the petrol-bomb attack on his house. Charles Makola decided to call it a day, but persuaded others from the township group to stand despite their disappointment about the 'bitter recommendations' of the commission. They were re-elected by their constituencies, as were most of the hostel group. As laid down in the constitution, the newly elected shop stewards then elected their office-bearers. The former township group felt that they could not stand for office-bearer positions because they were in a minority and 'you must come from the hostel and be a Pedi to qualify for a senior position in this union'; they also felt 'we had to give the other guys a chance to prove themselves and maybe they would give us the right direction'.[77]

The retrenchment strike: the township shop stewards re-emerge
However, the dynamics that had produced the split in the first place re-emerged, and the new shop steward committee did not last very long. According to the former township group, the new office-bearers from the hostels were unable to provide strategic direction or cope with disciplinary procedures in the company:

We had to work together now following the NUMSA constitution and policies but it was difficult for most of these guys who became shop stewards through force to adhere to the union policies and constitution, so they started by not attending meetings. They pulled out one by one, and then they finally vanished. We had to replace them and elect other office-bearers. And then they were silent.[78]

The final break took place at the end of 1991, during the first major strike since the 1987 lockout/strike, when workers launched a two-week strike against management proposals to retrench more than 500 workers. The strike appeared to be a display of militancy but, in fact, the union leadership inside Highveld Steel was divided and weak. Reluctance on the part of shop stewards to meet management was a sign that they lacked a strategy, that workers distrusted them and that the strike was being driven from below. On the one hand 'management was not moving', and on the other those who were to be retrenched 'were fighting tooth and nail' for their jobs.

Picketers monitored the steelworks entrance 24 hours a day and prevented vehicles from entering or leaving. The shop stewards would try to negotiate with management but had no control over the strikers and what was happening in the company premises. When they reported back to general meetings of their members, the retrenchees dominated discussion and prevented other members from speaking. Intimidation and violence had re-emerged among workers. The remaining office-bearers elected after the commission were unable to cope with the pressures – they simply 'were not there to lead the strike'. The chairperson attended negotiations at the start of the strike but as it became protracted 'he disappeared and he never came back into the union again'.[79]

Mosi Nhlapo, one of the artisan shop stewards from the township, decided the situation required decisive leadership:

It was tough, very tough. They had to run away. The strike was turning ugly because beatings were beginning to happen again. We were moving again to the 1987 period, and then one had to make a very clear decision that either we break the union or we break the strike. Someone had to take the lead and there was no one available. Everyone said no, they could not. I said, 'Okay, can I try?' That's when I was elected chairperson by the other shop stewards.

The shop stewards managed to push management to re-open negotiations and won a 'slight improvement' in the severance package. They recommended to the general meeting of members that management's offer be accepted and the strike ended. The meeting voted to accept their recommendation, but the retrenchees felt 'that they were being sold out'. The day after the strike ended, Nhlapo was cornered in the change-room showers by some of them 'with knives in their hands, wanting to stab me'. By chance, Jacob Msimangu, the former chairperson of the strike committee, came across them and was able to beat them off while Nhlapo escaped.[80]

In the aftermath of this strike, the artisan shop stewards re-emerged in the leadership of the shop steward committee. Nhlapo was confirmed as chairperson of the steelworks committee, Meshack Malinga was elected chairperson of the joint shop steward committee for the Highveld Group, and Jacob Skhosana and Ambrose Mthembu became key members of the executive. From now on, the strategy of NUMSA at Highveld Steel would be defined by more articulate and skilled shop stewards from the township, particularly artisans. Two of the leading figures in the former hostel group remained in the leadership of the committee: Johannes Phatlana as vice-chairperson of the joint shop steward committee and Ezekiel Nkosi (actually a township resident) as secretary of the steelworks committee. J.J. Mbonani, the 'bullfighter' from the hostels, was secretary of the joint shop steward committee. In an effort to overcome the division based on place of residence, the shop stewards engaged in a successful struggle for the right to meet at work during the 1990s.

Some of those who had 'vanished' before and during the retrenchment strike re-emerged as leaders of a new splinter union established during 1992: the National Union of Steel and Allied Workers (NUSAAW). It was recognised by the company despite having membership of about 100 – another sign of the readiness of management to encourage division among workers. The formation of a breakaway union did not mean that the divisions among members of NUMSA had been resolved. The accumulation of conflicts and internal struggles had left a deep legacy of distrust and bitterness among many migrants: the conflict between the strike committee and the shop stewards, the lockout/strike and dismissals, the 1990 split and its aftermath. The structural conditions that tended to marginalise unskilled migrants remained and would, if anything, become stronger. A significant grouping of migrant workers in the hostels continued to feel the township shop stewards were not trustworthy leaders. This was voiced by one migrant, although he decided not to join the splinter union:

> The shop stewards surprised us by misusing money. After that, we tried to expel them. We never found that money. Then in some departments they re-elected those shop stewards. That is when another union [NUSAAW] came in, it was for that reason. We said, NUMSA, we no longer trust you because you still have those people who squandered money. We did not really understand each other well with those re-elected shop stewards. So the shop stewards from the hostel withdrew. Every family can be fixed, and ultimately we will fix this. But some do not believe this, that is when they went out to join the other union, and it came in. As you can see, today there is lack of agreement.[81]

The township shop stewards, on the other hand, reported that 'some of the people that used to confront us directly have come to us confessing that they have watched us very closely and they are confident we have got the interests of the organisation at heart and that we are, in fact, the legitimate leaders'.[82]

Understanding violence between workers

Violence among workers is a repeated theme in the history of NUMSA at Highveld Steel.[83] Most social structures sanction the use of coercive measures against those who transgress its codes – what may be termed *legitimate coercion*. Thus the shop stewards and most members implicitly endorsed the use of legitimate coercion – that is, 'revolutionary bullying' – by the strike committee against workers who refused to behave according to collectively made decisions. But the notion of legitimate coercion implies that there are limits – defined by the codes and values of the social structure – beyond which coercion loses the sanction of the social structure in which it is embedded, and therefore its legitimacy. The violence that emerged and re-emerged during crisis moments for union organisation at Highveld Steel went beyond these limits. Workers adopted violent practices at moments when the union social structure became ineffective in the face of contending notions of union order. Violence was an indicator of breakdown in the cohesion of social structure, as contending factions sought to impose their version of order on the others.

However, it was not the case that all contestants deployed violence in equal measure against their opponents. It was specifically the groupings linked to the migrants in the hostels, to the militant youths of the township, to workers dismissed in 1987 and in 1991, to workers facing retrenchment, that did so. There was a combination of reasons for this. Most importantly, the migrant workers in the hostels were responding to a process of disempowerment. Relatively powerless in urban society, and experiencing a loss of power within the union, violent coercion appeared to offer a way to regain their control of the union and some degree of power within urban society. The more articulate and 'literate' shop stewards from the township had other sources of power: their mastery of the very practices and processes within the union – negotiation and the disciplinary procedures of the company, and the democratic procedures of the union – which disempowered the migrants. Violence did not promise to empower them; on the contrary, it threatened to destroy their power by undermining democracy, dividing workers and weakening or even destroying the union.

In their response to the loss of power, the Pedi migrant workers were able to draw on cultural resources and practices from community life in their rural areas – on the sanctions and codes of their rural social structures – to legitimise, or give meaning to, the violent coercion with which they tried to 'build the union'.[84] Their concentration in relatively easily monitored and controlled hostels also meant that coercion could more successfully maintain their unity. The militant youths (both those who worked at Highveld Steel and those who were jobless) tended to group themselves with the strike committee and the hostel shop stewards and also drew on the culture and practices of the youth movement, which sanctioned extreme violence against *impimpis* or traitors. This culture and set of practices was in turn shaped by the relative powerlessness of the unemployed youth in urban society, a powerlessness produced by apartheid, by their lack of access to work and incomes, and by the structure of the township family (Bozzoli 2000).[85]

In relation to the social structure of the union, the most disempowered of all were the workers who were dismissed in 1987, and those threatened with retrenchment in 1991. Exclusion from the workplace meant exclusion from the union and the loss of power within it. Having no recourse to democratic procedures or voice within the organisation, violence increasingly appeared to be the only option to construct or reconstruct their lost power. Not all migrant workers favoured the use of violence and not all township residents rejected it. Many of the workers in the hostels were deeply unhappy about the violence while a number of township residents participated in it. Nonetheless, it was the hostels that became centres for violent coercion within the union, and the shop steward leadership from the township, supported by a majority of township residents, who opposed it.

Conclusion

This analysis of the internal life of social movement unionism at Highveld Steel contrasts with the literature in several respects. In the first place, it reveals the union to have been as much a popular organisation as a class-based one, constituted through an amalgam of collective identities forged both beyond and within the workplace. Secondly, its internal organisational culture and practices, its goals, strategies, tactics and meanings were subject to continuous contestation and redefinition. Thirdly, and arising from this, the internal practices of the union were not unproblematically democratic and committed to open debate. Indeed, the failure of union democracy to empower the less literate migrant workers led them to resort to coercion to empower themselves. The thread of violence runs through the entire period of union formation covered in this book. Solidarity was forged through revolutionary bullying. Contending notions of union order generated intensely violent conflict along migrant/township resident and political lines.

Notes

1. Interview, Charles Makola, 14/5/94.
2. Interview, Frank Boshielo, 19/6/94; interview, Bob Moloi, 10/7/94; interview, Jacob Msimangu, 12/8/95; interview, Johannes Phatlana, 7/9/94.
3. Interview, Jacob Msimangu, 12/8/95.

4. Interview, Philip Mkatshwa, 7/7/94; see also interview, Ambrose Mthembu, 22/10/95.
5. Violence against non-strikers is 'a universal feature of industrial history' and only tends to decline with the institutionalisation of industrial and class conflict, for example through political enfranchisement, the protection of picketing, etc (Webster and Simpson 1991).
6. Interview, Philip Mkatshwa, 7/6/94.
7. Interview, Bob Moloi, 10/7/94.
8. Interview, Frank Boshielo, 19/6/94; see also interview, Charles Makola, 6/8/95 on the dynamics of negotiation.
9. Interview, Jacob Msimangu, 12/8/95.
10. Ibid.
11. Ibid.
12. Ibid; see also interview, Bunny Mahlangu, 8/11/93; interview, Gert van der Merwe, 29/11/95.
13. Interview, Philip Mkatshwa, 7/6/94; a second shop steward described an almost identical situation and commented that this was 'not covered by the law of the strike' (interview, J.J. Mbonani, 31/5/94).
14. Interview, Bob Moloi, 10/7/94.
15. Interview, Ephraim Kgole, 10/95; interview, Bob Moloi, 10/7/94; interview, Jacob Msimangu, 12/8/95.
16. Interview, Bunny Mahlangu, 4/5/95.
17. Ibid.
18. NUMSA generally tended to be based among migrant workers in the hostels in its early days (Sitas 1983; Webster 1985: chapter 9).
19. Interview, Charles Makola, 8/5/94; interview, Meshack Malinga, 12/5/94.
20. Meshack Malinga in interview, Mosi Nhlapo, 9/11/93; interview, Mosi Nhlapo, 8/5/94.
21. Interview, Tshagata, 10/95.
22. Interview, Frank Boshielo, 19/6/94; interview, Bunny Mahlangu, 4/5/95; interview, Charles Makola, 14/5/94.
23. Interview, Bunny Mahlangu, 14/5/95.
24. Ibid; see also interview, Bunny Mahlangu, 15/8/95.
25. For example, interview, Mosi Nhlapo, 9/11/93.
26. I am indebted for the insights discussed in the following two paragraphs to a series of discussions with William Matlala, Pedi migrant worker, labour photographer and cultural activist, and a former shop steward and hostel-dweller.
27. Interview, Hong Kong Kgalima, 10/7/94.
28. Interview, Ephraim Kgole, 10/95.
29. The importance of the dichotomy between local and outsider is demonstrated by an incident in the 1990s, when a group of Pedi migrants, unhappy with the way the shop stewards had handled a grievance, again accused the union of only looking after locals and threatened to resign from it. The Zulu shop steward they were speaking to responded that he too was an outsider in Witbank, having grown up in a township on

the East Rand. The migrants regarded this as significant information that suggested their accusations were misplaced, and apologised (interview, Mosi Nhlapo, 6/3/95). This story implies a greater significance for the local/outsider distinction than for urban/rural or Zulu/Pedi differences.

30. Interview, Barney Mashego, 13/10/95; interview, Bunny Mahlangu, 15/8/95; interview, Frank Boshielo, 19/6/94.

31. Interview, Bunny Mahlangu, 15/8/95; see also interview, Frank Boshielo, 19/6/94; interview, Barney Mashego, 13/10/95; interview, Ezekiel Nkosi, 5/5/94; interview, Johannes Phatlana, 7/9/94; interview, Tshagata, 10/95.

32. Beinart also points out that in a context of social dislocation and family breakdown, violence may be a means for young men to forge male identity and carve out social space, especially where they can draw on pre-colonial traditions with 'deep cultural markers which justify and shape the form of violence' (Beinart 1992: 481). The violence of the youth 'comrades' was as often directed towards the 'purification' and unification of a fragmented community as against the apartheid system (ibid: 483–4).

33. Interview, Charles Makola, 14/5/94. In the Witbank case the common allegiance of migrants and youth to the ANC provided a bridge between the two; where the migrant workers were Zulu-speakers and Inkatha was mobilising on an anti-ANC and anti-youth basis, the result was violent conflict rather than an alliance.

34. Interview, Jacob Msimangu, 12/8/95, 22/10/95.

35. Interview, Bunny Mahlangu, 4/5/95.

36. Ibid.

37. Interview, Frank Boshielo, 19/6/94; interview, Charles Makola, 8/5/94; interview, Barney Mashego, 13/10/95. In a union debate in the late 1980s, the Highveld region opposed a resolution that the union had failed to maintain the support of migrant workers, on the grounds that their regional secretary, Frank Boshielo, still lived in the hostels, that union meetings were based there, and that the hostel dwellers were highly active in the union and politically. For the East Rand see Mamdani (1996) and Segal (1992).

38. Interview, Hong Kong Kgalima, 10/7/94.

39. Interview, Jerry Mogoleko, 10/95; interview, Johannes Phatlana, 7/9/94; interview, Tshagata, 26/5/94.

40. Interview, Bunny Mahlangu, 4/5/95; interview, Charles Makola, 14/5/94, 6/8/95.

41. Interview, Mosi Nhlapo, 9/11/93.

42. Interview, Jacob Msimangu, 12/8/95.

43. Interview, Bunny Mahlangu, 4/5/95; see also interview, Bob Moloi, 10/7/94.

44. Interview, Jacob Msimangu, 12/8/95, 22/10/95; see also interview, Charles Makola, 6/8/95. There was also a limit to how much disorder could be tolerated by workers in the workplace: every stoppage diminished workers' earnings, and growing numbers of workers opposed the frequent stoppages called by the strike committee (interview, Charles Makola, 6/8/95).

45. Interview, Bunny Mahlangu, 4/5/95, 15/8/95; interview, Hong Kong Kgalima, 10/7/

94; interview, Bob Moloi, 10/7/94; interview, Jacob Msimangu, 12/8/95; interview, Johannes Phatlana, 7/9/94.

46. Interview, Bob Moloi, 10/7/94.
47. Interview, Bunny Mahlangu, 15/8/95; see also interview, Bob Moloi, 10/7/94; interview, Jacob Msimangu, 12/8/95.
48. Interview, Bunny Mahlangu, 4/5/95; interview, Bob Moloi, 10/7/94; interview, Mosi Nhlapo, 6/3/95.
49. Interview, Jacob Msimangu, 12/8/95; see also interview, Charles Makola, 6/8/95; interview, Mosi Nhlapo, 6/3/95.
50. Interview, Jacob Msimangu, 12/8/95; see also interview, Charles Makola, 6/8/95; interview, Bob Moloi, 10/7/94.
51. Interview, Ephraim Kgole, 10/95.
52. Interview, Mosi Nhlapo, 9/11/93.
53. Interview, Jacob Msimangu, 12/8/95.
54. Interview, Mosi Nhlapo, 9/11/93.
55. Meshack Malinga in interview, Mosi Nhlapo, 9/11/93.
56. Interview, Mosi Nhlapo, 6/3/95.
57. See Von Holdt (2000), especially chapters 8 and 9, for a full discussion of the position of black artisans in the union.
58. Interview, Mosi Nhlapo, 6/3/95; interview, Barney Mashego, 13/10/95. In the early 1990s, Makola was promoted to the position of industrial relations officer, in itself an index of the different opportunities available to more and less educated workers. The opportunities open to some workers would have a significant impact on the union during the 1990s.
59. Interview, Ephraim Kgole, 10/95; see also interview, Barney Mashego, 13/10/95.
60. This and the previous paragraphs are based on interview, Frank Boshielo, 9/93; interview, Ephraim Kgole, 10/95; interview, Bunny Mahlangu, 15/8/95; interview, Barney Mashego, 13/10/95; interview, Charles Makola, 8/5/94; interview, Jacob Msimangu, 22/10/95; interview, Ambrose Mthembu, 15/3/94, 26/4/94, 22/10/95; interview, Mosi Nhlapo, 9/11/93; interview, Ezekiel Nkosi, 5/5/94.
61. Interview, Jacob Msimangu, 22/10/95; interview, Ambrose Mthembu, 15/3/94, 26/4/94, 22/10/95; interview, Mosi Nhlapo, 9/11/93; interview, William Sehlola, 5/6/94.
62. Interview, Frank Boshielo, 9/93; interview, Bunny Mahlangu, 15/8/95.
63. Interview, Ambrose Mthembu, 15/3/94, 26/4/94, 22/10/95. The adoption of the rhetoric of the National Party regime when the social order of apartheid was under attack indicates how deeply the language of total confrontation – as a way of making sense of the crisis of apartheid social structure – had penetrated society; it also indicates the degree to which the union social structure had broken down, and the relationship of this to the political crisis. Some of the township shop stewards adopted a similar rhetoric, accusing the hostel group of 'destabilising' the union.
64. Meshack Malinga in interview, Mosi Nhlapo, 9/11/93; see also interview, Barney Mashego, 13/10/95.

65. Meshack Malinga in interview, Mosi Nhlapo, 9/11/93.
66. Interview, Mosi Nhlapo, 9/11/93; interview, William Sehlola, 5/6/94.
67. Interview, Ezekiel Nkosi, 5/5/94.
68. Interview, Ambrose Mthembu, 22/10/95; interview, Jacob Msimangu, 22/10/95.
69. Meeting held at hostel (shop steward minutes), 16 July 1990.
70. Interview, Meshack Malinga, 12/5/94; interview, Barney Mashego, 13/10/95; interview, Ambrose Mthembu, 15/3/94, 22/10/95; interview, Mosi Nhlapo, 9/11/93, 12/95.
71. Interview, Jacob Msimangu, 22/10/95; interview, Ezekiel Nkosi, 5/5/94; interview, Hendrik Nkosi, 26/10/95.
72. Interview, Mosi Nhlapo, 12/95.
73. Meshack Malinga in interview, Mosi Nhlapo, 9/11/93.
74. Interview, Mosi Nhlapo, 12/95; see also interview, Ambrose Mthembu, 15/3/94; interview, William Sehlola, 5/6/94.
75. Interview, Charles Makola, 8/5/94; interview, Ambrose Mthembu, 26/4/94, 22/10/95; interview, Mosi Nhlapo, 9/11/93; interview, Jacob Skhosana, 14/4/94; see also meeting held at hostel (shop steward minutes), 16 July 1990.
76. Interview, Ezekiel Nkosi, 5/5/94.
77. Interview, Mosi Nhlapo, 9/11/93; see also interview, Charles Makola, 8/5/94; interview, Ambrose Mthembu, 26/4/94.
78. Interview, Ambrose Mthembu, 26/4/94; see also interview, Mosi Nhlapo, 9/11/93.
79. Interview, Mosi Nhlapo, 12/95; see also interview, Ambrose Mthembu, 22/10/95; Highveld Steel, Founding affidavit, 6 December 1991.
80. Interview, Mosi Nhlapo, 12/95; see also interview, Frank Boshielo, 9/93.
81. Interview, Ephraim Kgole, 10/95.
82. Meshack Malinga in interview, Mosi Nhlapo, 9/11/93.
83. Violence was an increasingly prevalent element of industrial relations in the mid to late 1980s (see *South African Labour Bulletin* 1989 for an illuminating discussion of this trend).
84. Some of the Pedi migrants may have had direct experience of the Sekhukhuneland Revolt of 1958, when young migrant men spearheaded a struggle to reform the royal council and rename it Khuduthamaga (red-and-white-tortoise) in their struggle to reconstruct the institution of chiefly rule in the face of 'the Trust'. During a period when their way of life – their rural social structure – was under profound threat, Khuduthamaga 'mustered widespread popular support and participation' but 'was also a forum in which dissent was viewed with mounting hostility and in which the eradication of cleavages within the community became an overriding value' (Delius 1996: 133–4). Delius explains this in terms of the fact that 'their whole way of life faced destruction', popular interpretations of historical defeats as the consequence of 'internal divisions and conflicts', anxiety about the 'enemy within' in the form of witchcraft, and the persistence of the Pedi military tradition (ibid: 128–9). I would add traditional communal forms of authority, discipline and punishment (see first part of this chapter). The point is less whether there was any direct link between the

experience of Khuduthamaga and the conflict at Highveld Steel, than the repertoire of interpretations, codes and practices which existed in rural Pedi social structures and which formed a resource for men whose power was being undermined.

85. Delius finds a similar experience of disempowerment underlying the youth uprisings and witch killings in the Sekhukhuneland Revolt of 1986 (1996: 202–3).

CHAPTER 7

'Freedom is here, apartheid is finished'

NUMSA, transition and the new strategy
of reconstruction

> Now that we have a democratic government, we want to see it
> succeeding, and of course no political power can be maintained if
> there is no economic power. Our economy has been devastated by
> the system of apartheid, and we need to rebuild it now. So I believe
> that the culture definitely has to change from the culture of
> resistance and ungovernability to the culture of productivity.
>
> *Meshack Malinga, chair, joint shop stewards' committee, 1994*

When Nelson Mandela was released to tumultuous rejoicing in February
1990, workers in many factories organised celebratory demonstrations,
marches and stoppages – some lasting several days (Mondi 1990; Parfit
1990). The unbanning of the ANC, the SACP and the PAC was announced
at the same time. The 1994 democratic elections that followed a period of
protracted negotiations, disputes, deadlocks, mass action and a referendum
of the white electorate over the process of establishing a democratic
government, constituted a radical rupture in the colonial history of South
Africa.

For the first time, the colonised had breached the walls of political
exclusion – they were now citizens with the right to vote for government,
and they formed the overwhelming majority of voters. The new electorate
included the black working class, the members of NUMSA and other unions.
This change had a profound impact on the structure of social movement
unionism, which had been so strongly defined by the connection between
political struggle against apartheid and the confrontation with white power
in the workplace. Shop stewards and workers now saw it as necessary
to separate and redefine the politics of the union's relationship with

government and its engagement with management. This shift could be discerned in the changing attitudes of workers and the changing meaning of union activities for them, as well as in the adoption of new policies at a formal level.

The election of the ANC government – for which black workers campaigned and voted – constituted the moment of democratic incorporation of the black working class. Class incorporation is a contested process. The trade union movement developed a new *strategy of reconstruction* in order to contest and shape incorporation and the broader transition from apartheid. What was at stake was the nature of the post-colonial social order, and the idea of 'reconstruction' defined the kinds of contestations and accommodations that would characterise it.

The new strategy reflected the distinctive nature of the South African transition from apartheid to a post-colonial society. It has been – and continues to be – a transition akin to other transitions from colonialism, in that the entire system of social, political and economic relations and institutions was structured by colonialism and apartheid, and the transition is therefore a struggle between different forces over the nature and extent of the transformation of this legacy. In this, the South African transition differs substantially from other non-colonial transitions from authoritarian rule. The rest of this book examines in detail those struggles in the workplace, the community, the union, the ANC and the Witbank Town Council through which the old order was being transformed, and out of which the new order was emerging.

This book argues that the foundation for incorporation is established primarily at the political level of relations between classes and the state, rather than in the workplace. Workplace incorporation follows from such political incorporation. This chapter describes the adoption by COSATU and by NUMSA and its shop stewards and officials at Highveld Steel of the strategy of reconstruction and considers the implications of the new strategy for trade unionism.

The new meaning of the union

In the view of most shop stewards, the new political dynamics in South Africa changed everything. The movement towards a negotiated settlement and democracy implied a change in the nature of workplace struggle. Albert Makagula, a migrant shop steward, argued:

When Mandela came out of prison we realised the importance of negotiating issues first. If those fail, then we can go into the bush and fight [take strike action]. Mr Mandela's release brought a change in how things were done. It showed us the importance of negotiations. Before his release we never negotiated. We would just go into the bush and when asked why, we would tell them to release Mandela first.[1]

The transition to democracy meant South Africa was no longer a white man's country – and therefore Highveld Steel, as a part of the broader South African economy, was in some sense no longer a white man's factory. 'Killing the economy of this factory' would be 'killing the economy of the entire country'. Likewise, workers should start paying rent and rates in the township.[2]

These issues were not only of concern to the leading shop stewards. Tshagata, the migrant worker activist, expressed similar concerns:

It's different now because the government is ours. We must fight bearing this in mind. As for demands inside the firm, we are still demanding those previous demands because there is nothing which is really satisfactory. But you see us not demanding too much because if we were to strike for a long time we would destroy the government. Before, we were destroying the previous government using those tactics.

Asked whether this meant limiting the fight against the employers, he answered:

Actually, we do not limit it – as for fighting, we are fighting. But we no longer fight in the same manner as before, destroying things. If we say we are limiting, that won't be true, because we are still using the same power. But when considering our government, we think we must support it in a new manner, unlike before when we were *toyi-toying*. Because now, if I *toyi-toyi* while the government is mine it seems I'm not intelligent. So even if we take action, we just sit down to show that we have defeated the employer.[3]

Shop stewards and workers grappled with the complex tension between supporting government and fighting employers, demonstrating how broader political relations are inscribed within the social structure of the union through a process of social construction of the meaning of the union. On the one hand, their words reveal the desire to support the government and simultaneously continue the militant struggle for change in the workplace, where the apartheid workplace regime was relatively intact. On the other, they knew from their struggle against apartheid that workplace action has political and economic implications for government, and they wanted to find a different way of engaging in workplace struggle.

For shop stewards in particular, the new conditions implied a new concern with workplace procedure, and therefore awareness of common ground with managers:

> It's my duty to inform the employees what is wrong, what is right, what our constitution stands for. We are not there to fight man-agement, we are there to support our families. According to the Highveld rules, anything you do has to be done in the correct way. If someone is absent without permission he is supposed to be disciplined, otherwise you will find the whole workforce absent without permission. We are part and parcel of management, not officially, but according to our constitution as a union. It's playing a managerial role, to bring people in order. The difference is that management is giving you discipline and at the end you will be fired. My goal is different, I don't discipline, I'm helping the guy. To be a leader, you are supposed to see both sides. When the managers have left and I'm alone with my member I will tell him straight, you have done bullshit here, that is not the correct way to behave.[4]

In this shop steward's words there is a growing concern with legitimate procedures and 'correct' behaviour. Highveld Steel is no longer 'a white man's factory', but the place where workers earn wages to support their families. He grapples with the complexity of defending his members, persuading or compelling managers to conduct themselves differently, and constructing a new legitimate order in the workplace – an order that defines his own rights and duties as well as those of managers and workers. To do all of these he himself has to be a manager, managing relationships, people, conflicts and procedures. Clearly, the new conditions implied a greater degree of institutional participation, of negotiated accommodation, than previously.

There was no consensus among workers about these shifts. Some shop stewards, like J.J. Mbonani, complained that their members saw no reason to change. When he tried to explain to workers that procedures should be followed:

> They said, 'No, man, Mbonani has taught us about this action, we didn't know anything about strikes. Now he's telling us that we mustn't strike, we must negotiate. What is negotiate? What are we going to resolve out of that?' I said, 'Hey, Nelson Mandela has climbed to the position where he is now through negotiations, let's try it and see if it won't work.' But the people take a strike as something which just occurs at any time. If one feels oppressed, he just talks to his friend, they don't consult me. I'll find them dancing, on strike. The people don't understand the difference between the old government and this new one. We need more time to teach our people the differences.[5]

Shop stewards had mixed perceptions about the response of the general body of workers to the political transition in South Africa. Some commented that workers no longer had a fighting spirit, but were relaxing 'now that freedom is here and apartheid is finished'.[6] Others commented that 'some workers didn't know why we were fighting, and don't know why we now say they mustn't fight', and continued to draw on the repertoire of militant and unprocedural actions which developed during the 1980s.[7] These tensions and contradictions in workers' attitudes reflected the ambiguity, complexity and instability precipitated by the shifting meaning of trade unionism. The process of class incorporation was complex and contested, and opened up new challenges within the union.

Labour's new strategy of reconstruction: a national overview
At a more formal level too, the trade union movement responded proactively to the democratic transition by developing new policies and strategies.

COSATU adopted a *strategy of reconstruction* focusing on strategic engagement with the process of working-class incorporation in an attempt to shape its terms and the balance of forces that would emerge within institutions and relations underpinning post-colonial society. It became a member of the Tripartite Alliance with the ANC and the SACP – an alliance with an insurrectionary liberation movement was replaced by an alliance with a government-in-waiting. It also became an active participant in various forums where the new order was being negotiated.

COSATU's programmatic vision was crystallised in the Reconstruction and Development Programme (RDP) – initiated as a strategy to shape the policies of the ANC. In the end, the RDP was jointly drafted by COSATU and the ANC, and became the election manifesto of the Tripartite Alliance. The significance of these developments was that the union movement had shifted from a stance of all-out challenge to an economy structured by apartheid and capitalism, to a concern with the problems of economic reconstruction and industrial restructuring, and a quest for various channels and institutions through which to participate in national economic policy formulation. Concern with building institutions rather than destroying them, solving problems rather than precipitating crises, governing rather than opposing, had profound implications for organisational policies and practices, culture and identity.

As an affiliate of COSATU, NUMSA also grappled with the need to develop a new strategy in response to the changing political and economic landscape. Not only was the metal union a leading protagonist in the evolution of COSATU's strategy of reconstruction, it also developed policies for engaging with restructuring in the metal industry. Like other COSATU affiliates, NUMSA was faced with complex problems of company restructuring – retrenchments, outsourcing, new technology, reorganisation of production. The transition from a closed economy to an open one had severe implications for trade unions because of increasing competitive pressure on employers. The union began to develop a focus on skills formation, training, grading and narrowing the 'apartheid wage gap' as a strategy for addressing pressures for improved productivity (Von Holdt 1991a, 1991b).

NUMSA developed a programme of research groups for shop stewards (including two from Highveld Steel), which comprised seminars and overseas study tours to a number of countries, including Australia. NUMSA's strategic vision was strongly influenced by 'strategic unionism' as it had developed in Australia, and in 1992 an Australian unionist who had been closely associated with the development of strategic unionism was employed by NUMSA as a head office official. By the beginning of 1993, these internal processes had culminated in the adoption of a new negotiating strategy. This set goals to be achieved over a period of three years to replace the annual bargaining goals, and came to be known as 'the three-year programme'. In NUMSA's assessment, South African employers were choosing a strategy of 'lean production' in response to competitive pressures. This would, in the view of the union, entrench racial inequality. In contrast, the union strategy aimed to transform the apartheid workplace regime and construct a new non-racial order in the workplace based on workplace democracy, with the focus on 'intelligent production' rather than 'lean production'.[8]

The thrust of the bargaining strategy was to establish a new framework linking grading, training, skills development, pay and work organisation in the industry. Broadly speaking, the aim was to move from the highly differentiated, racist and anomalous system of 14 grades, to a five-grade system based on skills levels and known as 'broad banding'. Workers would have a clear career path up the grading ladder based on acquiring new skills through training. Wage gaps would be narrowed and wage levels would be determined by the levels of workers' skills. Restructuring would be based on more skilled work and higher value added as the workforce became more skilled. The shift away from narrow job demarcation would open the way for flexibility and teamwork based on multi-skilling and so would allow for a more competitive industry as well as greater job satisfaction.

The reconstruction strategy adopted by NUMSA shared the broader ambiguities of the RDP in relation to capitalism. On the one hand, it stressed that reconstruction was a strategy for achieving socialist goals, and it was based on building working-class power in society. On the other, it presented itself as a strategy for modernising and revitalising capitalism in the context of globalisation and increased competitive pressure. These ambiguities reflected the contradictory and contested nature of the process of class incorporation on the terrain of 'reconstruction'.

NUMSA's new strategy has been termed 'strategic unionism', based on the model of the strategic unionism developed by the Australian trade union movement (Joffe et al. 1995). Strategic unionism, itself an attempt to transplant the strategies of Scandinavian social democratic unionism into the Australian trade union movement, was a response to globalisation and industrial restructuring, and focused on industrial policy and workplace change (Ewer et al 1991). It was characterised by four features: union involvement in *wealth creation*, not just redistribution; *proactive* rather than reactive unionism; *participation* through bipartite and tripartite institutions; and a high level of union *capacity* in education and research ('Strategic unionism' 1989).

The strategy of reconstruction in Witbank: the political dimension

The dominant view among shop stewards and many workers was that the union movement should engage in a strategy of reconstruction that mirrored the strategy adopted by COSATU at a national level. This strategy, which was most coherently articulated by the shop steward leadership, most of whom were actively involved in the Tripartite Alliance as COSATU representatives, and some of whom occupied leadership positions in the local branch of the ANC, had the following elements:

- union commitment to political, social and economic development beyond the workplace;
- an alliance with, and participation within, the ANC;
- a strong role for organisations in civil society, including labour, in elaborating and implementing the RDP, and holding the ANC and government accountable;
- a strong role for labour in institution building, institutional transformation and democratisation in society;
- a continuing struggle for workplace change, with militancy, tactics and demands tempered in one way or another to avoid weakening the government or undermining the economy;
- recognition of contestation between labour and 'opportunists' in the ANC over the primacy of meeting the needs of the poor;
- recognition of contestation between labour and 'capitalists' both within the ANC and in society more broadly over development.

Strengthening and supporting the ANC, engaging and influencing it through the Tripartite Alliance and through becoming active members and leaders within it, would contribute organisational and negotiating experience, and ensure the ANC met the needs of the people. This was how the shop stewards explained their decision to stand as ANC candidates for the town council.[9]

This commitment to strengthening and influencing the ANC was marked with a degree of ambivalence. On the one hand, the shop stewards felt 'at home' in the ANC because 'it articulates the basic demands of the people' and the ANC and COSATU 'agree on issues'; on the other, they expressed a fear that the ANC might distance itself from the masses or the workers, and adopt policies more favourable to 'the capitalists':

> If we do not have our people inside there, if we are not involved as shop stewards, the ANC government can turn its back and follow the capitalists. It was very difficult for COSATU to convince the ANC to go along with the RDP.[10]

This was because there were 'opportunists' in the ANC who were pursuing their own interests and because many activists in the ANC failed to adopt democratic practices. It was to prevent this danger that it was so important for COSATU leaders to be deployed to work within the ANC. COSATU was like 'a mini-government because they have practical experience of democratic structures and the workers are the most democratic people in the country'.[11]

The shop stewards added that COSATU should not only rely on trade unionists *within* the ANC to ensure that it implemented the RDP, but that COSATU 'must maintain its independence and work as a watchdog of the ANC; whenever the ANC deviates, try to bring it back'. If the ANC failed to implement the RDP then 'hard luck, we will *toyi-toyi* against them'.[12]

In the view of the shop stewards, the transition to democracy was a breakthrough on the political front, but employers were not yet prepared to accept the need for change, both within the workplace and in contributing to the development of communities. Their concern was still 'only for profits, not to uplift the people of the country'. It was 'the duty of the companies that they must contribute in the community, because it is the community that is working for the companies'. During the apartheid era companies were able to hide behind the government, but the advent of democracy meant that an ANC government could 'assist us as COSATU to push companies' by applying pressure from above, both to contribute to the RDP and to accept the need for some form of democracy and improvement in working conditions in the workplace. At the same time, organised workers should apply pressure from below, linking their demands in the factories to RDP programmes in the community. This could create a new relationship between employers and unions.[13]

While the ANC was regarded as the leading organisation in the national liberation struggle, and as the natural ally of COSATU, the shop stewards demonstrated a critical awareness of the dangers of elitism, undemocratic and autocratic practices and 'opportunism' within the ANC, and the danger that the ANC could drift towards the agenda of business. In other words, policy and practices within the ANC were contested terrain, and workers and COSATU needed to remain vigilant in ensuring worker and popular interests were pursued.

There was, however, a minority dissenting voice among some shop stewards and workers, ranging from those who expressed stronger reservations about the ANC, to those who thought the ANC would not represent workers' interests and felt union strategy should not change. Among the former was J.J. Mbonani:

> After the unbanning of the ANC some of them were acting like bosses, and I hate that. When the leadership is speaking in front of the people, you'll find the guy is speaking like a king, or like somebody from heaven, not from the earth. This is the leadership who we knew ourselves.

This led him to conclude that 'we need to build COSATU stronger than before so that if our demands fail then we must be in a position to take a hard line' in relation to the ANC.[14]

Another shop steward expressed a strong scepticism about 'politicians':

> Maybe the Alliance should break off after the elections, and let COSATU be COSATU and the politicians be politicians. Politicians

are not predictable. Today they are like this, and tomorrow they are like other people – you won't know them. They are not like unions. We have got shop stewards who know exactly what is the mandate and are there to guide the workers. Now that we are the government, workers must go back to work and leave the politicians alone.[15]

This view resonated with another shop steward, who argued that an ANC government would not do anything to improve workers wages. The time-tested strategy of militancy would put pressure both on employers and the ANC to recognise workers' demands. Political exiles gained education while workers struggled and suffered inside the country, and even Mandela should be ignored when he advised workers not to strike because he was paid so much more than the ordinary workers. The town council should be left to the 'politicians'; shop stewards who were ANC politicians had divided loyalties and could not be trusted, and shop stewards should concentrate on representing workers interests, both in the workplace and in the community.[16]

This 'workerist' view tended to be based on a general suspicion of 'politicians' and political organisations rather than a specific critique of the ANC. Its adherents advocated that trade unionists should withdraw from active politics and concentrate on shopfloor issues rather than establish a political alternative. If necessary COSATU should put pressure on the ANC government from an independent position. In arguing for withdrawing from the Alliance, such shop stewards were articulating a formal position specific to NUMSA at the time;[17] but while the NUMSA resolution argued for the formation of a socialist political alternative to the ANC, these shop stewards tended to express a general reservation about politics and wanted to see a focus on trade union activities in the workplace and industry. Some argued that the union should not change the strategies evolved during the 1980s, but should continue to mobilise militant actions in pursuit of their demands.

This view was in many respects simply a stronger version of the critical attitudes displayed towards the ANC by most of the shop stewards, and there was no explicit disagreement or conflict among shop stewards over the strategy of reconstruction. However, it did point to some of the tensions inherent in the strategy, and when such tensions erupted in internal conflict this discourse would be available to those critical of the shop stewards or seeking to build their own power base for whatever reasons.

The new strategy of reconstruction provided the shop stewards with a framework for analysing the range of interests on the terrain of reconstruction, and the consequent need for contestation. As with the adoption of any new strategy, there were ambiguities and silences. Chief of these was whether the unions would be able to influence the policies and practices of the ANC as they hoped – whether the balance of forces within and around the ANC was propitious for their project – an issue that was raised most forcefully by proponents of the dissenting view and is explored in the next chapter.

The strategy of reconstruction at Highveld Steel: the workplace dimension

By 1993 the shop stewards at Highveld Steel and their regional organiser were articulating a radical vision of workplace democracy. Shop stewards talked about a quite diverse spread of goals, which they believed could reinforce each other: worker control of production, a say in the utilisation of profits, economic reconstruction, company competitiveness, overcoming the legacy of apartheid, and better training, skills and pay for workers. Different shop stewards emphasised different aspects of these goals but for the leading strategist among the shop stewards, Mosi Nhlapo, who was the chair of the steelworks committee, the chief goal was to extend worker power and control in the workplace. However, workplace reconstruction also had to benefit the community:

> Firstly, our goal is to give more control, more power, to the workers in their activities. Secondly, to make work easier for workers. One of the most important points is to change the relationship between management and workers, so that there should be mutual understanding between them. We want to make sure that at the end the workers benefit from the process of producing steel. The end result will be more productivity and better quality goods. You need to look at expansion of the factory to employ more. You must tie management to social programmes so that they are socially responsible. If you don't do that, whatever you are doing inside is

going to be doomed because those outside the factory will shout at you: you guys are getting so much money, you get houses, you're living well.[18]

The transition to democracy should not be confined to the political realm, but should be extended to the workplace:

The political structure outside is changing. We are now going to be involved in everything that is taking place in our country, and we feel as workers that we should also be involved in deciding what we want to see our company doing. We don't want to live in the past, where management had to think and decide for us.[19]

Decolonisation made the old apartheid workplace regime unsustainable, and created the opportunity to replace it with a new, democratic and non-racial regime in the workplace.[20] Apartheid had denied blacks access to skills and power, and democracy meant this must change. Just as the apartheid workplace regime had been linked to the political and social structures of apartheid beyond the factory, so the ending of apartheid outside the factory had to be linked to ending it within the factory.[21]

Political liberation meant not only that workers wanted more power, skill and control in the workplace, but also that the unions had a 'duty' to help rebuild the economy.[22] Reconstruction required a new culture of productivity among workers, and a new attitude to management – but it would not be easy to change the culture of resistance forged during the 1980s:

Now that we have a democratic government, we want to see it succeeding, and of course no political power can be maintained if there is no economic power. Our economy has been devastated by the system of apartheid, and we need to rebuild it now. So I believe that the culture definitely has to change from the culture of resistance and ungovernability to the culture of productivity. One must say that there are problems. It is difficult for the workers to change from that culture, the workers still believe that they must always resist anything that comes with management, be it right or wrong. A culture of resistance is inherent in the hearts and minds of the workers. I am sure to change that culture there has to be a process of learning.[23]

Democracy also meant that members should end their wildcat actions and start following procedures in the workplace.[24] The union could not focus solely on extending workers' power. The need to rebuild the economy implied that companies needed to become more productive to survive the increasing competitive pressures of globalisation.[25]

The goals of economic growth, benefits for workers, and job creation were interlinked.[26] Becoming competitive required a new system of production because 'the system we are using here in South Africa cannot compete in the global market'. Apartheid had bequeathed a legacy of unskilled and illiterate workers, and new technology would require new skills.[27] According to the new union programme, training and multi-skilling would meet the new goals *both* of empowering workers and improving their pay, *and* of improving productivity and quality, so building a strong and competitive economy.[28]

Multi-skilling and teamwork would also provide the basis for radical democracy in the workplace, with the devolution of power, skill and responsibility to the shopfloor, collective control of production and the elimination of supervision:

Our idea is that you take planning of work out of the offices and into the people. You set up work teams that are able to set their own targets, that can produce quality, that can run the show without the superintendent, the foreman, the assistant foreman standing there and telling you what the manager in the office is saying you must do. The office must give the production order to the people, and they should set their own priorities, their targets. There should be no supervisor within them. If they want a supervisor they can elect someone from amongst themselves. People must not feel a painful responsibility. When they wake up in the morning they should feel that they want to go to work, that they will enjoy it.[29]

Collective control of production should be matched by participation in the decision-making structures of management. The right to participate in making decisions at this level would make it possible for the union and its members to take responsibility for the performance of the company.[30]

The new strategy implied a different approach to collective bargaining:

The union was mainly concentrating on real worker issues, issues that were affecting the members in the factory. Once there was this realisation that you cannot divide the factory from the economics of the country, the approach changed. Merely by forming our own research groups, that's a pointer to say there's a change within the union, we've been unrealistic as a union. We have been a union that demanded this thing here and now, not understanding the problems within the demand, and how long it can take to achieve them. We were sort of negotiating uninformed about what we were proposing to employers. Research has shown us that you need to have a complete approach to things. This is changing the whole focus of the union.[31]

The new approach implied not only that the union needed to be more informed, more open to the concerns of management and more cognisant of the complexities and difficulties of meeting worker demands, but also that there was scope for constructing a shared interest in a more productive workplace, with increased benefits for workers and improved productivity for the company. A co-operative relationship between management and workers, based on compromise, was essential for reconstruction to be a success: 'As the union we can initiate, but if management does not agree, at the end of the day there will be no reconstruction programme.' The danger of not fighting for co-operation was that the union would be unable to protect workers from the hazards of unilateral workplace restructuring, such as health and safety risks or job loss. However, this co-operation could be quite limited since the two parties had different aims and the union would have to monitor and police agreements.[32]

Several of the shop stewards at Highveld Steel saw their strategy of democratising the workplace and improving productivity as having a socialist dimension, but were at the same time grappling with what socialism might mean in newly democratic South Africa.

The need to retain white skills and stability was a barrier to radical change. The union project for democratising the company was a way of gradually achieving socialist goals. In this light, the distinction between capitalism and socialism appeared to grow less:

> Socialism and capitalism are more or less the same. The only difference is that capitalism is a clique of people on top, running the economy, and socialism is about worker involvement. Even now, when we talk about worker involvement in terms of restructuring, it disguises that we are talking about socialism. We want to take decisions about profits, we want to take decisions how to run the factories. It disguises socialism.[33]

A second shop steward teased out this reformist theme in the direction of social democracy. If effective regulation of capital met the needs of the people, it should be regarded as socialism:

> If the people on the ground are satisfied with the way capital is used and are benefiting from that system in which capital is used, then I wonder what we are going to call it. If it is capitalism but the people are benefiting down there, then I think it is right. If it is communism and the people are benefiting, then I think it is right. As far as the basic principles of socialism are concerned, they are not applicable now.[34]

A third shop steward had come to an even more limited conclusion: socialism is 'managing our work, or what is it?'[35]

Problems with the new strategy

Despite their support for the three-year programme, shop stewards and officials recognised a number of problems with it, ranging from the process through which it was adopted, its complexity and the lack of union capacity, to doubts about its internal coherence, and the possibility that it could increase members' workload and lead to job losses.

The research groups had been introduced to ensure workers' involvement in developing the new strategy, but this generated tensions within NUMSA. They were developing policy for the union yet they were not constitutional bodies, nor were they elected. The elected union leadership resented the study trips and time off from work enjoyed by the research group participants. There were complaints that too much union money was spent on them. The research groups were first reduced in size, then scrapped.[36] The result, according to Nhlapo, who continued representing the union in meetings of the Metal Industries Training Board (MITB), was a further disempowering of workers.[37]

The concentration of increasingly complex expertise in fewer and fewer hands undermined democracy:

Information is concentrated in a few individuals. Decisions are no longer based on information, they're based on who says it. He might be complicated and say things you don't understand, but at the end of the day you are bound to agree with him because you don't understand. You don't have any way to say, No, I will debate it. That is the change in the union. Everything will be concentrated in the head office unless we do something very drastic.[38]

The rush to draft and adopt the three-year programme before collective bargaining in 1993 left many shop stewards and officials confused:

It was just discussed at head office level. When it came down to the regions, definitely the majority of the people did not understand what the hell was going on. We just went to our people and said, Listen, we want to reduce the grades, when there are five grades you'll get a lot of money. People said, 'Ja, we'll endorse it!' There was a rush to get this thing through the National Executive Committee and make it a proposal to the employers. It started to alienate our members from the structures and from everything, that's how we gradually lost touch with our members.

This was justified with a promise never before heard in NUMSA – that 'we'll discuss the demands with the members while we're discussing them with the employers'.[39] The development and adoption of the new strategy was highly controversial in the union:

The debate in NUMSA about this restructuring was a big debate. It nearly split the union. People just walked out of meetings. The question would be, 'Is this going to be socialism?' And no one could say yes, this is going to be socialism, we will move from here to here. The one who was asked that question would answer by asking another question: 'What do we do in the interim then? Do you think we must take up arms and fight the bosses and kill them and take over the factories? Do you think that's what you want?' Obviously we wouldn't agree to that. That debate was never finalised in the union. Whether at the end the strategy will achieve the goals that we are all striving for is not clear.[40]

This conflict echoes at a more ideological level the comment by the chairperson of the joint shop stewards' committee, quoted above, about the difficulty of replacing the 'culture of resistance' with a 'culture of productivity'. Clearly the new programme entailed a significant shift in strategy and organisational culture for NUMSA, which was reflected in something of an ideological crisis.

Quite aside from its political implications, the new programme was extremely complex and required both a sophisticated technical understanding of the issues, and a nuanced tactical and strategic ability. Shop stewards were quite frank about their weakness in regard to this:

It is confusing because we are not so clear, all of us, about this three-year programme. We still need more training so that we can understand the change of NUMSA. The people who understand this thing are very few in the union.[41]

Another shop steward expressed the view that there was only one shop steward, Mosi Nhlapo, 'who is well-informed about restructuring'.[42] Nor would workers necessarily elect shop stewards who had the skills or commitment to understand the new programme.[43] Notwithstanding these weaknesses, the leadership at Highveld Steel was a particularly talented and capable group of shop stewards who had been empowered by the participation of two of them in the research groups. They had more likelihood of successfully implementing the new programme than most other shop steward committees.[44]

Besides the complexity of the programme, there was the question of its coherence. As a programme it sought to achieve a diverse range of goals: laying the groundwork for socialism, increasing the power of workers on the shopfloor and in the company, improving the quality of working life, and making the company competitive. Could all of these goals be encompassed in one strategy? Were they compatible? If not, different understandings of the goals of the programme could make it difficult to implement. Even among the main union strategists at head office there were confusing differences of interpretation.[45]

The strategy entailed a tension between struggle and co-operation: co-operation to achieve competitiveness, struggle to enhance workers' power and lay a basis for socialism. Could these goals be reconciled? Nhlapo expressed reservations about the degree of co-operation that was feasible, because both the union and management wanted greater control over production:

> It depends whether the objectives of the strategy are still socialism. In the interim one envisages more co-operation, but management would like to see co-operation between management and *workers*, trying to sideline the union a bit. Management would like the result to be more co-operation, but no control for unions. A union that is said to be socialist would like to use its power to start driving the process. That is why there is no agreement, because there is uncertainty. We would say, but what is the strategy of management? Where do they want to lead us? Management would say, we must not involve the union too much, we must just consult them but it must end there.[46]

Whereas productivity could be a common goal 'whether you are a capitalist or a socialist', capitalists wanted the profits of productivity for themselves, while 'we would like to share the profit among the people who are making production'. It was to influence decision-making over how profit should be used that the union was demanding participation at the highest levels, not only on the shopfloor.[47]

For Nhlapo, there was also a disjunction between the socialist pretensions of the strategy and the lack of mobilisation in support of it: 'It's impossible to take a radical stance now, because the workers do not understand the strategy.'[48] The issue of power in the workplace was not explicitly addressed in the programme, and this gave rise to ambiguity (Von Holdt 1995). For some of the shop stewards it appeared possible to persuade management that worker control of production was in their own best interests. In the view of another, the *appearance* of ownership was an adequate goal: since 'ownership by workers is not practical' workers should 'have a feeling of ownership' and work 'as if it belonged to them'.[49] The similarity of these words to the discourse of new human resource management is striking. These ambiguities reflect an underlying ambivalence in the attitude of the trade unionists to incorporation and institutional participation. On the one hand, they realised that the strategy of reconstruction depended on such processes; on the other, they stressed the need for continuing with the practices of contentious mobilisation forged in the 1980s. Recasting these two dimensions of unionism for the new conditions created by democracy and reconstruction would be a difficult and contradictory endeavour.

Such contradiction did not only surface in ideological confusion or silences, but in the potential for confusion on the shopfloor. Most of the shop stewards acknowledged that company restructuring would increase productivity and therefore result in job losses, and explained that this problem could be resolved by expanding downstream production at the company, or providing substantial training programmes for retrenched workers to enable them to find jobs elsewhere. But in more reflective moments they acknowledged confusion about this issue:

> Really, I don't think I am qualified to say exactly what our position is going to be when that time comes. Even now it is my fear. Management was very pleased when a union official mentioned that when the steel industry restructures people lose their jobs. They keep on reminding us what he said, intimidating us. But still we are saying we must restructure.[50]

Other shop stewards voiced fears that the union programme would fail because workers would reject multi-skilling as loading them with extra work. After returning from a company-sponsored visit to steel plants in the United

States and Germany, shop stewards expressed anxiety about retrenchment and the increased workload and stress that could be the consequences of increased productivity. The result could be conflict and confusion on the shopfloor, divisions within the union, and the growth of rival unions.[51]

There were, therefore, anxieties among the shop stewards that the new NUMSA programme had been adopted too hastily, that it was extremely complex and that very few shop stewards or officials had sufficient understanding of it to negotiate or implement it in the workplace, and that it was contributing to a decline in union democracy. Technical complexity was compounded by diverse and possibly incompatible goals, uncertainty about the real objectives of the strategy, and a very real fear about the consequences of retrenchments and increased workloads, both for workers and the union.

Conclusion

The strategy of reconstruction provided a framework for contesting the process of working-class incorporation through attempting to ensure that workers' interests – and broader working-class interests – were recognised and accommodated. Its goals were to entrench workers organisational autonomy, power and voice in workplace and industry, and beyond this in the ANC, the town council and in the community. This would provide the basis for continuously negotiating, contesting and shaping reconstruction in post-colonial South Africa. It attempted to blend the established union vision, practices and meanings forged in the resistance of social movement unionism to apartheid, with new goals, practices and meanings required for reconstruction: on the one hand, transformation in a post-colonial society; on the other, competitiveness in a more exposed economy. This implied substantially recasting the relationship between institutional participation and contentious mobilisation.

The attempt to blend contradictory goals and practices accounts for the ambiguities and contradictions of the strategy – and the internal conflict and uncertainties articulated by unionists in this chapter. This illuminates what a major shift in strategy and vision entails for a mass organisation like a trade union. The social structure of a trade union is built around its vision and goals, and is embodied in its organisational culture and practices. The adoption of a new vision and goals necessarily entails a new organisational culture and practices, disturbing the social structure and provoking internal contestation and negotiation in which elements of the historically constituted social structure are carried forward in uneasy co-existence with elements of the new. This itself generates uncertainty and conflict. The danger is that it may so deeply undermine or damage core aspects of organisational culture that it weakens or destroys the organisation.

More specifically, the adoption of 'strategic unionism' by the Australian trade union movement was a project to reconstitute the terms of incorporation of the Australian working class under conditions of globalisation – but the tasks facing South African trade unions were substantially different: contesting and shaping the founding moment of class incorporation on the terrain of post-colonial reconstruction. Was 'strategic unionism' an adequate project for meeting this challenge?

The collective bargaining programme actually adopted by NUMSA had a narrower focus than the ambitious vision articulated both nationally and by the Highveld Steel shop stewards, and more closely resembled the programme of the Australian unions.[52] Imported into a social movement unionism with a more radical, militant, democratic and contested social structure than that of the Australian unions, it threatened to disrupt practices and cultures that had been forged over the previous decade of union struggle, undermining collective identity and solidarity.[53] Nor was it clear that the collective bargaining programme was adequate for the specific problems of the transition in the South African workplace – especially the prospect of retrenchment from restructured workplaces in a society already suffering from extraordinarily high levels of unemployment.

Notes

1. Interview, Albert Makagula, 29/3/94.
2. Interview, J.J. Mbonani, 7/6/94.
3. Interview, Tshagata, 10/95; see also interview, Ezekiel Nkosi, 5/5/94 and interview, Jerry Mogoleko, 10/95 for similar comments.
4. Interview, Philip Mkatshwa, 7/6/94; see also interview, J.J. Mbonani, 7/6/94; interview, Johannes Phatlana, 7/9/94.
5. Interview, J.J. Mbonani, 7/6/94.

6. Interview, Ambrose Mthembu, 26/4/94; interview, Ezekiel Nkosi, 15/4/94.
7. Interview, Hendrik Nkosi, 14/6/94; see also chapter 10.
8. This account of the new NUMSA strategy is based on Bird (1990); Joffe et al. (1995); Lloyd (1994); Von Holdt (1993a, 1995); and the interviews with shop stewards at Highveld Steel.
9. Interview, Ezekiel Nkosi, 9/3/94, 5/5/94, 23/11/95.
10. Interview, Ezekiel Nkosi, 9/3/94, 5/5/94.
11. Interview, Meshack Malinga, 15/3/94; interview, Leslie Nhlapo, 12/95; interview, Ezekiel Nkosi, 9/3/94, 5/5/94; interview, Jacob Skhosana, 26/4/94.
12. Interview, Ezekiel Nkosi, 9/3/94; interview, Jacob Skhosana, 26/4/94; see also interview, Meshack Malinga, 15/3/94; interview, J.J. Mbonani, 7/6/94; interview, Ambrose Mthembu, 26/4/94; interview, Ezekiel Nkosi, 5/5/94.
13. Interview, Ezekiel Nkosi, 9/3/94, 5/5/94; see also interview, Hendrik Nkosi, 15/4/94.
14. Interview, J.J. Mbonani, 7/6/94.
15. Interview, Jacob Skhosana, 26/4/94; see also interview, Phineas Mabena, 12/5/94.
16. Interview, Philip Mkatshwa, 7/6/94, 8/95.
17. This resolution was adopted by NUMSA and motivated at COSATU's 1994 congress, where it failed to find a second union prepared to support it. NUMSA later replaced this resolution with one endorsing the alliance.
18. Interview, Mosi Nhlapo, 8/5/94.
19. Interview, Jacob Skhosana, 26/4/94.
20. See also interview, Hong Kong Kgalima, 3/7/94; interview, Hendrik Nkosi, 14/6/94.
21. Interview, Ezekiel Nkosi, 23/11/95.
22. Ibid.
23. Interview, Meshack Malinga, 12/5/94, 14/5/94.
24. Interview, Ambrose Mthembu, 14/5/94; interview, Mosi Nhlapo, 10/7/94.
25. Interview, Mosi Nhlapo, 10/7/94.
26. Interview, Ezekiel Nkosi, 23/11/95.
27. Ibid; interview, Jacob Skhosana, 26/4/94; see also interview, Johannes Phatlana, 15/4/94.
28. Interview, Ezekiel Nkosi, 15/4/94; see also interview, Jacob Skhosana, 26/4/94.
29. Interview, Bunny Mahlangu, 12/5/94; see also interview, Ezekiel Nkosi, 9/3/94.
30. Interview, Ezekiel Nkosi, 15/4/94; see also interview, Johannes Phatlana, 15/4/94.
31. Interview, Bunny Mahlangu, 12/5/94.
32. Interview, Ambrose Mthembu, 26/4/94; interview, Johannes Phatlana, 15/4/94.
33. Interview, Ezekiel Nkosi, 23/11/95.
34. Interview, Ambrose Mthembu, 15/3/94.
35. Interview, Jacob Skhosana, 14/4/95.
36. Interview, Mosi Nhlapo, 15/3/94, 5/5/94.
37. Interview, Mosi Nhlapo, 15/3/94.
38. Interview, Mosi Nhlapo, 8/5/94.
39. Interview, Bunny Mahlangu, 12/5/94. Criticism of the way the three-year programme

was adopted was not confined to the Highveld region, but was common across the union (Von Holdt 1993a, 1995).

40. Interview, Mosi Nhlapo, 8/5/94.

41. Interview, Ezekiel Nkosi, 15/4/94; see also interview, Bunny Mahlangu, 12/5/94; interview, Ambrose Mthembu, 14/5/94; interview, Mosi Nhlapo, 15/3/94, 8/5/94.

42. Interview, Philip Mkatshwa, 7/6/94.

43. Interview, Mosi Nhlapo, 8/5/94.

44. Comments by NUMSA head office officials when the idea of a research project on Highveld Steel was discussed with them; see also interview, Bunny Mahlangu, 12/5/94; and personal observation.

45. Interview, Mosi Nhlapo, 15/3/94.

46. Interview, Mosi Nhlapo, 8/5/94.

47. Interview, Meshack Malinga, 12/5/94.

48. Interview, Mosi Nhlapo, 8/5/94.

49. Interview, Jacob Skhosana, 26/4/94.

50. Interview, Ambrose Mthembu, 26/4/94.

51. Interview, Philip Mkatshwa, 8/95; interview, Ambrose Mthembu, 26/4/94; interview, Ezekiel Nkosi, 15/4/94, 23/11/95.

52. This more ambitious and radical vision was reflected in the way the term 'strategic unionism' was used in the labour-aligned *South African Labour Bulletin*; for example, 'Strategic unionism is a strategy for far-reaching reform of the state, of the workplace, of economic decision-making and of civil society. It is a strategy driven by a broad-based coalition of interest groups, at the centre of which is the labour movement. Strategic unionism develops a step-by-step programme of radical reforms – each of which extends the arena of democratic decision-making, and deepens the power of the working class' (Von Holdt 1992: 33). This contrasts with the more conventional usage in academic articles in South Africa, such as Joffe et al. (1995).

53. Ironically, in the view of some critics the attempt to graft social democratic strategies onto the 'labourism' of the Australian unions also failed (see Ewer et al 1991).

CHAPTER 8

'The government is ours'

Shop stewards, reconstruction and class formation during the transition in Witbank[1]

> The difference is not between being a shop steward and being a councillor. The difference is the period we are coming from and the period we are in now. What is the role of the shop steward nowadays? Is the role of the shop steward just to stay in the factory and represent workers there, and lead some marches?

The strategy of reconstruction was designed to shape and contest processes of working class incorporation in post-colonial South Africa. This chapter assesses the success of the strategy in shaping reconstruction at a local level in the town of Witbank, and the impact on the union at Highveld Steel.

Leadership and democracy in the ANC branch[2]
The account in chapter 4 of union involvement beyond the workplace in the popular movement ended with the launch of the interim ANC branch in 1990. The NUMSA leadership in Witbank had been sidelined as community activists regrouped on the less repressive political terrain of 1989 in preparation for the unbanning of the ANC. This was a period of intense political and organisational activity in Witbank as activists sought to position themselves in a rapidly changing political landscape.

The newly launched interim ANC branch served as a platform for its chairperson, Benson Khumalo, to position himself in the regional politics of the ANC. He and other members of the Witbank executive spent most of their time in Nelspruit, and the Witbank branch of the ANC remained relatively inactive. NUMSA shop stewards were highly critical of this activist and his 'clique', and their track record in the UDF and the ANC:

He never wanted to work with us. He'd prefer to work with guys in Jo'burg and Pretoria and Nelspruit, neglecting the people of Witbank. He was once a secretary of UDF, although we couldn't understand why this guy became something big when there was nothing where he came from. Whenever he came to Witbank, he would come up with his own programmes and implement them halfway and leave us. He would come and cause problems here, so we had to deal with him and these other guys if we wanted to get Witbank right. He's not a democratic guy, he likes to do things for himself. He's a good guy. He's a hard worker and he's committed – the problem is that he does things for himself.

In the view of the unionists, the community activists constituted a clique which tried to control political activity: 'If you go to a civic meeting you would find them, you would go to an ANC meeting and you would find them, you would go to a UDF meeting and find them.' NUMSA unionists were accused of being 'workerists', and found themselves unable to speak in community meetings.

The ANC branch was still only an interim structure, and a launching conference, to be presided over by UDF national secretary Popo Molefe, was organised for early 1991. Only one member of the NUMSA group had managed to join the ANC, and he attended the meeting, determined to 'smash' the clique. He was able to use the classical tactics of the trade unionist – attention to constitutional procedure and detail – to do exactly that, and found himself elected to a new interim executive in an almost comical fashion:

When we came there the hall was full. People like the interim chairperson and the others wanted to be re-elected into positions, the way they were talking there. I decided, 'I'm not going to allow this thing to happen, but I don't know how to stop it!' And when we were about to start the elections for the new executive, I raised my hand. I asked if everyone who was in that hall had a card. I took out my card and I said, 'This is my membership card. I believe that only those who have membership cards are eligible to vote. Why don't we ask those with no cards to go outside?' Only to find there were only two of us with cards – myself and the chairperson.

The community activists pressed for elections to be held nonetheless; but Molefe declared this unconstitutional. A new interim executive was elected to recruit members, maintain proper membership and financial records and convene a new conference when at least 100 members had been recruited, as stipulated in the ANC constitution. The NUMSA activist was elected to this interim executive, and when the launching conference was finally held, he was elected vice-secretary. His comrade, a former Highveld Steel shop steward, was elected secretary: 'That is when we started emerging as the people who had direction, and we held very senior positions in the various organisations.'

The new leadership of unionists and community activists introduced a new culture into the ANC branch. Regular general meetings were held to discuss and plan activities and nominate candidates for the ANC election lists. Candidates, delegates and leadership began to be elected 'because of the work that they are doing, not because of who they are known by'. The unionists believed that they played an important role in forging this new culture, but it remained difficult to consolidate the different practices and styles of activists with different backgrounds. There was not only the different organisational and political culture of the union activists and the community activists; those with a background in MK, exile or Robben Island also had different 'cultures'. A commander from MK would 'be used to giving instructions and not listening to other people's fears'. Those from the Island or exile 'believed they had made more contributions to the struggle than anyone else; they expected a hero's welcome and they saw themselves as the ideal leadership, never concerning themselves about any democratic process that should take place before one could claim to be a leader'.

The influence of trade union activists in branch structures was not matched by the participation of union members in general meetings. Shop stewards expressed disappointment that despite a membership of more than 5 000, many of whom were union members ('more than two thirds of Highveld workers are card-carrying members of the ANC') general meetings were attended by only about 100 ANC members. The majority tended to be youths, unemployed residents and women, rather than union members.

The interventions of NUMSA shop stewards in the ANC contributed both to building the Witbank branch as a relatively dynamic and effective organisation, and to forging democratic organisational practices and culture. This facilitated local political activity, empowered local grassroots activists to participate in such activity, and enabled them to engage with transformation of the town council, and in the developmental challenges posed by the Witbank Development Forum. By engaging in this way, NUMSA shop stewards made a significant contribution to reconstruction through institution building and democratisation at a local level. The ANC was the key vehicle for establishing a new democratic order in Witbank.

The 1994 elections[3]

COSATU put a tremendous amount of resources and energy into the election campaign. It is fair to say that it was the federation's sole focus in the four months of 1994 leading up to the election in April. A National Elections Commission was formed, with Regional Elections Commissions, to co-ordinate the federation's campaign efforts and link these with the election structures of its Alliance partners. Shop stewards at Highveld Steel described the goals of their election campaigning as 'popularising the ANC, making sure that it is understood by the people and making sure that the ANC wins the election by a large majority'.

The region was divided into five sub-regions, each co-ordinated by an official or shop steward seconded full-time from the affiliates to work on the elections campaign. The chairperson of the Highveld Steel joint shop steward committee was included as a candidate on the ANC's provincial list, and was chosen as the co-ordinator of the Witbank sub-region. These structures corresponded to similar structures in the ANC and the SACP so co-ordination would be relatively easy. The COSATU election structures developed their own programme of activities, and then tried to co-ordinate this with the programmes of the Alliance partners, for example by inviting ANC activists and candidates to address COSATU meetings.

The COSATU region developed an intensive programme of activities – workers' forums, lunchtime meetings at the workplace, rallies, marches of the unemployed, women's prayer meetings for peace, meetings with small businesspeople, candidate walkabouts, door-to-door visits, voter education, mock elections, putting up posters – aimed at targeted constituencies such as workers, women, church congregations, the unemployed, business people, mineworkers, patients and nurses at hospitals, as well as the community in general. Every day in March and April was filled with such activities or with planning sessions.

COSATU and its affiliates did not only second officials and candidates to work full-time for the elections on COSATU salaries; they also made office space, photocopiers, faxes and telephones available. Shop stewards formed the organisational backbone for much of the campaign work, and their unions made up the pay they lost because of absence from work. Thus, at Highveld Steel the union negotiated the full-time secondment of the provincial candidate to the election campaign. The company agreed to continue paying his medical and housing benefits, but the union had to pay his salary. Four or five other shop stewards worked virtually full-time on the campaign, and also had to be paid for time away from the factory. One of NUMSA's two regional organisers was also seconded full-time to election work.

The unions also mobilised their organisational structures and networks in support of the ANC election campaign: workplaces and union and federation locals were used to recruit ANC members, conduct voter education programmes and mobilise workers to support the ANC. There were, however, gaps in the effectiveness of these structures and networks. While the most dynamic activists among the shop stewards were involved in a range of political activities beyond their workplaces, many of the other shop stewards found it difficult to mobilise their members for election activities. At a NUMSA shop steward local meeting held in March, it emerged that in the Witbank area only Highveld Steel had arranged any activities, and that few companies had managed to implement any voter education. Ordinary shop stewards appeared confused or anxious about how to arrange such activities, and many cited management's lack of co-operation or insistence that voter education should be undertaken by neutral bodies, as reasons for their inactivity. Shop stewards at Highveld Steel experienced the same problem, but organised the mock elections for lunchtime, secure in the knowledge that shift-workers, with the defiance customary at their company, would find time to leave their jobs and participate as well.[4]

The involvement in election campaigning generated organisational problems for the union in the workplace. The fall-off in union activities and meetings at Highveld Steel, and the protracted absence of senior shop stewards, weakened the organisation and left room for those with grievances against the shop steward leadership to exploit them. During the week immediately preceding the elections virtually all active shop stewards were absent from the steelworks, leaving only one 'reliable' shop steward in the workplace. 'Just imagine if some problem blows up, there is only one shop steward for 3 000 members,' commented one shop steward. A problem did blow up. The entire workforce in Iron Plant One, where there were growing tensions between groups of workers and the shop steward leadership, stayed away for two days over the elections in April, in contravention of COSATU policy and the agreement reached between shop stewards and management at Highveld Steel. This incident is further explored in chapter 10.

During the period of election campaigning there was a noticeable increase in shop stewards' criticism of the ANC. Closer involvement with the world of politics was not inspiring. The process of selecting candidates for the provincial list was fraught with struggles and power-mongering, which saw the provincial candidate from Highveld Steel at the bottom of the list with no chance of making it to the provincial assembly. Such struggles generated tensions between different groupings within the ANC and the Alliance, and raised questions over the credibility of the list. After a meeting with the group of COSATU candidates on the provincial list, one shop steward commented on his despondency, and described problems of ambition, power-seeking, and positioning to get close to the provincial premier-to-be amongst the senior politicians in the province.

During the period of the elections, the inauguration of Nelson Mandela as president, and the formation of the national and provincial governments, many of the politically active shop stewards expressed scepticism about the intentions of the ANC, about national and provincial cabinet and civil service appointments, and about whether the former COSATU regional secretary, who was appointed MEC for economic development in Mpumalanga, intended to represent union interests. Some commented that there was too much focus on reconciliation and too little on reconstruction. Another thought it was time to form a workers' party. Yet another expressed his intention to tell the new premier when he addressed the COSATU regional congress that it was difficult for the unions to learn how to support a government rather than opposing it, and ask him why he was making it even more difficult for the unions to learn how to change.

Nonetheless, the shop stewards continued to support and work for the ANC. There was much to celebrate – an overwhelming victory against apartheid – and new tasks of implementing the RDP, as well as new opportunities for talented individuals. On the evening when the election results were finally announced, the Witbank ANC executive and some of the shop stewards were enjoying a celebratory *braai*[5] in KwaGuqa township. During Mandela's victory speech they heard singing from all over the township. Someone came with a message that the community was gathering in the stadium, 'waiting for the leadership to come and address them'. However, *en route* to the stadium they heard that people were marching towards the 'white' town of Witbank. The leadership drove in that direction and managed to convince the marchers to follow them back to the KwaGuqa stadium, fearing that the march into the white town 'was going to be a mess-up, especially at night, we were going to experience a big problem'.

At the stadium the Alliance leadership had a different problem: 'We didn't have a sound system. We had these small loudhailers and the stadium was packed. They couldn't hear us, but eventually we managed to cool them down, and then we asked them to disperse and told them that meetings and rallies would be arranged where they would enjoy everything, and we would give them the results of the election.'

For both activists and the community, the ANC victory marked the triumphant end to centuries of colonialism and apartheid. The spontaneous march of the community out of the black township of KwaGuqa and towards the white town symbolised this. But the shop stewards and activists knew that the elections were also 'just the beginning'. Their efforts to convince the township marchers to turn back to the stadium, to 'cool them down' with inadequate loudhailers, and their promise of formal celebrations in place of spontaneous action, were perhaps symbolic of the complexities and compromises of this beginning, involving as it did the institutionalisation of popular politics. Soon afterwards the chairperson of the joint shop steward committee would leave the company, not as a Member of the Provincial Legislature (MPL), but as a civil servant responsible for implementing the RDP in the provincial administration. Other Highveld Steel shop stewards would turn their attention to the local development forum and to the countrywide elections for local government.

The recognition by the trade union movement that the ANC was the key vehicle for establishing a new post-colonial order in South Africa accounts for its massive contribution of resources, and the enthusiastic participation of shop stewards in the election campaign. The participation of trade unionists in the first democratic election in South Africa did far more than simply contribute to the victory of the ANC. In their role as Alliance campaigners, organisers and strategists, as voter educators and election monitors, they made an impressive contribution to ensuring that the elections were successful in reaching the widest possible number of voters, thus helping build the institutions of constitutional democracy. They used their organisational, strategic and communication skills to inform the widest number of workers and residents of the importance of the elections, and of how to vote, and in doing so channelled the popular political energy of the 1980s into the institutional politics of the emerging democracy in South Africa.

The Witbank Development Forum[6]
From the early 1990s, Highveld Steel shop stewards were involved in development projects and forums beyond the workplace, both as COSATU representatives and as activists within the ANC. Two shop stewards from Highveld Steel participated in the Witbank Development Forum as ANC representatives, and one of them chaired it. The secretary of the shop steward committee, in his capacity as chairperson of the COSATU local, represented the federation in an initiative to establish a skills training centre in Witbank, and when this project grew in size and was brought under the umbrella of the Development Forum he became the COSATU representative on this.

The shop stewards saw the forum and its initiatives as ways of implementing the RDP, mobilising resources, pressuring local companies to contribute to development, and ensuring that worker and popular interests were served. The forum liaised with local organisations and companies, government agencies and the Development Bank. After the 1994 elections, the training centre project was able to gain financial support of several million rand from the Department of Labour, and was established as the regional headquarters of its training institutions. The new training centre provided technical training in bricklaying, carpentry, plumbing, electrical installation, dressmaking and fashion design, diesel and petrol mechanics, panel-beating and spray-painting. The Reconstruction and Development Committee (RDC), as the development forum was renamed, was also planning to establish a Housing Support Centre, and a Local Business Centre together with an industrial hive, to facilitate the development of small builders, manufacturers and other small businesses. Two of the RDC projects were co-ordinated by shop stewards from Highveld Steel, and others were co-ordinated by an activist from the South African National Civics Organisation (SANCO) and a shop steward from COSATU's teachers affiliate.

Although these developmental initiatives were not monopolised by COSATU shop stewards, they played an important organising and strategic role in their development. Their organisational experience and commitment, their vision of development and the thinking about the RDP that had evolved within COSATU, all equipped them to play an important role in building developmental institutions and capacity in the community. They were able to engage with the initiatives and resources of both the state and business, and channel these into projects facilitating the formation of small businesses, job creation, skills formation and the delivery of housing. In a society sorely lacking in entrepreneurial, managerial and strategic skills, the qualities of the COSATU shop stewards gave them access to many new opportunities. At the time, one of the Highveld shop stewards was considering a suggestion that he apply for the full-time job as manager of the industrial hive. He articulated this as an important strategy for ensuring that the projects retained a progressive direction.

The local town council[7]

In 1993 the government passed legislation that imposed a duty on local government to form forums to negotiate the formation of new transitional local councils, with the 'non-statutory parties' consisting of community organisations and political parties representing those who had been excluded by apartheid. A forum was established at Witbank early in 1994, a process that was driven by the non-statutory parties from the township, since the Witbank Town Council, controlled by the Conservative Party, was extremely reluctant to undergo 'transformation'. The core group of NUMSA shop stewards and former shop stewards from Highveld were active in this process as ANC members.

When the transitional council was established towards the end of 1994, two shop stewards and a former shop steward from Highveld Steel became councillors in the non-statutory delegation. During the year of its existence, the transitional council was able to redirect some municipal resources towards the township – tarring roads, for example – and facilitate some development projects.

Nationwide elections for local government took place in November 1995. The new councils would combine councillors elected from specific constituencies or wards (the ward councillors) and councillors elected according to proportional representation. The ANC proportional representation councillors were elected at a conference attended by delegations from the Tripartite Alliance and the civic organisation. The selection of ward candidates took place through a process of ward general meetings for ANC members, nominations and ward conferences where members chose their candidate. Two Highveld Steel shop stewards, a former shop steward and a Highveld worker were chosen.

As with the national elections in 1994, COSATU put significant resources into the local government elections. In Witbank the ANC won 19 seats out of 30, and 12 of the ANC councillors were members of COSATU affiliates. Nine were NUMSA members, of whom two were officials and four were workers at Highveld Steel (the two officials were compelled to resign from NUMSA immediately, as the union had adopted a resolution that officials could not become councillors). The shop steward councillors saw their election as an opportunity to make workers' concerns felt in the council, to shape reconstruction and development in the local economy, ensure the RDP was implemented, and to link the wage demands of workers to broader social wage issues. The council should be a vehicle for 'gaining control' of the local economy through redirecting the resources, rates and taxes of the council to provide services such as electricity, water, rubbish removal, sanitation, and tarred streets with street lamps in the township and informal settlements. The council should encourage companies to establish sports facilities, swimming pools and so on in the township, as they had previously in the white town. An RDP department would be established in the council to implement RDP projects, liaise with civil society through the RDC, facilitate development projects in the community and encourage business to contribute.

One of the shop steward councillors argued that it was 'politically correct' for shop stewards to be councillors, as workers' living standards were determined not simply by their wage incomes, but by social wage policies of government, including taxation, rates and services:

Now the choice is, are you going to stay there at the factory and always organise marches against the council because their rates are too high? Or are you going to get inside the council and influence the debate over rates, and make sure that the whole struggle of the living wage is realised, not only through people marching, but also consulting with them and accommodating everyone? The difference is not between being a shop steward and being a councillor. The difference is the period we are coming from and the period we are in now. What is the role of the shop steward nowadays? Is the role of the shop steward just to stay in the factory and represent workers there, and lead some marches?

As a shop steward and a councillor, he had raised council issues with workers in general meetings at Highveld Steel, explaining why workers should pay council rates and tariffs, and providing the opportunity for workers to raise their problems with the council. He could then try to address these, and report back to members in the factory. Shop steward councillors could also play an important role in building partnerships between the council and the companies where they worked. The shop steward councillors did not think that time constraints should pose a problem, particularly if there was a strong shop steward team in their workplace and a strong councillor team in local government. They conceded, however, that union organisation was in fact weak.

The dissenting view identified in the previous chapter surfaced in the contrary argument, strongly expressed by one shop steward, that wearing 'two hats' as shop steward and councillor posed serious problems for workplace organisation. Shop stewards who were in the leadership of the ANC branch, or who were ANC councillors, would, he argued, have divided loyalties and could not be trusted to represent the best interests of workers. He criticised such shop stewards for persuading workers at Highveld Steel not to launch a wage strike with the argument that a strike would not help the democratically elected government to improve people's lives or finance the RDP. Similarly, he criticised shop stewards for accepting the proposal by the transitional town council to equalise the rates paid in the township and the town by increasing rates and levies in the township. Although the COSATU local and a general meeting of township residents had agreed to the increases, he argued that this was meaningless, as most people continued to boycott paying rates and levies in any case. The new geographical mobility of blacks was also fragmenting once-unified community interests – several of the leading shop stewards and skilled workers had bought or rented company houses in town, and they could no longer be trusted to protect township interests.[8] The 'first person to be reconciled' was the businessperson, and whites in general.

> We are paying for democracy. When you disagree with their arguments, they say, 'You are outdated, you don't understand politics, you are not talking like a leader.' To me, being a leader does not mean that I am supposed to accept everything that is coming from the ANC. Most of our shop stewards are active ANC members, they have got seats outside the union. I don't say you must not have an alliance with the ANC. I am also an ANC member. But the ANC must not drive us. They must not call our leader for discussion, and when he comes out from that door he doesn't look people in the eyes. Then you know that something has been done behind that door. That's what is happening.

Shop stewards should still be active beyond the workplace, but as representatives of workers, not of government. The town council 'should be left to politicians'.

The significance of the views of this shop steward is that they indicate the presence among workers of a discourse of distrust towards 'politicians', and scepticism about the ANC and its ability to make a difference to workers' lives, which could be mobilised against shop stewards who were politically active, as we shall see in chapter 10. It also held the potential for mobilisation against the broader alliances and developmental concerns of reconstruction, and for building an alternative, economistic unionism focusing only on the immediate workplace and wage interests of workers.[9]

The councillor who argued that it was 'politically correct' for shop stewards to become councillors recognised the existence of this discourse and its dangers, and had articulated similar views during an earlier interview when the position of the shop steward leadership at Highveld Steel had seemed quite precarious in the face of numerous challenges from workers in the plant. Then, on the verge of becoming a councillor in the transitional council, in the midst of acute organisational contestations in the workplace, he used the interview to explore the dilemmas and contradictions of his rapidly changing social identity. It would be 'laughable' to have a councillor or mayor in overalls. The councillors would have to make the council work, and ensure that 'people must be responsible'. This would mean increasing council tariffs and insisting that residents paid. If shop steward councillors objected that the unemployed and poorly paid workers could not afford the tariffs, they would be outvoted and in the end would be forced to justify the position of the council. On the other hand, the councillor's stipend was 'good money' and there would be family pressure to accept it. Workers, though, would know the shop steward was getting extra money while they were complaining of lack of service; this 'might just be pouring petrol on a small fire'. For all these reasons shop stewards would have to choose whether to remain shop stewards or become councillors; they could not do both.

There was some truth in these views. The tension between taking responsibility for building new institutions and accommodating diverse interests on the one hand, and mobilising workers in defence of their interests on the other, was a real one. The existence of blue-collar workers as town councillors also offended the hierarchies, privileges and statuses structured by South African society. The human resources manager at Highveld Steel made this quite clear, urging those who became councillors to accept promotion into the ranks of management: 'Obviously he's viewing the councillor in the old light, as someone who wears a tie, who is much respected, who does not mix with ordinary people. He put it very clearly that he does not think that he'll manage to work with us as councillors and shop stewards. He does not want to see us being shop stewards anymore.'

For a significant number of workers, too, workers who became councillors had risen in the hierarchy of society and become subject to new interests, concerns and loyalties, crossing the boundary defining workers' solidarity. They could no longer be fully trusted as worker leaders. Ironically, as if to underline the difficulty of inverting class hierarchies without a systematic struggle to transform them, by the end of 1998 only one of the councillors from Highveld Steel was still a worker there, and he was not an active union member.

Despite their success in becoming councillors, and their commitment to ensuring that the council implemented the RDP, extended services to those who had previously been excluded, and facilitated development, there were major obstacles in the way of implementing such a programme. The institutional structure and practices of the council, and the distribution and organisation of power in the ANC, acted to constrain the power of councillors. The lack of cohesion among trade unionists on the council, and their tenuous links with COSATU, further limited their ability to impact on it.

The practices and procedures of the council concentrated enormous power in the hands of the mayor, the chairperson of the executive and the heads of departments. The 'parliamentary' nature of council rep-resentation – representation in the form of political parties – distinguished the democracy of local government from the direct forms of representation in union democracy, and structured debate in a way that appeared to disempower councillors. One shop steward recalled clashing repeatedly with the hierarchy in the transitional council, where he was a councillor: 'I used to go there with the democracy I know – when there's an item on the table you can influence it, but in this council you can't do that. In each and every council meeting I had to be called to order.'

The hierarchical concentration of power continued in the new council. The heads of departments prepared the items for the agenda. The mayor chaired council and executive meetings. The council executive was formed by the ANC, as the party with a council majority. The chairperson of the executive committee was vested with the powers to drive executive and council meetings: 'He's the one who leads from the agenda, and says what position he wants adopted. The way the council functions, the chairperson has got those powers. Once he's put his views on the table you cannot challenge it, you've just got to accept it. If you challenge his position that's a problem, because you are from the same organisation and you're challenging the chairperson that you've put there with decision-making powers.'

The same problem existed in council debates. Some issues were decided on in the executive, others would go to open debate in the full council. Even here, the mayor and the chairperson of the executive had powers to determine the nature of the debate and individual ANC councillors were unable to contradict positions adopted by the organisation's leadership. The relation of councillors to the council bureaucracy also disempowered councillors. Council rules prohibited councillors from contacting departmental heads directly. Even the mayor and chairperson of the executive were only permitted to approach departmental heads through the town clerk:

> According to how this council functions, there's no way that it is going to deliver. All of the heads of departments are white, they don't understand the RDP. They still operate in the old way, and bring reports as they brought them in the past. The agenda items are designed by the various departments, and we have got to take decisions based on what they are saying, that's all. Therefore there is no clear programme that you can put in place.

It was therefore essential to reform fundamentally the way the council operated, both in council meetings and in the relations between councillors and the council bureaucracy. The prospects for this did not seem good, because of the way power was distributed and structured in the council and the ANC. In the union, all delegates to higher structures were accountable to the lower structures that nominated and mandated them. In the ANC, on the other hand, 'all the powers' were given to the executive, and there was 'no clear link of accountability' to the structures. Powerful leaders in the ANC could act like bosses, issuing instructions to their supporters. Activists with union roots entering this world could not operate as they did in the union. They had to find their place within political networks, and establish relationships with those who were able to exercise influence or power.

Without a coherent strategy from COSATU or the ANC, it would be impossible to reform the council. The chairperson of the executive was himself a former Highveld Steel activist, and had the power by virtue of his position in the council and as an influential figure in the ANC branch to lead a reform of this institution, or so his comrades thought. However, his very position linked him into ANC networks, and he seemed 'comfortable' with the status quo. Other ANC councillors were either new and did not yet understand the functioning of the council, or were reluctant to challenge the most powerful figure in the council and the branch. Moreover, the old opponents of the Highveld Steel shop stewards, a grouping of community activists, former exiles and political prisoners who had organised against them during 1989–91, were still present and lobbying to oust the current branch leadership. Overt conflict between the activists with roots in trade unionism in the face of this threat would be dangerous.

Finally, COSATU, which had the potential for serving as a rallying point for unionists in the council, was too weak to play this role. Its chairperson put this forcefully:

> COSATU has got a chance to drive and control this council, but they are not going to do that because COSATU is really, really dying. The last five meetings of the local were cancelled because no one showed up. I am the chairperson of COSATU, I run all over the show trying to represent COSATU and I report nowhere. At the RDC there is no COSATU either. COSATU is sinking, the affiliates are no longer taking COSATU seriously – they think now that they have freedom there is no reason for attending meetings.

The social structure of the ANC was still highly fluid and contested, as the organisation was the key agent in the process of elite-formation through which new black classes were emerging. It was the key to access to new jobs, opportunities for enrichment, and control over sources of patronage. A stable political elite had not yet established itself together with a set of codes and steps through which political careers could be advanced. Power struggles were therefore intense. Those with union origins found their identities shifting. Unionists who were absorbed into this world of politics rapidly lost any coherence they might have as a group, and lost touch with their base – especially in the absence of an institutionalised linkage to COSATU. One of the shop steward councillors described how this process had neutralised a comrade:

> He has lost touch with the real issues faced by workers now, and

he's lost touch with debates in NUMSA and COSATU, he's dead now. He has moved towards internal ANC politics. Although he does not agree with everything the ANC does, he would like to protect ANC positions. He's operating just like the guys in the province are doing, like the guys in the ANC national office are doing. Mandela said power is sometimes corruption, and I agree with him.

Entry into the world of politics took unionists away from the world of workers. Indeed, this rupture started the moment the unionists were nominated as ANC candidates for the town council. None of them informed their members or discussed their nomination with them, despite their allegiance to principles of accountability; nor did the shop steward committee as a whole discuss the implications or report to the membership. One candidate explained that it was an ANC matter, over which the union had no discretion. Within two years, all of the trade unionists, including the Highveld Steel shop stewards, who became councillors or political leaders in the ANC, had ceased to be unionists.

The result of these pressures was that 'the group that we've been through all these things with is in a way cracking now'. Instead of growing and attracting activists, forming the basis of an alternative network, the Highveld Steel group stagnated and its activists were absorbed into other networks. It appeared that the union movement could not provide adequate political resources – influence and power – to compete with other networks in the ANC.

Thus, despite its successes, the group of Highveld Steel shop stewards remained a small and tenuous one, and not even all those from NUMSA who were involved in politics could be regarded as part of it. As one of them commented wryly:

> The group does not expand although one believes that it is an ideal group to lead this area, but the problem is no one knows about it and it's not recognised by anyone. We took it upon ourselves that it is our responsibility to make sure that NUMSA's democratic practices are being practised wherever we go. Maybe we are wrong somewhere. That's why we don't have a crowd of people around us.

So it's just a useless group that keeps barking when there are problems and cannot solve them.

Despite the lack of coherence among the group from the unions, there was tension within the ANC branch about the high number of those with union roots in leadership positions. Others in the branch wanted access to power and the opportunities to participate in the processes of elite-formation, and rallying opposition to trade unionists accused of 'workerism' might bear fruit. There was also a hint of involvement from figures at the provincial level, who might wish for a more pliant branch in Witbank. Many of the Highveld Steel shop stewards' old opponents, who had tried to gain control of the civic and the ANC branch between 1989 and 1991 were still present, and in late 1995, were caucusing to replace the branch executive. In the words of one of the shop steward councillors:

Some comrades around here are saying that they must do away with this unionism in the ANC ranks, but they are failing because they are only a few people and the COSATU guys are very popular among the people. We are straight and we know our job, because of the leadership training we received in the union. How do you put your case in front of the masses? How do you explain things to the masses? That counts. If you are not well trained, if you are not a skilled negotiator, you are not going to be able to put your case clearly to the people. So they are unable to remove us.

This confidence was misplaced. Politics was different from trade unionism. Despite their strengths, many of the branch executive, including the former Highveld shop stewards, were ousted in early 1998 by their opponents, a group which included another former NUMSA shop steward who was also a councillor. According to the deposed leadership, the new branch leadership was motivated by the desire for access to jobs and resources. The branch collapsed when the constitutionality of the branch elections was contested, and the provincial ANC had to establish a task team to explore ways of resolving the conflict.

The participation of the shop stewards in the town council contributed to institution building and transformation, as well as to the shaping of a democratic perspective and practices. However, the town council was the key political institution at a local level, where individuals and the networks they were part of could gain access to status, patronage, opportunities, resources and jobs. The contestation over positions, practices and power was correspondingly intense – more so than in the other areas we have discussed – and reached deeply into the structures of the ANC and the Tripartite Alliance. This limited the effectiveness of the shop steward councillors in building and transforming the institution and its practices. Moreover, even while they remained active trade unionists, the shop steward councillors found it increasingly difficult to maintain a link between their union base and their political activities. The realities of organisational and political dynamics within their political party, the ANC, took precedence over their ability or even willingness to try to represent their union base. Their coherence as a group of unionists was fragmented as they became subject to the exigencies of leadership and politics within the ANC. At any rate, by the end of 1998 only one of them was still employed at Highveld Steel, and he was by then a manager. The idea of labour leadership in local politics had not been realised.

Impact on the union at Highveld Steel

While union structures at Highveld Steel played such an important role 'producing leadership' for institutions and organisations beyond the workplace, this took a heavy toll on the capacity and coherence of workplace organisation in the company. This took three forms: the involvement of the most experienced shop stewards in issues beyond the workplace, thus weakening workplace organisation; the complete loss of such shop stewards when they took up other jobs and pursuits in politics and business; and the internal tensions that the mobility and political involvement of shop stewards generated within the social structure of the union at the workplace.

It was common cause among shop stewards that the involvement of their leadership in the elections campaign had weakened the union and was the reason for complaints among members. One former shop steward commented that the union was becoming weaker and members were complaining that shop stewards 'are working for the ANC, not for them as workers in the plant', and argued that 'shop stewards should concentrate on the work situation rather than the politics of our country, otherwise for sure issues at work are going to suffer'. Shop stewards who were politically involved responded that it was essential to ensure the election victory of an ANC that would implement the RDP, and that after the elections things would return to normal.[10]

Things did not return to normal. The chairperson of the joint shop steward committee left for a job in the provincial administration. Other leading shop stewards became increasingly active in the affairs of the ANC branch, the transitional town council, and development projects. Then came the local government elections at the end of 1995, and the election of the chair and secretary of the steelworks committee as town councillors. In the course of 1997, the chairperson applied successfully for a managerial position at Highveld Steel, and the following year the secretary resigned as a shop steward and then from the company in order to pursue political and business interests. It was not only shop stewards who moved out of the union. Two NUMSA organisers resigned when they were elected as councillors, as stipulated in union policy, and one of the regional organisers, a former chairperson of the shop steward committee, applied successfully for a managerial post in another company. Shop stewards also began to be promoted internally to supervisor and other managerial positions.

This loss of the most experienced shop stewards and officials had a devastating impact on workplace organisation at Highveld Steel, not only because of the loss of skills – which undermined the project of recon-struction in the workplace – but also because of the impact it had on collective solidarity in the workplace. This issue is taken up in chapter 10.

Conclusion

The strategy of reconstruction was designed to shape the process of constructing post-colonial society and, in doing this, to shape the process of working-class incorporation in order to institutionalise its influence and power. Thus, the Highveld Steel shop stewards were motivated by a vision of reform driven by the labour movement, of union activists participating in political organisation and socio-economic development while retaining a strong, accountable relationship with their base of organised workers. They were successful in their contribution to building new institutions of democracy, and struggled to forge a culture of democracy within them and implement a vision of development through them. In doing this, they made an important contribution to establishing the new post-colonial and democratic order.

However, over the period of the transition the link between the politically active shop stewards and the trade union movement became increasingly tenuous until, by 1998, the union movement in Witbank had virtually no representation in the two centrally important political institutions in the town – the ANC branch executive and the town council. Thus in the space of four years it could no longer be said that the union movement was a dynamic influence on local political, developmental or community events. While, as individuals, many of the former unionists would carry with them a commitment to the vision and practices they had learnt in the unions, this commitment was rapidly compromised by their entry into a political world structured in a very different way to the world of unionism they had left. The trade union movement had been incorporated into the newly institutionalised democratic politics, but had failed in its endeavour to establish a strong institutional base for shaping and contesting the terms of incorporation and the goals of politics.

Not only had the unionist politicians ceased to be unionists, but their exodus had weakened the trade union; the irony was that the union's contribution to building institutions in society beyond the workplace had simultaneously weakened the union itself as an institution. It lost its most experienced and skilled shop stewards and suffered new strains over the allegiances and trustworthiness of shop stewards.

The distinction between the trade union strategy of reconstruction considered in this chapter, and the social movement unionism of the 1980s, was substantial. Firstly, the strategy of reconstruction entailed a focus on institution building in place of the popular mobilisation of social movement unionism. There was, of course, also continuity, as the trade unionists drew on their experience of institutional innovation – as well as on their leadership, organisational and negotiating experience – forged in their struggle to create a new workplace order in the 1980s, but there was a fundamental recasting of the relation between the *institutional* and the *movement* aspects of trade unionism with the strategy of reconstruction.

Secondly, there was a dissolution of the intense popular identity and solidarity that was forged both outside and inside the union during the 1980s, an increasing distance between the leadership who governed and those on whose behalf they governed. Together with this went the greater salience of individual ambitions and careers, and the relations and networks in which these individuals were embedded. In other words, the structure of politics had altered fundamentally, and this in turn had an impact within the social structure of the union as both shop stewards and their members became aware of the opportunities for political careers and the new allegiances that this implied.

Finally, while the ongoing contestation over practices and tactics between trade unionists and community activists recalls the contestations of the 1980s, the trade union movement was increasingly absent as an organisation in the conflict between individuals. This process ultimately concluded with the absorption of the trade unionists into the internal social structure of the ANC and the end of a strong trade union role in local politics.

Notes

1. Activists quoted in this chapter remain anonymous, as some are still involved politically.
2. This section of the chapter is based on interview, Charles Makola, 14/5/94; interview, Meshack Malinga, 15/3/94; interview, Mosi Nhlapo, 9/11/93, 8/5/94.
3. The account in this section is based on interview, Meshack Malinga, 15/3/94; interview, Ezekiel Nkosi, 9/3/94, 5/5/94; interview, Jacob Skhosana, 26/4/94; COSATU, Regional voter education/elections programme (mimeo); NUMSA shop stewards local, 9 March 1994.
4. NUMSA shop stewards local, 9 March 1994; interview, Ezekiel Nkosi, 9/3/94, 5/5/94.
5. *braai*: barbeque.
6. The account in this section is mostly based on interview, Ezekiel Nkosi, 5/5/94, 26/5/94, 23/11/95; but also on interview, Meshack Malinga, 15/3/94; and interview, Ambrose Mthembu, 26/4/94.
7. The following account is based on interview, Ephraim Kgole, 10/95; interview, Veli Majola, 26/10/95; interview, Meshack Malinga, 15/3/94; interview, Philip Mkatshwa, 8/95; interview, Mosi Nhlapo, 10/7/94, 12/95; interview, Ezekiel Nkosi, 23/11/95; interview, Hendrik Nkosi, 26/10/95; interview, Johannes Phatlana, 12/10/95.
8. Many of the black artisans took advantage of the company offer to buy or rent houses on the company housing estate in the white town of Witbank. Shop steward artisans were cautious about taking this up, knowing that 'workers look critically at such issues, they don't just accept that', but some were 'brave' and bought houses; one who did so, prudently placed his mother there and continued living in the township himself.

Tension over this was defused during the clash between MWU and NUMSA in 1993 (see chapter 9), when shop stewards joked with their striking members that they had not only to 'fight the *boers*' at work, but also to go and sleep with them in Witbank at night. Such relief could only be temporary. Former shop stewards who landed better-paying jobs in the civil service, management or provincial legislature were able to move further afield, into the suburbs 'where managers live'. See interview, Mosi Nhlapo, 10/7/94.

9. Of four other shop stewards and workers who expressed a view on this issue, two – both migrants – thought it was a good thing for shop stewards to be elected as councillors, as 'they are the people who know poverty' and could perhaps encourage the council to solve workers' problems 'before action becomes necessary'. The other two opposed the idea of shop stewards being councillors as 'they cannot do both jobs'.

10. Interview, Ezekiel Nkosi, 9/3/94, 5/5/94; interview, William Sehlola, 5/6/94.

CHAPTER 9

Fighting for 'the law of freedom'

The workplace regime, incorporation
and the strategy of reconstruction

Before, the manager would interfere with our work in many ways –
even though we knew what we were supposed to do. Multi-skilling
and teamwork are important, in this way we are more protected
and we can protect each other. The way we now work at the iron
plant is one of the ways I hope to see democracy in the workplace
because I find myself feeling happy with the way we work. There is
no harassment from white people.

Albert Makagula, migrant worker and shop steward

The democratic breakthrough provided the basis for working-class
incorporation at the political level. This chapter turns to the question of
incorporation in the workplace. In parallel with its goals beyond the
workplace, the strategy of reconstruction was designed to shape the terms
of workplace incorporation by institutionalising the autonomy and the
influence of worker organisation. This chapter describes the union's struggle
to implement its strategy at Highveld Steel.

The chapter starts by identifying the most important features of the
workplace regime in the early 1990s, and argues that these constituted a
neo-apartheid workplace regime. Integral to the neo-apartheid workplace
regime was a process of decomposition generated by the tension between
racial structures of power in the workplace and the democratic breakthrough
at a political level. This tension created the pressure for transformation,
for the search for a post-apartheid workplace order through which black
workers could be incorporated into the workplace regime. Three contending

projects for the establishment of a post-apartheid workplace regime can be identified at Highveld Steel. Management sought to impose discipline and co-operation through a project of *authoritarian restoration*. The NUMSA shop stewards attempted to negotiate the transition to a post-apartheid workplace regime characterised by co-determination and worker control through *negotiating reconstruction*. A third project emerged out of the initiatives of a progressive manager to cultivate *wildcat co-operation* as the basis for workplace incorporation, by constructing a coalition of local interests among black workers independently of the union.

The neo-apartheid workplace regime
Racial assault and racial solidarity: NUMSA vs MWU in 1993[1]
In mid-1993 a white worker using a public phone at the steelworks punched a black worker who was cleaning the area, breaking four of his teeth. A disciplinary inquiry dismissed the white worker, but he was reinstated when his union, the white Mine Workers' Union (MWU), took the case on appeal.

Black workers immediately launched a wildcat strike, demanding that the white worker be removed. Management acceded. The next day MWU members fetched the white worker from his home and launched a wildcat strike demanding his immediate reinstatement. The following day both NUMSA and MWU were on strike. Black workers were searching through the plants for the white worker, banging walls and machines threateningly with pangas and, in the words of a NUMSA shop steward, the strike 'was becoming a little bit dangerous'. Feeling threatened, MWU called the Afrikaner Weerstandsbeweging (AWB – a militant white right-wing organisation) to 'please come and protect our people', and a group of armed and uniformed white 'commandos' arrived at the company. The company called the police in, and eventually the situation was defused with an agreement that the white worker would be suspended while management and the MWU worked out a severance package.

The Witbank office of an official of the right-wing MWU gave some sense of how deeply racism and apartheid history were ingrained in the culture of white workers and their union. The office, visited in 1993, was filled with the icons of apartheid, and of a white man's biography in a white man's country: a photograph of the architect of apartheid, Hendrik Verwoerd; a large model of a boer ox-wagon on a table; on the wall several brass images of wild animals, and one of two hands meeting in prayer; on another table a small replica R1 military rifle with a plaque inscribed with the words 'Border Duty' – rich with meaning for white South Africans. Other military images included an air gun mounted on the wall, and a replica canon on a table. This was a man who remembered war and needed to show he was ready to fight. The icons of a mineworker were inserted among those of apartheid: four old brass mine-lamps and a lump of ore arranged on a white lace tablecloth on a third table. And most explicit of all, a poster referring to an informal discourse usually omitted from the formal language of apartheid, but underpinning it: it depicted a row of figures starting with a baboon on all fours, then a stooped cave-man, followed by a somewhat less stooped 'kaffir', and finally an erect white man. This poster, in the office of a white man in 1993, who had been a worker at Highveld Steel from 1985–91, and was now an official of MWU, indicates the kind of racism experienced in work relations between black and white.

Racial tension was, if anything, exacerbated by changes inside the workplace, as well as by broader political change in the country. Black workers were acutely aware of the new democratic order that was emerging from the negotiations between the National Party (NP) government and the ANC. Racism was intolerable in this changing political context. Indeed, what was foremost in the minds of black workers was the justice of fighting for the implementation of an important company policy that banned assault. As a worker put it: 'What caused us to have a stoppage is that a law has been established that if a person hits another, he gets fired.' Management was still applying a different law to blacks and whites.

White workers, on the other hand, were feeling increasingly embattled both in the 'white man's country' where democracy threatened to overwhelm the protections of apartheid, and in the workplace where their power was being eroded and NUMSA was campaigning for the right of black workers to use the previously segregated facilities of whites. NUMSA's response to the reinstatement of their fellow white, and management's response to NUMSA, epitomised their vulnerability and provoked them to un-accustomed militancy in defence of their position.

Although the strike suggested that little had changed in the workplace, the reality was more complex. Six weeks later NUMSA and MWU launched a legal strike together in support of a wage increase. The shifting balance of power in the workplace and in South African society more broadly had created a fluidity in social identities unknown during the rigidities of the apartheid era.

The racial division of labour

Although the level at which blacks were employed was slowly drifting upwards as discussed in chapter 2, in the early 1990s the main outlines of the racial division of labour were still in place. Before the mid-1990s management seemed to show little commitment to changing this. It was the basis for the racial structure of power, and the racial differentiation of incomes and benefits among company employees, and accounted for the bitterness among workers that the racial order in the workplace had barely changed. Black and white staff were still on racially defined payrolls, and were members of separate benefit funds with different benefits. Hourly-paid workers were also still on separate racially defined payrolls. The racial structure of power was intact. More than 90 per cent of supervisors, and virtually all line managers above that, were still white.[2]

In the experience cited by the shop stewards, promotions were still influenced by favouritism and racial discrimination even in the absence of formal job reservation. They were demanding the right to participate in the process to ensure it was fair.[3]

Racial segregation

Despite the repeal in the 1980s of legislation that required segregated facilities (see chapter 2), Highveld Steel continued to maintain segregation into the early 1990s. In 1991 the company agreed to desegregate all facilities but failed to enforce this policy. This fuelled the militant response of workers to management:

> The policy says all facilities will be multiracial. Shop stewards asked what would happen if black workers went to the white showers and the whites started trouble. Management said they can't control that. We said, 'Put some security there, put out a brief that anyone found guilty of starting such trouble would be disciplined.' They wouldn't do that. You find that some foremen have got the key to a particular toilet, and that key is rotating amongst the white artisans and blacks

must use the other toilet. The company would not take a stand about that. These are very small things that people may overlook, but they are the real issues people see as apartheid. When you have a dispute with management they start to think of those small things and get furious.[4]

Where black workers were well organised and confident, they took the initiative in desegregating toilets, showers and mess-rooms simply by making use of them. In other areas workers were scared to challenge whites.[5] Either way, workplace relations continued to be infused with racial tensions, and the racial underpinnings of the workplace order continued to inflame relations with management.

Trade union rights
The establishment of NUMSA at Highveld Steel, and its recognition by management, had brought about substantial reforms to the despotism of the apartheid workplace regime. Basic union rights had been established: the election of shop stewards as the representatives of union members, the deduction of union dues, collective bargaining over wages and conditions and representation by shop stewards in formal disciplinary and grievance procedures.

Nonetheless, these rights were circumscribed by several company restrictions on union activities. While shop stewards were allowed time off for union training, there was no provision for paid time off, nor was there agreement about the right of the shop steward committee to meet regularly during working hours, nor was the committee provided with an office or telephone. Most importantly, management effectively refused permission for the union to hold general meetings during working hours. It was extraordinary that one of the biggest industrial companies in South Africa, owned by the country's biggest conglomerate, continued to withhold what had been recognised as basic rights in many workplaces during the 1980s and were increasingly common during the 1990s.

When there was a burning issue to address, shop stewards defied the company by calling general meetings during working hours, which meant every such meeting was an illegal stoppage. They also decided to hold weekly committee meetings during working hours. On occasion disciplinary action was taken against them, which led to stoppages in their support. Instead of basic agreement on the ground rules for union rights and powers in the workplace, there was continuous contestation and defiance.[6]

Shop stewards and organisers concluded that the company was essentially anti-union:

> If you allow the union to have meetings at the company during working hours, it's like allowing your enemy to plan how to kill you inside your house. That's how they look at the union. You cannot talk to them about a programme for change. We have been making requests, requests, requests to talk to the MD. To them he is God, who are you to talk with him?[7]

The racial structure of power in the workplace

Despite the promotion of a handful of black foremen, the racial structure of power remained intact in the early 1990s. Racial dynamics in the workplace reflected the persistence of the racial structure of power. Mosi Nhlapo, an artisan and chairperson of shop stewards, contrasted the relationship of white and black artisans to their white foreman:

> The foreman is a Kruger, the artisan is a Van der Merwe.[8] When he goes to the foreman's office he will sit on a chair and talk to the foreman. Sometimes they will talk about what is happening where they live. But when I go to the foreman's office I must stand up and talk about work. The relationship is different between me and the foreman and Van der Merwe and the foreman. Always I make sure that I work harder so that I can avoid going to the foreman's office.[9]

This racially defined managerial authority was not only inclined by its nature to racial discrimination – as the racial antagonism of the 1993 strike demonstrates – but was distinguished by a range of other features that sprang from its racial nature: it was authoritarian, hierarchical, characterised by favouritism, lack of skill in managing people, and frequently ignorant about how the labour process was actually performed. A kiln operator in Iron Plant One – a relatively skilled job – described his frustrations as an educated young black man:

I started working on the kilns, only to find ourselves being supervised by people who have never been at school, people who could not write, people who don't understand things, people who don't want to listen, people who don't want to communicate with us. We find it very difficult. Even if you see something wrong that you have to explain to them, they don't take that at all. So you just have to keep quiet. Wherever they don't understand something, they don't ask the operators. They just impose instructions without consulting us, although we are the people who do the job. The job of foreman needs a person who can organise, a person who can plan, with a great skill for communication, but my foremen, most of them, lack those qualities. They don't have leadership qualities.

The problem was that poorly educated whites, or men from other plants with no experience of kilns, were appointed as foremen. Such a man would then consult a fellow white, the superintendent who 'has old information because things have changed through technology', rather than consulting the black operators. The kiln operator described a dispute where the kiln's monitors were giving misreadings and the foreman and superintendent, without consulting him, had the monitor removed when, according to the operator, it should simply have been repositioned. The operator – who had two kilns to run – then had to check the kiln flame manually, which wasted time and resulted in poor production, wastage and a costly increase in the furnace's consumption of electricity. In the experience of this operator, simply promoting a few blacks as foremen did not improve supervisory practices. Since these blacks were likely to have been promoted through favouritism, they were insecure and tended to adopt the decision-making style of their white colleagues and superiors. The hierarchical and authoritarian style of management affected not only the relations between workers and supervisors but also the entire co-ordination of production:

People do not work to improve production. We have a mechanical department, an instruments department and the production department. If ever there's something wrong, each side will defend itself, without looking at the value of discussing and overcoming the problem. Why? Because the fitter does not know how to operate the kiln, and I know how to operate the kiln but I'm not a fitter. I cannot look where he is working because I don't know what's happening. He also cannot try to pry into my job because he does not know how to operate the kiln. So we cannot overcome the problem. Everyone is trained at different things.[10]

The apartheid workplace regime was not only a racially oppressive way of controlling people but had widespread ramifications for the production process and efficiency in the workplace. Apartheid had produced an authoritarian layer of white supervisors who thought 'nothing good can come from a shop steward', who wanted 'always to remain on top and be the only one who knows what is happening' and policed workers 'as if he is having a *sjambok*, rather than working as a team leader'.[11]

Many of the black shop stewards repeated this critique of the apartheid production regime, describing supervisors as ignorant, unskilled, promoted because of their colour, making 'racial utterings', allocating dirty, unpleasant jobs to black workers, and masking their incompetence by drinking endless cups of tea in their offices and issuing instructions without understanding problems. Several told stories of how maintenance work was delayed because the decision had to be passed up a long line of command, or how machines were jammed or broke down because supervisors overrode the decision of an operator. Workers related stories of poor-quality production, of management complaints about the high costs of wastage, and of defective orders returned by customers.

Production losses were not only caused by poor relations between black and white, but by poor management, lack of commitment and nepotism among whites. Workers – black and white – contrived to damage machines so as to stop production and rest, or display displeasure at management decisions. Workers and foremen – black and white – colluded in ensuring overtime was authorised, and then *braaied* and drank instead of working. A white supervisor described how one manager ensured that Highveld Steel bought sand from a particular farmer, and was rewarded with invitations to shoot kudu on his farm. This 'kudu sand' was of the wrong quality, and tended to explode when the molten iron ran over it. 'That's only a small thing,' he hinted, 'there are bigger things.'

Continuity and change: a neo-apartheid workplace regime
By the early 1990s, the combination of union-driven reforms and the structural features of the apartheid workplace regime had produced contradictory results. NUMSA had succeeded in curbing dismissals. There were proper disciplinary and grievance procedures and reduced harassment, job reservation and favouritism. Through stoppages and negotiation workers had won the right to shift allowances, adequate work clothes, cabins in which to shelter from cold weather in exposed workplaces, pulpits on machines, heaters and fans in cranes and other workstations, and stoves in the workplace where shift-workers could cook lunch.[12] Many stressed that they were now treated as human beings to the extent that white foremen and black workers could make tea for each other 'without fearing that one will poison the tea'; blacks and whites 'are now able to share a glass of water because of the union'.[13] Furthermore, the link between the apartheid workplace regime and the apartheid state had been severed by the democratic transition.

But while the union had reformed the apartheid workplace regime, the structural features of this regime had persisted into the new South Africa: the low wages of unskilled black workers, discrimination in promotions and access to training, the racial structure of power in the workplace, and so on. The migrant activist Tshagata captured this with great clarity:

> Amongst us there hasn't been satisfaction with our employer at the firm even in a single day. He has never done something better for us, because he treats a black person very badly. I have been living here in the hostels for 19 years. Where will I get the money to buy a house, because the little money I get is enough for buying a bag of mielie meal only? I worked for years and even now I have got nothing, so what kind of enjoyment can I say I feel? I would be lying if I said that when the union came in, the employer discussed something better with us. The union, if I remember, changed minor things, not big ones, all the minor things which troubled us, so that we could co-operate somewhere and listen to each other with white men. Those are the things which the union did. Today I see myself as a human being because of the union. I'm able to be viewed as an employee. But the union still has a job to do, because there are

issues we failed to solve before, which the old government as well
as the employer denied us, which even now we are still negotiating.
We have written them down, we have not forgotten.[14]

The Highveld workplace in the early 1990s was no longer the classic
apartheid workplace regime, yet it was profoundly structured by the legacy
of that regime. It can be characterised as a neo-apartheid workplace regime,
an essential feature of which was the contradiction between racial structures
of power in the workplace and democracy beyond it – a contradiction that
generated a process of decomposition.

The decomposition of the workplace regime in the 1990s

As the outlines of a new political order began to emerge from the political
negotiations beyond the workplace, so the existence of core features of
apartheid within the workplace became increasingly untenable. A further
deterioration of discipline and authority in the workplace signalled the
decomposition of a regime that had become increasingly incoherent during
the period of militant unionisation in the 1980s. This decomposition was
most apparent in the front line of supervisory relations in the workplace,
between artisan assistants and artisans, and between workers and their
foremen. Workers demonstrated their rejection of the racial structure of
power with stoppages and strikes, and frequent references to Mandela and
the ANC symbolised the importance of political changes beyond the
workplace. Nhlapo noted that artisan assistants were beginning to display
open defiance of instructions by whites. Political change increased their
confidence, as they showed by plastering their helmets with ANC stickers.[15]

In the words of a shop steward in the General Maintenance and
Planning Department (GMPD), actions were becoming worse 'because
nobody's afraid now – he knows for what reason he is striking'.[16] In flat
products foremen responded to workers' requests or queries with provocative
comments that they should ask Mandela or the ANC. Workers downed
tools, demanding the dismissal of a particularly bad offender.[17]

A shop steward in the structural mill commented:

The workers are starting to victimise the foremen. The foreman
gives an instruction and the worker just does nothing. When the

foreman threatens him with discipline, he says 'you can do whatever you want but we are going to fight'. The foremen are complaining that they are under attack here.[18]

The decomposition of the workplace regime was apparent not only in deliberate confrontation with supervisors but in the general increase in disciplinary problems described by one shop steward:

The unbanning of the political organisations gave the workers a wrong impression. They thought that now we are going to rule the country and we can do anything that we want. People come to work drunk. They stay away from work without permission. A person can get a warning at a disciplinary inquiry, and next week he is absent for another three days. They take advantage of the union because they know it will represent them. And on the other side, the whites are scared of NUMSA, scared that disciplinary action will cause a strike. Discipline is breaking down because people are taking it into their own hands.[19]

White supervisors endorsed the view that there had been an erosion – and finally a virtual collapse – of discipline:

In the past we didn't take shit from anybody – if you were very lucky you got maybe two warnings. On the third one, you were out. But nowadays a guy gets disciplinary forms over and over, but nothing happens to him. He gets his representative and off they go to the office, and he gets shit out, and next week is the same thing. It's getting worse and worse everyday because nothing happens to that guy. If one or two get fired, the others will see what happens and they will do the job properly because they will be scared.[20]

A second white supervisor echoed this: 'As soon as you start with disciplining, the people just laugh at you because you never get the support from management.'[21] He described the gradual erosion over the years of the foreman's power to control workers:

The foreman was completely responsible for the section and for his

people. Now you're still responsible, but you can't tell them what to
do. You don't have the power to do it. In the past, if the guy did not
listen to you immediately you could give him a hard time. You could
warn him, and that was that. You could take his weekend away, or
fine him some money. That's how it worked in the past – you can't
do it anymore. We had the *baas-boy* system. The person who
laboured under that *baas-boy* could ask him for a day off, and the
baas-boy had the power to give it to him. Even the foreman hasn't
got that power now. That's totally wrong. If someone was giving
the *baas-boy* problems he would go to the foreman and tell him he
has warned the guy several times. Then the foreman could give
him a warning. Now they've taken it away, there's no more *baas-
boy*. In the past the foreman was responsible for holding inquiries –
they took it away. Why, I don't know, they never explained that to
us. Management took everything away.

The foreman had less power than the workers he supervised because they
had a union to ensure they were listened to. This foreman blamed the
increasing employment of black workers and management's fear of strikes
and political change.

The management strategy of authoritarian restoration[22]
Management attempted to stem this process of decomposition and restore
order on the shopfloor by unilaterally imposing a new disciplinary procedure
in late 1994. The new code increased the disciplinary powers of the foremen,
reduced the procedural protections for the workers and whittled away at
their right to be represented by a shop steward.

The shop steward committee responded by referring the dispute to the
Industrial Council. At the dispute hearing the union induced the company
to make concessions, and outstanding issues were referred to the Industrial
Court. The shop stewards were using institutional procedures to block and
dilute management's new code but this did not mean that they would
collaborate with management attempts to reconstitute discipline on the
shopfloor. In a strategy identical to that of the 1980s, they were negotiating
without recognising the legitimacy of management's right to discipline:

We've made them shift some of the things they had in there, but we've not agreed that it's binding on us. Even after the court case there's no way we'll sign the code. We'll follow the procedure if it suits us – if it does not, we'll say it's not binding on us.

Shop stewards did not confine their resistance to formal, institutional procedures; they took their resistance into the workplace, where they mobilised their members against the new procedures. Where shop stewards were bold and their members militant, they refused to co-operate with the new procedures and threatened stoppages. Supervisors and managers avoided trying to implement them. In Iron Plant One, white foremen complained that they were also opposed to the new procedures because workers would not accept them, and ended up joining NUMSA.

In similar vein, management tried to impose co-operation. In 1993, after the shop stewards had presented the bargaining proposals of their reconstruction strategy, the human resources manager told them that the company wanted to introduce green areas as a forum for communication.[23] When the shop stewards raised questions about the purpose of the green areas, and their relation to the structure of supervision, they were told the green areas were non-negotiable. The shop stewards made it clear that they would mobilise against them until they were properly negotiated, not because they were opposed to green areas but because they believed they should be negotiated together with the union's proposals for workplace change. Management wanted to implement green areas in isolation, 'as an island, they don't want to link it with anything – with training, grading or production'.

The shop stewards' campaign against the green areas was generally successful, not only because of the resistance of workers but also because managers and supervisors, locked into the authoritarian and non-participatory practices of the apartheid workplace regime, could not comprehend a process of participation. It was not difficult to discourage workers from attending green area meetings, as they quickly concluded that they were intended to buttress authority in the apartheid workplace regime instead of dismantling it. A migrant worker observed:

We have realised that the green area is taking us nowhere. We would like a green area which accords everyone the right to know everything about the firm and about production. We left the green area when we saw there is no way it can help us, because it is still oppressing us. It is taking us back to that apartheid of theirs, not in the direction which we as workers want.

Another shop steward described how green areas simply became another forum for foremen to issue instructions as they always had, with no attempt to solve problems collectively:

The foreman just comes and tells us, 'Look, yesterday we rolled so many cobbles [reject structural steel]. Please, today don't do any mistakes. Fine. Do you hear me?' We say, 'Fine, let's go.' The siren blows, we go back on duty. Here come more cobbles . . .'

Another element of management's strategy was to use natural attrition to gradually reduce the number of workers, over time increasing workloads and introducing multi-tasking in an effort to cut costs and increase productivity.[24] Along with this the company started outsourcing 'non-core' functions such as the canteen and housing maintenance, and there was a gradual increase in the use of casuals. These were all strategies of authoritarian restoration, which the shop stewards sought to regulate by negotiating new agreements, with some success.

The management strategy of *authoritarian restoration* failed to incorporate workers because management practices were still embedded in the structures and culture of the apartheid workplace regime. The strategy constituted an authoritarian attempt to preserve a neo-apartheid workplace regime. The decomposition, inefficiency and continued exclusion of black workers in the neo-apartheid workplace regime meant that there were increasing pressures to break with the neo-apartheid workplace and construct a new post-apartheid workplace.

NUMSA's attempt to negotiate reconstruction
The joint working groups: paralysis over reconstruction[25]
At the 1993 wage negotiations, NUMSA presented Highveld Steel with its proposals in the form of the union's three-year programme to replace the apartheid workplace regime with a new high-skill, democratic regime. Management refused to negotiate the proposals but suggested that joint

company-union working groups be established to discuss them. After a short work stoppage, management agreed that the number of grades in the grading structure would be reduced from fourteen to eight and three working groups were established. The first was to implement the new grading structure, the second was to draft an agreement governing relations between the company and the unions, and the third was to focus on new work organisation and productivity.

The formation of the joint working groups appeared to herald the possibility of negotiating the transition to a post-apartheid workplace regime. Instead, they were marked by deadlock, paralysis and frustration. Management and NUMSA tried to use these forums to implement contending notions of transformation. NUMSA shop stewards were seeking to prevent management from implementing unilateral change: they wanted co-determination of change strategies and a high degree of worker control in production. Management wanted to regain control of the workplace. They wanted a free hand to test new strategies, and they wanted shop steward co-operation in implementing them.

In the restructuring group, for example, 'management comes with proposals, with the view that we must accept them and help implement them, not discuss them'. Furthermore, management was continuing to implement restructuring in the plants, 'whether we like it or not, whether we have an agreement or not'. For the shop stewards, then, 'the challenge is can we stop them, can we counter them in various ways so that they begin to respect us?' Nhlapo had no expectation that an agreement with management would emerge from this process – it was simply an opportunity to block management and educate workers. This meant the working group had no potential for satisfying either party.

The union proposals for moving towards a new workplace regime were never discussed in the working groups. There was no attempt to develop common ground for establishing a new regime, and no agreement on the purpose, procedures or goals of the groups.[26] A process marked by such fundamental contention over transformation had little prospect of ushering in a new workplace regime. In Nhlapo's view, managers' continued belief in a formalistic approach was bound to fail:

You can put all the documents that you want in place, and think that the courts are going to help you, but these workers are not going to co-operate, not now. When they experience problems they forget about agreements. And if we start reminding them that we've got this agreement, they will say no, we will put that agreement aside. We want to deal with management. It's because for years management has been taking us to court instead of resolving our problems. Even if the court says we're wrong, the problem remains. That's why the procedural agreement is a waste of time.

The process of engaging with the working groups also revealed serious capacity weaknesses in the union. There was no one the shop stewards could rely on for advice or support. National officials consistently failed to attend meetings where they were expected. Bunny Mahlangu, the regional organiser who understood the NUMSA programme, was overextended, and then resigned from the union to take up a managerial position in another company in early 1995. Nhlapo was the only shop steward able consistently to engage proactively with management. He reported to the shop steward committee:

The work is killing me. I am alone. The last meeting of the grading committee was cancelled because I was absent. I am carrying my union, I am carrying the other unions, and I'm carrying management.

These weaknesses meant that the union was unable to develop proposals alternative to those put forward by management in the working groups. Nhlapo felt that management, on the other hand, was no longer simply reacting in an ad hoc way to production problems or union demands, but was beginning to develop the capacity for a strategic approach to restructuring. He was acutely aware of the ambiguities and contradictions in the reconstruction strategy and the confusion this generated:

I'm not sure whether the working groups are negotiating forums. Are we supposed to reach consensus, or does our view of socialism involve struggle? Can we strike for real participation in decisions, or can we only participate on the shopfloor in green areas? We have never negotiated these issues in our bargaining forum, and in the working groups you have to be diplomatic. We don't have guidelines for these questions.

While the shop stewards wanted to forge a completely new workplace regime on the basis of negotiated co-operation, management appeared unable to imagine negotiating the shape of a new dispensation with black workers or their union. At stake was power and control. The result was stalemate and increased disorder. In the end, each of the three working groups was closed down or suspended indefinitely.

A final attempt to negotiate reconstruction: a model agreement?[27]

By mid-1995, there seemed to be little prospect for co-operative agreement between management and unions at Highveld Steel. The three working groups were defunct and management opened the house agreement negotiations by withdrawing its commitment to implementing a five-grade system, which in Nhlapo's opinion 'removed the principle of the NUMSA programme for overcoming the apartheid work organisation'. However, management surprised NUMSA by proposing a new agreement of intent to govern restructuring in the company. This sought to overcome the conflict and paralysis in the working groups in two ways. Firstly, it proposed that 'in view of the uncertainties, the lack of trust and inadequate benchmarking', management and unions should jointly decide on a pilot project in a specific plant and focus their energies on this. The limited scope of such a project might reduce the fears of both management and shop stewards. Secondly, the project would be overseen by a joint management-union steering committee. This implied institutionalising a high degree of union influence, which management hoped would persuade the union to drop its strategy of resistance.

The shop stewards saw this as a promising offer and proceeded to develop proposals to amend the document 'to suit our own thinking and make it possible for us to achieve our goals'. The two key clauses finally accepted by the company effectively gave the union a veto over change in the workplace by stating that 'no other change would be implemented with regard to work reorganisation without reference to the joint management-union steering committee' and adopted the principles of co-determination –

'the full and equal participation' of the unions in 'the conception, development and implementation of any changes, and the sharing of information pertaining to this programme'. These were the clauses that made shop stewards feel 'we are going to get our leverage to deal with management'. The agreement appeared to hold the promise of a new beginning, in which unions and management could negotiate a transition to a new workplace order acceptable to them both. However, profound disjunctures undermined this promise. There was still no substantial shared ground on how the workplace should change or what the goals should be. The shop stewards had fought to include clauses that pointed in the direction of their vision – but this did not mean that management understood or accepted the implications of such clauses. Furthermore, despite the protracted negotiations and the signing of the agreement, senior management was still not committed to co-operation. The problem was that other options were beginning to emerge, options that seemed more attractive because they promised to secure managerial control and sideline the union by cultivating 'wildcat co-operation'. Thus management continued to pursue such projects, and even initiated a major new project at Vantra, without involving the unions, after the agreement had been negotiated. When the full steering committee finally met, Nhlapo observed: 'Things are just as they used to be – management is supposed to make the decisions and we must accept them.'

How can this anomaly be explained? The same senior managers who had negotiated the agreement were undermining it. In the view of the shop stewards, even the general manager and the human resources manager who had negotiated the agreement were profoundly ambivalent about it. On the one hand, they knew that 'the rules of the game have changed now' and accepted that they had to co-operate with the union. On the other hand, they were still unable to grasp what this really meant, so 'it is a shift, but a shift that is on paper'. It had been explained to some of the stewards that the executive committee of the company did not fully support the 'paradigm shift', and managers down the line were likely 'to block everything we try to come up with'. The majority of managers from top to bottom of the company were seemingly unable to transcend their history as agents of the apartheid workplace regime.

Clearly the shop stewards were facing a tough battle to ensure that the agreement actually had meaning in the workplace. The problem was that the union lacked the capacity to take up this battle. In the first place, the shop stewards were operating without any support from regional or head office officials[28] and had effectively been doing so for about two years. They found that union policies were too broad and generalised to help them in implementing workplace strategies and engaging with management, and were forced to improvise. The handful of shop stewards who had the confidence and skill to do this was growing ever smaller. Nhlapo, the key strategist and driver of the shop steward committee, was increasingly involved in local politics as well as in union work at a national level; from early 1996 he was seconded full-time to work on a National Training Board (NTB)[29] project in Johannesburg and was able to spend very little time at Highveld Steel. Other shop stewards were increasingly involved in political careers or positioning themselves for promotion within the company. These weaknesses meant that, at a certain point, shop stewards lost faith in the strategy and even in the union. Nhlapo articulated this at the end of 1995: the union could continue to paralyse management initiatives but had no alternative initiatives of its own:

The first step is to make sure that within Vantra nothing happens. You block their initiative, use your old tactics, call strike action, make sure that a similar thing does not happen in GMPD. Then force them to implement the agreement by forming the steering committee. Then once you've done that, I don't know what the steering committee is going to do. That is how far I can think about this thing – block Vantra, block GMPD, then establish a steering committee – don't ask me then what. That's precisely the problem because from here . . . what?

The union had no guidelines for how to participate in green areas, how to form teams without being 'divided by capitalist ideas', how to negotiate production bonuses or profit-sharing. While management was building on experience, engaging at the NTB, learning from other companies both in South Africa and abroad, and developing their strategies, the handful of union officials who were familiar with union thinking on these issues were leaving NUMSA and COSATU. The result was that the shop stewards could not move from shaping the process of engagement with management to shaping the content.

The NUMSA attempt to negotiate a strategy of reconstruction with management failed. The ambiguities and contradictions in the strategy played a role and it may be that the overriding concern of the shop stewards with the issue of who drove change, and with asserting union power in the company, prevented them from seizing opportunities to make gains through co-operating with management initiatives. The lack of union capacity was also vitally important. But the most important factor was the limited nature of management's vision. They proved incapable of grasping the opportunity presented by the shop stewards' commitment to negotiate the transition to a post-apartheid workplace order.

In the rest of this chapter we turn from the level of formal negotiations between management and unions to examine the struggle over contending projects for transformation and incorporation on the shopfloor.

Contending strategies in the workplace: reconstruction on the tap floor

The shop stewards – Nhlapo in particular – made several attempts to implement the union strategy on the shopfloor in specific workplaces,[30] but were successful in only one case, the tap floor in Iron Plant One. There the collective solidarity and militancy of the workers, reinforced by the sophisticated strategising of Nhlapo and the presence of an innovative manager, resulted in a different way of organising work.[31]

When Nhlapo heard in 1992 that the tapping crews on the iron plant tap floors beneath the six furnaces were initiating frequent stoppages in support of their demands for upgrading their jobs and improving their wages, he thought it might provide an opportunity to engage management. The job of the tapping crews was to open the tap-hole when the smelt was ready so that the molten iron and slag could run out of the furnace, separate in the brick-and-sand gutters or launders, and pour over the edge of the tap floor into the waiting slag-pots and iron-pots. The slag was dumped and the molten iron was transported to the steel plant for processing into steel and vanadium slag. The tapping crew drilled the tap-hole open, monitored the separation of iron and slag by the skimmers in the launder, released the flow of separated iron into the iron-pot at the right moment, and tried to prevent spills. After the tap, their job was to clean the launders of iron and slag, clean up any spills that occurred when slag or iron overflowed the launders, and then prepare the launders and skimmers for the next tap.

Conditions on the tap floor were arduous and dangerous in the extreme. Workers had to wear thick protective suits because of the heat of the molten iron and the danger of spills. Dehydration and heat exhaustion sometimes caused workers to collapse; workers were injured and on occasion had died in spills. One of the tap floor workers described these conditions:

> I am used to the place so I can work there with ease, but for a new person it is a very dangerous place. Whenever you are on the tap floor you should always do what the people who work there do, not run away or take the wrong direction.

The tap floor was a harsh working environment, not only because of the physical conditions, but also because of treatment meted out by supervisors:

> It was tough on the tap floor. If they regarded you as cheeky they would send you there. If you complained about wages you were sent there as well. It was a white-dominated working site, it was an apartheid workplace. The treatment there was not fair.

Most of the tappers were illiterate migrants, many of them Pedi-speakers. Many had worked on the tap floor for long periods of their working lives. During the late 1980s, with the change in the company's recruiting policy, relatively highly educated young township residents had begun to appear on the tap floor, but they were promoted fairly quickly to operate the kilns or furnaces. Each tapping team was led by a *baas-boy* or *induna* – an institution that seems to have lasted longer here than elsewhere. When the furnace operator decided that the smelt was ready for tapping, he informed the foreman, who instructed the *baas-boy* to start tapping. The *baas-boy* told the members of his team to get ready while he drilled open the tap-hole. The tapping team members were graded as labourers on grade 14, while the *baas-boy* was on grade 13. Absenteeism was fairly high, and, after they had finished tapping their furnace, tappers in one team were frequently instructed to join another team and assist with tapping a second furnace. This was a sore point with workers, who felt entitled to rest between taps because of the gruelling nature of their work.

The tappers were known for their high level of solidarity and militancy – as Nhlapo put it, 'that's where the strength of the union is'. They felt that the harsh conditions of their work merited higher wages, and during 1990 they launched a series of small stoppages demanding to discuss their problems with their manager. Eventually they were promoted – the tappers by one grade and the *baas-boy* by three. This exacerbated the tappers' grievances, and they demanded to be promoted three grades themselves. Although the *baas-boy* was supposed to open the tap-hole, all the tappers knew how to perform this task. It had long been a custom on the tap floor that if the *baas-boy* was not present, the foreman would instruct another member of the team to do so. But now they refused on the grounds that they were not paid to perform this task:

> Management would come and just point at anyone and tell them to do the job. So we realised that we have the same knowledge, but we are not paid for the work. That is why we came up with this grievance, after realising that we knew the same thing.

Management bent company policy and offered to pay the tapper who filled in for the *induna* an acting allowance at the higher rate. This worked for three months before the tappers again refused to co-operate:

> If the *baas-boy* was absent no one would open the tap-hole. The operator could not move from his pulpit and come down to the tap floor. So he would phone the superintendent. The superintendent, not knowing the skills of opening the tap-hole, would phone the manager, and he would come and start begging the guys to open the hole. But they would just sit down and say, 'You do it. Once the tap-hole is open we will work. But now the tap-hole is closed and there is no one to open it.' If the manager called another *baas-boy* to come and do it the guys would threaten to walk off the floor. If management tried to discipline a worker who refused to open the tap-hole or refused to assist another team, all of the workers on the tap floors would leave their work and go to the inquiry, and say, 'We are going to witness this inquiry'.

It was at this point that Nhlapo intervened. Since the tap floor occupied a key place in the production process any delay brought the entire steel plant to a standstill, so management was under intense pressure to resolve the workers' grievances. The iron plant manager agreed that the tappers could be upgraded to grade 12 but insisted that it should be paid for by reducing the number of workers per team. The numbers had been reduced from nine to seven in the 1991 retrenchments, and mechanical grabs had been introduced to help clean the workplace after tapping. Management proposed that the size of the teams be frozen at their new levels, and justified this by arguing that the grabs had reduced the workload. Since this would not entail any fresh reduction, workers 'were ready to fall for it' until Nhlapo pointed out that it could intensify work because the grabs were subject to frequent breakdowns, and that it would make it more difficult, when market conditions improved, to re-engage their former workmates who had been retrenched.

Instead, Nhlapo proposed to the tappers that work be reorganised so that they operated as self-directed teams. Job descriptions should be expanded to include drilling open the tap-hole for tapping, using the special gun for shooting open the tap-hole when it was blocked, repairing the brickwork in the launders, minor welding work, and checking and replacing the safety screens. All tappers should be trained in these tasks and in leadership and team skills, and upgraded to grade 10. There should no longer be a *baas-boy*, but each team should elect its own leader and this position should be rotated. The workers agreed. This seemed like a proposal that would not only satisfy their demand for more money but also alter the racial and skill hierarchies of the apartheid workplace, and it was attractive to migrants who were located at the bottom of the apartheid hierarchy:

> Mosi came to our rescue with the suggestion that since there were jobs that whites were doing that we could do, why don't those jobs be done by us, so that our wages can also be equal to theirs.

While the proposal was put to management, workers applied their work-to-rule tactics to the grab. Whenever the grab ceased functioning – which was frequently – the team would down tools until two extra workers were found or the grab was repaired. At about this time Mike Bowker,[32] an innovative manager from flat products, was shifted to the iron plant. He proved to be more open to co-operation with the shop stewards and welcomed suggestions. He agreed to get rid of the grabs and expand the teams again, and motivated acceptance of proposals for teamwork and upgrading to senior management. Agreement was reached on a two-month training programme for all tappers. It was a radical break with the organisation of the apartheid workplace regime. For most of the unskilled migrants on the tap floors it was the first training they had received. This was the case for Albert Makagula, a migrant who had worked there for 10 years:

> We only realised how well we do the job after we had been for training. What has improved now is the sense that we all have equal knowledge and everyone knows what to do, and there are no conflicting ideas on the job that we are doing. That is the fulfilling thing, that everyone knows exactly what to do and why, and that's why it's better now.

The training, upgrading and increased pay for tappers implied a recognition of the skills, experience and importance of a group of black workers who had been least acknowledged in the apartheid workplace. According to collective memory on the tap floors, white workers had once been responsible for opening the tap-holes, and the black workers who replaced them had been paid much less: 'Throughout the years we were paid in a discriminatory way. Now for the first time we succeeded in forcing management to pay us equally with the whites.' The tappers had also won the right to 'job ownership', defined by a job in a particular team on a specific tap floor. Tappers could no longer be instructed to assist in another team whose members were absent. Instead, workers from the preceding and following shifts would be requested to work 12-hour rather than eight-hour shifts to cover absenteeism, which meant increased overtime pay.

The culture of solidarity on the tap floor that had always been strong was reinforced by the new way of working. The workers there felt it was important for new workers to share their experience:

> The new people who come in should also go for the same training, so that whatever they are paid and whatever job they do is equal to

everyone else. That is what the fight is all about now, that every person who comes into the job should also go for training.

The creation of self-directed teams was a direct challenge to the racial structure of power centred on the foremen – and management resistance to removing them indicates how important they were to the practices of the apartheid workplace regime:

> We said, okay, remove this foreman, because when there are problems, when there is spillage, this foreman just stands there and says, *Werk! Werk! Werk!*[33] – but he has got no idea how to do this work himself. Remove this foreman, he must never be in contact with these people. The furnace operator, let it be his responsibility to move from his pulpit and tell the tappers that it is time to tap. So when there are problems the operator and the tapping team can communicate, unlike the foreman who just gives instructions and goes away – when there are problems there is no one to talk to. It was a tough battle. Management said, 'No, this foreman is important.' We said, 'He has got no role here.' Eventually management agreed and the foreman was removed.

The importance of the new way of working, in Makagula's view, was that workers could control their work and protect each other from the racism and victimisation of management:

> Before, the manager would come to tell us to start tapping and would interfere with our work in many ways – even though we knew what we were supposed to do. Multi-skilling and teamwork are important, in this way we are more protected and we can protect each other. The way we now work at the iron plant is one of the ways I hope to see democracy in the workplace, because I find myself feeling happy with the way we work. There is no harassment from white people.

Instead of being oppressed by the foreman, workers could develop their own leadership skills:

If workers are scattered and there is a job that needs to be done, the leader is the person who organises everyone and calls them together and tells them what to do. If management comes about a problem in the plant, or wants to know why a particular worker is absent, then he knows who to speak to. That is why there has to be a leader at all times. The former *baas-boys* are still with us, and probably they are happier than us with the new arrangement, because it used to be very difficult for them.

Another tap floor shop steward, Hendrik Nkosi, commented on how workers' attitude had changed with the transformation in the structure of power:

Before, the *baas-boy* was part and parcel of the foreman. The foreman had to assist the *baas-boy* because the people didn't do the job properly. The people were not working properly – not to say they didn't know the job, but the *baas-boy* was driving the people and the people were fighting the bosses. Now people are doing the job properly, the people are happy about this system. They assist the team leader, whereas they never helped the *baas-boy*. I don't see the foreman's job at the tap floor now, he's got nothing to do.

Nkosi also described the collective resolution of disciplinary problems:

The leader calls the whole team to say, 'Let's talk with this gentleman', because he has come late many times, or maybe when he's present he is not doing the job properly. 'Let's find out from him what his problem is.' So the team sits down and talks to him.

If that didn't solve the problem the leader would call some members from another team to assist, or even involve a shop steward. This was a process of trying to solve the problem through discussion rather than punishment. Management's disciplinary procedures remained in place if the workers could not solve the problem. Nkosi stressed that this approach also protected workers from managerial discipline – something that had been of concern to workers since the 1980s:

It is important to understand that if the man is absent and he didn't report to the team, the team can't defend him from management's disciplinary inquiry because they can't explain why he is absent.

There were limitations to the tap floor experiment. For Nhlapo, there had not been a shift to real multi-skilling. He would have liked to see the tappers trained to operate the furnace as well, thus abolishing the distinction between tappers and operators, but the tappers' lack of formal education made this impossible. Welding was not included on the training course and, in practice, the tappers did not patch the launders. Several of the tappers confirmed that they had not learnt new work skills on the training course since they already had the skills to do their job. What was new was the training in leadership skills, and information about how the furnace worked. Other than that, the chief contribution of the training course was that it gave formal recognition to the informal skills of the workers.

The new organisation of work on the tap floors was not based on a reorganisation of work and production in the entire plant. This rendered it vulnerable to erosion over time. The migrant worker activist, Tshagata, moved to the tap floor after the new arrangements had been put in place, because he had heard that the pay was better. He did not receive any training, and commented that the racial division of labour persisted because the task of shooting open the tap-hole if it was blocked was still reserved for a white foreman:

We blacks mainly work for the whites. I must go and select the gun and place it properly for him so that he can shoot. The white man will just come and shoot, and this job of shooting is not really work. After he has finished he goes away, and I continue with the work.

Despite the limitations, the union was able to combine the traditional militancy and solidarity of the tap floor workers with the insights of its new programme in constructing a new regime on the tap floors, even if it was only an enclave in the still-intact broader workplace regime. As one of the iron plant shop stewards put it: 'We have taken the workers out of their Egypt, now they are in Jerusalem.' This enclave was not insignificant, incorporating some 160 workers on three shifts. The new regime dismantled the racial hierarchy of skill, income and power, and replaced it with the collective organisation and control of their work by black workers, nurturing workers' solidarity, democracy and leadership skills. Work teams elected and rotated their own leaders, removing the racist and authoritarian power of the foreman. Workers endeavoured to resolve problems of discipline and performance collectively, building their collective solidarity and protecting each other against managerial discipline. While the new regime entrenched a greater sphere of workers' control over their work, it also created the possibility for greater co-operation with management.

Workers did try to extend their control over discipline – in co-operation with management – but this revealed the instability of the new enclave. It started with the continuing problem of endemic absenteeism on the tap floors. Bowker and the tap floor shop stewards discussed this and reached agreement that the tap floor workers should establish their own disciplinary committee with the authority to punish persistent absenteeism with suspensions of up to several days without pay. In return management would suspend its own disciplinary procedures. Iron plant workers and shop stewards adopted this strategy, which had parallels with practices during the 1980s, to protect themselves from excessive work and their workmates from final warnings and dismissals.[34]

However, the arrangement proved deeply unstable. Nhlapo argued that management should be responsible for discipline because it paid workers' wages, that it was 'immoral' for workers to discipline another worker, and that it would cause division and cliques among them. One of the iron plant shop stewards commented that worker-controlled discipline had not been fairly applied. Some workers were treated leniently while the disciplinary committee punished others harshly, and there were no clear procedures or rights to representation. The disciplinary committee ultimately became a source of contention between workers and management when workers tried to use it to enforce solidarity during a wildcat strike, and it was disbanded.

Nonetheless, Tshagata for one regretted that workers' control of discipline had ended. It protected workers' jobs and pointed to a regime governed by 'the law of freedom':

I'm sad about the end of that committee. It was able to consider that the children of the worker should continue to eat because when he came back from suspension he was not dismissed. In my view it was good because it accorded with the law of freedom.

Events on the tap floors demonstrated the potential of reconstruction to meet some of management's concerns as well as create a domain of democracy and worker control. The strategy provided a set of resources for contesting the form of workplace incorporation and establishing considerable autonomy and worker control, but it was dependent too on innovation and co-operation from management. It proved unsustainable because wider co-operation could not be established.

Contending workplace strategies: wildcat co-operation in Iron Plant One[35]

The iron plant also became the site for the most comprehensive management initiative to construct a new workplace order on its own terms. The common factor was Mike Bowker. He was appointed works manager at Iron Plant One during 1992. In the shop stewards' experience he was different from any other manager at Highveld Steel, keen to innovate and experiment, open to discussion and consultation with the union and the shop stewards. His style was different – he interacted with ordinary workers on the shopfloor and visited shop stewards at home.

Bowker's strategy for eliciting co-operation was to work with groups in different sections of the plant on ways to reorganise work, without the constraints of negotiating with the union over the broader implications of local changes. He would identify common interests through a process of negotiation and consultation with workers, and try to accommodate their demands – usually for increased pay – by linking these to a reorganisation of the work process. In this way the workers would be won over to his goals of increasing efficiency and reducing costs, through increased levels of skill, pay and responsibility. In driving this process, Bowker could build a worker constituency supportive of his vision of workplace change, weakening the union's links to its own constituency and the shop stewards' ability to challenge his project and drive their own. Through this kind of participation, Bowker could ensure management retained control over workplace restructuring and over production.

Nhlapo first became aware of Bowker's plans when these were presented at the company-level restructuring committee. He thought they were 'a marvellous proposal' promising 'very significant changes that I can call real restructuring' which had the potential to reduce the high level of waste product in the iron plant. Despite his enthusiasm Nhlapo was concerned about Bowker's reluctance to discuss the broader implications. He also feared the impact of increased efficiency on staffing levels. Finally, there was no discussion about how workers would benefit from increased profits:

> This means more profits. Now, how do you benefit from these profits? By upgrading two people and employing two extra foremen? Until we are involved in how the profits are distributed, I don't think we should co-operate with management.

As important, if not more so, were his concerns about the politics of workplace change. Management did not see the restructuring committee as a forum for discussing and negotiating proposals but expected shop stewards to endorse and help to implement management ideas. It was important for the union 'to counter them in many ways so that they can begin to respect us' and so compel them to accept that change had to be negotiated. Workplace change was as much about the balance of power and control as it was about grading or efficiency. This also applied to Bowker's proposals, since he showed little inclination to negotiate with the shop steward leadership, preferring to interact with the shop stewards in the iron plant and win them over to his proposals.

Meanwhile, Bowker was busy building other constituencies for change in the iron plant, bypassing the shop steward leadership who were 'frustrating' him. He was able to construct support for his vision of restructuring the work of kiln operators, furnace operators and hot-charge car drivers in Iron Plant One by encouraging participation and accommodating immediate concerns.

His first opportunity came when black kiln operators complained that as white kiln operators were replaced by blacks, management also did away with the kiln attendants. This meant the operators had to perform extra tasks, like cleaning their workplaces or unblocking the chutes that fed the kilns, which made it impossible to control the kilns properly and resulted in poor production. Frustrated by management's lack of response, a shop steward on the kilns proposed in a meeting with management that a working group should be established to investigate the problem and propose solutions. A shop steward from the furnaces added that they had a similar problem with a shortage of operators. The shop stewards and Bowker agreed that two working groups should be established, one for the kilns and one for the furnaces. The kiln working group consisted of the shop steward, seven rank-and-file workers, the superintendent and the assistant manager. The furnace group had a similar structure. The shop stewards saw these working groups as participative structures where managers and workers should combine as a team, rather than negotiating as representatives.

According to the kiln shop steward:

> It was an idea that flashed into my mind – that if we continue to put the whole problem on management they will do nothing. We better get ourselves involved. There is no win, no lose, in actual fact. When we are disputing on a certain issue we are trying to find a solution, we are not trying to win. What are you going to win there? We all win if the solution is found, we all lose if there is no solution, because the problem will still be there.

Although he regarded the working group as a union structure, the shop steward did not feel it necessary to discuss this initiative with the rest of the shop steward committee beyond the iron plant:

> We have support for this throughout iron plant, but the other divisions don't know anything about it because this involves the problems of iron plant. It's just a working group, we have agreed with management.

The shop steward in the furnace working group agreed that the participatory forum should transcend the usual bargaining relationship between managers and unionists, but found that the manager was unable to do this:

> I found something which is not right. The manager who was chairing the meeting was separating himself from us, from the team. He was talking on behalf of management, which means that we're supposed to talk on behalf of the workforce, which is wrong. I told him that

we're supposed to forget that you are a manager and I am a shop steward. We're coming to try and solve the problems of these people, all of us, as a team.

These two quotes show how 'wildcat co-operation' facilitated the emergence of new non-union collective identities among workers. There were two aspects to this. Firstly, in their desire for a different relationship with management – an aspiration for management to co-operate with them – workers distanced themselves from the union and its bargaining stance so as to build a 'team' with management. Secondly, workers and even shop stewards started to distance themselves from the union as the representative of the general interest of all workers in the company, and constituted themselves into smaller, more local groups with specific sectional work-interests – iron plant workers, or kiln workers and furnace workers.[36]

Bowker clearly succeeded in sorting out the problems in the furnace working group: a year later the shop steward reported that the working groups had developed a successful proposal to solve the shortage of labour by employing and training a new category of workers called swingmen. The swingmen formed a flexible, multi-skilled group of workers who could be deployed wherever there were shortages – to the kilns, furnaces or hot-charge cars. Twelve attendants were trained and upgraded for this position. The furnace shop steward counted this as a success: workers had been upgraded, the workload of operators had improved and management and workers had co-operated fruitfully. The only problem was that the new multi-skilled workers were graded and paid two levels below the operators, although they were even more skilled. The shop steward did not see this as a major problem: he and other shop stewards had 'as the union' demanded that this anomaly be addressed. Bowker had satisfied them by promising that it would occur once the restructuring of work in the iron plant as a whole had been completed – again, successfully establishing a constituency in support of his programme of restructuring.

While the furnace shop steward was pleased with the success of the working groups, one of the white foremen who had joined NUMSA argued that the shop steward leadership was correct, and that management had pulled the wool over the workers' eyes. The swingmen were happy because they had been upgraded, but their presence was allowing management to continue reducing the numbers of other workers, some of them – kiln and furnace operators, furnace attendants, hot-charge car drivers and radial gate attendants – paid more highly than the swingmen. Swingmen had applied for vacant positions as kiln or furnace operators, but were refused and the posts were kept vacant. Contractors were being brought in to do work previously done by furnace attendants. Management was planning a programme of automation that would do away with hot-charge car drivers. In other words, it was slowly implementing a programme to create a smaller, multi-skilled and flexible workforce that would simultaneously reduce costs and increase responsibility. The iron plant shop stewards, focused on immediate and local concerns and grievances, were missing the broader picture and failing to protect the collective interests of all iron plant workers. Bowker had successfully mobilised localised interests in 'wildcat co-operation' and undermined the union as the representative of the broader collective interest of workers.

This tendency was exacerbated by the new opportunities for talented black workers – and especially shop stewards with leadership skills – to benefit from upward mobility in the restructuring process. The kiln shop steward was promoted into the ranks of management and shifted to a different plant. The furnace shop steward – who had started out as a shop steward on the tap floor – was regularly appointed an 'acting foreman', and expected to be promoted as a full-time foreman. Co-operation with management clearly held potential for the advancement of their personal careers.

Initially, the furnace shop steward commented on the dangers of Bowker's style and of working with management as a team:

> He's clever. If you talk with him you're supposed to be very careful. He tries to pull you from your side to be with him now, to be on the management side. If you don't look carefully, you can't see him pulling you from that side. He wants to use you. He knows that if he gives a report together with you to the workers, they will accept it. Maybe later they will say this thing was not right. They are going to fight with you then, not with him.

But a year later, he was convinced that fundamental changes had taken place:

Racism is totally changing. The management and workers are friends. If the foreman makes tea he doesn't make tea for himself only. He asks all of us whether we want tea. Before, the foremen did not talk with the tapper. Now they talk not only about work, but generally. The whites are coming to NUMSA. And they even come to my home to visit me, these whites. Before, I was the enemy to them.

This also meant the role of the shop steward had changed:

There are no more disciplinary inquiries. The foremen can solve problems with the workers. For the past ten months nothing has been required of me as a shop steward. Now you can't tell the management, I want this because I'm black. No, you're supposed to think now. The time for fighting is past. Now you can negotiate. The door is open. If there is something you are not happy about you can go and talk about it.

White foremen were able to use the new relations that emerged from wildcat co-operation to re-establish discipline on a new basis – very different to the attempted solution of *authoritarian restoration*. The shop steward could restore the foreman's link to a culturally alien workforce, lost when the *baas-boy* was 'taken away', as one foreman explained:

We solved it our way. We went to the shop steward and told him we've got a problem and asked for help. It's an easier way, because we don't know their languages. The easiest way to solve problems is to go to the shop steward with the guy and the shop steward can explain in his own language. Then we sit down and explain to each other what the problem is.[37]

Another white supervisor commented on how he was having to learn new ways of relating to black subordinates – with a note of surprise that the world had not collapsed:

The black, if he was calling 'Gert', there was shit. It was 'baas Gert' or nothing. Nowadays they call you by your name and each and everybody is getting used to it, and things are running smoothly. That's quite normal now, things that weren't happening in the past. Okay, there were some problems in changing over, but not serious, and after that things carried on.[38]

By the end of 1995, Nhlapo had to acknowledge that Bowker 'has managed to get me out of his way'. The group of energetic new black foremen appointed by Bowker supported the new way of working. Like the kiln and furnace operators, the hot-charge car drivers supported Bowker's restructuring plans because it meant increased wages and responsibility for them. Nhlapo 'doubted' whether the iron plant shop stewards were still really union representatives since they too had been won over to Bowker's idea. Nhlapo's absence from the factory on the NTB project had given Bowker crucial space:

He had all these plans a long time ago, but he was blocked. We said we need to have an agreement before he can implement them. Now if I come in there I'll come in as someone who's trying to block progressiveness from Bowker. We're divided in iron plant. Most blacks want this thing in place, most whites are saying no to this thing.

In the view of the iron plant shop steward, a new workplace regime had been constructed through co-operation between workers, shop stewards and management. In the view of the shop steward leadership, through the process of 'wildcat co-operation', management in the iron plant had managed to undermine the collective identity of the union, elicit new collective identities outside the union, and co-opt the shop stewards. The result was management control over restructuring, which held potential dangers for workers, and the inability of the union to contest, negotiate or put forward its own demands in relation to restructuring. Workplace restructuring was removed from the terrain of company-level negotiations where safeguards could be built in, long-term goals established, and the distribution of increased profitability negotiated.

Wildcat co-operation proved a successful strategy, from management's point of view, for incorporating black workers and forging a post-apartheid workplace regime while neutralising union resistance. While it preserved managerial domination, it did so by accommodating some of the demands and aspirations of black workers for a changed workplace, and so accorded them the opportunity to influence it, albeit from a subordinate position and informally rather than through the structures of the union.

Legacy of the apartheid workplace regime: a stalemate in reconstruction

The failure of the union strategy to transform the workplace, and the failure of managerial strategies of authoritarian restoration, resulted in a general stalemate, notwithstanding the successful implementation of wildcat co-operation in one or two plants, which meant that the neo-apartheid workplace regime – including its tendency towards decomposition – remained in place.[39]

This chapter opened with the description of a strike over racial assault. A second costly strike three years later, in September 1996, revealed continuing racial tension around power, authority and procedure.[40] Again the strike was sparked by a white supervisor assaulting a black labourer. This case read like a carbon copy of the confrontations of the 1980s and repeated the patterns of the 1993 strike against racial assault, minus the militant involvement of the MWU and the AWB.[41] Clearly important elements of the neo-apartheid workplace regime were still present in 1996, six years after the unbanning of the liberation movement and more than two years after the democratic elections. The arbitrator's ruling supported the union: the white supervisor was guilty of assault and the black labourer was not guilty. The case suggests not only that racial assault was still a factor on the shopfloor, but that managers continued to support white supervisors against black workers and apply discipline in a racially discriminatory way, and that despite a professed concern about the high incidence of assault on the shopfloor, senior management was prepared to support white managers without question through a costly 12-day strike. The persistence of racial tension on the shopfloor seems to have been invisible to senior white managers and, in a newspaper advertisement, the company blamed the union for behaviour which was discouraging investors and 'very damaging to the entire national effort'. It appeared insensible to the irony of building a 'national effort' on the foundations of the apartheid workplace, which the company was implicitly defending.

The persistence of important features of the neo-apartheid workplace regime ensured the continued illegitimacy of the regime in the eyes of workers. This is implicit in the workplace behaviour of the black worker and the strikers' behaviour. They ignored the dispute provisions of the new 1995 Labour Relations Act as well as a court interdict instructing them to return to work. The company complained that the union showed 'disregard for agreed procedures' and 'for the law', and that workers 'barricaded roads, manhandled and threatened employees going to work, hijacked contractors' vehicles and damaged a number of vehicles'. As Nhlapo commented earlier, when provoked, workers would put aside any agreement or procedure in order to 'deal directly with management'. The cost to the company was high, both directly through the strike, which was estimated to have cost R30 million, and through ongoing inefficiencies.

The continuity of racial conflict should not, however, obscure a growing fluidity in workplace racial relations. Six weeks after the strike described at the beginning of this chapter, NUMSA and MWU went out on a joint strike over wages. By 1995 several white workers had left MWU and joined NUMSA, particularly a group of iron plant foremen who felt threatened by Bowker's restructuring plans. The easing of racial tension was facilitated by both of the more co-operative projects (negotiated reconstruction and wildcat co-operation), and in turn made them more viable (see Von Holdt 2001). Thus both stalemate and fluidity could be found within the workplace regime, and its final shape was not yet settled.

Notes

1. This section is based on interview with a group of shop stewards, 2/9/93; interview, Andre Vermaak, 9/93; also interview, Ambrose Mthembu, 15/3/94; interview, Ezekiel Nkosi, 9/3/94; interview, Jacob Skhosana, 14/4/94; interview, Tshagata, 26/5/94.
2. Interview, Frank Boshielo, 9/93; interview, Gert van der Merwe, 29/11/95; interview, Albert Makagula, 29/3/94; interview, Marcus Moswane, 21/8/95; interview, Mosi Nhlapo, 15/3/94; interview, Ezekiel Nkosi, 9/3/94; interview, William Sehlola, 5/6/94. See chapter 2 for figures.

3. Interview, Ambrose Mthembu, 14/5/94; interview, Ezekiel Nkosi, 9/3/94; interview, Johannes Phatlana, 15/4/94; interview, Jacob Skhosana, 26/4/94.

4. Interview, Bunny Mahlangu, 12/5/94.

5. Interview, Frank Boshielo, 9/93; interview, Phineas Mabena, 12/5/94; interview, Veli Majola, 26/10/95; interview, Jacob Skhosana, 14/4/94.

6. Interview, Ambrose Mthembu, 22/10/95.

7. Interview, Bunny Mahlangu, 15/8/95.

8. Afrikaans surnames.

9. Interview, Mosi Nhlapo, 15/3/94.

10. Interview, Paxon Mokoena, 14/6/94.

11. This and the following two paragraphs are drawn from interview, Gert van der Merwe, 29/11/95; interview, Hong Kong Kgalima, 3/7/94; interview, Ambrose Mthembu, 15/3/94, 14/5/94; interview, Mosi Nhlapo, 8/5/94; interview, Ezekiel Nkosi, 9/3/94, 15/4/94; interview, Hendrik Nkosi, 14/6/94; interview, Johannes Phatlana, 15/4/94; interview, Jacob Skhosana, 14/4/94, 26/4/94.

12. Interview, Phineas Mabena, 12/5/94; interview, Ezekiel Nkosi, 9/3/94, 5/5/94; interview, Johannes Phatlana,15/4/94. Shift-workers work an eight-hour shift without a formal lunch break. The regular day shift-workers work a nine-hour day with a lunch break in the canteen.

13. Interview, Ephraim Kgole, 10/95; interview, J.J. Mbonani, 31/5/94; interview, Jerry Mogoleko, 10/95; interview, Hendrik Nkosi, 14/6/94; interview, Johannes Phatlana, 7/9/94.

14. Interview, Tshagata, 26/5/94; see also interview, Philip Mkatshwa, 8/95.

15. Interview, Mosi Nhlapo, 15/3/94.

16. Interview, Hong Kong Kgalima, 3/7/94.

17. Interview, Ezekiel Nkosi, 3/9/94, 15/4/94. This taunt was reported from several plants, for example, interview, Johannes Phatlana, 7/9/94.

18. Interview, Johannes Phatlana, 15/4/94.

19. Interview, Ezekiel Nkosi, 15/4/94; see also interview, Mosi Nhlapo, 8/5/94.

20. Interview, Gert van der Merwe, 29/11/95.

21. Interview, Bossie Bezuidenhout, 29/8/95.

22. The following account of the disciplinary initiative is drawn from Highveld Steel joint shop stewards' committee meeting, 12 November 1994; interview, Bossie Bezuidenhout, 29/8/95; interview, Ambrose Mthembu, 22/10/95; interview, Mosi Nhlapo, 8/5/94, 6/3/95, 12/95; interview, Hendrik Nkosi, 26/10/95; interview, Johannes Phatlana, 12/10/95. The account of the green areas is drawn from interview, Ambrose Mthembu, 15/3/94; interview, Mosi Nhlapo, 15/3/94, 8/5/94, 10/7/94, 6/3/95; interview, Ezekiel Nkosi, 9/3/94, 5/5/94, 26/5/94, 23/11/95; interview, Johannes Phatlana, 15/4/94; interview, Tshagata, 10/95.

23. 'Green areas' are forums for participatory management, where workers and their supervisors discuss production problems.

24. See Von Holdt (2000: 282–7) for a fuller account of these processes and contestation over them.

25. This section is based on Highveld Steel shop stewards' meeting, 19 May 1994, 12 November 1994, 9 December 1995; interview, Ambrose Mthembu, 22/10/95; interview, Mosi Nhlapo, 10/7/94, 6/3/95, 12/95; Highveld Steel letter, 29 April 1994: Appendix C: Technical negotiating structures.

26. I am referring here to the lack of a common underlying understanding on these issues; there was a formal agreement according to which each technical committee would meet at least once per fortnight, decision making would be by consensus, agreements and disagreements would be referred to a steering committee, and unresolved issues would be referred to mediation or arbitration.

27. This section is based on Highveld Steel shop stewards meeting, 9 December 1995; interview, Ambrose Mthembu, 22/10/95; interview, Mosi Nhlapo, 12/95; interview, Ezekiel Nkosi, 23/11/95; Approach to multi-skilling: NUMSA (prepared by shop stewards in March 1995); Agreement of intent: efficiency improvement programme (draft 6 July 1995 and final draft with structures and procedures, 9 September 1995); Workplace changes (shop stewards' response to July draft of above, n.d., handwritten); Into the bushes (document prepared by shop stewards in early 1997 for *bosberaad* [brainstorming meeting] with management).

28. The two head office officials responsible for Highveld Steel, and who had indicated in 1993, when this research project was first mooted, that the company could become a pilot project for the implementation of the union strategic vision, were never available to the shop stewards at Highveld Steel. One left the union shortly after, and the other was constantly needed in national level negotiations before he too left the union. When the shop stewards had finished negotiating the agreement of intent, the national organiser and regional organiser responsible for Highveld Steel refused to sign on behalf of NUMSA, citing the clause on redundancies as unacceptable. The shop stewards were scathing in their response, pointing out that the organisers had failed to attend negotiations, that the clause stipulated consultation on retrenchment and that in any case the house agreement laid down procedures for negotiating retrenchment, and argued that their agreement was superior to what the national union had achieved in the Industrial Council. Eventually NUMSA did sign.

29. The NTB was established as part of the ANC government's drive – influenced by COSATU's policies – to raise the level of skills in South African industry.

30. See interview, Mosi Nhlapo, 15/3/94; interview, Ezekiel Nkosi, 9/3/94.

31. This account of the struggle to construct a new order on the tap floor draws from interview, Veli Majola, 26/10/95; interview, Albert Makagula, 24/3/94, 29/3/94; interview, Mosi Nhlapo, 15/3/94, 8/5/94; interview, Hendrik Nkosi, 26/5/94.

32. Not his real name.

33. *Werk! Werk! Werk!*: 'Work! Work! Work!'

34. This kind of negotiated control of discipline seems not to have been unusual in this period; see for example Von Holdt (1994, 1996). See also chapter 3, pp. 79–82.

35. This and the next section are drawn from interview, Bossie Bezuidenhout, 29/8/95; interview, Paxon Mokoena, 14/6/94; interview, Mosi Nhlapo, 8/5/94, 10/7/94, 6/3/95,

12/95; interview, Hendrik Nkosi, 14/6/94, 26/10/95; interview, Gert van der Merwe, 29/11/95; conversation with Mike Bowker, iron plant manager, 24/3/94.

36. These alternative team and sectional collective identities exist in one form or another in most workplaces, and unionism needs to find effective ways to engage them and incorporate them into its project – especially where management seeks to mobilise them to its own ends, as current human resource management practices tend to do.

37. Interview, Bossie Bezuidenhout, 29/8/95.

38. Interview, Gert van der Merwe, 29/11/95.

39. See for example interview, Mosi Nhlapo, 12/95.

40. This account is based on the arbitrator's award (faxed mimeo, reference no. GAR 001597); *Business Day* 1/11/96, 5/11/96, 12/11/96; *The Star* 7/11/96; Highveld Steel 'Cautionary announcement' advertisement in *Business Day* 13/11/96; NUMSA advertisement in *Business Day* 13/12/96.

41. A black labourer went to the shop to buy bread for tea. On his return he was confronted by his white chargehand for being absent from work without permission, and was assaulted by him. He lodged a grievance. At a disciplinary inquiry both were dismissed for assault. On appeal both were reinstated with final warnings. Some 2 000 NUMSA members launched an immediate strike, demanding the dismissal of the white supervisor and the reinstatement of the labourer with a clear record. After a week the company reached agreement with NUMSA that the dispute should be referred to an arbitrator, but would not agree to the union's demand that, should the arbitrator find that the workers were correct and that the company had failed to apply its disciplinary procedure fairly, its members should be paid for their time on strike. As far as the workers were concerned, they were being forced yet again to take action to compel the company to respect its own policies. After several more days on strike, the company accepted this demand too. The arbitrator agreed with the workers, finding that on the labourer's return from the shop the chargehand had grabbed him and begun to force him towards his office. The labourer was justified in resisting this assault by attempting to push the chargehand away, whereupon the chargehand hit the labourer on his cheek with his fist hard enough for a doctor to record bruising and laceration. The white chargehand was therefore guilty of assault and the labourer not guilty. The arbitrator did, however, comment that the labourer's attitude to work and supervision was 'reprehensible'. He was frequently absent from his workplace without permission and his attitude 'indicated an arrogant disregard of his duties as an employee'.

CHAPTER 10

'Amabhova revolt against the union'

The fragmentation and erosion of worker solidarity

> We are going to lose our shop stewards. We have identified others
> to stand as shop stewards, but they are unwilling. People believe
> that in order to be promoted you have to be a blue-eyed boy in the
> eyes of management. I don't believe that there will be people strong
> enough to stand up. It means all that has been achieved is going to
> be lost. *Sidwel Nkosi, active member*

Social movement unionism was a complex amalgam of popular, class and
workplace identities. This accounted for both the intense solidarity of the
trade union movement in the struggle against apartheid in and beyond the
workplace, and the high level of internal contestation and even violent
conflict between contending factions. During the 1990s, the democratic
breakthrough, new processes of class formation, and the contradictory
practices of management in the neo-apartheid workplace regime –
authoritarian restoration and wildcat co-operation – led to the dilution
and fragmentation of solidarity in the social structure of the union.

Challenges from the iron plant
The concerned group: echoes from the past?
During the first democratic elections in South Africa in April 1994, workers
in the iron plant launched a two-day stayaway to ensure that everyone
could vote. In the days preceding the elections the workers in the iron
plant – particularly the migrants on the tap floors – had become concerned
about how workers who lived in faraway rural areas would vote. By this
time the shop steward leadership at Highveld Steel was working full-time

on the ANC election campaign, so there was no one to answer their questions. At a general meeting in the iron plant, workers decided that a stayaway was the only solution, thus flouting union policy.

The remarkable feature of this stayaway was the workers' rejection of 'interference' by shop stewards. When the only senior shop steward left at the steelworks remonstrated with the iron plant leadership, he was told that he and the other shop stewards were mistrusted and the iron plant workers 'are going to do things on our own'. After the elections, when the secretary of the shop steward committee tried to discuss the stayaway with those in the iron plant, he was told 'this thing has got nothing to do with the union, it is our thing of the iron plant, please excuse us'.[1] The stayaway was clearly more than simply a wildcat action – it was also a rejection of the union, or at least of the shop steward leadership in the company.

The stayaway and the interactions which accompanied it were the product of two organisational initiatives rooted in the iron plant. While these two groups had similar concerns and some overlapping membership, they were also quite distinct and evolved in different directions. The first was the concerned group which first emerged in Iron Plant One at the beginning of 1994.[2] A group of workers who were dissatisfied with the performance of the shop stewards came together, and established links with dissatisfied workers in other plants, with the aim of 'addressing these issues straight to our leadership'. A key figure in this process was Jacob Msimangu, former chairperson of the strike committee in the 1980s. The concerned group was born out of distrust of the shop steward leadership: they 'were easily communicating with management and we don't have a report back'; they were not achieving anything through negotiations; they were no longer mobilising workers around wage negotiations as in the past; the shop stewards were using their positions as 'a platform for their own political gain'; and their absence from work on political and union business was paralysing the union because ordinary shop stewards did not have the authority to negotiate major issues with management. There were rumours that the shop steward leadership had been 'bought' by management.[3]

The concerned group accused the shop stewards of failing to address their concerns:

We said from now onwards we are members of the union, but we don't recognise our leaders. We do our things according to the union constitution, but the only link with the union will be with the organiser. Then if we have a problem we nominate people to talk with our own divisional management concerning that. That is why we had the stayaway in Iron Plant One. And then the shop stewards wanted to intervene and we said, no, this is our own thing. We did it on our own. Then we chased them away.[4]

For the shop steward leadership, the emergence of the concerned group was a source of great anxiety. It seemed to them that the divisions of 1987 and 1990–91 were surfacing again. The rumours and allegations against them echoed those of the strike committee and the hostel group in earlier conflicts. The man who had been the chairperson of the strike committee appeared to be the main instigator of the concerned group. Some of the iron plant shop stewards were associated with the concerned group, as were former shop stewards from that and other plants. The signs indicated that the concerned group 'are planning to make a coup, to take out all the shop steward committee and replace them'.[5]

Msimangu denied any resemblance between the strike committee and the concerned group – the latter was 'only focused on our internal problems, that there's a crack, so let's close it'. But he acknowledged that the legacy of the earlier divisions still had an extremely potent resonance among members: 'Even in our general meetings workers are saying, we don't forget what happened in 1987, that thing of the strike committee is coming back.'[6]

Unskilled migrants and the 'action committee'
The second initiative was the action committee on the tap floor, which grew out of similar issues at around the same time as the concerned group.[7] However, its focus was local rather than company-wide, seeking to address the marginalisation and disempowerment experienced by the unskilled, illiterate and predominantly migrant workers on the tap floor. The action committee was both a response to grievances about the shop steward leadership, and a response to the perceived ineffectiveness of the local iron plant shop stewards in negotiating with the iron plant management.

According to Tshagata, a founding union member and long-standing activist who had recently moved to the tap floor:

> This committee was started because our iron plant shop stewards were not trusted by the office-bearers. They were saying that our shop stewards take decisions on our behalf. So we decided that we – the workers – should meet and form a committee that will go to the office-bearers and tell them what we as workers want.

Another worker on the tap floor emphasised the weaknesses of some of the iron plant shop stewards:

> My shift had shop stewards who were afraid to face management, who were only representing management's position to us, instead of representing our position to them. The one was always on management's side, he was just trying to get a promotion, and indeed he succeeded at last. We decided to establish a committee of workers who'll be able to face management. I was one of those chosen, as a delegate and not a shop steward.

The promotion of shop stewards was a recurring theme in workers' expressions of distrust. The action committee met several times with the chairperson of the shop steward committee to demand that five of its delegates accompany the negotiating team in the annual round of collective bargaining to ensure that the shop stewards represented them properly – just as the strike committee had done almost ten years before (see p. 151). This demand was eventually agreed to.

There was, therefore, a fluid and overlapping series of organisational initiatives among workers in the iron plant. Only one or two of the shop stewards were trusted by the tappers. The shop stewards from their own ranks were discredited, and they did not believe that the shop stewards from the furnaces and kilns understood their problems, apart from Hendrik Nkosi who had worked on the tap floor. On the other hand, there were tensions between the iron plant shop stewards and the shop steward leadership in the steelworks.[8] On the tap floors the disciplinary committee (see previous chapter) and the action committee overlapped. The concerned group consisted mostly of operators and artisans, although at least one member of the action committee also regarded himself as a participant. The concerned group and the action committee were a response to similar concerns about the office-bearers and the lack of service from the union, and they converged on the election stayaway, but most of the time they seemed quite remote from each other.

Although the iron plant was regarded by the shop steward leadership as the source of a general challenge to their leadership – as in the days of the strike committee and the hostel committee – the distinct organisational forms in the plant illustrated the cleavages that arose among workers as a result of the internal differentiation of the workforce. Many interviewees referred to the specific culture of the illiterate, unskilled, mostly Pedi migrants concentrated on the tap floor. In the words of a shop steward on the kilns:

> They are very militant, those people. They have their own strategy of showing they want a manager – they leave their work and call him to come. It's not good, there are procedures that should be followed. The person who is directly involved in the problem should call the shop steward, he's the one who can solve it.

For another worker, an unskilled labourer, this special culture was an attraction:

> I wanted to work there because they were highly unionised, it was not easy to be victimised because one always had the support of the other workers. The people at the tap floors are the guys who knew the struggle, they have suffered a lot under apartheid. They are willing to fight to ensure that the changes that they have won are not taken away from them.

Their harsh working conditions, their strategic location in the production process, their mutual dependence on the work team in the labour process, their own history of struggle, their shared sense of themselves as migrants among whom Pedi culture was predominant, and their sense of losing power within the union they had founded, produced a strong collective solidarity and militancy among the tappers. They preferred direct action and self-representation to handing matters over to shop stewards and procedures over which they had little control and from which they were alienated by language and education. The disciplinary committee, the action committee and the election stayaway were manifestations of this culture.

For the tappers the meaning of the union had less to do with the structures and constitution of NUMSA than with their own collective solidarity and militancy. When the chair of the shop stewards said 'he did not know where our committee came from because the union constitution only allows for shop stewards', the action committee objected:

> We could not reach agreement with the shop stewards because we believe that we as workers are the basis for the union, it is there because of us. If we have a problem we have to solve it in our own way. We can solve the problem with our shop stewards, or with the action committee, because it is publicly known.

The rise and fall of the concerned group

The shop stewards committee held at least two meetings with the concerned group at which the latter aired their complaints. The shop stewards invited the members of the concerned group to 'boost the committee' by standing for election as shop stewards in their workplaces. The concerned group demanded that the office-bearers should stand down. The meetings broke down in arguments – identical to those between the hostel and township groups in 1990 – over the union constitution and procedures governing union representation in the workplace.

Shop stewards and regional officials were highly suspicious of the motivations of the concerned group. The regional organiser, Bunny Mahlangu, tried to find out the core concern of the group:

> It's difficult to say where this thing is coming from. You get a lot of different stories. Even the perpetrators of this thing seem to be ducking and diving the real issue.

Mahlangu and the shop stewards identified disgruntled individuals in the group: one who was jealous because he had not been chosen for training; another who was in danger of dismissal for absenteeism and was looking for ways to protect himself; a third who had always quarrelled with shop stewards and was suspected of collaboration with management. Some of them were former shop stewards 'and then they ran away, and now they come and accuse the shop steward committee of not working'. Others were happy to attack the shop stewards but always refused to stand for election. There were even two current shop stewards 'who had sidelined themselves'.

Finally, a general meeting was convened for the concerned group to voice its criticisms of the shop stewards. The meeting was particularly interesting for what it revealed of the tensions and dynamics within the union. The chief dynamic was the attack by the migrant workers – the constituency of the action committee on the tap floor – on the concerned group, whom they saw as typically vacillating, unreliable representatives of the more skilled local workers from the township, and their defence of the shop stewards. Also interesting is the shop stewards' sense of the precarious nature of the union order among workers, under constant siege by anti-union *amabhova*[9] among their members. Mosi Nhlapo described the meeting:

That concerned group was nearly *sjambokked*, man. These workers just said to them, 'Look, if you've got any grievances, take them to your shop steward. This is not the place where we're going to discuss these grievances. If you've got problems with your shop steward, go to your plant and elect another shop steward. Don't come with shit here.' People who want to revolt against the union, we call them *bhovas*. A *bhova* is a big ugly dog. All the time it was the people who stayed in the hostel who were *bhovas*, who never wanted the union to operate as it is operating now. Now you've got a new kind of *bhova*, guys from the township who have serious complaints about the union. The guys from the hostel were saying these guys from the township must be dealt with now, in this meeting, you must just *bliksem*[10] them. And they were generalising that everyone from the township must just be *bliksemmed*, you cannot deal with such people. Now the thing is turning round, because these are the guys that were real *bhovas* in 1987. Tshagata was one of the biggest *bhovas* you've ever known in your life, but Tshagata was the first guy who spoke, speaking against these other *bhovas* and telling them, look, you keep quiet. We're going to *sjambok* you, we cannot continue with such people who cannot behave themselves. This shows that Tshagata understands the union now, you can leave him in whatever situation, he's in Iron Plant with those *bhovas* now but he's able to defend the union.[11]

Nhlapo attributed some of this change to the five members of the tap floor action committee who had insisted that they accompany the shop stewards to negotiations:

> They had demanded the right to speak in the negotiations, but they had nothing to say because we were saying everything that should be said. At the end they had to go back to their committee and report that negotiations are what they've seen, the shop stewards are not selling out as they've been told.

As a result, the action committee and its militant migrant constituency turned against the concerned group. The shop stewards were fighting for them, and more than any other workers they appreciated the necessity of unity and collective solidarity if workers were to be protected from management. The old suspicion of township residents as unreliable elements and the source of weakness and division surfaced again. They had come to accept the shop steward leadership from the township, but other township residents were suspect. The most effective way to assert discipline and maintain union unity was to resort to the *sjambok* again.

The shop stewards were elated. Their leadership had been affirmed, and the concerned group defeated. However, a month later they faced a new crisis when workers at the flat products division launched a wildcat strike and rejected the NUMSA shop stewards. The concerned group resumed its attack. It was in a mood of crisis that workers gathered at a general meeting to discuss what to do about the flat products strike. The concerned group accused Nhlapo and Malinga of undermining the union by not calling general meetings to report on negotiations with management, and of selling out the union. It was a heated meeting. For every attack, the constituents of the office-bearers would rise to defend their shop stewards. Bunny Mahlangu and Frank Boshielo were booed and shouted down. At one point a worker – later found to be a non-member – stood up and said that the shop stewards should be killed because they were betraying the workers. Eventually the meeting resolved to elect five workers – two of whom were members of the concerned group – to work with the shop stewards and accompany them in negotiations over the flat products strike to ensure, yet again, that they did not sell out.

After the flat products strike had been resolved, by-elections were held in several constituencies to increase the strength of the shop steward committee. Some members of the concerned group were elected. By early 1995, several of them 'have already disappeared', and it had become clear to Nhlapo and other shop stewards that some of the concerned group had been motivated by a belief that shop stewards had access to opportunities to become small business contractors to the company. Some of the concerned group had put proposals to management for outsourcing certain operations. Msimangu, one of the concerned group who had been elected a shop steward, had a proposal to run an outsourced petrol station. When he discovered the shop stewards had no authority over such issues, he asked them for advice on how to proceed. By the end of the year he had been chosen by management to run a small soap factory to supply Highveld Steel, and he resigned. Six months later the business had folded. And so the concerned group petered out.

The action committee continued on the tap floors. While its constituency had come out in support of the shop steward leadership and against the concerned group, they continued to distrust and bypass most of the shop stewards in the iron plant. They approached Nhlapo several times asking him to remove two of the shop stewards, but refused to organise by-elections to elect new shop stewards.[12] They persisted in their sense of themselves as migrants marginalised in urban society and, they suspected, in the union too. Nhlapo described a confrontation between himself and Tshagata, the erstwhile *bhova* turned union-supporter whose suspicions of the union leadership had resurfaced, over whether a tap floor worker had been adequately represented in a disciplinary inquiry:

Tshagata was saying that Veli is from Transkei, he is not from Witbank, that is why we never wanted to represent him properly. We explained that we did. Tshagata said again, us guys who come from outside Witbank, we're not going to join this union. This union is for people who stay in Witbank. All these things started again. I must say I was angry and emotional. I said, look, if that's the way you want to run this union, I'm quitting. Immediately he apologised very sincerely. But this thing, that they're from the homelands, is still there.[13]

The turmoil in the iron plant reflected the widening differentiation between black workers with contrasting working conditions, prospects and aspirations. The concerned group was located among more skilled workers with prospects for advancement through wildcat co-operation – the most successful instance of which evolved in the iron plant – and whose attack on the shop steward leadership was motivated at least in part by the desire to gain access to opportunities for upward mobility. In contrast, the unskilled migrant workers on the tap floors had no prospect of workplace advancement, and responded to the trend of upward mobility with disenchantment towards shop stewards and township workers. They established separate structures, under their own control, to defend their interests in the workplace and union.

While the concerned group and the action committee had different objectives and trajectories, they both drew on repertoires of contention established through the internal contestation of the 1980s in order to organise and mobilise in the 1990s – a strategy which was facilitated by the persistence of the neo-apartheid workplace regime. What made the current situation different from the 1980s was the partial withdrawal or disengagement of the various *amabhova* from the union. Their focus on local problems and personal ambition formed the basis of a new sectionalism among workers. For some members of the concerned group, the shop stewards committee constituted a route to new opportunities. The action committee, on the other hand, did not claim to be shop stewards – i.e., to represent a contending notion of the union as during the 1990 split – but were satisfied to form their own distinct structure within the union. This was a manifestation of the dilution and fragmentation of the union's social structure.

NUSAAW and the strike at flat products[14]
In July 1994, the workers in the flat products division launched a wildcat strike. Like the workers in the iron plant during and after the election stayaway, they rejected the role of NUMSA and its shop stewards. The

organised grouping opposed to the shop stewards in flat products was the tiny splinter union, the National Union of Steel and Allied Workers (NUSAAW),[15] which the remnants of the hostel group had formed when they broke away from NUMSA in 1991.

By 1994, NUSAAW was a tiny group, consisting of some 60 to 90 workers. Most of its members were in flat products. NUSAAW was too small to have any significant impact on negotiations or unionism at Highveld Steel but it was a nuisance to NUMSA. Throughout 1994, there were rumours that NUSAAW was trying to extend its influence in the company. Its members were active in organising a wildcat go-slow in the flat products slabyard early in the year, and led a wildcat stoppage in the steel plant a few months later.

Two grievances had been festering in flat products before the wildcat strike. Workers on the strip-mill were required to clean under the furnace – a dirty, heavy job – when the mill was down for maintenance. They objected because white workers were exempted from this duty, and demanded extra pay. Both NUMSA and NUSAAW had attempted to negotiate these grievances with management but without success. The second grievance concerned the workers on the burning-bed where the rolled plate was cut to length; they believed they were on lower rates than workers doing similar jobs elsewhere in the steelworks, an anomaly that seemed to date back to the time when white workers were replaced by black workers and wages were reduced. They too had been trying to negotiate with management.

According to some accounts, the workers on the strip-mill were given warnings for refusing to clean under the furnaces; according to others, an assistant manager started an argument with the burning-bed workers. The grievances were in any case very similar: both concerned unfair wages determined, at least in part, by racial discrimination. Workers 'started collecting each other and walking out'. Neither of the two NUMSA shop stewards was on duty – Ezekiel Nkosi was on a union training course in Durban and Philip Mkatshwa was working a different shift – and NUSAAW was able to take advantage of this. Without disclosing that they were shop stewards, NUSAAW activists argued that shop stewards and unions should be kept out of the dispute and that the workers of flat products should act independently. When Mkatshwa arrived for his shift, and found the plant on strike, he was told not to interfere because he was not trusted.

The workers formulated their demands, all focusing on money. A NUMSA member commented that the demands 'would make you laugh because they were practically impossible'. They then elected a delegation of five workers, several of whom were – unbeknown to most workers – NUSAAW shop stewards, to meet management. As Mkatshwa explained: 'Workers were confused, they didn't understand who was driving the car. If you start talking about money they will strike for those demands.' The delegation was under strict instructions not to negotiate but to bring senior managers to flat products to negotiate directly with the strikers. When the managers arrived they told the workers that they could not negotiate in this fashion. There were specific forums to negotiate wages, they said, and both NUMSA and NUSAAW knew the correct procedures. The response of the flat product strikers was remarkably similar to that of the iron plant workers:

They said that they do not belong to any unions now. They are there as the employees, not as union members, so management must not now involve the unions. They must come and solve their problems.

The workers settled in for a sleep-in strike, to prevent management from deploying the maintenance workers to keep production going.

Why were the flat products workers so ready to reject involvement by NUMSA and its shop stewards? They cited similar concerns to those of the iron plant strikers. One reason was their frustration at the fruitlessness of the shop stewards' negotiation with management:

We put the union aside. We thought if it was approached in this manner we will bring down the managers, so that they would understand quickly that what we want is our own, because if we always send the shop stewards they may think this comes from the union, not from us.

Suspicion of the shop stewards was also a factor:

We wanted management to respond to us directly, without the unions, because the shop stewards used to come back saying that management refuses to give us the increase, and we thought that somehow, somewhere, there might be something, you see?

The two workers quoted were both unskilled Pedi migrants, both of whom had been involved in the hostels movement against the township shop stewards, and were sympathetic to those who had formed NUSAAW.

Workers were impatient for changes, as Mkatshwa pointed out: 'As black people we are still disadvantaged. Our aim is to live the life of the people, and you cannot live the life of the people on empty pockets. The workers must get something from management to live their lives.'

But NUMSA had been unable to deliver, partly because management was intransigent and partly because union capacity was so limited. Instead of the six shop stewards in flat products required by the union constitution, there were only two. Ezekiel Nkosi was frequently busy outside the workplace on political and community projects and Mkatshwa was not familiar with the complex new NUMSA strategies. NUMSA was also vulnerable because of its participation in restructuring committees that were delivering nothing to the shop floor, while NUSAAW 'can sit outside and accuse it of selling out'.

Immediately the strike started, management called the NUMSA shop stewards and asked them to help end it. However, the shop stewards and officials did not have access to the workers and knew that to arrive at the plant in the company of managers would only reinforce workers' suspicion. Moreover, they told management, NUSAAW had been recognised by the company so the strike was management's problem. Bunny Mahlangu, the NUMSA organiser, described the union's strategy:

I said to myself, maybe we should leave these workers until they burn their fingers – once their fingers are burning I'm sure they'll accept us as the union. Now there was a sort of power struggle between NUMSA and NUSAAW. We wanted to intervene when people were in real trouble, so that we could help them out of the problem and NUMSA could be seen to be a better union.

The stalemate at flat products lasted several days. Eventually management issued an ultimatum and then announced that the strikers had been dismissed. A contingent of police moved onto the company premises to prepare to evict them. Inside the plant the workers started to turn to the NUMSA shop steward, Philip Mkatshwa, for advice:

> They realised they were in deep shit, and they started to remember my words. They came to me straight and said we realise what we have done is wrong. Let's sit down like men and talk because now we are losing our jobs. Go in now and talk to management.

Meanwhile, outside the plant, the NUMSA shop stewards asked management to delay the eviction while they tried to resolve the problem. The leadership of the strike were 'starting to panic' in the face of the mass dismissal and police presence, and were now keen to meet the shop stewards. There was 'a lot of to-and-fro, communicating with management and these guys'. Communication was the beginning of negotiation, and eventually the NUMSA shop stewards were able to negotiate reinstatement of the strikers with no adverse conditions, and secure an agreement that a joint management/shop steward committee should be formed in flat products to address workers' grievances. Union order had been restored: workers acknowledged the importance of the union and the distinction between members and non-members, affirmed the shop steward leadership and their success in protecting the dismissed workers, and rejected NUSAAW. NUMSA emerged strengthened. NUSAAW, on the other hand, was described as 'the living dead'.

Despite this success, the almost identical events at flat products and the iron plant – worker sectionalism and their readiness to reject the intervention of their union, and the salience of networks forged in past conflict – suggested that the collective identity of workers was in a state of flux, and that the social structure of the union was undergoing deep processes of dilution and fragmentation.

The neo-apartheid workplace regime and the rejection of shop stewards

A major reason for the tenuous nature of the shop stewards' leadership in the workplace, and the precarious state of internal order in the union, was the persistence of the neo-apartheid workplace regime as reflected in the

management strategy of authoritarian restoration. Management intransigence had created enormous frustrations for workers and shop
stewards – a frustration which had generated internal conflict since the
divisions of the 1987 lockout. For Bunny Mahlangu, the divisions of 1990
and 1991, and those of 1994, 'seem to be part of the same process; nothing
has changed'. The leadership of the concerned group had told him:

> We're not fighting the shop stewards, we are trying to find ways to
> confront Highveld management. We don't get anything at Highveld,
> and now we on the floor are frustrated. Maybe our frustration is
> what makes us think the shop stewards are not taking care of us.
> We at Highveld are so frustrated, we even think of just burning
> down Highveld Steel and forgetting about it.

It was this frustration 'that is causing division in the union – people just
want to fight among themselves, and they all say they're doing it for the
benefit of everyone'.[16]

The internal differentiation of African workers into migrants and urban
residents had been integral to the structure of the apartheid workplace
regime. Over time the situation of the migrants in the workplace and in
the community had, if anything, worsened. As the company started
promoting black workers into more skilled positions it recruited fewer
migrants. With the ending of influx control, and the popular pressure
exerted in KwaGuqa for stepped-up recruitment of locals, Highveld Steel
ceased recruiting in the rural areas. In the early 1990s, the number of
migrants in the Highveld Steel workforce fell gradually from above 2 000
to about 1 500.

By 1990, the company was only recruiting workers with a standard 6 or
higher qualification. By the mid-1990s, the requirement was a standard 8.
Men from the rural areas with little or no education – who had previously
been the majority of black workers at the company – could no longer find
work at Highveld Steel.[17] Inside the steelworks, the unskilled migrant
workers were still locked into their position at the bottom of the division of
labour. A migrant worker, one of the flat products strikers, described his
bitterness:

I'm approaching 19 years working for Highveld. I just collect scrap like a person who is disabled or very old or with no use in the firm. Since I have worked at Highveld I have got nothing, there is nothing which the company did for me. Even if they say next year there will be a change, I no longer have any hope. My future at Highveld is no longer there.[18]

With the end of influx control some migrants moved into the township or the shack settlements, bringing their families or establishing new ones. For the migrants who continued to stay in the hostels, conditions became worse. Highveld Steel had stopped managing its hostels in 1988, handing responsibility back to the KwaGuqa council. The town council failed to regain the administrative control it had lost in the later 1980s, and people without shelter, including local technikon students, simply occupied empty rooms as they wished, without paying rent. The hostel staff had been reduced, and the superintendent replaced with a senior clerk. The council no longer knew who was staying there or collected rent, and ceased providing maintenance or repairs.[19]

The goal of many migrants remained the maintenance of their homes, family resources and communal life in the rural areas. The hostels, despite the degradation of hostel life, provided a cheap way to live and work in the city. The vulnerable position of the migrants in the urban community was reflected in their fears that the new, democratically elected town council would respond favourably to demands in some township quarters for the hostels to be demolished. The conversion of some of the hostels into family units in the early 1990s could, they feared, be a sign that they were in danger of losing access to a place in the town.[20] These workers, who still constituted a significant part of the workforce in many plants at Highveld Steel, formed a militant stratum of union members whose place in the neo-apartheid workplace regime and the unions had, if anything, worsened, and who readily drew on the repertoire of militant and unprocedural wildcat actions forged in the 1980s to make their grievances known.

It was frustration with the neo-apartheid workplace regime that led to wildcat strikes and challenges to the leadership and the constitution of the union. There were always *amabhova* among the workers, ready to disrupt union structures and procedures in fresh attempts to challenge managerial power. While the shop stewards were trying to reform the workplace regime through negotiation, the dissidents were drawing on the repertoire of militant ungovernability forged in the struggles of the 1980s.[21] But those who rebelled against the shop stewards could provide no alternatives to the union, and to the powers and constraints that defined the shop stewards' role, for engaging management. This was experienced directly by individual rebels who became shop stewards. When a militant activist in the tap floor action committee appeared to be in danger of dismissal, his comrades elected him as a shop steward as a form of protection. He commented:

As a shop steward, I have to follow the rules, although I do not agree with some of them. Rules involve agreements which have been made between management and the union. For instance, if you want to engage in a strike you have to follow procedures. If workers decide to engage in a work stoppage in my presence, I will be asked why I allowed that to happen. I think the rules are going to bind me. It was better when I was not a shop steward because I had no knowledge of the rules. The shop stewards are the ones who know the rules, and now I have to follow them. And if I do, my fellow workers may start questioning me.[22]

The five workers who were elected to monitor the shop stewards had a similar experience. Having accompanied the shop stewards to several meetings with management they 'started to understand the dynamics and difficulties of negotiating, and when they came to report to people they were starting to talk the same language as the shop stewards'. When they reported that the shop stewards were actually doing a good job they were seen 'as having been bought by management together with the shop stewards'.[23]

Thus rivals like the concerned group and NUSAAW were out-manoeuvred and disappeared, or were absorbed into the structures of the union, and the latter emerged from each crisis as the only force able to win concessions from management, maintain worker unity and defend their interests. Nonetheless, currents of suspicion and dissidence persisted in the workplace. These currents had sources in the divisions of the 1980s, but it was the current structural tensions in the role of the shop stewards that kept them alive. The observations of an active member in flat products provide a striking insight into this dynamic:

> Ordinary people, particularly the old ones and the uneducated ones, they look upon a shop steward as an opportunist, as a person who is there not only to service them as employees, but who is there for promotions, for recognition from management. They know for a fact that there is no single case they can win without a shop steward, but when it comes to things like benefits, promotions and so on, then automatically they change their minds. While, on the other hand, management looks upon a shop steward as the first enemy in the company – that is why, when it comes to promotions, he is the last man to be considered. Shop stewards are dealing with people who are weathercocks, who can easily be moved from one point to another. You cannot say they distrust the shop stewards entirely because they are on and off. Trust among illiterate people is very difficult to achieve – you've got to prove yourself.[24]

The notion of workers as 'weathercocks', unreliable and fickle in their loyalties, surfaced frequently in the conversation of shop stewards. Members were gullible, easily misled by demagogues, prone to becoming agents of *disorder* in the union. Talking about the wildcat strike in the flat products division, the secretary of the shop steward committee remarked that 'it is easy to confuse our members, they are so easily swayed or I can use the term stupid – they just follow anyone'.[25]

This deep tension between shop stewards and rank-and-file members repeated the tensions of the apartheid workplace during the 1980s. It was a manifestation of the contradictions of transition: the persistence of the neo-apartheid workplace regime provoked workers to draw on the repertoire of actions and anti-shop steward discourse forged in the 1980s, while wildcat co-operation fostered new aspirations and identities. Shop stewards on the other hand, inspired by the vision of reconstruction, attempted to negotiate a new workplace order. This tension reflected a disjunction between democratic incorporation at the political level and contradictory processes of exclusion and incorporation in the workplace.

The new upward mobility of shop stewards[26]

The neo-apartheid workplace regime was not the same as the apartheid workplace regime. All *amabhova* agreed on one point: shop stewards could not be trusted because they were pursuing promotion. This was a new allegation, unknown during the 1980s, and it reflected a profound new reality in post-apartheid South Africa. From 1994 onwards, the senior shop stewards at Highveld Steel were increasingly thinking about careers beyond the union. Options ranged from town councillor, civil servant or politician in the provincial legislature, to manager in the local training and development initiatives or simply going into business. Within the company there were opportunities for promotion to foreman, industrial relations or safety officer or even managerial positions. While this was frequently articulated in terms of service to the community or political activism, underlying it was the reality that factory workers moving into any of these positions would significantly improve the income, material circumstances and the future prospects of themselves and their families. They would be moving out of the working class into the middle classes, thereby becoming beneficiaries of the rapid process of class formation that accompanied decolonisation. Many of the more highly paid workers took advantage of the company offer to buy or rent houses on the company housing estate in the 'white' town of Witbank – residential dispersal reinforcing the dispersal of solidarity in the union.[27] The impact was described with some bitterness by a shop steward who, without career prospects elsewhere, stayed behind:

> Most of our shop stewards are online to government. Everyone is looking at green pastures, you see. And when they leave to government or to promotion, there is no one to close the gap, because they have all the information. In future we will become weaker and weaker. You can hide these things, but at the end of the day, they will come out.

These new opportunities and ambitions – which were closely linked to processes of wildcat incorporation – had a deep impact on individual shop stewards as well as on the institution of the shop steward committee and its relation to the members it represented. The perception that shop stewards were using their position to pursue promotion or new careers, and were no longer representing members' interests, was a common factor in the wildcat strikes. It also underlay tensions over political participation.

These new dynamics also had an impact within the shop steward committee, on its culture of shared commitment to the workers and the struggle, and on the consciousness of individual shop stewards. While a sense of these shifts could be gleaned from informal conversations with and between shop stewards, one shop steward who was acutely aware of the dilemmas he and his comrades faced was brutally honest about how the culture and vision of the union and the shop stewards was changing. According to Mosi Nhlapo:

> The politics of today is about how much money you have, how beautiful your car is. It's no longer about how you develop the economy and how you look at the interests of the poorest. It's about self interest. I also want to be myself. I've been a shop steward for a long time, and I've gained nothing from it except the politics and experience that I have.

Nhlapo was describing the culture and ethos of a new black elite. For the moment his skill and position of power as the shop steward chair, his interest in the role, and his commitment to workers, unionism and socialism kept him a shop steward, but these could not last. He sensed a general decay around him in the union movement. Those who had taught him and others about socialism had disappeared, and references to socialism had become purely rhetorical and without anchor in the programmes of the union movement. He frequently expressed the view that the union was 'dying' or 'finished' because shop stewards, worker leadership and officials were looking elsewhere to further their careers:

> Sometimes I say to myself a very clever group of people came to us and said there is something called communism or socialism. The more things are unfolding in front of my eyes, I tend to believe someone was lying to me. There's nothing like socialism. The SACP, in our area it's finished. Even the SACP guys in parliament are tamed. What happened? Someone fooled me. If socialism exists, why don't we continue that route? If I announce that I'm not a

shop steward tomorrow, I'm telling you I'll get a very high position in management. Maybe what keeps motivating me to be a shop steward is my belief that we've got a programme of socialism and one must keep on, things will clear up and we'll start to implement it very soon. If there's anything like socialism I must start searching for it now. But those guys that would lead us, that would make us believe that there's something called socialism, they are not here. They are no more. We are left by ourselves now.[28]

Nhlapo also described tensions within the shop steward committee over its opposition to the company's strategy of outsourcing service functions to small contractors. Like members of the concerned group, some of the shop stewards saw this as an opportunity to become small contractors themselves: 'They want to see themselves tomorrow owning these small enterprises. They see you as blocking them. The more you talk about these issues the more they say you want to remain poor – just remain poor and leave us alone.'

It was not only new opportunities and ambitions that were eroding the commitment of the shop steward committee and propelling the most skilled and experienced shop stewards out of it. It was becoming increasingly difficult to recruit new and committed shop stewards. In the new political climate of the 1990s most workers lacked the commitment to take on the demanding and difficult role of the shop steward.[29] Many of those with leadership potential who would have become shop stewards in the 1980s preferred, in the light of the new opportunities opening up for blacks at work, to pursue careers outside the union. An active member in flat products expressed his concern at the difficulty of recruiting workers with leadership skills as shop stewards:

We are going to lose shop stewards like Ezekiel Nkosi because there are many developments taking place in our country. He has got a number of offers outside. The other shop stewards as well. Even myself, I don't think I will be around there for a long time. We have identified others to stand as shop stewards, but they are very unwilling. People believe that in order to be promoted you have to be a blue-eyed boy in the eyes of management. I don't believe that there will be people strong enough to stand up. It means all that has been achieved is going to be lost.[30]

The new opportunities and ambitions opened up for workers by the democratic transition had a profound effect on the social structure of the union and on the institution of the shop steward committee that was at its core. The process of class formation that accompanied the birth of post-colonial South Africa reached deep into the social structure of the union, diluting solidarity, altering the relations between workers and changing the *meaning* of the shop steward committee in the workplace. Insofar as the culture of collective solidarity and the mutually affirmed commitment to the workers' struggle had been undermined by a new culture of individual self-advancement, the social structure of the union had undergone a process of erosion.

The strategy of reconstruction and the loss of vision[31]
NUMSA's new three-year programme was more complex than anything negotiated before by the union, and it placed more difficult demands on the shop stewards. At most, three or four of the Highveld Steel shop stewards – all but one of them artisans – had sufficient technical understanding, negotiating skill and conviction about the importance of the programme as a proactive vision, to engage consistently in the struggle to persuade or force management to implement aspects of it. One person, Mosi Nhlapo, the chair of shop stewards, emerged as the key figure leading the committee in this process.

The programme sharpened the differentiation between shop stewards on the basis of skill, experience and ability. It empowered a few to challenge and engage management and workers on issues of workplace restructuring, and disempowered the rest who felt unable to actively implement or participate in the programme. It thus reinforced the other factors altering the dynamics within the shop steward committee. The complexity of the programme, and the drawn-out process of engaging management on it, made it extremely difficult to forge real mandates in general meetings or to report back effectively. The dislocation between shop stewards and members grew as workers' grasp of what was being negotiated and its implications became more tenuous. This had a serious impact on the social structure of the union, reinforcing the trend towards fragmentation and the dilution of solidarity: the lack of accountability of shop stewards, and their failure to report back to members was a constant refrain in the various challenges to the leadership of the shop stewards described in this chapter.

But the three-year programme did not only contribute to the changing relationships between shop stewards in the shop steward committee, and between them and their members. As the union lost key strategists from the head office, regional offices and workplaces from 1994 onwards, it became less and less able to implement or support its own strategy – and, perhaps, less committed to it. This contributed to a growing sense that the union had lost its vision. This was the conclusion drawn by Nhlapo towards the end of 1995 – in a statement all the more remarkable for the fact that it was made when the union strategy appeared to have reached its highpoint at Highveld Steel with the negotiation of the agreement of intent: 'We have in some way lost direction. I have lost direction, I'm not sure whether I know where we want to go. I wish we could retreat.'

This loss of vision was related to several different factors: the lack of expertise in the union, a sense that the union strategy was failing both at Highveld Steel and nationally, and that the union lacked the strategic capacity to reassess it and find a way forward; the decay of the social structure of the union; and confusion in the workplace about the appropriate response to the new conditions. Lack of capacity and vision within the union were also linked to the bigger problem of ambiguities and contradictions in the strategy of reconstruction. How should the union be responding to the contradictions of transition in South Africa, to the tension between the new and the old, between justice for workers and the pressure of competitiveness? According to Nhlapo:

This transition is going to confuse us all. What is our ultimate objective? When do we say that the struggle is over now because we've reached our objective and we need to change the way we do things? Although already we have started changing the way we do things . . .

This was not only an abstract political question; it had strategic implications.

How should the union respond to competitive threats from cheaper steel? Supporting increased productivity could undermine the organisation:

> I know the implications of competition, but the ordinary worker might not know them. Do I go to him and say, let's go on strike comrade – whereas I know this is going to undermine the company? Do I go and motivate him to work harder – and when he asks what he is going to get at the end of the day, I say, nothing comrade, you just have to make sure your job is secured. You cannot address such questions in a general meeting. After we've spoken they'll say, see he's joined the bosses already.

Such problems were aggravated by the differential impact of management's new strategies on workers with different levels of education:

> Now the unskilled members, the militant members, they don't see their way through the career path, and they start fighting, saying we've been fighting the struggle with you guys, we've made sure democracy is installed in this country, but we've benefited nothing. While other workers are happy. They'll tell you that our struggle was against apartheid, and now that apartheid has been dismantled, what more to you want?

The three-year programme was also likely to aggravate divisions by drawing a distinction between workers facing retrenchment as a result of productivity improvement and those who stood to benefit from such improvement. The erosion of democracy discussed in chapter 7 meant that workers were demobilised. In Nhlapo's view the only way to galvanise the social structure of the union and rebuild the collective solidarity on which it was based was to revert to more traditional forms of mobilisation and 'to pull a huge strike next year'. Otherwise, 'we won't be able to get that unity that we had in the past years – guys are just going to be drifting in different directions'. However, even such a strategy evoked ambivalence: 'But you should be careful how you mobilise, because if you do it roughly you are going to revive all those wildcat strikes again.'

The shop stewards, and the union more broadly, were unable to find a way of rooting the new vision and programme in the organisation and mobilisation of members – which had been the key to NUMSA's vitality. The weaknesses and tensions in the shop steward committee – and the distraction of shop stewards by their interest in other things – made it impossible to develop a coherent strategy to deal with these challenges.

Management intransigence at this particular company played its part in the failure of the strategy of reconstruction, but the strategy itself, by fragmenting and eroding the values and practices central to the union social structure, played an important part in weakening the union and rendering the strategy ineffective. This failure further demoralised the shop stewards and contributed to their sense that they had lost direction. In view of this loss of vision it is not surprising that Nhlapo accepted promotion into management towards the end of 1997.

Conclusion

Wildcat strikes and challenges to shop stewards reached their peak in 1994, a year of heightened volatility because of the political drama of the first elections. The open manifestation of conflict served, however, to delineate the contours of deep and ongoing divisions in the workplace and the union.

In some ways the internal conflict of the 1990s resembled the internal contestation of the 1980s. However, despite drawing on repertoires of the past, it was quite distinct. Democratic incorporation and the new tensions over political involvement, the salience of promotion, upward mobility and class formation, the impact of wildcat co-operation, were all new factors. The new collective and individual identities were characterised by a degree of partial disengagement or withdrawal from trade union identity. Internal conflict was less a struggle between contending notions of union order and practice than a struggle to assert or defend specific local and personal interests within the union and the workplace. The intensity of such conflict was less, just as the intensity of solidarity was less. The transition replaced the class compression of apartheid, characterised by a closed class structure defined by race, with an open and porous structure characterised by class fragmentation, new class formation and class mobility, thus undermining the historically constructed collective solidarity of social movement unionism. The end of apartheid created scope for the rapid formation of a black elite within which new class forces were crystallising: a bourgeoisie, a political elite, and managerial and professional middle-classes. Talented shop stewards, with their skills and experience, were swept up in this process, weakening the union and introducing new dynamics and tensions into it.

Nor was the union successful in forging a new strategy of reconstruction. The essentially collective nature of trade unionism means union strategies are deeply embedded in the social structure of the unions that adopt them. Trade union strategies do not consist merely of a set of technical goals and capacities, but are intimately linked to the internal distribution of power, to organisational identity and culture, to goals and meaning. The strategy of reconstruction – or more specifically, strategic unionism – redistributed power within the union at all levels, both national and local, to those with expertise. The attempt to graft a highly complex 'strategic unionism', developed in the more institutionalised and well resourced social democratic unions of industrial society, onto the more volatile, militant unionism of South Africa with its large proportion of unskilled workers and faced with the challenges of transition from apartheid, proved unsuccessful.

Notes

1. Interview, Meshack Malinga, 12/5/94; interview, Mosi Nhlapo, 8/5/94; interview, Ezekiel Nkosi, 5/5/94.
2. Interview, Jacob Msimangu, 12/8/95, 22/10/95.
3. Interview, Jacob Msimangu, 12/8/95.
4. Interview, Jacob Msimangu, 22/10/95.
5. Interview, Bunny Mahlangu, 12/5/94; interview, Ezekiel Nkosi, 15/4/94, 4/5/95.
6. Interview, Jacob Msimangu, 12/8/95.
7. This account of the action committee and the culture of solidarity on the tap floors is based on interview, Veli Majola, 26/10/95; interview, Paxon Mokoena, 14/6/94; interview, Jacob Msimangu, 22/10/95; interview, Mosi Nhlapo, 8/5/94, 10/7/94; interview, Ezekiel Nkosi, 5/5/94; interview, Jacob Msimangu, 22/10/95; interview, Hendrik Nkosi, 26/5/94; interview, Tshagata, 10/95.
8. Interview, Jacob Msimangu, 22/10/95; interview, Hendrik Nkosi, 26/5/94.
9. *ibhova/amabhova*: township patois for bulldog, epitomising a vicious, aggressive animal.
10. *bliksem*: 'hit'.
11. Interview, Mosi Nhlapo, 10/7/94.
12. Interview, Mosi Nhlapo, 6/3/95.
13. Ibid.

14. This section is based on interview, Ephraim Kgole, 10/95; interview, Bunny Mahlangu, 4/5/95; interview, Philip Mkatshwa, 8/95; interview, Jerry Mogoleko, 10/95; interview, Marcus Moswane, 12/8/95; interview, Sidwel Nkosi, 26/8/95.

15. The National Union of Steel and Allied Workers was formed as a small breakaway from NUMSA at the giant state-owned steelworks, Iscor.

16. Interview, Bunny Mahlangu, 12/5/94, 15/8/95; see also interview, Philip Mkatshwa, 8/95.

17. This and the previous paragraph are based on interview, Moses Nkabinde, 12/5/98; interview, Paxon Mokoena, 14/6/94. One worker from outside Witbank, who found temporary accommodation in the hostels, reported that the company had instructed the labour office to refuse employment to anyone with a hostel address (interview, Paxon Mokoena, 14/6/94).

18. Interview, Ephraim Kgole, 10/95.

19. Interview, Moses Nkabinde, 12/5/98; interview, Leo Makwakwa, 12/5/98; interview, Adam Engelbrecht, 12/5/98.

20. Interview, Mosi Nhlapo, 6/3/95; interview, Johannes Phatlana, 12/10/95; interview, Tshagata, 26/5/94, 10/95; see also chapter 2.

21. See interview, Phineas Mabena, 12/5/94.

22. Interview, Veli Majola, 26/10/95.

23. Interview, Bunny Mahlangu, 4/5/95, 15/8/95.

24. Interview, Sidwel Nkosi, 26/8/95.

25. Interview, Ezekiel Nkosi, 23/11/95.

26. Apart from other interviews cited in the text, this section is based on interview, Mosi Nhlapo, 8/5/94, 6/3/95; interview, Ezekiel Nkosi, 23/11/95.

27. See Chapter 8, note 8.

28. Interview, Mosi Nhlapo, 10/7/94; see also interview, Ambrose Mthembu, 22/10/95. The issue of socialist beliefs is scarcely mentioned in this study, despite its significance to the culture of social movement unionism, because shop stewards referred so seldom to it in relation to the struggles of the 1980s. This may have been because Witbank was somewhat remote from the main urban centres where socialism was most discussed – which itself casts doubt on the depth of such beliefs, or at least the meaning of these beliefs. It only emerged as an issue for the new group of shop stewards who began to participate in national union affairs from about 1989, and then mostly in relation to the new strategy of reconstruction.

29. See, for example, interview, Bunny Mahlangu, 12/5/94; interview, Ambrose Mthembu, 26/4/94.

30. Interview, Sidwel Nkosi, 26/8/95.

31. This section is based on interview, Mosi Nhlapo, 6/3/95.

CHAPTER 11

'Today I see myself as a human being because of the union'

The future of the workplace, the future of the union

Now, you go to the workers and tell them 'Mandela is President, now they must work harder'. Then they say 'Mandela is President but nothing has changed. The whites are still getting more money'. I went into the shop where Phineas [a black artisan] works. It was quarter to nine, we take tea time at 9 o'clock. They were already in the mess room, eating, Phineas and some simple labourers. At that time all the whites were still working. I said, 'Shit Phineas, I never expected this from you guys. You know our NUMSA programme says that workers must be motivated.' One of the labourers said, 'Look, we voted Mandela into power, and unless we see serious changes we're not going to change the way we operate, we're going to continue as we are continuing now. We don't see your national programme. We can work hard, but give us money. Why is that white getting more money than I am?' You can say, 'No, there are things that you don't understand. Those guys are trained artisans, and you guys are just simple labourers.' But they say, 'Who's working hard? I'm working hard.' *Mosi Nhlapo, shop steward chairperson*

This book demonstrates that the South African transition consists not simply of an elite pact engineered at the commanding heights of society, but is characterised rather by transformations which reach deep into society, by intense contestation and conflict over such transformations, by the long time span over which they occur, as well as by the disjuncture between transformation in different institutions and at different levels of society. This study reveals a process of fragmentation, erosion and dissolution of old social structures, and attempts – contested attempts – to forge new ones. In the gap between the old and the new, in the conflict between the old and the new, and between contending versions of the new, emerges a kind of interregnum characterised by uncertainty and disorder, which recalls Durkheim's concept of *anomie*[1] – and accounts, at least in part, for the sense of disorientation and dislocation induced by the South African transition: a sense both of dramatic change and of continuity and stasis. Such processes are not confined only to the institutions that are the subject of this study, but occur in many others.[2]

These features are explained by the colonial nature of the South African transition, and by the profound processes of decolonisation and recon-struction that it entails. This also explains the salience of post-colonial class formation and the significance of the democratic incorporation of the working class – both processes that are marked by contending projects, by upward mobility, by dramatic change and seeming stalemate, and that take place in many different sites: in the political arena at both local and national levels, in the workplace, and in communities. Given these characteristics, the South African transition can only be understood through complementing analysis of the institutional summits of society with an analysis from below, as this book attempts to do. Likewise, successful resolution of the profound conflicts over contending projects of transformation can only occur through the meshing of policy initiatives from above with negotiated accommodation from below.

In undertaking an analysis from below, this book tells a story of extraordinary innovation and collective agency on the part of workers as they struggled to shape their world – a theme that runs like a thread through the entire period of long transition at Highveld Steel. In the early 1980s, they built their union as a weapon to combat the arbitrary racial despotism which oppressed them, constructing new institutions to govern their collective relations with each other as well as engaging in fierce struggles to establish new procedures, new notions of fair treatment, and new rights in the workplace. It was workers, not managers, who fought with great determination and courage to replace the practices of apartheid with the outlines of a new managerial order in the workplace. Simultaneously, acutely aware of the link between their oppression in the workplace and the broader system of apartheid, they struggled to overturn the world of apartheid they lived and worked in. They participated in and struggled to shape the popular movement in the community, and mobilised highly charged confrontation with white power in the workplace.

It was through the trade union, through the way it empowered them and gave them voice, that workers were able to recover their humanity in the face of apartheid. Tshagata described this with great clarity: 'Today I see myself as a human being because of the union.'[3] Albert Makagula, also an illiterate migrant worker in the iron plant, a man whose family life had been devastated by poverty, elaborated on this: 'Now that we are in transition towards a new South Africa, some of us feel we are already in the new South Africa because of what the union has done for us. Now you can actually tell the white man what you want, you can speak for yourself. Those things were impossible in the dark years of the past, especially for the people before us, our fathers.'[4]

But the collective activity of black workers did not forge an un-problematic solidarity; rather it generated intense conflict as different groups of workers did battle over contending notions of social order within the organisation they had created. This was a period of heightened political consciousness, of heightened dynamism, popular agency and organisational innovation that threatened to tear the trade union apart. And yet black workers and communities did overturn the world of apartheid. Collective struggle, collective innovation – not only at Highveld Steel, but in a myriad workplaces and communities across South Africa – unravelled the apartheid system by producing a state of chronic defiance and deep disorder from below, and thereby created the pressure for negotiated transition to democracy.

Transition ushered in new conditions, new contestation. Again, workers responded with formative efforts to shape transition itself and the new world emerging from it. The strategy of reconstruction formulated in union head offices was a complex and sophisticated programme – but underlying it was a simpler response to radically new conditions, articulated by ordinary workers: they, who had contributed so much to the popular assault on apartheid, had much to contribute to transforming society – and if they did not engage, there were plenty of others who would shape things in their own interests, leaving workers the losers.

Trade unionists made an important contribution to establishing the democratic institutions of post-apartheid South Africa: organising voter education; building the ANC and campaigning for it; transforming the town council. In the workplace they demonstrated an impressive capacity for creative struggle, fighting to desegregate facilities, to recast the practices of supervision and to negotiate new relationships and new work organisation. But their efforts to continue shaping reconstruction foundered on bitter reefs: on the one hand, the intractability of the old in the form of management intransigence; on the other, the dynamic force of class formation unleashed by the new, which gradually fractured the solidarity of the union and structured power within the ANC in such a way as to absorb and neutralise trade union influence. The collective agency of worker struggle and innovation was eroded by a new agency – that of individual self-advancement. While workers continued to participate in the construction of new practices and relations in the workplace, this was reactive to management initiatives rather than proactive as the strategy of reconstruction had required.

What, then, of the future? What are the possible outcomes of these new processes and contestations on the terrain of post-apartheid reconstruction? Have black workers in South Africa irrevocably lost their capacity to shape society from below? But before addressing these questions, we must ask how we are to understand the significance of the Highveld Steel case study. How representative is it of broader trends?

Ungovernability and the transition: broader trends

Supporting evidence for both the politicisation and disorder of shopfloor relations, and for heated contestation that at times broke out into violence between, variously, shop stewards and militant youth, different ethnic groups, migrants and politically militant township residents, and between rival trade union factions, is provided by the studies of both Maller (1992) and Moodie (1994), by a number of articles in the *South African Labour Bulletin* (see especially 1989), by the mine workers strike of 1987 (Baskin 1991: 275–6), and by the events of the Mercedes Benz sit-in strike in 1990 (Von Holdt 1990). The two major studies of trade unionism under apartheid that argue the contrary belonged to the early 1980s, before ungovernability emerged (Friedman 1987; Webster 1985).

There is also a growing body of evidence for the erosion of union solidarity in the transition. Buhlungu (2001) has systematically surveyed the negative impact of the upward mobility of union officials on organisational culture and the emergence of new fracture lines in internal solidarity in four COSATU affiliates. A sample of episodes of 'ungovernability' in the South African trade unions over the transition is also suggestive. In 1994, 2 000 truck drivers surprised their union by organising the blockade of a major transport route under the name of a new rank-and-file movement (Mtshelwane 1994). In 1996, the National Union of Mineworkers (NUM) was sidelined at Rustenburg Platinum by a non-union 'Workers' Committee' which led a wildcat strike over pensions. The result was mass dismissals, division and a continuing violent conflict that claimed several lives and extended into the rural areas of the Transkei (South African Labour Bulletin 1996). In 1997, 7 000 workers at Harmony gold mine went on strike against a productivity agreement signed by the NUM, forcibly evicted the NUM shaft stewards and announced the formation of an alternative union branch (*Business Day* 21/11/97). In 1999, workers at Volkswagen SA downed tools, demanding that NUMSA reinstate eight shop stewards who had been expelled from the union (*Business Day* 20/7/99). This has since led to a split, dismissals, and the formation of a rival union (Buhlungu 2001).

Thus there is considerable supporting evidence that the trends analysed in this study are broadly representative rather than idiosyncratic.

The future of the workplace regime

This study characterises the workplace at Highveld Steel in the period during and after the negotiated transition to democracy as a *neo-apartheid workplace regime* – an unstable transitional regime in a state of disjuncture with the broader socio-political changes in post-apartheid South Africa. It describes three contending projects for establishing a post-apartheid workplace regime through the incorporation of black workers.

The first was a management project of *authoritarian restoration* that attempted to restore managerial authority without negotiating structural changes to the racial order in the workplace. It tended to generate formal and informal resistance from black workers and a high degree of alienation, as illustrated by the quote at the beginning of this chapter. Should it remain the dominant project at Highveld Steel, the incorporation of black workers would remain *partial*. Their alienation from and resistance to incorporation would make it difficult for management to mobilise compliance and co-operation in production; informal resistance, informal work control and informal negotiation with supervisors would emerge as distinguishing features of work organisation. On this basis, too, trade unionism would have the potential to sustain a relatively militant defence of worker interests and resistance to managerial initiatives, whether on a formal or informal (wildcat) basis.

The second project was the NUMSA strategy of *negotiated reconstruction*. Except for the enclave on the tap floors of Iron Plant One, the strategy failed in the face of managerial intransigence and the lack of capacity within the union. Nonetheless, the implications for workplace incorporation can be drawn out from the tap floor experiment. Negotiated reconstruction implies the incorporation of workers through negotiating a process of workplace change that takes account of both the interests of managers and those of workers, and creates the basis for productive co-operation. Simultaneously, however, it establishes a high degree of worker autonomy and control within the production process, based on both work group and trade union organisation, which provides a platform for workers to influence the workplace regime, engage with management and co-operate in production. Thus the strategy of reconstruction implies the simultaneous incorporation and collective autonomy of black workers on the basis of strong, proactive trade unionism.

The third project was that of *wildcat co-operation* through which progressive managers were able to use mostly informal negotiation with individuals and work groups to establish coalitions for change. The basis for wildcat co-operation was the very real interest of black workers in ending incompetent, authoritarian white supervision, and in securing access to training, improved pay and personal advancement. Rapid upward mobility served as a dynamic underpinning workplace incorporation. Wildcat co-operation negotiated a way forward from the neo-apartheid workplace regime to a new post-apartheid workplace regime, but on an informal basis that retained managerial control and tended to sideline the formal structures and involvement of the union. Thus wildcat co-operation constituted a potentially successful strategy for incorporating black workers on the basis of co-operation between managers, individual workers and work groups, and weakening or undermining the union.

Highveld Steel is a large complex consisting of different plants and divisions. This created the scope for different experiments and different outcomes in different workplaces, depending on the variable capacity for innovation on the part of individual managers and trade unionists. At the end of the period covered by the study (1996), the overall situation at Highveld Steel was characterised by stalemate between the managerial strategy of authoritarian restoration and the NUMSA strategy of negotiated reconstruction. In at least one plant, wildcat co-operation looked promising as a strategy for incorporating black workers while retaining managerial control, and there were signs that a growing number of managers would pursue this option. While the union initiative had run out of steam, and the shop stewards' ability to block management initiatives was looking increasingly tenuous, authoritarian restoration itself appeared to be an untenable strategy in the face of worker alienation and resistance.

However, over the longer term matters appeared less clear cut. In 1998, after this study was completed, Highveld Steel successfully increased productivity, using voluntary retrenchment and attrition to reduce the workforce by about 750 workers, or 11%. In September 1999, the company announced it would retrench a further 600 workers. Although it withdrew this decision, according to shop stewards it was continuing to increase the workload and introduce labour-saving technology. The weakening of union solidarity left the field relatively open for management to impose authoritarian solutions. Indeed, one of the former shop stewards commented recently that the transition had 'liberated' management to take back many of the gains won by workers.

More generally, across South Africa permutations of these three strategies were being explored and implemented in different workplaces. In a strong variant of authoritarian restoration, companies in many sectors were vigorously pursuing a strategy of casualisation, outsourcing and downsizing in an effort to reduce costs, undermine trade unionism and restore an authoritarian managerial style and the kind of labour flexibility that characterised the apartheid workplace (Kenny and Webster 1999; Theron 2003). In workplaces with more innovative managers, the various permutations of wildcat co-operation provided a feasible strategy (Buhlungu 1996, 2000). In the few workplaces where more vigorous and proactive unionism retains its strength, compromises around a strategy of negotiated reconstruction may have made some headway.[5] State intervention in the form of the legislative and institutional reforms of the Labour Department – the Labour Relations Act of 1995, the Skills Development Act of 1998 and the various institutions for fostering skills development, the Employment Equity Act of 1998 – create the framework for negotiated reconstruction,[6] although union weakness and employer intransigence make this the least likely outcome. Without strong worker engagement from below, as this book so clearly shows, such reforms will remain paper tigers. They may, however, create favourable conditions for wildcat co-operation to flourish wherever innovative managers exist.

The concept of a transition from the apartheid workplace regime to a post-apartheid workplace regime assumes that workplace industrial relations takes the form of a nationally distinctive pattern of relations and institutions captured in the concept of a workplace regime. In the case of Highveld Steel the three projects identified in this study appear as alternatives, and indeed in some respects they are, particularly in medium to large scale traditional enterprises. But looked at more broadly, a complex new pattern may be emerging which combines all three projects in a differentiated hierarchy of workplace/employment relationships consisting of a core of more highly skilled and stable workers surrounded by successive layers of more and more peripheralised or externalised workers. Thus in a traditional manufacturing enterprise, for example, there may be a core of 'permanent' employees as well as numerous non-permanent 'casual' workers of various kinds. Beyond this, workers in 'non-core' functions may be externalised into more or less stable service companies – for example catering, security and maintenance companies. Some workers are even further peripheralised into labour-broking companies, into 'self-employment' – owner-drivers for example – or into informal homeworking or sweatshops, as for example in the footwear industry (Mosoetsa 2000).

This kind of corporate restructuring is driven not only by post-colonial contestation, but by other dimensions of the triple transition, economic transition in particular. Increasing competitive pressure in domestic and international markets, as well as globalised management practices, combine with post-colonial contestation as companies seek to increase productivity and avoid the costs, risks and difficulties of incorporating black workers. Such processes of industrial and corporate restructuring entail a reconfiguration of the workplace regime and a growing differentiation among workers. Casualisation and externalisation constitute a new strategy for avoiding the incorporation of (mostly black) workers, intensifying their workloads and reducing job security through a market-driven authoritarian restoration reminiscent of the flexibility afforded by the old apartheid workplace regime. While in both core and non-core workplaces workers continue to experience highly racialised forms of domination and control (Webster and Omar 2003: 17), in at least some of the former incorporation of black workers remains a prime concern, and managers are making use of new human resource strategies such as teamworking and increasing skills in order to elicit wildcat co-operation. Where unions retain their strength they may seek to negotiate reconstruction.

These processes of restructuring and reconfiguring the workplace regime continue to be shaped by contestation and negotiation in a myriad workplaces across South Africa. Overall, though, their impact is to reduce worker solidarity and negotiating power.

The future of trade unionism

In response to the moment of democratic incorporation of the working class, NUMSA and COSATU developed a new strategy of reconstruction for contesting and shaping the process and mode of incorporation. The implication of this was a shift from social movement unionism characterised by the militant resistance of workers excluded both politically and in the workplace, to a new form of unionism characterised by participation and engagement with both the state and management. The strategy attempted – at least rhetorically – to blend elements of social movement unionism with new strategic elements designed to guide union engagement with post-colonial reconstruction on the one hand, and to respond to the increased competitive pressures of globalisation on the other. In this it was a response to the contradictory pressues of the triple transition. The result was a high level of contradiction, ambiguity and uncertainty in the trade union strategy – which tended to undermine the solidarity and cohesion of the union social structure. But trade unionism was also profoundly weakened by deeper social processes underlying transition and post-colonial reconstruction. Primary amongst these were dynamic processes of new class formation that facilitated the upward mobility of shop stewards and more skilled workers both in the workplace and outside it. In a workplace marked both by the persistence of the neo-apartheid workplace regime and by upward mobility and wildcat co-operation, class compression was replaced by class differentiation, fragmentation and the dilution of solidarity. The strategy of reconstruction unravelled in the face of management intransigence and the loss of union capacity and solidarity.

At the heart of the changing social structure of trade unionism was the internal differentiation of black workers in terms of contrasting interests and prospects, the resulting fragmentation of solidarity, and the erosion of the role of the shop stewards committee as representative and champion of workers. Different layers of workers responded differently to practices and grievances in the workplace. While some with prospects of upward mobility might become agents of incorporation through wildcat co-operation, others were alienated from incorporation and developed a militant response to the neo-apartheid workplace regime and to authoritarian management strategies. Meanwhile, the shop steward leadership attempted to shape incorporation by implementing the strategy of reconstruction, both beyond the workplace in the community and the town council, and within it, before themselves moving onward and upward. These contrasting pressures and responses suggest a future trade unionism marked by inconsistent responses and alternating between quiescence, defensive strategies, wildcat militance, and attempts at proactive engagement with reconstruction.

It must be emphasised that this is a transitional situation, and there are different potential trajectories for trade unionism over the longer term. The legacies of social movement unionism and of the strategy of reconstruction remain alive within the trade union movement, and constitute resources for reinvigorating it. At some point the process of rapid class formation characteristic of post-colonial reconstruction is likely to slow down – or rather, the process of upward mobility from the working class into the new elite will slow down as the social distance between the working class and elite grows greater and the black middle class and nascent bourgeoisie become more capable of reproducing themselves without recruiting from other classes to the same extent. When this point comes, the dynamic of internal fragmentation is likely also to diminish, and it will become possible to reforge worker solidarity. It would be hazardous to predict whether such unionism will consist of a defensive and narrowly focused collective bargaining unionism, a new variant of social movement unionism adapted to conditions of (at least partial) working class incorporation, a new variant of the strategy of reconstruction, or some permutation of these possibilities.

Of particular importance will be union responses to the processes of workplace restructuring described above. Unless they are able to draw on their social movement unionism past to develop innovative strategies for organising and mobilising the casualised, externalised and more peripheral workers – something they show little sign of doing at present – they will be unable to contest corporate reorganisation, and will remain confined to core workplaces and their core workers.

In short, the challenge for the trade union movement will be to find new ways for workers to assert their humanity through trade unionism. Put differently, the question is whether workers will continue to shape the formation of a post-apartheid workplace regime through their own formative, active efforts, as they did through the long transition from apartheid. Where authoritarian restoration has been imposed through corporate restructuring, workers may have lost virtually all scope for collective or individual resistance – indeed, this is precisely the aim of such restructuring. For the many workers in more stable workplaces prospects are not so bleak. They are likely to continue playing a part in the construction of a new workplace order, even if only in the negative. Thus, if authoritarian restoration becomes the dominant managerial strategy, workers will give life to a resistant, defensive and unproductive work culture, as the workers quoted at the beginning of this chapter make clear. If a more innovative, productive workplace regime is to emerge, workers will have to be involved, whether through their organisations or in other ways. This book has shown that attempts to reform workplace order from above – whether by legislation or by company policy – remain a dead letter unless and until given life by the actions and struggles of workers.

Postscript

Readers who have by now followed the lives and struggles of several Highveld Steel workers and shop stewards through a decade and a half will want to know where these activists and key informants are presently. Mosi Nhlapo, former chairperson of the steelworks shop steward committee and chief strategist of reconstruction, is a manager at Highveld Steel. Tshagata, the founder member and migrant activist, is still working in the iron plant as a tapper. J.J. Mbonani, the 'bullfighter' and founder member, resigned as a shop steward so he could devote more time to his lay preaching. He is now a supervisor at Transalloys. Johannes Phatlana was dismissed for breaking company regulations in his shop steward activities, a case he is still fighting. Ambrose Mthembu is a branch organiser for NUMSA, and Frank Boshielo, founder member of NUMSA, its first organiser at Highveld Steel, and NUMSA regional secretary for most of the period covered in this book, recently left the union to head a business initiative to create downstream manufacturing businesses in nearby Middelburg. Bunny Mahlangu, the militant former shop steward chairperson and then regional organiser for the union now runs his own business; as does Ezekiel Nkosi, the former shop steward secretary who led wildcat actions in flat products after the 1976 uprisings, before the union appeared in Witbank. Meshack Malinga, the former chairperson of the joint shop steward committee, also runs his own business. The former shop stewards have lost touch with Jacob Msimangu, the former chairperson of the strike committee and leader of the concerned group, whose soap manufacturing enterprise failed. Charles Makola, for a long time the shop steward who provided intellectual leadership to the shop steward committee, and the first chairperson of the Witbank COSATU local, is a senior civil servant in the provincial government.

Notes

1. See Burawoy (1972) for a discussion of *anomie* in the context of upward mobility, class formation and decolonisation on the Zambian copper mines.
2. On the Land Bank, see Dolny (2001); for struggles over land, see Steinberg (2002).
3. Interview, Tshagata, 26/5/94.
4. Interview, Albert Makagula, 24/3/94.
5. There is some anecdotal evidence for this; it needs, however, to be substantiated.
6. This is not surprising, as the chief architects of the Labour Department strategy are former unionists, many of them from NUMSA.

Bibliography

Interviews

NUMSA

Frank Boshielo, 9/93, 19/6/94 (NUMSA regional secretary and union founder at Highveld Steel, migrant worker).

Hong Kong Kgalima, 3/7/94, 10/7/94 (NUMSA shop steward).

Ephraim Kgole, 10/95 (NUMSA member, migrant worker).

Phineas Mabena, 12/5/94 (former NUMSA shop steward and active member, artisan).

Bunny Mahlangu, 8/11/93 (with Victor Kgalima), 12/5/94, 4/5/95, 15/8/95 (NUMSA regional organiser, former chairperson of the Highveld Steel shop steward committee; Kgalima: NUMSA head office official, former shop steward at Highveld Steel).

Veli Majola, 26/10/95 (NUMSA member).

Albert Makagula, 24/3/94, 29/3/94 (shop steward, migrant worker).

Charles Makola, 8/5/94, 14/5/94, 6/8/95 (personnel officer, former vice-chairperson of the Highveld Steel shop steward committee, former chairperson of the COSATU local, ANC branch leadership).

Meshack Malinga, 15/3/94, 12/5/94, 14/5/94 (chairperson of the Highveld Steel joint shop steward committee, NUMSA regional vice-chairperson, artisan, ANC branch leadership).

Barney Mashego, 13/10/95 (NUMSA regional organiser, former NUM shop steward, community activist, ANC branch leadership).

J.J. Mbonani, 31/5/94, 7/6/94 (secretary of the Highveld Steel joint shop steward committee, secretary of the COSATU local, migrant worker).

Sam Mkhabela, 1/6/94 (UDF activist, former artisan and NUMSA member).

Philip Mkatshwa, 7/6/94, 8/95 (NUMSA shop steward).

Jerry Mogoleko, 10/95 (NUMSA active member, migrant worker).

Joe Mokoena, 12/10/95 (community activist, former NUMSA shop steward, former NUMSA local organiser).

Paxon Mokoena, 14/6/94 (NUMSA shop steward).

Bob Moloi, 10/7/94 (NUMSA member, former Highveld Steel shop steward committee chairperson).

Marcus Moswane, 21/8/95 (NUMSA active member).

Jacob Msimangu, 12/8/95, 22/10/95 (former chairperson of the strike committee, member of the concerned group).

Ambrose Mthembu, 15/3/94, 26/4/94, 14/5/94, 22/10/95 (NUMSA shop steward, artisan).
Mosi Nhlapo, 9/11/93 (with Meshack Malinga), 15/3/94, 8/5/94, 10/7/94, 6/3/95, 12/95 (chairperson of the Highveld Steel shop steward committee, NUMSA regional chairperson, artisan, ANC branch leadership).
Ezekiel Nkosi, 9/3/94 (with Philip Mkatshwa), 15/4/94, 5/5/94, 26/5/94, 23/11/95 (NUMSA shop steward, secretary of the Highveld Steel shop steward committee, chairperson of the COSATU local, ANC branch leadership).
Hendrik Nkosi, 26/5/94, 14/6/94, 26/10/95 (NUMSA shop steward).
Sidwel Nkosi, 26/8/95 (NUMSA active member).
Johannes Phatlana, 15/4/94, 7/9/94, 12/10/95 (NUMSA shop steward, vice-chairperson of the Highveld Steel joint shop steward committee, migrant worker).
William Sehlola, 5/6/94 (NUMSA member, former NUMSA shop steward and secretary of the Highveld Steel shop steward committee, former migrant worker).
Jacob Skhosana, 14/4/94, 26/4/94 (NUMSA shop steward, artisan).
Tshagata, 26/5/94, 10/95 (NUMSA active member, migrant worker).

Interview with a group of shop stewards (Meshack Malinga, Mosi Nhlapo, Ambrose Mthembu, Ezekiel Nkosi), 2/9/93.

White trade unionists/foremen

Bossie Bezuidenhout (pseudonym), 29/8/95 (white foreman, NUMSA member, former MWU shop steward).
Gert van der Merwe (pseudonym), 29/11/95 (white foreman, MWU member).
André Vermaak, 9/93 (MWU organiser, former white worker at Highveld Steel).

Witbank City Council officials

Adam Engelbrecht, 12/5/98 (Witbank Town Clerk, acting).
Leo Makwakwa, 12/5/98 (Head, Witbank Housing Department).

Management

Moses Nkabinde, 12/5/98 (Highveld Steel recruiting officer, retired).

Documents

NUMSA (nd). Commission Report.
Highveld Steel. Application in the industrial court of South Africa held at Pretoria, case no 11/2/1277, 19 May 1988.
—— Founding affidavit, 6 December 1991.
Highveld Steel and Vanadium Corporation (HSVC). Annual Reports.
—— (nd). Highveld Steel and Vanadium Corporation (brochure).

Books, articles, theses and unpublished papers

Adler, G. (1993). 'Skills, control, and "careers at work": possibilities for worker control in the South African motor industry' in *South African Sociological Review* 5 (2).

—— (1994). ' "The factory belongs to all who work in it": race, class and collective action in the South African motor industry, 1967–1986'. PhD dissertation, Political Science Department, Columbia University.

Adler, G. and E. Webster (1995). 'Challenging transition theory: the labour movement, radical reform, and transition to democracy in South Africa' in *Politics & Society* 23 (1), March.

—— (2000a). 'Social movement unionism in South Africa: a reassessment where it all began'. Paper presented at the American Sociological Association, Washington.

—— (2000b). *Trade unions and democratization in South Africa, 1985–1997*. London: Macmillan.

Adler, G., J. Maller and E. Webster (1992). 'Unions, direct action and transition in South Africa' in N. Etherington (ed). *Peace, politics and violence in Southern Africa*. London: Hans Zell Publishers.

Africa Perspective (1983). 'Colonialism of a special kind and the South African state: a consideration of recent articles' in *Africa Perspective* 23.

Bacon, N., P. Blyton and J. Morris (1996). 'Among the ashes: trade union strategies in the UK and German steel industries' in *British Journal of Industrial Relations* 34 (1), March.

Baskin, J. (1991). *Striking back: a history of COSATU*. Johannesburg: Ravan Press.

—— (2000). 'Labour in South Africa's transition to democracy: concertation in a third world setting' in G. Adler and E. Webster (eds). *Trade unions and democratization in South Africa, 1985–1997*. London: Macmillan.

Beinart, W. (1992): 'Introduction: political and collective violence in southern African historiography' in W. Beinart, T. Ranger and R. Turrell (eds). *Journal of Southern African Studies Special issue: political violence in Southern Africa* 18 (3), September.

Belanger, J., P.K. Edwards and L. Haiven (eds) (1994). *Workplace industrial relations and the global challenge*. Ithaca, New York: ILR Press.

Benjamin, P. (1987). 'Trade unions and the industrial court' in G. Moss and I. Obery (eds). *South African Review 4*. Johannesburg: Ravan Press.

Beynon, H. (1973). *Working for Ford*. London: Allen Lane.

Bird, A. (1990). 'NUMSA's vocational training project' in *South African Labour Bulletin* 15 (1).

Bonner, P. and V. Ndima (1999). 'The roots of violence on the East Rand, 1980–1990'. Seminar paper, Institute for Advanced Social Research, University of the Witwatersrand.

Bonnin, D.R. (1987). 'Class, consciousness and conflict in the Natal Midlands, 1940–1987: the case of the BTR Sarmcol workers'. MA dissertation, University of Natal.

Bozzoli, B. (2000). 'Why were the 1980s millenarian? Style, repertoire, space and authority in South Africa's black cities' in *Journal of Historical Sociology* 13 (1).

Budlender, D. (1983). 'The Factories Act 1918–1945' in *South African Labour Bulletin* 8 (7).

Buhlungu, S. (1996). 'Trade union responses to participatory management: a case-study'. MA dissertation, University of the Witwatersrand, Johannesburg.

—— (2000). 'Trade union organization and capacity in the 1990s: continuities, changes and challenges for PPWAWU' in G. Adler and E. Webster (eds). *Trade unions and democratization in South Africa, 1985–1997*. London: Macmillan.

—— (2001). 'Democracy and modernisation in the making of the South African trade union movement: the dilemma of leadership, 1973–2000'. PhD thesis, University of the Witwatersrand, Johannesburg.

Burawoy, M. (1972). 'The colour of class on the copper mines: from African advancement to Zambianisation'. Zambian Papers No 7, Institute of African Studies, University of Zambia, Lusaka.

—— (1979): *Manufacturing consent: changes in the labour process under advanced capitalism.* Chicago: University of Chicago Press.

—— (1985). *The politics of production: factory regimes under capitalism and socialism.* London: Verso.

—— (1989): 'Marxism without micro-foundations: Przeworski's critique of social democracy' in *Socialist Review* 89 (2).

Central Statistical Services (1980). Census. Pretoria.

—— (1985). Census. Pretoria.

—— (1991). Census. Pretoria.

Cohen, R. (1991). *Contested domains: debates in international labour studies.* London and New Jersey: Zed Books.

Cooper, D. (1991). 'Locating South Africa in the Third World: comparative perspectives on patterns of industrialisation and political trade unionism in South America' in *Social Dynamics* 17 (2).

COSATU (1997). Report from the September Commission. Johannesburg: COSATU.

Crankshaw, O. (1997). *Race, class and the changing division of labour under apartheid.* London: Routledge.

Cressey, P. and J. MacInnes (1980). 'Voting for Ford: industrial democracy and the control of labour' in *Capital and Class* 11.

Dauskardt, R. (1994). 'Outside the metropolis: the future of South Africa's secondary cities'. Urban Foundation Research Report 9, Development Strategy and Policy Unit of the Urban Foundation, Johannesburg.

De Villiers, D. and M. Anstey (2000). 'Trade unions in transitions to democracy in South Africa, Spain and Brazil' in G. Adler and E. Webster (eds). *Trade unions and democratization in South Africa, 1985–1997*. London: Macmillan.

Delius, P. (1996): *A lion amongst the cattle: reconstruction and resistance in the Northern Transvaal.* Johannesburg: Ravan Press, Oxford: James Curry, Portsmouth: Heinemann.

Dolny, H. (2001). *Banking on change.* Johannesburg: Viking.

Edwards, P.K. (1990): 'Understanding conflict in the labour process: the logic and autonomy of struggle' in D. Knights and H. Wilmott (eds). *Labour process theory.* London: Macmillan.

Edwards, P.K., J. Belanger and L. Haiven (1994). 'Introduction: the workplace and labour regulation in comparative perspective' in J. Belanger, P.K. Edwards and L. Haiven (eds). *Workplace industrial relations and the global challenge.* Ithaca, New York: ILR Press.

Eidelberg, P.G. (2000). 'The Tripartite Alliance on the eve of a new millennium: COSATU, the ANC and the SACP' in G. Adler and E. Webster (eds). *Trade unions and democratization in South Africa, 1985–1997.* London: Macmillan.

Ewer, P., I. Hampson, C. Loyd, J. Rainford, S. Rix and M. Smith (1991). *Politics and the Accord.* Leichhardt, Australia: Pluto Press.

Fanaroff, B. (1987). 'Interview' in *South African Labour Bulletin* 12 (4).

—— (1992). 'Interview' in *South African Labour Bulletin* 16 (8).

Fine, A. and E. Webster (1989). 'Transcending traditions: trade unions and political unity' in G. Moss and I. Obery (eds). *South African Review 5.* Johannesburg: Ravan Press.

Foster, J. (1982). 'The workers' struggle: where does FOSATU stand?' in *South African Labour Bulletin* 7 (8).

Friedman, S. (1987). *Building tomorrow today: African workers in trade unions 1970–1984.* Johannesburg: Ravan Press.

Friedman, S. and M. Shaw (2000). 'Power in partnership? Trade unions, forums and the transition' in G. Adler and E. Webster (eds). *Trade unions and democratization in South Africa, 1985–1997.* London: Macmillan.

General Workers Union (1983). 'General Workers Union on the Democratic Front' in *South African Labour Bulletin* 9 (2).

Genovese, E.D. (1976). *Roll, Jordan, roll: the world the slaves made.* New York: Vintage Books.

Gordon, R.J. (1977). *Mines, masters and migrants: life in a Namibian mine compound.* Johannesburg: Ravan Press.

Götz, G.A. (2000). 'Shoot anything that flies, claim anything that falls: labour and the changing definition of the Reconstruction and Development Programme' in G. Adler and E. Webster (eds). *Trade unions and democratization in South Africa, 1985–1997.* London: Macmillan.

Gramsci, A.H. (1971). *Selections from prison notebooks.* London: Lawrence and Wishart.

Green, P. (1986). 'Trade unions and the state of emergency' in *South African Labour Bulletin* 11 (7).

Hart, G. (2002). *Disabling globalisation: places of power in post-apartheid South Africa.* Pietermaritzburg: University of Natal Press.

Hocking, A. (1998). *Act of faith: the story of the Highveld group.* Bethulie: Hollards.

Hyman, R. (1971). *Marxism and the sociology of trade unionism.* London: Pluto Press.

—— (1975). *Industrial relations: a Marxist introduction.* London: Macmillan.

Innes, D. (1984). *Anglo: Anglo-American and the rise of modern South Africa.* Johannesburg: Ravan Press.

International Labour Organisation (ILO) (1997). 'The iron and steel workforce of the twenty-first century'. Report for discussion at the tripartite meeting on the iron and steel workforce of the twenty-first century: what it will be like and how it will work. Geneva: ILO.

Jennings, N.S. (ed) (1997). 'Steel in the new millennium: nine case studies'. Working paper, Sectoral Activities Programme, ILO, Geneva.

Joffe, A., J. Maller and E. Webster (1995). 'South Africa's industrialisation: the challenge facing labour' in S. Frenkel and J. Harrod (eds). *Changing labor relations in industrializing countries*. Ithaca, New York: Cornell University Industrial and Labor Relations Press.

Jourdan, P. (1993). 'South Africa's mineral beneficiation industries – and the potential for mineral-based fabrication industries'. Unpublished first draft, Industrial Strategy Project, Johannesburg.

Kay, C.Y. (1994). 'Conflict and compliance: the workplace politics of a disk-drive factory in Singapore' in J. Belanger, P.K. Edwards and L. Haiven (eds). *Workplace industrial relations and the global challenge*. Ithaca, New York: ILR Press.

Keegan, T. (1996). *Colonial South Africa and the origins of the racial order*. Cape Town: David Philip.

Kenny, B. and E. Webster (1999). 'Eroding the core: flexibility and the resegmentation of the South African labour market' in *Critical Sociology* 24 (3).

Knights, D. and H. Wilmott (eds) (1990). *Labour process theory*. London: Macmillan.

Kuruvilla, S. and B. Mundell (eds) (1999). *Colonialism, nationalism and the institutionalisation of industrial relations in the Third World*. Stanford, Connecticut: JAI Press.

Labour Monitoring Group (LMG) (1985). 'The November stayaway' in *South African Labour Bulletin* 10 (6).

Lambert, R. (1990). 'Kilusang Mayo Uno and the rise of social movement unionism in the Philipines' in *Labour and Industry* 3 (2 & 3).

Lambert, R. and E. Webster (1988). 'The re-emergence of political unionism in contemporary South Africa?' in W. Cobbett and R. Cohen (eds). *Popular struggles in South Africa*. Trenton, New Jersey: Review of African Political Economy/Africa World Press.

Lane, T. (1974). *'The union makes us strong': the British working class, its politics and trade unionism*. London: Arrow Books.

Leger, J. (1992). '"Talking rocks": an investigation of the *pit sense* of rockfall accidents amongst underground gold miners'. PhD thesis, University of the Witwatersrand, Johannesburg.

Lings, K.S. (1990). 'An economic analysis of the iron and steel industry in South Africa'. Occasional paper 7, Nedcor Group Economic Unit, Johannesburg.

Littler, C.R. (1982). *The development of the labour process in capitalist countries*. London: Heinemann Educational Books.

—— (1990). 'The labour process debate: a theoretical review 1974–88' in D. Knights and H. Wilmott (eds). *Labour process theory*. London: Macmillan.

Lloyd, C. (1994). *Work organisation and world class management: a critical guide*. Johannesburg: Red Earth Publications and South African Labour Bulletin/Umanyano Publications.

Lodge, T. (1986). 'Mayihlome! – let us go to war!: from Nkomati to Kabwe, the African National Congress, January 1984–June 1985' in *South African Review 3*. Johannesburg: Ravan Press.

—— (1989). 'People's war or negotiation? African National Congress strategies in the 1980s' in G. Moss and I. Obery (eds). *South African Review 5*. Johannesburg: Ravan Press.

Lopez, S. (2000). 'Social movement unionism in the USA' in *RC 44 Newsletter*. Labour Movements Research Committee (RC 44) of the International Sociological Association, August.

Maller, J. (1992). *Conflict and co-operation: case studies in worker participation*. Johannesburg: Ravan Press.

Mamdani, M. (1996). *Citizen and subject: contemporary Africa and the legacy of late colonialism*. London: James Currey, Kampala: Fountain, Cape Town: David Philip.

Marais, H. (1998). *South Africa: limits to change: the political economy of transformation*. Cape Town: University of Cape Town Press, London and New York: Zed Books.

Maree, J. (1993). 'Trade unions and corporatism in South Africa' in *Transformation 21*.

Marx, K. (1976). *Capital Vol 1*. Harmondsworth: Penguin Books.

Mayekiso, M. (1996). *Township politics: civic struggles for a new South Africa*. New York: Monthly Review Press.

Mondi, L. (1990). 'Mandela release: workers celebrate' in *South African Labour Bulletin* 14 (7).

Moodie, T.D. with V. Ndatshe (1994). *Going for gold: men, mines and migration*. Johannesburg: Witwatersrand University Press, Berkeley: University of California Press.

Moody, K. (1997). *Workers in a lean world: unions in the international economy*. London: Verso.

Moore, B. Jr (1978). *Injustice: the social bases of obedience and revolt*. London: Macmillan.

Morris, A. (1990). 'The complexities of sustained urban struggle: the case of Oukasie' in *South African Sociological Review* 2 (2), April.

Mosoetsa, S. (2000). 'South Africa: moving into the fourth world?' in *South African Labour Bulletin* 24 (1).

Moss, G. and I. Obery (1987). *South African Review 4*. Johannesburg: Ravan Press.

Mtshelwane, Z. (1994). 'Truckers blockade: "If you leave your base, others will fill your space"' in *South African Labour Bulletin* 18 (5).

Munck, R. (1987). *Third world workers and the new international labour studies*. London: Zed Books.

Murray, M.J. (1994). *Revolution deferred: the painful birth of post-apartheid South Africa*. London and New York: Verso.

NALEDI (National Labour and Economic Development Institute) (1994). *Unions in transition: COSATU at the dawn of democracy*. Johannesburg: NALEDI.

Nichols, T. and H. Beynon (1977). *Living with capitalism: class relations and the modern factory*. London: Routledge and Kegan Paul.

Njikelana, S. (1984). 'The unions and the Front: a response to the General Workers Union' in *South African Labour Bulletin* 9 (7).

Nolutshungu, S.C. (1983). *Changing South Africa*. Cape Town: David Philip.

Parfit, J. (1990). 'Release of Nelson Mandela: workers respond in the Eastern Cape' in *South African Labour Bulletin* 14 (7).

Pityana, S.M. and M. Orkin (eds) (1992). *Beyond the factory floor: a survey of COSATU shopstewards*. Johannesburg: Ravan Press.

Przeworski, A. (1989). 'Class, production and politics: a reply to Burawoy' in *Socialist Review* 89 (2).

—— (1991). *Democracy and the market: political and economic reforms in Eastern Europe and Latin America*. Cambridge: Cambridge University Press.

Robinson, I. (2000). 'Is neo-liberal restructuring promoting social movement unionism in the USA and Canada?'. Paper presented at the American Sociological Association, Washington.

Rosenthal, T. (1997). 'Steel in South Africa: Iscor' in N.S. Jennings (ed). Steel in the new millennium: nine case studies'. Working paper, Sectoral Activities Programme, ILO, Geneva.

Scipes, K. (1992). 'Social Movement Unionism and the Kilusang Mayo Uno' in *Kasarinlan*, Third World Studies Centre, University of the Philippines, 7 (2–3).

Seekings, J. (2000). *The UDF: a history of the United Democratic Front in South Africa 1983–1991*. Cape Town: David Philip, Oxford: James Curry, Athens: Ohio University Press.

Seidman, G. (1994). *Manufacturing militance: workers' movements in Brazil and South Africa, 1970–1985*. Berkeley: University of California Press.

South African Labour Bulletin (1987). 'NUMSA calls off the strike' in *South African Labour Bulletin* 12 (6/7).

—— (1989). 'Focus on violence in the workplace' in *South African Labour Bulletin* 14 (3).

—— (1996). 'Amplats: an avoidable tragedy' in *South African Labour Bulletin* 20 (5).

Segal, L. (1992). 'The human face of violence: hostel dwellers speak' in *Journal of Southern African Studies* 18 (1).

Sitas, A. (1983). 'African worker responses on the East Rand to changes in the metal industry, 1960–1980'. PhD thesis, University of the Witwatersrand, Johannesburg.

Steinberg, J. (2002). *Midlands*. Johannesburg: Jonathan Ball.

'Strategic unionism: ACTU/TDC Mission to Western Europe' (1989). Document reproduced in B. Ford and D. Plowman. *Australian unions: an industrial relations perspective*. Melbourne: Macmillan.

Swilling, M. (1983). '*Umzabalazo wabasebenzi*: the politics of working class struggles in Germiston, 1979–83'. Honours dissertation, University of the Witwatersrand, Johannesburg.

—— (1984). 'MAWU split' in *South African Labour Bulletin* 10 (1).

—— (1988). 'The United Democratic Front and township revolt' in W. Cobbett and R. Cohen (eds). *Popular struggles in South Africa*. Trenton, New Jersey: Review of Political Economy/Africa World Press.

Tarrow, S. (1998). *Power in movement: social movements and contentious politics*. Cambridge: Cambridge University Press.

Theron, J. (2003). 'Employment is not what it used to be'. Draft paper presented at The changing nature of work research workshop, Department of Labour, the National Institute for Economic Policy, and the Sociology of Work Unit.

Thompson, E.P. (1971). 'The moral economy of the English crowd in the eighteenth century' in *Past and Present* 50.

—— (1991). *Customs in common*. London: The Merlin Press.

Thompson, P. (1990). 'Crawling from the wreckage: the labour process and the politics of production' in D. Knights and H. Wilmott (eds). *Labour process theory*. London: Macmillan.

Thompson, P. and E. Bannon (1985). *Working the system: the shop floor and new technology*. London: Pluto Press.

Van Zyl Slabbert, F. (1992). *The quest for democracy: South Africa in transition*. London: Penguin.

Von Holdt, K. (1988). 'Trade unions, community organisation and politics: a local case study on the East Rand: 1980–1986'. Labour Studies Research Report 3, Sociology of Work Unit, University of the Witwatersrand.

—— (1990). 'The Mercedes Benz sleep-in' in *South African Labour Bulletin* 15 (4).

—— (1991a). 'From resistance to reconstruction: the changing role of trade unions' in *South African Labour Bulletin* 15 (6).

—— (1991b). 'Towards transforming South African industry: a "reconstruction accord" between unions and the ANC?' in *South African Labour Bulletin* 15 (6).

—— (1992). 'What is the future of labour?' in *South African Labour Bulletin* 16 (8).

—— (1993a). 'New plan from NUMSA' in *South African Labour Bulletin* 17 (2).

—— (1993b). 'Alusaf: violence and racism in northern Natal' in *South African Labour Bulletin* 17 (3).

—— (1993c). 'Frame: shopstewards make proposals' in *South African Labour Bulletin* 17 (3).

—— (1993d). 'Unilever: testing worker participation' in *South African Labour Bulletin* 17 (3).

—— (1994). 'NUMSA workshop' in *South African Labour Bulletin* 18 (4).

—— (1995). 'NUMSA's three-year programme: addressing the question of power?' in *South African Labour Bulletin* 19 (2).

—— (1996). 'Empowering the supervisor at SA Engineering' in *South African Labour Bulletin* 20 (2).

—— (2000). 'From resistance to reconstruction: a case study of trade unionism in the workplace and the community (1980–1996)'. PhD thesis, University of the Wiwatersrand, Johannesburg.

—— (2001). 'White workers and trade unionism in a changing South Africa: a case study of the construction and contestation of racial solidarity in the workplace'. Paper presented at the conference The burden of race: 'whiteness' and 'blackness' in modern South Africa, 5–8 July, History Workshop, University of the Witwatersrand.

—— (2002). 'Social movement unionism: the case of South Africa' in *Work, Employment and Society* 16 (2).

Waterman, P. (1984). *For a new labour internationalism*. The Hague: ILERI.

—— (1993). 'Social movement unionism: a new union model for a new world order?' in *Review*, a journal of the Fernand Braudel Center, XVI (3).

—— (2001). 'Trade union internationalism in the Age of Seattle' in P. Waterman and J. Wills (eds). *Place, space and the new labour internationalism.* Oxford: Blackwell.

Webster, E. (1984). 'A new frontier of control? case studies in the changing form of job control in South African industrial relations' in *Second Carnegie Inquiry into Poverty in South Africa.* Cape Town: University of Cape Town (also published in *Industrial Relations Journal of South Africa* 6 (1) 1986).

—— (1985). *Cast in a racial mould: labour process and trade unionism in the foundries.* Johannesburg: Ravan Press.

—— (1988). 'The rise of social movement unionism: the two faces of the black trade union movement in South Africa' in P. Frankel, N. Pines and M. Swilling (eds). *State, resistance and change in South Africa.* London: Croom Helm.

—— (1999). 'Defusion of the Molotov cocktail in South African industrial relations: the burden of the past and the challenge of the future' in S. Kuruvilla and B. Mundell (eds). *Colonialism, nationalism and the institutionalisation of industrial relations in the Third world.* Stanford, Connecticut: JAI Press.

—— (2002) 'Manufacturing compromise: the dynamics of race and class among South African shop stewards in the nineties' in R. Baldoz, C. Koeber and P. Kraft (eds). *The critical study of work: labor, technology and global production.* Philadelphia: Temple University Press.

Webster, E. and G. Adler (1999). 'Towards a class compromise in South Africa's "double transition": bargained liberalisation and the consolidation of democracy' in *Politics & Society* 27 (3), September.

—— (2000). 'Consolidating democracy in a liberalizing world: trade unions and democratization in South Africa' in G. Adler and E. Webster (eds). *Trade unions and democratization in South Africa, 1985–1997.* London: Macmillan.

Webster, E. and C. Lipzig-Mumme (2000). 'Recasting labour studies in the new millennium'. Paper delivered at the World Congress of Sociology, International Sociological Association, Montreal.

Webster, E. and R. Omar (2003 forthcoming). 'Work restructuring in post-apartheid South Africa' in *Work and Occupations.*

Webster, E. and G. Simpson (1991). 'Crossing the picket-line: violence in industrial conflict' in *Industrial Relations Journal of South Africa* 11.

Wolpe, H. (1975). 'The theory of internal colonialism: the South African case' in I. Oxaal, Barnett and Boath (eds). *Beyond the sociology of development.* London: Routledge and Kegan Paul.

Wood, G. and C. Psoulis (2001). 'Mobilisation, internal cohesion, and organised labour: the case of Congress of South African Trade Unions' in *Work and Occupations* 28 (3).

Index

absenteeism   46, 81–2, 249, 252, 256
action committee   271–4, 276–8
advancement, self   287–9, 300
African National Congress (ANC)   2, 4,
  23–4, 89–90, 105–8, 110–14, 123,
  159, 181–2, 186–92, 201, 205–16,
  218–26, 231, 238, 270, 300
  and union rift   221–2
  Youth League   169
Afrikaner Weerstandsbeweging (AWB)
  230–1
amabhova   275–8, 284, 287
ANC   *see* African National Congress
Anglo American Corporation   15, 133
anomie   298
apartheid   1–8, 11, 21–4, 27–55, 61, 77–8,
  100, 105, 120–2, 143, 147, 159, 168,
  174, 181–4, 193, 211, 233, 269, 298–9
  facilities in factory   1–2, 30, 77–8, 232,
  300
apprentices   47–8
artisans   28, 47–8, 82, 102, 139, 165–6,
  172, 232, 238, 290, 297
assaults   125, 129, 131, 139, 162–3, 168
  racial   72–3, 77–8, 129, 230, 234, 264
Australia, trade unions   187–8, 202
authoritarian restoration   230, 240–2,
  262, 264, 269, 301–3, 305–7
automation   261
Azanian People's Organisation (AZAPO)
  90

baas-boys   28, 35–7, 68, 73–4, 83, 240,
  249–51, 254 *see also indunas*
baaskap   32–3, 68, 72, 74, 76
Bank Colliery   92
bargaining, collective   7

bhova   see amabhova
black consciousness   22, 90
Black Local Authorities (BLAs)   22, 95,
  115–16
bonuses   34, 247
Boshielo, Frank   55, 64, 79, 82, 97, 106,
  136, 150, 164, 167, 276, 308
bourgeoisie   293, 306
Bowker, Mike   251–2, 256–65
boycotts   22, 90–5, 109, 216
Boyd, Leslie   62, 128
bus burning   93, 157, 159

capitalism   196
Chamber of Mines   133
class structure   4–5, 10, 182, 187, 287,
  290, 293, 298, 305–6
communication   35 *see also* languages
communism   196, 288
concerned group   270–1, 274, 276–8, 283,
  285
Congress of South African Students
  (COSAS)   90, 107
Congress of South African Trade Unions
  (COSATU)   19–20, 23, 96–105, 108–
  14, 120, 141, 182, 186, 188–91, 208–
  10, 212–14, 216, 218–22, 247, 301, 305
  and Co-ordinating Committee   96–109
Conservative Party   213
COSATU   *see* Congress of South African
  Trade Unions
Council of Unions of South Africa   97

Defiance Campaign, 1989   109
democracy   6, 53, 82, 105, 112, 148, 160,
  165–8, 181–90, 193–4, 216–18, 224–5,
  242, 256, 292, 299

democracy, ANC   205–8, 210
Detainees' Parents' Support Committee
    90
Detainees' Support Committee   90
detention   89–90, 103
Development Bank   212
discipline   75, 78–83, 129, 137, 139–40,
    142, 148, 156–7, 162, 184, 237–40,
    256, 262 see also sjambok
    hostels   44
dismissals   37–8, 72–3, 120, 122–5, 127,
    129, 132, 138–40, 230, 237, 282, 301

education   48, 89–90, 93, 102, 155, 188,
    235, 255, 274, 283 see also training
efficiency   257–9 see also productivity
elections, 1994   4, 181, 208–12, 223, 269,
    300
electricity payment   92–3
elite
    black   5, 288, 293, 306
    political   220–2
elitism   190
Employment Equity Act   304
ethnic groups   44, 66, 157–8, 300 see also
    under tribal names, e.g. Pedi
ethnic identity   35

Factories Act   29–30, 55
Federation of South African Trade Unions
    (FOSATU)   97
Ferrobank industrial area   14
Ferrometals   127–9
franchise   4, 181
freedom   229–65

General Maintenance and Planning
    Department (GMPD)   238, 247
globalisation   186–8, 194, 202, 305
government, ANC   182
green areas   241–2, 244, 247

Harare Declaration, 1989   121
Harmony gold mine   301
hegemony   4, 39
Highveld Administration Board (HAB)
    13, 41, 43–4, 89, 95

Highveld Steel and Vanadium Corporation
    11–12, 14–19
    bus service   93–4
    facilities   1, 29, 77–8, 232
    lockout, 1987   132–7, 140–1, 161–4,
        166, 283
    maintenance   276
    production   16–19, 199–20
    reconstruction in the workplace   73–
        84, 182–4, 192–6, 229–65, 298–304
    strikes   101–2, 123–43
    and unions   20–1, 63–8, 96–101, 107,
        110–12, 147–75, 198, 207–15, 221–4,
        269–93
    workplace   27–55, 119–20, 224, 229–
        65
hostels   13, 40, 43–5, 48, 95, 100–2, 106–
    8, 134, 136, 140–1, 148, 152–9, 161–
    3, 165–70, 172–5, 237, 275, 279, 281,
    283
housing   43
Housing Support Centre   213

impimpis   158, 162, 174, 305
incorporation   4–5, 53–5, 61–3, 182, 287,
    293
    workplace   5, 46, 182, 229–30, 286,
        301–2, 305–7
indunas   35–8, 44, 74
Industrial Conciliation Act   28
Industrial Council   54, 62–3, 67, 121,
    125–6, 139–42, 166, 240
Industrial Court   28, 62, 139–40, 240
industrial relations   53–5, 67, 76, 79, 120,
    123, 135, 166, 243, 304
influx control   13–14, 48, 63, 95–6, 102,
    283–4
informal settlements   1, 14, 102, 214
Inkatha   107
Internal Security Act   114
intimidation   151–3
iron production   17, 248–9

job
    creation   194
    description   75, 251

losses 200
reservation 28–9, 77, 232–7, 255

kangaroo courts 94, 161
Kgalima, Hong Kong 105
kgoro 154–7
Khumalo, Benson 64, 96–100, 107, 109, 111, 113, 205–6
KwaGuqa 13–15, 40–1, 43, 50, 90–3, 95, 99, 106, 108, 211, 283
Town Council (KTC) 93, 95, 284

labour
immigrant 47
migrant 13–15, 40–8, 99, 101–2, 106–8, 112, 147–8, 152–9, 163, 166–9, 172–4, 249, 251, 269, 277–8, 281, 283–4, 299, 300
racial division 27–40, 46–9, 123, 232, 283
semi-skilled 28–9, 34, 40, 46–50, 102
urban 40–8
labour movement 12, 224
labour relations 140, 192, 262–3, 300, 304
Labour Relations Act (LRA) 61–3, 67, 70, 76, 121, 133, 139, 141, 265, 304
Landau Colliery 92
languages 35, 40, 45, 157–8, 262
leadership 114, 139, 148, 153, 166, 171, 184, 190, 207, 223, 235, 253–6, 289
liaison committees 53–5, 61, 63, 67
liberation movement 19, 21–2, 49, 105, 122, 148, 157, 186, 190, 264
literacy 41–2, 153, 155, 157, 166, 174, 194, 273
local government 201, 208, 213–23, 300
see also Black Local Authorities; KwaGuqa, Town Council
local government transitional council 213–14
lockout, 1987 132–7, 140–1, 161–4, 166, 283

Mahlangu, Bunny 119, 127–8, 130–1, 134–5, 138, 151–2, 158, 161, 167,

172, 244, 274, 276, 282–3, 308
Majola, Veli 277
Makagula, Albert 182, 252–3, 299
Makola, Charles 64, 69, 70, 96, 98, 110–11, 113, 120, 124, 132, 138–9, 166, 170, 308
Malinga, Meshack 103, 110, 139, 165, 276, 308
Mandela, Nelson 51, 83, 105, 122, 181–3, 185, 191, 210–11, 238, 297
manhood 156–7
Mapochs mine 14, 21, 130, 151–2
Mashego, Barney 96–7, 99, 109–12
mass action 90, 98
Mass Democratic Movement (MDM) 23, 109
Masters and Servants Act 32, 56
MAWU see Metal and Allied Workers Union
Mbonani, J.J. 50–3, 64, 72, 99–100, 106–7, 110, 123, 139, 172, 185, 190, 308
Metal and Allied Workers Union (MAWU) 17, 19–21
Metal Industries Training Board (MITB) 197
middle class 294, 306
Mine Workers' Union (MWU) 11, 230–2, 265
MK see Umkhonto we Sizwe
Mkatshwa, Philip 279–82
Mkhabela, Sam 96
Mokoena, Joe 71–3, 90
Molefe, Popo 206–7
Moloi, Bob 55, 64–5, 132, 149, 151
Msimangu, Jacob 150, 158, 172, 270, 277, 308
Mthembu, Ambrose 81, 110, 139, 172, 308
MWU see Mine Workers' Union

Naidoo, Jay 114
National Housing Trust 95
National Party 168, 231
National Training Board (NTB) 247, 263
National Union of Metalworkers of South Africa (NUMSA) 11–12, 17, 30, 46,

50, 55, 61, 63, 96–8, 106–8, 124–7,
138, 181–7, 197–202, 205–9, 242–5,
247–8, 274, 278–82, 290–4, 297, 301–
3, 305–8
discipline   81, 160–1
division   79, 82, 109–14, 164–73
formation   19–21, 154, 159
Highveld Steel Commission of Inquiry
169–70
membership   38, 65–8, 241, 260, 262
political activity   213–14, 221–2, 224
recognition by Highveld   67, 71–2, 76–
7, 143, 233
strikes   101, 103, 126–33, 135, 152,
230–1, 237, 239, 265, 276
National Union of Mineworkers (NUM)
7–8, 20, 92, 96–7, 133, 301
National Union of Steel and Allied
Workers (NUSAAW)   172–3, 278–
82, 285
nationalism
African   4
Afrikaner   4
Ndebele   44, 50
necklacing   91, 100
negotiation   121, 124–6, 134, 136, 142–3,
148–52, 155, 158, 160–1, 174, 182–5,
187, 201, 237, 240, 257, 262, 270, 276,
278, 280, 282, 285, 302
New National Party   4
Nhlapo, Mosi   80–1, 110–13, 138–9, 171–
2, 192, 197–9, 234, 238, 243–8, 250–
1, 255–8, 263, 265, 275–7, 288–93,
307
Nkabinde, Moses   102
Nkosi, Ezekiel   50–2, 66, 90, 172, 279,
281, 289, 308
Nkosi, Hendrik   254, 272
NUM   see National Union of
Mineworkers
NUMSA   see National Union of
Metalworkers of South Africa

Oppenheimer, Sir Harry   15

Pan-Africanist Congress (PAC)   89, 181

parliament, tricameral   22
Pedi   40, 44–5, 66, 107–8, 155–9, 164,
168, 170, 174, 249, 273, 281
Phatlana, Johannes   110, 139, 172, 308
police   52, 72, 74, 89, 91–2, 94–5, 99–
101, 103–4, 106–7, 120, 129–32, 137,
230, 282
popular movement   89–91, 96, 113, 119
power
economic   181
management   137, 142, 239–42
people's   93, 119
political   181, 294
racial   30–40, 54, 66–70, 73–9, 85,
122, 135, 181, 193, 232–8, 253, 256,
264, 298–9, 301, 305
worker   123, 128, 136, 139, 148–53,
158, 174–5, 183, 192–4, 199–201, 224,
256, 299
productivity   40, 82–4, 121, 134, 152,
181, 186, 192–5, 199–201, 235–6, 242,
247, 254, 258–9, 265, 292, 301, 303–
4
profits   258
promotion   34, 261, 272, 286–7
public holidays   121, 124

race relations   233–6, 265
racism   2, 27, 33, 48, 68, 71–2, 153, 187,
230, 237, 253, 262, 279 see also power,
racial
Rand Carbide   14–15, 42, 50–2, 64, 67,
72, 99, 127, 130–1
rates, payment   215–16
Reconstruction and Development
Committee (RDC)   213–14, 220,
257–8
Reconstruction and Development
Programme (RDP)   186–90, 211–14,
219
recruitment
labour   41–2
union officials   289
unions   64–5, 113
rent payment   92–3, 95, 183, 284
resistance politics   89–96

restructuring, workplace   2, 186, 187,
   188, 195, 196, 198, 200, 243, 244,
   245, 257, 258, 260, 261, 263, 265,
   281, 290, 304, 305, 307 *see also*
   strategy of reconstruction, workplace
retrenchment   62, 171–2, 200–2, 251,
   292, 303
Rietspruit Opencast Collieries   96
riots   *see* uprisings
Robben Island   207
Rustenburg Platinum   301

Samancor   128
Sebabi, David   63
Sebatakgomo   108
Sehlola, William   64, 110, 139, 168, 170
SEIFSA   *see* Steel and Engineering
   Industries Federation of South Africa
Sekhukhuneland Revolt, 1958   108, 179
service companies   304
shop stewards   7, 12, 61–4, 67–79, 81–3,
   85, 96–8, 101, 103–4, 106, 110–13,
   119–20, 159–75, 195–8, 200–1, 205–
   26, 232–4, 238–48, 252, 256–63,
   269–86, 290–4, 300–3
   committees   20–1, 96, 120, 148–55
   council   98, 102–6
   councillors   218, 221–4
   elections   67
   local government   213–19
   politics   181–92
   research group   186–7
   strikes   124–42
   training   20, 68, 112
   upward mobility   287–90, 301, 305–6
sjambok   51, 74, 81–2, 100, 129–32, 152,
   156, 160–2, 164–5, 168, 275–6
Skhosana, Jacob   172
skilled workers   *see* workers, skilled
skills   27–9, 47–8, 67, 187, 193–4
Skills Development Act   304
social structure, racial   27–40, 85, 147,
   298
socialism   81, 187, 196, 198–9, 244, 288–9
South African Boilermakers' Society
   (SABS)   54–5, 65–6

South African Communist Party (SACP)
   108, 181, 186, 208, 288
South African Congress of Trade Unions
   (SACTU)   49
South African National Civics
   Organisation (SANCO)   213
South African Youth Congress   90
Soweto   50, 52, 89, 124
Spitzkop   130
state of emergency   23, 91, 125
status, men   156
stayaways   89, 98–107, 109, 125, 269 *see
   also* strikes
Steel and Engineering Industries
   Federation of South Africa (SEIFSA)
   62, 67, 128
steel production   16–17
strategy of reconstruction   181–202, 205–
   26, 229–65, 286, 290–4, 299–308
   iron plant   257–64
   negotiated/ing   230, 242–8, 302–5
   tap floor   248–57, 302
   workplace   192–7, 200–1, 224, 229–57,
   307
strike committee   79–80, 82, 120, 129–
   39, 148–58, 169, 173–4, 272, 285,
   292, 300–1
strikes   23, 62, 70, 73, 120–41, 148–50,
   161–4, 171–2, 183, 185, 215, 231,
   238–9
   1993   234, 264
   1994   278–82, 286
   1996   264–5
   Durban, 1973   20, 22, 49, 53
   mine workers, 1987   300
   wildcat   50, 70, 151–2, 158–65, 194,
   230–1, 256, 270, 276, 284, 287, 293,
   301
'struggle' holidays   124–5, 141
swingmen   260–1

tap floor production   40–3, 248–55
township/hostel conflict   40–6, 101–2,
   157, 163–70, 173–5, 276–8, 281, 283
townships   13–14, 22, 40, 153–9, 183
   development   214

maintenance   95
services   214
unrest   91–5, 102–3, 300
trade unionism   *see* unionism
training   28, 42, 46–8, 186–7, 194, 200,
    212–13, 237, 251–3, 255, 302
swingmen   260
union leaders   170, 198, 233
Transalloys   130–1, 308
transformation
social   3, 9, 182, 201, 297, 298
town council   208, 213, 222
workplace   11, 229, 243, 248, 254
transition   2–5
economic   3, 182, 188, 193–4, 201
political   3, 181–2, 185, 188, 193, 205–
    6, 225, 229
social   3–5, 9, 181–202, 291, 297
triple   3, 304, 305
workplace   5–8, 53, 71, 85, 187–8,
    202, 229–30, 243, 246, 286, 291, 299,
    301–6
Transvaal Provincial Administration   95
tribalism   101, 107, 155–6
Tshagata   183, 237, 255–6, 271–2, 275,
    277, 299, 308

UDF   *see* United Democratic Front
Umkhonto we Sizwe (MK)   22, 90, 207
unbanning political organisations   239
Unemployed People's Congress (UPCO)
    90, 99, 109, 113
unemployment   202, 208
ungovernability   22–3, 91–6, 103–5, 111,
    114, 119–43, 153, 158, 161, 181, 285,
    300–1
union law   159–61
unionism   4, 7–11, 34, 38, 49, 54, 61–2,
    68, 71, 85, 96–114, 181–2, 185, 188,
    225, 299, 307
social movement   119–23, 143, 147–75,
    269, 305–7
social structure   147–75, 184, 201–2,
    223, 226, 269, 278, 282, 290–4, 299,
    305–6
strategic   196–202, 204, 302, 305

transition   8–11
unions, power loss   263–5, 269–94, 300,
    302–3, 305
United Democratic Front (UDF)   21–4,
    90, 93, 96–8, 105, 108–9, 111, 113–
    14, 205–6
Co-ordinating Committee   90, 91, 96–
    101, 104, 109
uprisings   50, 61, 105
Soweto   49–50, 52, 89

vanadium   14–15
production   16–17, 248
Vantra   4, 130–1, 246–7
Verwoerd, Hendrik   230
violence   50, 91–2, 105, 148–51, 153, 162,
    168–9, 171, 173–5, 300–1
Volkswagen strike   301

wages   14, 28–9, 34, 42, 47, 50–1, 54,
    106, 120, 132–3, 139, 162–3, 184,
    187, 191, 197, 214–15, 231, 233, 237,
    248, 250–2, 260–1, 263, 265, 279
wealth creation   188
whites   1, 27–55
Wiehahn Commission   19–20, 22, 47,
    61–3, 76, 78, 84, 133, 140
wildcat co-operation   230, 257–65, 269,
    278, 286, 293, 302–6
Witbank   13–14, 27, 29, 89–102, 108–14,
    134–6, 141, 157, 159, 164, 188–92,
    205–26, 277, 287
Witbank Development Forum   208, 211–
    13
Witbank Parents' Crisis Committee   90
Witbank Town Council   13, 182, 189,
    201, 208, 213–24, 300
Witbank Youth Congress   90, 92, 109,
    113
witchcraft   94
work ethic   81–4, 193, 297
workers, skilled   193–4, 200, 252–3, 278,
    283, 304–5
working class   4, 41, 43, 49, 182, 187, 201,
    205, 229, 298, 306
working conditions   190

workplace, future   297–308
workplace regime   229–65
  apartheid   5–8, 27–55, 73–8, 82–5,
    119–43, 154, 184, 193, 223–4, 236–7,
    241–2
  decomposition, 1990s   238–42
  neo-apartheid   229–32, 237–8, 242,
    264–5, 278, 282–7, 301, 306
  post-apartheid   243–57, 264, 301–7
  see also transformation, workplace

Xhosa   40, 44–5, 66, 158

Young Christian Students   96

Zulu, Clement   92, 114
Zulus   35, 44–5, 107, 135, 157–8